D1599949

Vigilant Memory

Vigilant Memory

*Emmanuel Levinas, the Holocaust,
and the Unjust Death*

R. CLIFTON SPARGO

CABRINI COLLEGE LIBRARY

The Johns Hopkins University Press
Baltimore

✳61445803

© 2006 The Johns Hopkins University Press
All rights reserved. Published 2006
Printed in the United States of America on acid-free paper

2 4 6 8 9 7 5 3 1

The Johns Hopkins University Press
2715 North Charles Street
Baltimore, Maryland 21218-4363
www.press.jhu.edu

Library of Congress Cataloging-in-Publication Data
Spargo, R. Clifton.
Vigilant memory : Emmanuel Levinas, the Holocaust, and the unjust death /
R. Clifton Spargo.
p. cm.
Includes bibliographical references and index.
ISBN 0-8018-8311-3 (hardcover : alk. paper)
1. Lévinas, Emmanuel. 2. Holocaust, Jewish (1939–1945). 3. Grief.
4. Bereavement. 5. Elegiac poetry. 6. Ethics. 7. Conduct of life. I. Title.
BF575.G7S63 2006
152.4—dc22   2005024562

A catalog record for this book is available from the British Library.

In Loving Memory of My Father,
Robert Clifton Spargo
1941–2005

Contents

Acknowledgments

I am grateful for the contributions made by the following people either directly to this book itself or to the advancement of my thought and scholarship during the writing of it: Leslie Brisman, Susan Brisman, Bill Brown, Anne-Lise François, Kevis Goodman, Geoffrey Hartman, Peter Hayes, Sara Horowitz, Christine Krueger, Walter Benn Michaels, Anne Ream, Margaret Reid, Jahan Ramazani, and Michael Rothberg. In graduate school Henry Pickford, in the context of many extended conversations about philosophy and literature and through a Yale college seminar we co-taught on the Holocaust, effectively introduced me to the work of Emmanuel Levinas. I benefited immensely from conversations with a Levinas reading group at the Whitney Humanities Center at Yale University in 1993–94 (sponsored by David Bromwich) and farther down the road from conversations with Brad Hinze, George Justice, Aimee Pozorski, and Michele Saracino, also as part of a Levinas reading group, and from many hours of discussing Levinas with Michele, whose dissertation (now a book) on Levinas and the theologian Bernard Lonergan I helped direct.

Much of the research for this project as well as the early stages of its composition were executed under the auspices of the Pearl Resnick Fellowship at the Center for Advanced Holocaust Studies of the United States Memorial Holocaust Museum in 2000–2001. My deep gratitude to the Resnick family as well as to the superior staff of the CAHS—especially to Robert Ehrenreich, Wendy Lower, and Paul Shapiro for facilitating and deepening my engagement with the broader field of Holocaust Studies. I'd like to thank my editor Michael Lonegro for expertly overseeing the publication of this book as well as Trevor Lipscombe of the Johns Hopkins University Press for his early sponsorship of the manuscript, my copy editor Elizabeth Gratch, and the excellent editorial staff at the press. Two anonymous readers made insightful, challenging, and highly practical suggestions for improving the manuscript, and I hope they will find their perspectives addressed (if not always in full) in this final offering.

I want to sound two special notes of appreciation—for the contribution of Michael Bernard-Donals to this project at several key stages and for the opportunities he provided to present my work on ethics and the Holocaust, most particularly by inviting me to give one of the keynote addresses for a conference on "Out of Europe: History, Exile, and Memory after 1945" at the University of Wisconsin–Madison in April 2004; and for the extraordinary degree of collaborative generosity exhibited by Amelia Zurcher, who offered insightful and practical readings of the manuscript at several stages and helped me aspire throughout to—and I hope to attain at least in part—a delicate balance between philosophical precision and clarity of expression.

Finally, by dedicating this book to my father, whose support and generosity I can only barely acknowledge by such an honor, I also dedicate it to my mother, his collaborator in all things. I feel fortunate to have had the opportunity to share this book's basic argument with my father only a month before his sudden death, and even more fortunate that my father—hardly a philosopher or literary critic, who throughout the conversation kept challenging me to put what I was saying in language that salespeople and factory workers could understand (a challenge I'd like still to take up)—perceived the link between ethics and politics I was advocating and saw the immediate relevance of my argument to our contemporary political context. In this way, even before publication this book had its first reception.

Abbreviations

WORKS BY LEVINAS

AICH   "As If Consenting to Horror," *Critical Inquiry* (Winter 1989):
            485–88.
AQE   *Autrement qu'être ou au-delà de l'essence* (The Hague: Martinus
            Nijhoff, 1974).
D   "Dying For . . ." (1987), *Entre Nous: On Thinking-of-the-Other*,
            trans. Michael B. Smith and Barbara Harshav (New York:
            Columbia University Press, [1991] 1998), 207–18.
DF   *Difficult Freedom*, trans. Seán Hand (London: Athlone Press,
            [1963, 1976] 1990).
DR   "Diachrony and Representation" (1985), *Entre Nous: On
            Thinking-of-the-Other*, trans. Michael B. Smith and Barbara
            Harshav (New York: Columbia University Press, [1991] 1998),
            159–77.
DT   "Death and Time," a lecture series given at the Sorbonne in
            1975–76, *God, Death, and Time*, trans. Bettina Bergo (Stanford:
            Stanford University Press, [1993] 2000).
EP   "Enigma and Phenomenon" (1965), trans. Alphonso Lingis,
            rev. Robert Bernasconi and Simon Critchley, *Emmanuel
            Levinas: Basic Philosophical Papers*, ed. Adriaan T. Peperzak,
            Simon Critchley, and Robert Bernasconi (Bloomington:
            Indiana University Press, 1996), 65–77.
FC   "Freedom and Command" (1953), *Collected Philosophical
            Papers*, trans. Alphonso Lingis (Dordrecht: Martinus Nijhoff,
            1987), 15–23.
IIRB   *Is It Righteous to Be? Interviews with Emmanuel Levinas*, ed.
            Jill Robbins (Stanford: Stanford University Press, 2001).

LR   *The Levinas Reader,* ed. Seán Hand (Cambridge, MA: Basil
          Blackwell, 1989).

NC   "Nonintentional Consciousness" (1983), *Entre Nous: On
          Thinking-of-the-Other,* trans. Michael B. Smith and Barbara
          Harshav (New York: Columbia University Press, [1991] 1998),
          123–32.

NI   "No Identity" (1970), *Collected Philosophical Papers,* trans.
          Alphonso Lingis (Dordrecht: Martinus Nijhoff, 1987), 141–51.

OTB   *Otherwise than Being or Beyond Essence,* trans. Alphonso
          Lingis (The Hague: Martinus Nijhoff, [1974] 1981).

PD   "The Philosopher and Death" (1982), *Alterity and
          Transcendence,* trans. Michael B. Smith (New York: Columbia
          University Press, [1995] 1999), 153–68.

S   "Substitution" (1968), trans. Peter Atterton, Simon Critchley,
          and Graham Noctor, *Basic Philosophical Writings,* ed.
          Adriaan T. Peperzak, Simon Critchley, and Robert Bernasconi
          (Bloomington: Indiana University Press, 1996), 79–95.

TE   "Transcendence and Evil" (1978), in Philippe Nemo, *Job and
          the Excess of Evil,* trans. Michael Kigel (Pittsburgh: Duquesne
          University Press, 1998), 165–82.

TEI   *Totalité et infini: sur l'extériorité* (The Hague: Martinus
          Nijhoff, 1961).

TI   *Totality and Infinity: An Essay on Exteriority,* trans. Alphonso
          Lingis (Pittsburgh: Duquesne University Press, [1961] 1969).

TO   "Time and the Other" (1947), *Time and the Other, and
          Additional Essays,* trans. Richard A. Cohen (Pittsburgh:
          Duquesne University Press, 1987).

US   "Useless Suffering" (1982), *Entre Nous: On Thinking-of-the-
          Other,* trans. Michael B. Smith and Barbara Harshav
          (New York: Columbia University Press, [1991] 1998), 91–101.

WORKS BY OTHERS

AING   Berel Lang, *Act and Idea in the Nazi Genocide* (Chicago:
          University of Chicago Press, 1990).

DR   Karl Barth, *Church Dogmatics,* ed. G. W. Bromiley and T. F.
          Torrance, vol. 4, pt. 1: *The Doctrine of Reconciliation* (1953),
          trans. G. W. Bromiley (Edinburgh: T. and T. Clark, 1956).

E	Alain Badiou, *Ethics: An Essay on the Understanding of Evil*, trans. Peter Hallward (New York: Verso, [1993] 2001).
GM	Friedrich Nietzsche, *On the Genealogy of Morals and Ecce Homo*, trans. and ed. Walter Kaufmann (New York: Random House, 1967).
P	Plato, *Phaedo*, in *Euthyphro, Apology, Crito, Phaedo, Phaedrus*, trans. Harold North Fowler, Loeb Classical Library (Cambridge, MA: Harvard University Press, 1999).
PLP	Judith Butler, *The Psychic Life of Power: Theories in Subjection* (Stanford: Stanford University Press, 1987).
RA	Giorgio Agamben, *Remnants of Auschwitz: The Witness and the Archive*, trans. Daniel Heller-Roazen (New York: Zone Books [1998], 2002).
SA	Primo Levi, *Survival in Auschwitz: The Nazi Assault on Humanity*, trans. Stuart Woolf (New York: Collier Books [1958], 1961).
Sh	Primo Levi, *The Drowned and the Saved*, trans. Raymond Rosenthal (New York: Simon and Schuster, [1986], 1988).
SS	Walter Benn Michaels, *The Shape of the Signifier: 1967 to the End of History* (Princeton, NJ: Princeton University Press, 2004).
SW	Sarah Kofman, *Smothered Words*, trans. Madeleine Dobie (Evanston, IL: Northwestern University Press, [1987] 1998).

Vigilant Memory

Introduction

Until the latter half of the 1980s, during the almost twenty-year heyday of high theory in the American academy, the general perception was that ethics and theory were in some basic way at odds with each other. If anything, what Geoffrey Galt Harpham calls the "Theoretical Era (c. 1968–1987)" instituted the Nietzschean suspicion that ethics was a fraudulent discourse, masking the concrete arrangements by which those who are powerful advance their own privilege in society under the guise of the universal dictates of law and principle. In this view, ethics seemed to partake of a "pre-theoretical arrogance."[1] As a discourse framing far-ranging, generalized values, ethics was either nothing more than a distraction from the conditions of its own origin—which is to say, part of the delusive privileging of the speech act as constitutive of presence (roughly, Jacques Derrida's complaint against the Kantian categorical imperative)—or nothing less than an ideological rationalization of the political and socioeconomic structures by which the masses are oppressed in any given society (roughly, Fredric Jameson's estimation of morality's real worth).

What brought the orthodox theoretical ban on ethics to an end, according to Harpham, had much to do with the 1987 discovery of the wartime journalistic writings of Paul de Man. Interpreted as symptomatic of deconstruction's larger failing, de Man's early collaboration with Nazism symbolized high theory's talent for suspending the ethical moment of decision in favor of perpetual critique. Suddenly, after 1987, the contributions of poststructuralist theory—say, the achievement of having foregrounded the necessarily self-reflective aspects of our cultural immersion in language or of having exposed the self-contradictory past of the regulatory functions of religion, philosophy, literature, and history—seemed in retrospect to conceal theory's own deep complicity with historical expressions of power, even at their most terrible, absolutist limit. No doubt, the antitheorists opportunistically seized the moral high ground from the preeminent discourse of deconstruction, which seemed otherwise undefeatable, but the final result was clear in at least one respect: "ethics was on the agenda" (21). Or, perhaps we should insist, still reflecting the terms of Harpham's own argument, that ethics was again on the agenda. Indeed, ethics had never been as off the agenda as it had once seemed.

It is somewhat ironic that the specter of the Holocaust, by haunting not only de Man's own scholarly reputation but the entire professional status of deconstruction and the high-theoretical enterprise, should serve in Harpham's narrative as the site for the renewal of ethics, since it is not at all clear that those who, in the wake of the de Man controversy, sought to devenerate the status of theory in the American academy did so because of their special affinity for Holocaust memory. Nevertheless, the rise and fall of de Man's status was indicative of the surprising moral leverage the Holocaust had suddenly achieved in American culture during the decade that included the Yom Kippur War of 1973 in Israel, the airing of Gerald Green's miniseries *Holocaust* on television in 1978, and in that same year President Jimmy Carter's establishment of a presidential commission to plan a Holocaust memorial in Washington, D.C. Occurring nearly a decade later, with Holocaust memory still on the rise, the de Man controversy might mark a quasi-epochal transition with regard to the status of theory in the American academy, to be measured, if only anecdotally, by whether doctoral students of major English and philosophy departments would have felt in the year 2000 anything like the shame they would have felt in 1985 for not knowing, perhaps never having read, the work of Derrida. At the nearer end of a now twenty-year epoch of killing off theory, one might take the often tastelessly dismissive response to Jacques Derrida's death in autumn 2004 to be indicative of how far the star of theory had fallen.[2]

Also remarkable, in and of itself, was the fact that the Holocaust should have served throughout the de Man controversy as what Jeffrey Shandler has called a master moral paradigm.[3] For there is little consensus, if any at all, that the Holocaust can be readily repaired to the discourse of ethics. To offer but one example, when in 1998 Lawrence Langer criticized Tzvetan Todorov's attempt to elaborate the terms of moral life in the concentration camps, Langer's skepticism was firmly rooted in a doubt he himself had helped establish—namely, that there could be any rapprochement between the ordinary parameters of social knowledge and the Holocaust as a catastrophic abyss of meaning. What Langer most lamented was that Todorov should, by concentrating upon the structure of deliberation and decision so central to ethical thought, try to restore the appearance of choice to a situation in which all language

of choosing was a form of doublespeak, a mock-solicitation of the victims to cooperate in a fate they could not possibly escape.[4] Primo Levi, in describing the "gray
zone" of morality inhabited by the victims of the camps, asserted that he knew of no
human tribunal fit to sit in judgment of victims who had perhaps been made complicitous with their oppression, but only as a result of first being forced so far beyond
the social bounds determining ordinary humanity as to render their behaviors ines-
timable by everyday moral standards.[5] And much as Theodor Adorno hypothesized
a rift forever inscribed within the category of culture as a consequence of the Shoah,
Giorgio Agamben has more recently insisted, with exegetical fidelity to Levi's work,
that the camps, as measured especially by the unrecountable witness of those living
dead euphemistically termed *Muselmänner*, were "the site of an experiment in
which morality and humanity themselves [were] called into question."[6] At the very
least, then, it must strike us as odd that a historical event so often used to denote a
historical moment wherein the language of ordinary moral judgment failed (perhaps permanently) should yet achieve the status of a moral signifier by which judgment could be rendered on de Man and all who shared his methodology even if not
necessarily the deplorable ideology of his early wartime writings.[7]

Even in its supremely negating connotations, however, the Holocaust has been
infused with persistent, if not altogether transparent, cultural meanings. Thus, according to an ethical valence that has become almost interchangeable with the word
Holocaust, the Nazi genocide quickly became an event signifying insistently apart
from our ability to formulate any positive ethical statements about it—whether these
be imagined as attempts to describe the event experientially from within its history
or as efforts to contain it retrospectively, perhaps within a system of progressive moral
knowledge, before setting it back within the parameters of common, or commonsensical, judgments.[8] If such a formulation of the Holocaust's surprisingly ethical
signification begins to sound a bit Levinasian, this is because I wish also to suggest
that, in addition to the coincidental timing of theory's demise and the Holocaust's
accrual of cultural importance in the United States, we might add to Harpham's narrative about the return of ethics circa 1987 at least one other significant event: namely,
the retrieval of Emmanuel Levinas as a significant interlocutor in intellectual conversations informed by French poststructuralism. In postwar France, Levinas's importance had been generally acknowledged for a great many years, but despite Derrida's
"Violence and Metaphysics" (1964, 1967), which as Robert Bernasconi suggests
influenced the terms for the reception of Levinas in the English-speaking world,
Levinas's impact on the importation of French theory had been relatively minimal.[9]
Then, at about the time of which Harpham speaks (perhaps as part of the same cultural crisis pertaining to theory's legitimacy), all this began to change. Suddenly

Levinas also was on the agenda, and nowhere more obviously than in the work of Derrida himself. Indeed, by reemphasizing the technique of *clôtural* reading, Derrida foregrounded, as Simon Critchley has aptly pointed out, ethical concerns that had (always) informed his textual hermeneutics.[10] Insofar as deconstruction expressed discomfiture with the regulatory aspects of philosophical, cultural, linguistic, and literary epistemes, Derrida began to emphasize the deconstructive resistance to totalizing discourse as a mode of ethical dissent, a resistance that might even seem consistent with liberal ideology. Also newly acknowledged was the fact that deconstruction's characteristic unease with the truth claims of language and with culture's regulatory enterprise owed a dialogic debt to Levinas's own stated distrust of the projects of representation and systemic knowledge. The introduction of Levinas into the theoretical conversation, during an era in which theory was dramatically on the wane, had the effect of associating Levinas with theory in a manner that, depending on one's point of view, might have served to rehabilitate theory or to throw Levinas into a theoretical wilderness he'd never imagined as his proper terrain.

If we approach this same cultural moment from a different angle, this time viewing it within a Cold War framework, we might instead choose the year 1989 to denote not so much the end of theory as the return of ethics. I have in mind here roughly the objections to the Levinasian project offered by Alain Badiou. According to Badiou, who interprets our present hegemonic, late capitalistic era as a turning from the revolutionary potential of 1968, ethics was recuperated not merely coincidentally when imperialistic, Western culture conquered its primary opponent—or, should we say, lost its only viable point of resistance.[11] In the so-called post-ideological era—or what Walter Benn Michaels, ironically following Francis Fukuyama's construct of the "end of history," has called "posthistoricism"—Kantian morality with its universal respect for the law was returned to preeminence; and, bolstered by the renewed vogue for ethics, individualist subjects proved to be forgetful of both the trenchant critiques of universalistically construed humanity (by, say, Foucault, Althusser, or Lacan) and of collectivist political paradigms.[12] The discursive culprit for Badiou is the language of human rights, which coincides all too neatly with the spread of late capitalism. In Badiou's estimation the prestige of ethics and a focus on human rights seem interchangeable, mutually dependent on our own purported, a priori ability to define evil. Ethics begins by taking for granted the fact of evil, and law (or its internationalist counterpart, human rights discourse) positions itself against evil, obligating us, according to a circular logic, precisely because it allows us to define evil. In recent years Badiou's critique, originally written in 1993, has come to seem prescient. Even a reader highly skeptical of Badiou's Maoist leanings would have to account for the eerie harmony between President George W. Bush's confident pronouncements against an "axis of evil" and the American political right's subsequent rationalizations of a war in Iraq fought under entirely false pretenses. By repeatedly reminding the American public after the war had begun (with reasons altogether different from those deployed to justify the invasion) about Saddam Hussein's awful record on human rights and his history as a genocidal dictator, the Bush administration effectively leveraged the concept of internationalist duty, despite having respected none of its obligatory procedures. The president's ability to mouth the language of human rights might demonstrate just how well ethical language conforms to legitimating discourses of Western self-interest, to say nothing of our imperialistic confidence that, in our goodness, we can identify and conquer evils in less developed, less civilized countries.

Not only is such behavior consistent with Badiou's estimation of Western culture's predominant understanding of ethics, but it is entirely symptomatic in his view of the reasons for the renewed ascendancy of ethics. In our contemporary, once-again-ethical epoch, politics gets subordinated to ethics. Under the auspices of ethics, Badiou supposes, our behaviors are motivated by the split phenomenality of our humanity—which is to say, the split between our recognition that human beings are (always potentially) victims and our globalizing answer to this fact. In our acts of judgment we identify with the suffering of others, who are not just coincidentally those who are less privileged and less advanced than we. Then, from our position of every cultural advantage, we who belong to the already universalized, benevolent West intervene in a situation that we also loathe, in large part because it exemplifies a barbarity we long ago put behind us. According to the basic logic of human rights, the fundamental right, then, is a right to non-evil. But what this means pragmatically is that our ethical vigilance will be on behalf of conditions and ideational commitments already extant in Western culture: "What is vaunted here, what ethics legitimates, is in fact the conservation by the so-called 'West' of what it possesses" (E 14).

There are a good many Levinasian resonances implicit in the category of ethics as Badiou initially defines and protests it in *Ethics: An Essay on the Understanding of Evil* (1993)—some of which, indeed, exert more influence on Badiou's own counter-proposal than he might wish to admit (specifically, I address the conflict between Badiou's account of the culture of victimization and the question of victim-subjectivity in Levinas's work in chap. 3). Yet, when Badiou introduces Levinas directly, he does so unflatteringly, describing him as head of an alternate school of ethics that, despite its opposition to Kant's school of morality, has only reinforced the conventional opposition of ethics to politics. Ultimately, he sees every argument for an ethics based on the recognition of difference—whether advocating tolerance for the immigrant, opposing racism and sexism, or pushing a respectful multiculturalism—as owing its philosophical prestige to Levinas. Yet, almost as soon as Badiou makes this association, he qualifies it in a twofold sense. First, he finds that ethics as a respect for difference deconstructs itself as nonsense according to the strawman categories—fanaticism, racism, identitarian fixity—to which it is typically opposed. Next, he admits that, from a philosophical perspective, the so-called ethical respect for other cultures must be accounted for as "strikingly distant from Lévinas's actual conception of things" (E 20). This concession is more than incidental, and I wish to emphasize it for the clarifying light it sheds on my own project.

Immediately after this concession, Badiou offers a fairly faithful account of Levinas's rigorous resistance to the philosophical realm of sameness (or, *la même*), suggesting why it is that Levinas's hope of reorienting philosophy from the perspective of the other is necessarily susceptible, as Levinas well knows, to the fact that every other can be perceived through resemblance or through a conceptual knowledge running back toward sameness. As Badiou aptly infers, nothing guarantees that the other shall be experienced according to the primordial distance or nonidentity by which she is purportedly signified in the Levinasian system. Able to offer only a metaphysical guarantee of otherness, Levinas devotes even the facticity of the other to a principle that exceeds it, which Badiou rather too neatly decides is, if not God himself, at the very least a "religious axiom" (E 22). In this way, as he effectively bypasses the elaborate process by which Levinas reinterprets religious idiom through the primacy of the ethical relation, Badiou accounts for Levinas's category of the altogether-other as merely a mystificatory version of difference. If you suppress the "religious character" of such an ethics, what you are left with, Badiou declares, is a "pious discourse without piety, a spiritual supplement for incompetent governments, and a cultural sociology preached . . . in lieu of the late class struggle"—in short, a language that mystifies our real political accountability for creating just social structures and makes our responsibility seem as mysterious to us as our own ideological commitment to the structures of power by which we already benefit (E 23). It is hard to know exactly whose simplification of Levinas is at work here—whether this is Badiou's own critically reductive reading or perhaps his parroting of a misreading offered by those who find their commitment to traditionally liberal politics reaffirmed by Levinasian ethics. After initially declaring that Levinasian piety once severed from its religious moorings becomes mere bunk, Badiou slides into a lament against the cultural discourse of difference, deciding that the advocates of an ethics of difference show their hand by what kinds of difference they will in fact tolerate, and speculates that the condition for obtaining ethical respect might read as follows: "Become like me and I will respect your difference" (*E* 25).

By first admitting that Levinasian ethics is, in philosophical terms, not readily reconciled to the varieties of identity politics with which it has sometimes been associated, and next proceeding nevertheless as though such a misapplication of his thought were Levinas's most concrete legacy, Badiou implicitly poses a challenge to all subsequent critical study of Levinas. Indeed, if Badiou's objections are not just caricature—and I believe they are not—then Levinas must be made answerable also to an apolitical or post-political trajectory that has seemed, for detractors as well as enthusiasts, to characterize his ethics. Badiou's critique lays the ground, then, for much of this book's dialectical method. On the one hand, I wish to argue for an abiding relevance of Levinasian ethics that cannot be canceled simply by introducing political concerns or matters he fails to take direct or proper account of. Not everything that is political is stated as such, and in this book I honor a view Levinas held of his own work, namely, that ethics can stand for the function of critique in relation to politics and also, as a result of the necessarily unrealized dimension of every ethical obligation, as the place from which politics begins.[13] That persistent dialectic—according to which ethics unmakes the conclusions, doctrines, and hazards of politics even while politics always invents itself anew as based in the anterior and often unrecognized ethical structure of all responsibility—runs throughout Levinas's work; and it is at least part of my intent here to lay bare some of its implications. On the other hand, the argument of this book does not proceed as though my primary task were to paraphrase Levinas or apply him to those ethical scenarios or political situations not directly taken account of by his work. Although I do not finally join ranks with Badiou and others such as Gillian Rose, Gayatri Spivak, and Slavoj Žižek who have interrogated the usefulness of Levinasian ethics, I do take account of many of the objections frequently leveled against Levinas, even as I also (more consistently in chaps. 3 and 4) maintain a critical perspective on Levinas's philosophical arguments and simultaneously investigate the cultural logic inscribed upon the figures he uses for ethics.[14] According to this methodology, I attempt to study Levinas's ethics from a theoretical, explicitly political standpoint and also to elaborate those places where his modes of argument get enfolded into other contested categories of culture. In this respect *Vigilant Memory* sketches what might be called a *critical ethics*, based in a rereading of Levinas's philosophy according to its patterns of submerged argument and its not altogether consistent figurative logic, but finally also according to its unrealized, sometimes contradictory politics.[15]

RE-THEORIZING ETHICS

Ironically, one result of introducing Levinas into a narrative about the changing face of theory since 1987 or 1989 is to return us, albeit through a slightly different lens, to that aforementioned, long established antinomy between ethics and theory. Although Levinas is among the most stylistically and cognitively difficult of the post-structuralist philosophers (quite capable with his severely appositional and paratactic syntax of giving Derrida a run for his money when it comes to the density of his sentences), he is not, strictly speaking, a high theorist. What the term *theoretical* signifies for Levinas is an aspect of language that systematizes knowledge, drawing up its rules and principles in such a way as to abrogate and overly determine the human other for, through, and to whom language speaks. As such, theory is indicative of a Western propensity to abstract knowledge until it becomes irresponsible to those originary significations from which language emerges. Although ethics persists at the level of what Levinas calls in his late work the *Saying* rather than the *Said* function of language, theory dedicates itself to the quintessential aspect of the Said, the pure tendency (suspect as all pure tendencies must be) to generalize knowledge and to forsake the particulars of relationship. Yet, for my purposes, what seems most important with regard to Levinas's contact with high theory is the eminent function in his work of ethics as critique.

Phrased succinctly and perhaps too axiomatically, the aspect of critique in Levinas's work is generated by the following principle: *the obligating force of an obligation necessarily fails to coincide with its expression.* In the phrase "its expression," *its* might refer either to the obligating force or to an enacted obligation. What the historical project of morality has typically tried to do is reconcile the force and instance of obligation by way of a rationalizing, ideational framework for moral obligation. Whereas Levinas also discerns a gap between the force of ethics and morality's normative expressions, and additionally emphasizes a gap between the aspects of obligation (say, between the formally assigned duty and the historically situated responsibility), he allows the gap itself to serve a signifying function. In that gap is the distance of alterity, an aspect of responsibility that cannot be enfolded into intention or charted and thus contained as part of a system of knowledge. One way to understand the structural gap that begets responsibility is in temporal terms, and, as Dennis Keenan points out, Levinasian critique is characterized by a distinct construct of temporality. Keenan distills the temporal structure of Levinasian ethics to what he calls, translating Levinas, the "not yet of dead time," which structures all obligation.[16] Emphasizing the sense in which ethics in its signifying force is always unrealized,

Keenan summarizes a paradox whereby any moment in which obligation seems to have been met can only prove, since obligation must still persist in order to signify, that it lies yet or always elsewhere. As Levinas overtly states in *Otherwise than Being or Beyond Essence* (1974), the method of skepticism is relevant here, both as that which is again legitimated by Levinas's estimation of ethics and also as an analogous mode of inquiry within the tradition of philosophy.

In skepticism our concern for the truthfulness of any statement perceives an impossibility (denoted under the aspect of faith or inherited knowledge) upon which the statement is based. As Levinas similarly charts a structural resistance within knowledge, which he will rename ethics, he does not rely on what he understands to be the mistake of skepticism. Every time skepticism insists upon the impossibility of a stated truth, it has opened itself to a critique unmasking the skeptical statement as riven by the contradictory condition of its own utterance.[17] Skepticism is for impossible truth against the readily possible truth, but has nowhere to stand. Whereas skepticism proves open to refutation precisely because it gets locked into a principle of simultaneity, thus adhering too much to the "at the same time" by which all contradictions are gleaned, Levinas instead discerns a dislocating temporality behind every representation or statement, behind being itself (*OTB* 7). Most consistently, he calls this paradoxical notion of temporality "diachrony." Referring to the future, which is never as simple as what will happen, and referring to a past that is never quite exhausted by our understanding of what has already happened (the "so it was" statement of history), Levinas persistently characterizes diachrony as a functional resistance to all chronology. It is the very principle by which any event and our understanding of it refuse to align in the instant.[18] If skepticism contests the order of knowledge by remaining immanent to such an order, only a skepticism that can be shown to take its cues implicitly from elsewhere—which is to say, only a mode of inquiry legitimated by that which is outside of, or otherwise than, being—can elude the fate of being refuted on the basis of the very logic it has contested. As such, skepticism might signify, even without fully elucidating the value of its own significance, the abiding possibility of ethical critique.[19]

In response, then, to the problem of how the obligating force of ethics might still signify even though neither the obligation nor the expression can ever be adequate to the signifying force, Levinas supposes that the estranged temporality of responsibility preserves the force of ethics. While conceding the inadequacy of—indeed, the necessary failure of—every stated, conceived, or enacted instance of obligation, Levinas supposes that the immediate, contingent inadequacies of morality prove the greater calling of responsibility, which is always other than or anterior to its occasion. In what follows I will attempt to link the diachronic dialectic of the Levinasian

project to a mode of historical memory and to associate it with a more practical horizon for politics. Presumably, if ethics depends upon recognizable and enactable obligations, then even in its most extraordinary connotations our responsibility might
always be subsumed by the ordinary workings of social consciousness, or by a politics aiming pragmatically, or merely conventionally, beyond rigorous ethical questions. The signifying force of ethics must be without practical force in the real world;
otherwise the language of *ought* or the vocation of responsibility would not be
required. We can only be obligated to do that which the regulatory, practical social
forces in our lives do not already guarantee, or at least make likely, that we will do.

To the extent that our responsibility must always be negotiated within the realm
of pragmatic necessity, such that we are likely to project our ownmost interests into
the ideal realm of duty and to intervene on behalf of others so as to defend principles that align with our interests, Badiou's concern necessarily resurfaces. Is not
ethics primarily a mystification of what we already hold dear and only choose to
see as categorically important? Does not ethics lend itself to being equated with
neoconservative or neoliberal social codes that have presided over the renascence
of morality in contemporary United States culture? Is not ethics a language that
defines familial loyalty as a first principle, with the sentiments of nationalism (distilled during the war in Iraq into the motto "Support Our Troops" etched on yellow,
ribbon-shaped car magnets) a not so distant second? What could ever prevent us
from perceiving so-called obligating force only where we want to, or where the logic
of an imperialistic, capitalistic nation-state wants us to? Bearing just such reservations about ethics in mind, I emphasize how fully invested a Levinasian view of
ethics is in the renewable endeavor of critique, which by definition discomfits any
alignment of ethics with a conservative construct of morality such as that which is
hypothesized by Badiou.

I use the notion of ethical force advisedly. As a consequence of the contemporary
demystification of ethics—as a result, in other words, of our necessary participation
in an era that, as John D. Caputo phrases it, has brought about the "end of ethics"—
the problem of force is a pointed one, upon which the ethereal balloon of ethics
might seem finally to burst.[20] Blending the language of Derrida and Levinas,
Caputo argues for obligation against ethics or for the gifted dimension of ethics—in
other words, for that which cannot be squared with the merely dutiful connotation
of obligation.[21] The generosity of ethics, which Levinas derives from the definitional
excess inhering in the Good, is always about doing more than what is required. It is
precisely because we have become so jaded about what is required of us and how
it came to be required—in short, because we are both aware and mistrustful of the
sociopolitical force behind every notion of duty—that exorbitant responsibility

denotes the only real possibility for ethically meaningful acts in a post-ethical era. Ironically, or not so ironically, Caputo's call for the end of ethics pronounces a way of still doing ethics after we have admitted in our postmodern era that ethics as morality, or as Kantian duty, has failed its historical mission.

It is tempting to attribute the problem of force to the universalism of Kantian ethics, and thereafter to hypothesize an ethics free from such presumptive, oppressive, and impractical notions about how morality binds us. Yet, though the problem of force is indeed quintessentially Kantian and has inspired great doubt in contemporary ethicists, it also persists within the very possibility of ethics. For Kant ethical force differentiates itself from the multiplicity of subjective interest or the practical misuse of reason by being based in ideality. As Kant refers the construct of duty beyond a subject's private perception of what she must do to the generalizing framework of the categorical imperative, he separates a merely contingent sense of urgency, as also any response that is practically motivated, from what we might call a durable obligation. Such an obligation is defined by the possibility that it can be generalized and that, as Bernard Williams savvily observes, an agent might not be able to act upon it in any given situation. For Kant a subject who acts ethically acts upon principle, motivated by the thought that she must do such and such—which is also to say that she must do what another (or any) reasonable person would also be required to do. From the premise of interchangeability (the notion that another person would also be required to do this) we progress to the general principle: any person finding herself in this situation and able to recognize the relevant principle must act accordingly, at least insofar as she is able to do so. All of this leads to a familiar Kantian axiom: *I know that I am responding to a moral obligation when I do that which I do not wish to do, or that which I cannot not do and still consider myself to be a moral person.* The force of the generalizable obligation depends upon its exterior relation to a subject's immediate, interiorly motivated concerns. And thus, the force of any moral obligation resides in an aspect of transcendence, which is to say, in the obligation's superiority to all practical necessities or habitual behaviors.

Much of the field of contemporary ethics, which is as diverse and theoretically complex as the field of literary theory, has yielded the construct of Kantian obligation back to an implausibly universalistic past. As we have come to define morality from the historicist standpoint and thus to align all claims for universalist obligations with discernible (if not always transparent) cultural norms, the work of critique has become ever more closely associated with the demystification of morality. According to Hobbes's account of regulatory justice, the law is based upon the fact that we are all naturally self-interested, competitive beings and so presumes as its very structure an analogous premise of social competition, even as it defines the possibility of cooperation precisely by delineating the requirements of obligatory force, thus deterring, limiting, or containing the cultural play of self-interested behavior. Like Hobbes before him, Nietzsche advocated a construct of justice openly harmonized with social constructs of power. Since morality had served historically as a veil concealing the individual will to power, as also the social function of force behind every enacted obligation, the value of obligation (thanks especially to Judaism and even more so to Christianity) was over time completely inverted. Not only was morality's attempt to describe the force of obligation as though it were opposite to socially enacted power an empty endeavor; it was obviously a falsification of reality. In the Nietzschean view we become newly required, in the name of justice, to expose the structure of force behind every moral statement, even as we suppose that there can be no real difference between moral and politically leveraged force. Indeed, by offering a slightly caricatured reduction of Levinasian ethics, or the ethics of difference with which it is sometimes associated, Badiou reenacts just such a well-worn mode of Nietzschean critique.

Along not altogether dissimilar lines, Bernard Williams proposed from within the field of ethics a critique of the construct of moral obligation, in which yet again the question of force, though approached from a different angle, was relevant. In Williams's work—I wish to highlight here the essay "*Ought* and Moral Obligation" (1981) as a highly representative, concise example—the *ought* of moral obligation is persistently interrogated via the perspective of an individual who might be hypothetically obligated by such a consideration but who turns out to be just as compellingly motivated by an array of practical social interests that concern him.[22] Any difference between the practical *ought* and so-called *ought* of moral obligation disappears under close scrutiny—or we might say more accurately that the two *oughts* frequently coincide to an extent that seems significantly detrimental to the qualitative character of the moral *ought*. It is part of Williams's working method to rehabilitate the province of ordinary thought, including the requirements of everyday life and those motivations made meaningful by being commonly enacted as part of an agent's life project, so as to reveal the Kantian moral *ought*'s disregard for a field of experience contextualizing so-called moral rationality. Every event of the practical *ought* is governed strictly by possibility, as also by an exclusivity (in the sense that it is relevant to an agent particularly) and by its pertinence to a project with which the agent is identified. All of these factors distinguish it from the impractical, generalizable, altogether transcendent function of the highly moral obligation—but, then, only so far: "of course in the deliberations of an agent who is morally motivated, or in advice given to such an agent, an *ought* of moral obligation and the practical *ought* will often coincide. Moreover, that must be so, to some considerable extent, if there is to be a working system in which moral considerations have any force. They have force only because a fair proportion of agents a fair proportion of the time grant them force in their deliberations" (120). Even moral obligations, Williams asserts, work back toward the enactable possibility of the practical *ought*; otherwise we could not attribute any real force to them. As he appeals to the question of force, Williams presumes that a moral obligation obtains its prestige in some strong proportion to its hypothetical forcefulness, and, say what we will, in the end forcefulness has to refer to that which actually compels us in everyday life. By a circular logic he associates with the system of morality itself, Williams argues that the quality of force in the moral obligation is derived from the momentum, or moving inertia, of past behaviors.[23]

Thus, the failure of an obligation ever to get beyond its own immediate exigency is at the heart of Williams's critique of ethics. As soon as we extrapolate from the practical circumstances of any obligation to produce a general principle, already the principle has lost its particularity as an obligation. The problem with the generalized obligation is that it cannot be acted upon as such. Not only is it governed by highly contingent circumstances, but it has to be embedded in a set of practical considerations in order to be realized. Although it might appear that Williams's commitment to pragmatism positions him against a theoretical understanding of obligation, it is worth noting that his revaluation of contingency and his commitment to a demystifying critique of normative, received knowledge are simultaneously legitimated by the complementary, high-theoretical praxis associated with such figures as Nietzsche, Derrida, and Foucault. Only when theory is equated with a mode of discourse dependent on the capability of rationalist conjecture to elaborate exhaustive explanations of phenomena is it characterized by its striving for completeness. What the revolution of deconstruction brought about (as a further step in the progress of the skeptical tradition) was a contrary, also theoretical movement—indeed, an emphasis Walter Benn Michaels and Steven Knapp associated in 1981 with the reign of theory while calling for its end—by which we might interrogate the workings of systemic knowledge and disrupt the conventional stabilities of intentional conceptualization so as to question the harmonious reduction, or abstracted paraphrase, linking the generalized idea to a particular occasion or significance.[24]

What meta-ethical ethicists such as Williams or Caputo share, even though they begin from extremely divergent philosophical priorities, is an objection to morality's capacity to function as an impersonalist, generalizing, or abstract (in their estimation, theoretical) system. In this view what is left out of theoretical conjecture is the radical contribution of contingency, the immediate forcefulness by which obligations obligate, without ever permitting us the time to refer to a scale of priority or to suppose deliberatively pure motives. Contemporary meta-ethical critique thus recommends that ethics as a discourse should distrust its traditional commitments and question its devotion to all principles elaborated at the expense of practical decision making or of a realistic politics constituted within diverse cultural contexts. Attempting to locate obligation elsewhere than with virtue and universalizing constructs of the Good, Caputo proposes starting with those "who are beset by evil demons on every side, . . . with the disasters who are as often as not, maybe more often (I have not taken a survey), the victims of the Good (somebody's Good)" (*Against Ethics* 35). As I will suggest hereafter, and as Caputo surely recognizes, this is not an un-Levinasian move. Yet, despite his overtly Levinasian influences, Caputo wishes also to stress that he has parted with Levinas, who remains too committed to the Good, too pious (which is also, we recall, one of Badiou's objections). Like Badiou, Caputo sees Levinasian ethics as immersed in, if not altogether characterized by, its religious idioms. I have no reason to defend the pious Levinas, although such defenses have been offered and might even appear to legitimate Badiou's conflation of Levinasian responsibility with a religious rationale. Instead, I proceed largely in the opposite direction, questioning whether Levinasian ethics has much at all to do with piety and finding those moments (addressed in greater detail in chaps. 3 and 4) wherein his rhetoric becomes again enfolded in piety to be in contradiction to the most responsible horizon of ethics. But we should also emphasize that the ground of Badiou's and Caputo's contention with Levinas pertains to the question of contingency. Thus piety, in their critical usage, serves as a shorthand for any construct of a responsibility launched elsewhere than in the immediate circumstance, or for that sense of obligation that, while it impresses itself upon the subject in immediacy, would also lay claim to the force of an enduring, noncontingent, universally valid decree.

THE LANGUAGE OF THE OTHER

Levinas will cooperate only so far with a demystification of morality that lends itself to a pluralist, relativist, nonuniversalizing discourse of difference as the ground of responsibility, a discourse that would quickly start to resemble, as Badiou intuited all too well, late liberalism. In speaking of late liberalism, I allude to Jameson's understanding of "late capitalism" and thus to a philosophy that might ultimately cooperate with the overextension of the liberal nation-state in history and with the revalorization of nationalism that coincided so dramatically with the ascendant prestige of ethnic difference in the late twentieth and early twenty-first centuries. For Caputo, who might be characterized as a deconstructive pluralist, it is preferable to be late liberals—distrustful of our founding principles and ideologies, newly responsive to the multiplicity of obligation—than to risk any reversion to authoritarian, even totalitarian systems of social morality. Yet, as leftist critics such as Žižek have pointed out, such appeals to the specter of totalitarianism have consistently served in the late twentieth century to reinforce the mythology of the liberal nation-state, as though any social policy obviously on this side of totalitarianism might mark itself as progressive by contrast.[25] Levinas's persistent suspicion of totality has been sometimes associated with the specter of totalitarianism, even to the point where Levinasian thought might be characterized as political according to the implicit memory of the totalitarian state embedded within his ethics.[26] It is precisely along such lines that Levinas's objections to the totalizing tendency of all philosophically systemic knowledge, whether ontological or epistemological, have been linked to a kind of antitheoretical particularism, as though Levinasian ethics were largely continuous with Kierkegaard's reservations about Hegelian idealism.[27] In such a scheme the other encountered in relationship is preeminently singular, and responsibility for her is constituted as though it reflected the unique individuality of each other person who might become obligatingly meaningful in our lives if only we were willing to cede to her exceptionality. When Levinas refers to the other in her height or in his apparent poverty, when he speaks in the biblical idiom of taking responsibility for the widow and the orphan, the particularity of the other who suffers appears to be that which obligates the self, as though Levinasian responsibility discerned centrally the exceptional, immediate demand of obligation.

Any attempt to align Levinasian alterity with a particularity indicative of the multiplicity in being or symptomatic of the diversity of cultural differences forsakes, however, Levinas's own rejection of such a straightforwardly liberal option in an essay such as "The Ego and Totality" (1954). Perhaps more important (since, his objections notwithstanding, Levinas's philosophy might still serve the predominant liberal social order), our seeing the radical of alterity as though it were coextensive with the unique individuality of each person, or the unpredictable contingency of every situation, suggests a mode of aristocratic democratization, according to which the distinctive individual obtains significance precisely by being made symptomatic of an ennobling currency of virtue. In Nietzsche, as also in Foucault and perhaps to some extent in Williams, the critique of morality proceeds by exposing the self-contradictory valences and politically dishonest function of morality as a system. Partly marked by a fondness for the rigors of antiquated Greek culture, such suspicion of normative morality returns us explicitly in Nietzsche (implicitly in the others) to an appreciation for those who are strong in character and thought, who are always, not merely coincidentally, those individuals privileged enough by social rank to assign themselves responsibilities within the political system. There can be little doubt that in the American cultural context our system of rights has been well served by just such a possibility. Our narratives of social ascendancy typically democratize, according to a mythical logic that many conservatives now euphemistically legitimate through the notion of meritocracy, by discovering again or for the first time the worth of an individual who was always inherently better than the adverse condition by which he or she was, for a time, mistakenly characterized. The selective importation of Nietzsche into the American individualist tradition is often attributed to H. L. Mencken, and at the very least one might remark with regard to this confluence that Mencken's purportedly iconoclastic, fiercely individualistic brand of Nietzschean Americanism was based in a complex, mythicizing reclamation of aristocratic heritage. So, too, in the late twentieth century Alan Bloom's donning himself in the cultural splendor of ancient Greece resonated with the American public of the Reagan era, as *The Closing of the American Mind* hypothesized an aristocratic legacy that might once have belonged to American culture, according to which each reader, cooperating with the resourcefulness of American myth, might demonstrate an individualized merit.[28]

I do not wish to reduce every argument for radical particularism simply to a nostalgic fondness for the individual, who is perhaps necessarily a sign of our nostalgia for aristocratic constructs of character. Rather, my point in offering such anecdotally metonymic evidence of the American enchantment with distinguished particularity is to suggest that any attempt to bind the particular of responsibility to the unique individuality of the other runs necessarily toward a selective hypothesis. One might well indeed demystify much of what counts within the field of morality by emphasizing how neatly our cultural values correspond with our interests, how predictably the responsibilities we select reinforce such values, or how the individuals for whom we admit obligations affirm our already constituted, exclusive constructs of community. In this view critique would be associated with ethics primarily by being opposed to it, so that the forcefulness of obligation would seem its most conspicuously false gesture, with ethics serving either as a veil for genuine political force (as Nietzsche proposes) or as that which converts the necessarily contingent motivation into a durable principle (as Williams argues). Since Levinas can be read as though he advocated a preference for the individualized situation of ethics over against the impersonal, generalizable rule, as though what he meant by alterity were necessarily bound up with social constructs of difference that are never quite fully other than sites of liberal heritage, my contention here cannot be uncontroversial. Nevertheless, I maintain that any reading of Levinas as the defender of cultural difference, or as the advocate of responsibility construed through particularist attachments, involves us in a liberalizing misapplication of Levinasian ethics and may thus cancel the most significant import of Levinasian critique.

In Levinas critique proceeds not as though it were opposed to ethics but as though it were an emanation of ethical responsibility. In short, ethics begets critique. There can be little doubt that Levinas, as does Nietzsche, Williams, and Caputo, finds fault with both philosophy and the system of morality. Yet, whereas other meta-ethical ethicists have framed their critique of morality by attempting to liberate us from obligation (Nietzsche), or to liberate obligation from the implausible idealisms (Williams) or foundationalist origins (Caputo) to which it has been shackled, Levinas does not attempt so much to overturn morality as to reinvigorate it via a point of exteriority that, in having been thus far conceived, has never been exterior enough. In Levinasian responsibility we venture outside the permissible limits of exteriority's obligating force (for instance, as Kantian duty) to find ourselves far more obligated than we imagined, subjects suddenly not to obligations of our choosing but, rather, to what lies beyond our culturally self-limiting constructs of obligation. There is, as Levinas repeatedly insists, an anarchic dimension to responsibility. This does not amount finally to moral relativism, or to an ethics to be discerned contingently as a respect for the differences of other individuals. Any ethics so conceived would functionally resolve itself in the play of identity (albeit a demystified identity, apparently lacking the traditional resources of virtue or moral idealism). Much of the post-Kantian critique directed at morality has borne such a supremely individualist imprint, as though morality's greatest flaw were that it could not greatly enough honor the diversity of human experience. In the cultural-critical vein the impulse against normativity has often characterized critique as if it were always the equivalent of antitheoretical methodology, an effort, in short, to honor (as is the case with Foucault's Nietzscheanism) the contingent particulars of history without generalizing them across time, unless perhaps to demonstrate how they have cumulatively and ideologically constructed present identity. In Levinas, however, responsibility has priority over identity in such a way that it signifies the breakup of all conventionally prior constructs of identity. This must be true not only for the subject but also for the other.

An ethics contradicting a subject's identity while affirming the other's identity as based, say, in cultural difference would be either philosophically contradictory or merely politically contrary, unable to sustain the ground of its critique. For Levinas the other who obligates does so with no conceptual or characterizing control of the responsibility she imparts. The responsibility she signifies is altogether alterior to the identity of the subject she obligates but also alterior to her own significance as other. It is the other through whom responsibility is issued, yet in a basic sense it is the structural dimension of responsibility that obligates. Thus, I wish to maintain, responsibility begets a form of critique that is also rigorously theoretical insofar as it calls for us to make political systems answerable to the responsibilities they have constitutively neglected. It is far too easy (as Badiou has done) to underestimate the systemic implications of Levinasian ethics on the ground that Levinas laments the philosophical and moral system without proposing a substitute system and without concretizing the nature of the alterity that inspires all ethical thought. However, if the force of the other proceeds not as an exception supremely individualistic in nature but, rather, as one that is connotatively systemic, that demands not the forgoing of political justice but its basic reconception, then the reputation of Levinasian ethics, at least insofar as Badiou's critique has influentially characterized it, will have to be significantly revised.

To put it most succinctly, we could say that the sociality of the other, what Kevin Hart also calls a "forgotten sociality," is the site of ethical force.[29] This book is devoted to recovering the force of sociality behind Levinasian ethics as well as to discerning in what sense such an ethics could ever be said to have force in the political world. Perhaps the most characteristic move of Levinasian ethics derives from its willingness to admit the paradoxical forcelessness of all obligation: ethics is that which can make us do nothing. Its meaning cannot be resolved in pragmatic consequentialism, as though responsibility were always only that which we have, to some extent, already enacted in the world. For any such Nietzschean attempt to square responsibility absolutely with enacted political wills would abandon the scene of concrete suffering and thus also the genuine historical reality of those others who constitute the greater portion of collective humanity, who have not been realized in history. The historical reality of others involves both contingent and systemic (as opposed to necessary) circumstances, but, whereas much poststructuralist theory (perhaps most prominently in the work of Derrida and Foucault) emphasizes the contingent determinations of persecuting force, I want to suggest that for Levinas social injustice and oppression are preeminently systemic and thus interpretable as the sites where justice turns from, rather than toward, the ethical significations from which it arises. For its part ethical critique always proceeds implicitly from the memory of the injustice done to others in the past as also from our vigilant concern for injustices perpetrated in the present political moment. Ethics is not simply a form of politically motivated dishonesty to be genealogically charted or an obligation to be discerned in the unpredictable particular instance of injustice. Neither is it a piety about difference amounting to a de facto acceptance of the forward necessity of the capitalist nation-state. Conceiving of ethics as such is Badiou's largest mistake, unless of course he should prove to be right.

ETHICS AS CRITIQUE

If there is some truth to Badiou's assumption that Levinas legitimated the ethics of difference in France, when it comes to the American scene—and my concern here is especially focused on Levinas's relevance for debates in the American intellectual context—the order of this process was inverted. However we account for Levinas's recently ascendant reputation in the American academy, the turn to a Levinasian ethics emanating from that which is altogether-other lagged behind the deconstructive obsession with difference and critical explications of the differences pertaining to gender, race, and multiculturalism, almost as though Levinas were merely adding— once it had become commonplace for academics on the cutting edge of theory to express weariness with ubiquitous, always-more-demanding *others*—an extra dose of otherness to those already evolved discourses.[30] There is something ironically appropriate about Levinas's belated arrival on the American scene, that the philosopher of whom Derrida so reverently declared he would not alter a word (almost as though Levinas could be exempted from deconstruction) should be received only after deconstruction was on the wane and after postcolonialism, as the latest-to-arrive discourse of difference, had asked us to consider whether it was ever possible for the subaltern to speak in the dominant language of the West; and there is something uncannily disconcerting about the fact that this supreme advocate of an ethics pertaining to the always unrealized, anterior, not-yet relation should be introduced rigorously into our conversations about alterity when otherness was already passé.

Still, if by a certain literary historical narrative theory came and went in the United States without Levinas, his work should not be understood as altogether determined by its cultural reception, which is to say, as fully implicated in the cultural politics of identity from which his reputation no doubt benefited. There can be little question that much of Levinas's recent popularity has been dependent upon a revaluation of Jewishness in contemporary philosophy, both as a point of revered difference (especially within Christian philosemitic discourses) and as a positive expression of cultural heritage (within literary-critical discourses concentrated on ethnicity). The temptation is to invoke Levinas's Jewish writings as though the philosophical writings could be summarily characterized from the perspective of identity. That there should be cross-fertilization between the two realms—specifically, between Levinas's cultural, often religious Jewish writings and his rigorous philosophical assessment of ethics as that realm that philosophy had almost from its inception, with repetitive splendor, forsaken—seems inevitable. Even a thumbnail sketch of Levinas's biography makes the point for us. He wrote the greater portion of one of his earliest philosophical studies, *Existence and Existents*, while imprisoned in a Jewish prisoner of war camp in Germany, accorded the rights of the Geneva Convention of 1917 as a military combatant. Prior to the war he had taught at the Alliance Israélite Universelle in Paris, and after the war he took an appointment with the Oriental Israelite Normal School, also a branch of the Alliance. Throughout the 1950s he undertook studies of the Talmud and gave his first public lecture on the Talmud very close to the time he published his first major philosophical monograph, *Totality and Infinity* (1961). It is only reasonable to ask how his practically engaged Jewishness and his memory of the Holocaust shaped his philosophical thought.

Even so, the place of the Holocaust in all of this is not simple. Although I take to heart Jill Robbins's point that we should not read the Holocaust as though it were the determinative influence on Levinasian ethics, I follow Robert Eaglestone in wishing not to underestimate the forceful coincidence of the Holocaust and ethics at key moments in his work.[31] Right away we notice that the Holocaust for Levinas is focused not by cultural priorities but, rather, by ethical, even implicitly universalist ones. The dedication of *Otherwise than Being* to the six million who died as a result of antisemitism, that great hatred of the "other man," provides a historical connotation that, if applied too hastily, might even seem to predetermine many of his subtle figures for the Holocaust as weighty allusions. I am not contending that the Holocaust is the precipitate cause of Levinas's ethics, as if his entire project were traumatically determined by Holocaust consciousness. Such a move would greatly oversimplify on both ends—providing at once an explanatory rubric for reading Levinas that overlooks his deep engagement with the long history of Continental philosophy while also making the Holocaust function too readily as an explainable event through which a vocabulary of moral action or ethical relationship relevant to our everyday lives might be articulated. If only because the Holocaust informs Levinas's work without ever becoming the explicit content of his philosophizing, we have to respect the distance Levinas maintains between the immediate figurative terms he employs for the ethical relation and the history they indirectly evoke.

Nevertheless, although Levinas does not concern himself with practical applications of ethics, his weighted and controversial turns of phrase have already begun the work of application, if only in reverse. For Levinas responsibility is never just a figure, and indeed a naïve literalism preoccupies his overly insistent figures, quite as though history could impose itself, becoming manifest in the figures, as an interruptive force. Throughout *Vigilant Memory*, then, I pay special attention to the patterns of figuration that mark ethics in the Levinasian project. Often what Jill Robbins calls

the "ethicofigural" aspects of Levinas's writings are devoted to phenomena of unpleasure, those recurrent traces of a demand enacted exteriorly, by which ethics is
persistently impressed upon us, whether in the very midst of potential devastation or
in our witness to it. Levinas's ethicofigural terms, ranging from *substitution*, *persecution*, and *accusation* to *traumatic commanding* and *taking hostage*, are by no means
innocent of their historical and political connotations, and for the purposes of this
study I assume that they draw upon, as their most obvious historical example, sufferings based in the Holocaust.[32] These terms bring to mind actual moments in which
the other dies, invoking the historical specter of the unjust death as they make overt
a significance inherent in every death of the other—namely, that it is first and fore-
most an injustice. For Levinas the death of the other occurs in a moment of impossible contemporaneity, a moment historically shadowed by the Holocaust. According to this argument for impossible simultaneity, Levinas makes mourning a figure
for the past having everything to do with the injustice of the present.

   Throughout this book I interpretively elaborate the historical resonances of
Levinas's figurative language, and yet I do not simply impose a literary reading on
Levinas, who pronouncedly distrusted literature for its capacity to obscure the straightforwardness of ethical obligation. There is at times an almost willful component to
Levinas's distrust of rhetoric and literature, a distrust, as Robbins has argued, that is
simply not sustainable: Levinas's language must dip into the well of rhetorical stratagem, even of literary affect, to demonstrate the ethical premises of signification
itself.[33] Indeed, the literariness of his language often provides the very means by
which its practical dimensions as ethics can be discerned. At least one function of
the figure, as a complement to its historicity, is to trace a rupture in language's conceptual seamlessness and turn us again to the necessary situatedness of ethics. In this
view metaphoric logic does not set up an analogous realm forever resistant to the real
world of reference or to the relational affect imposed by the other but, instead, functions as a figurative system by which responsibilities can again be denoted as though
they had survived the persistent cultural history of philosophy's forgetfulness of the
other, of politics' seeming disdain for alterity. Metaphor's transgressiveness is always
also a retrieval of language's genealogy, which in Levinas necessarily returns us to the
hypothesis that address determines all language as for-the-other.[34]

   According to Levinas, the sign of ethics is forever concealed by the progressive
function of knowledge or by any politics that presumes sameness where no such
ground exists. Yet the signifying force of ethics always emerges once more, almost as
though it were pronounced by a violent rupture in language and being, in the necessary repetition of the ethical scenario, casting us back upon that determinative
structure of language which is the face-to-face relationship.[35] Or, in the terms of

paradox that characterize so much of Levinasian ethics, we might say, *unease is the very sign of the ethical.* Ethics is not a yearning for imaginary harmony, for an ideal condition that has been lost or forever displaced. It is not an idealistic project in the sense that it can be foreseen, planned, and fulfilled. It pertains always to memory's unseating of what it resolves. Ethics is the other's resistance to all benevolent or malevolent intention. As soon as one settles the score with unease (say, by acting benevolently on behalf of another person), one has moved beyond the originary claim of ethics, yet without ever escaping its reach. For Levinas the relation to the other persists in language as a contra-diction (as a Saying within the Said) of all those ways in which a subject has been culturally constructed and codified as well as of all those concepts received as though they were tantamount to reality. Every reality established by language as such is like the province of literature as Plato imagined it: an escape from the originary significations of a reality to which one must in the end always return. Discomfited in our belief that obligation is contractual and directly measurable, we find that responsibility can be neither anticipated nor enacted in perfect proportion to a self's intentions or experiential understanding or extant citizenship.

In this sense the poststructuralist mistrust of philosophy's confident espousal of universalistic principles is evident in Levinas, but philosophical praxis is not finally dissolved for him in light of contingent truths to be worked out immediately, situationally, and provisionally. For Levinas the obligation proceeding from the other remains universally binding for every subject because we enter into language under the signification of ethics. Thus Levinas's commitment to the universalistic nature of responsibility (which is, in a strictly philosophical sense, a metaphysical premise of his work) points us to those operative or functional universals already at work in socially determined knowledge and in the political organization of both oppression and justice. By virtue of its status as that which signifies apart from our deeds and even our recognitions, ethics commands attentiveness to the political conditions that delimit responsibility, or to what we might think of as a set of contingently developed beliefs that obtain the values of universals insofar as they are applied systemically.

One aspect of the current state of Levinas studies challenged by this book, then, is our tendency (as I've already suggested) to locate responsibility as separate from systemic thought, as though the critique of ethics did such damage to universal signification that even responsibility and the question of injustice were rendered immeasurable except via relativistic cultural norms. By this logic it might seem that the predominant tendency of all sociopolitical organization was to mute the calling of responsibility. Such a view might well complement what antiphilosophical philosophy attributes to the influence of contingency, or the unpredictable sway of any event by or in which responsibility might be signified. So immense do the trappings of normative Western culture and our discursive regimes seem that even Badiou, while lamenting the identity-ridden, particularist tendency of the new vogue for ethics legitimated by Levinas, predicates a turnaround for ethics on the contingent event through which truth arises. Ethics, according to Badiou's recuperating emphasis, should be a fidelity to the unpredicted event with its new requirements of truth. In other words, he can project an ethics on the side of systemic thought only by first abrogating the extant norms of what he sees as an obviously unjust system. Such a dialectical balance between a newly situated responsibility and obsolete, oppressive systemic norms shares the apocalyptic character of Christian theology (Badiou even cites Paul's conversion as an example of such forward-thinking ethical fidelity), and is also not altogether un-Levinasian.

In those such as Badiou who dismiss Levinasian ethics as unshakably metaphysical, implicitly characterizing him as a mildly Christianized Jewish Talmudist whose thought is irreconcilable to the necessarily pragmatic praxis of politics, their dismissal may take on the character of an evasion. Consider more closely Badiou's charge that Levinas must be held accountable for dismantling the philosophical category of sameness, the only ground by which we might aspire to universalistically achieved aspects of truth and by which we might thus redress the real consequences of injustice in the world. Badiou wants to have it both ways, referring to established cultural beliefs (so often understood as though they were universals) as antithetical to truth and then hypothesizing the transformative dimension of truth, which arises contingently through events and must for the sake of justice universally compel those who recognize it. In Badiou our capacity to redress oppression entails a commitment to truths that break with normative understanding and in so doing appeal to what holds human persons in common, thus newly forging the terms of universalism. Without mitigating their philosophical differences—without, that is to say, deploying the false compromise whereby two philosophers, though they themselves cannot see it, are interpreted to be saying the same thing, only in different ways—I am attempting here to draw out the also universalist aspirations of the Levinasian project, specifically insofar as ethics demands, at least implicitly, a critique of systemic political practices and calls furthermore for redresses in the realm of justice that must necessarily be systemic. Treating a range of vaguely situational scenarios that seem as readily locatable in historical circumstances of extreme injustice, Levinasian ethics is not simply reformative, seeking redress for the contingently determined disfranchisement of those who suffer in the present moment, as though their suffering were accidental and systemically unpredicted. Instead, Levinas consistently refers us to those who were never franchised, to the victims occupying a realm that is, from an existential perspective, not in any way temporary or merely the product of the social malfunctioning of justice. Even if he does not delineate a practical political ethics, Levinas implies that the suffering of the other, which is the unnegatable facticity of ethics, must have political meaning. In her alterity the other is not merely a relativized difference, not the function of culture or an inverted identity-position. Rather, the other for whose suffering we are inherently responsible approaches from outside knowledge, from outside the political system as though she were, at the same time, intentionally excluded by it.

In other words, responsibility depends in no way upon the contingent circumstances by which it occurs or by which we recognize it. In its universalistic aspect, Levinas presumes, responsibility precedes even the moment of its purported occurrence. And I wish to suggest that this apparently metaphysical premise of a supererogatory other has a corollary for Levinas in the systemically perpetuated suffering of those who remain entirely alien to political justice—not through any admirable, estimable quality of cultural difference but through the politically determined facticity of injustice they endure. At least in part this is the consequence of a supremely historical consciousness, honed on the facts of the Holocaust, embedded in all of Levinas's metaphysical, or rhetorical, insistences.

POST-1945 MEMORY

If this is the case, however, it is true nevertheless that any attempt to draw out the implications of the Holocaust for Levinas's work must honor, as I have already suggested, the author's own strategy of referring to the Holocaust by rhetorical indirection, through figures of rupture and unpleasure. The Holocaust is never directly spoken in Levinas's philosophical work, a fact owing as much to Levinas's insistently nonhistoricist philosophical method as to his respect for the victims who have been silenced and should not be presumptively ventriloquized. As I discern an ethical specificity inscribed upon Levinas's figures for ethics, informed by historical consciousness and bearing always on our systemic view of politics, I am fully aware that I am interrogating conspicuous silences, which are frequently logical and ideological gaps, in Levinas's own work. Still, as the Holocaust is alluded to with ever greater frequency in the latter half of Levinas's career, ethics is informed by imperatives that keep us mournfully mindful of the Nazi genocide. To the extent that the Holocaust is invoked as a superfluous sign of injustice, it characterizes the precariousness of ethics within philosophy as though ethics must run parallel hereafter to the political questions raised by post-1945 memory. In this respect ethics must be understood as a realm of thought, or a realm presignifying thought, in which the cultural space of the victim remains significant, in which the one whose injustice cannot be simply articulated through representation or by our ordinary categories of justice persistently impresses herself upon the very meaning of justice.

In giving concrete historical expression to what remains largely implicit and figurative in Levinas's own philosophy, I would like to think of my hermeneutic as not so much a presumptive attempt to speak for the victims of political injustice (a method that would necessarily maintain the priority of an experiential logic) as an insistence, already implicit in Levinas, that our attention be turned to them through the memory of injustice. Especially from within an extended cultural moment in which debates about whether particularist modes of memory (described sympathetically or critically) should be necessary to our concepts of justice in democratic society, and during which the experiential self-understanding of the victim has been made to stand for the political meaning of systemically determined injustices and oppression, my study of the sociality of Levinas's figurative language may function as a timely intervention, not least of all by identifying some of the faulty assumptions now directed at victims and the facticity of injustice. In this respect this book responds to what we might distinguish as three contemporary strands of critique (aspects of which are evident, for example, in Badiou's characterization of Levinas) pertaining to the usefulness of the cultural memory of injustice as a mode of political discourse:

1. There is, first, a reigning assumption that memory and history make difficult bedfellows, and the attempt in recent years to explore the dynamics of collective or cultural memory has come under fire from empiricist advocates of history and pragmatic devotees of politics alike. Much of the contemporary theorization of memory—whether as an emanation of trauma, as a rhetoric of witness or testimony, or as a collective account of the historical and political significances pertaining to the construction of any community or just society— has arisen through discussions of the Holocaust's continuing relevance to our culture. Increasingly of late, however, this debate has been informed by perspectives unsympathetic to the contemporary cultural significations of the Holocaust.[36] Stated most reasonably, this suspicion is a political one, casting doubt as to whether the cultural uses to which the Holocaust has been put (say, in America, where it is not even an indigenously inspired memory) are entirely appropriate to its history. What have sometimes followed such historical skepticism are deeper misgivings about the obligatory relevance of the Holocaust as amoral signifier. From a strictly cultural perspective, the critics of Holocaust politics would remind us that the Holocaust is only relevant if

we say it's relevant, and in the opinion of at least a few the time has come, because of the perceived political uses to which the Holocaust has been put, to say it is not nearly as relevant as it has been made to seem.

2. This suspicion of the Holocaust runs sometimes, though quite imperfectly, parallel to a critique that has been brought to bear on identity politics, at times from the conservative right and at other times from neo-liberalists and neo-Marxists. Their worry is that the articulation of a politics based in ethnic particularisms will prove fragmenting—either to what some (on the right) perceive as a largely laudable capitalist economy already functioning well enough via the mythic suppositions of our individualistic culture by incrementally extending its liberties and rights to those previously left out of the picture; or to what others (on the left) perceive as the theoretical premises and still-to-be elaborated constructs of justice based in measurable, correctable imbalances in wealth or political stature among different segments of democratic populations.[37] According to these emergent lines of critique, to base politics on anything but the hypothesis of equality is already to concede the ground of justice politics has achieved or might one day achieve—the most obvious difference between the right and the left on this front being the perception of how well politics has already succeeded in creating the conditions for justice. The appeal to identity as based in ethnic particularism locates the meaning of political conduct and motives outside the apparent commonality of the public sphere, suggesting (with perhaps too much Nietzschean confidence) that each individual, as a reflection of his heritage or her shaping by affiliation and group identifications, proceeds from a set of motivations and interests that are not adequately measured by extant sociopolitical discourse. The advocates of identity politics would remind us that positionality within culture has everything to do with the political principles one advocates and that the set of values so far formulated by Western democratic—or, more specifically, American—culture has been construed so as to confer benefit on those who are in a privileged position, already within the political mainstream. Those most critical of this newly espoused cultural orthodoxy (which is not nearly so well established as some of its critics try to make it appear) would point out that it has become complicit with a mystification of identity, much to the detriment of any pragmatic discourse about unjust conditions. Not only is there a danger that identity becomes a sentimentalizing, rationalizing narrative about origins, reifying certain premises such as race as though they were biologically and biographically determined realities, but there is the further danger that by transforming the language of political rights into a set of essentializing affilia-

tions, identity politics serves the status quo culture rather than attacking its unjust conditions. If heritage can be made a matter of pride, to be leveraged and marketed by capitalist economy, then the cultural myth of individualism is only reinforced by the resources of identity: the problem with the poor is not that they do not have enough money; it's that they do not have enough pride in themselves and in the public status of their ethnic group. Any mode of cultural memory based in identity is by definition a testimony against the real facts of social inequivalence, since the individual who can draw upon the resources of group identity is always already greater than the real conditions of economic injustice or social oppression that determine her.

3. The third critique involves a strange conflation of the previous two, according to which it is observed that the memory of injustice serves the politics of identity. Among those who have expressed their reservations about the cultural status of Holocaust memory and cultural politics of identity, the perception is that injustice and identity have become so far interfused as to obtain the status of a mutual heritage.[38] The most obvious sign of this critical position might be the contemporary use of the epithet *victim* (as in "victim politics") or any number of hybrid victim terms (such as *victimhood*, the *culture of victimology*, or *cries of victimization*) in a disdainful or dismissive matter. According to a certain line of cultural commentary and popular ideology, victims have become mere opportunists, seizing the moral high ground of their historical, social, or interpersonal oppression as a means to obtain privileges in the public sphere. In this mode of cultural criticism there is a redoubled cynicism: the cynicism of the critic who supposes that victims are merely dishonest agents is perhaps only a rationalization of a cynicism that perceives in victims people who would exploit their suffering, or their perceived suffering, for political gain. Any attempt by the victim to address the systemic sources of her suffering or to seek redress in the public sphere for an injustice done to him might, by such a logic, be discounted as opportunism. Thus a basic suspicion persists that the memory of injustice has become a heritage, and this charge pertains notably to contemporary critiques charging that the term "Holocaust" has become synonymous with mythic valences that render service to Jewish identity.

Insofar as the present study tries to expand the theoretical suppositions of ethics so as to make Levinas's work conversant with a range of contemporary conversations, it should not be viewed as an attempt to invoke Levinas as having already provided answers to any of these debates. To do so would involve a pat theorizing of

Levinas in a manner his ethical philosophy deeply resists and would also require an ahistorical simplification of contemporary culture as though, by a kind of inverted Hegelianism, our conceptual answers already presupposed the form of every cultural problem. Nevertheless, a reading of Levinas in light of a set of contemporary American intellectual debates may result in a recognition that the terms of our debates are partly anticipated by central aspects of his work.

Even as contemporary multicultural politics attempts to extend what many of its advocates perceive to be the most productive horizon of liberal pluralism, Levinasian ethics cannot find its true significance in a politics of diversity, in the belief that being conscientiously located in one's own tradition of identity might make one necessarily respectful of the manifold alterity of others and their diverse constructions of belonging. Such a view of Levinas might enfold his thought within the framework of cultural or ethnic studies, such that the meaning of his ethical pronouncements would be inherently on the side of his cultural locatedness as a Jew, to be explained, say, in terms of Hebrew scriptures or the Jewish tradition of interpreting the Talmud.[39] In Levinasian ethics there is no identity—neither Greek nor Jew—from which responsibility begins. Levinas repeatedly makes the point, as for example in an essay such as "No Identity" (1970), that a subject rooted in identity has knowledge of herself in her own freedom, so that she is necessarily forgetful of an originary signification by the other. In *Otherwise than Being* he insists that ethical relationship, which is the anterior condition of our humanity, is principally structured via a subjectivity already in relationship to the other, referred to itself by way of its responsibilities: the subject that is for itself only in having always been for the other. If, then, there is in Levinasian ethics a particularist rhetoric, it is a particularism hypothetically exempting itself from identity. Even in the concrete moment of face-to-face relationship by which ethics obtains its meaning, an alterity preempts the other's own self-understanding. Ethics is not a gesture of humility by which a self would yield to another person's opinion about ethics or to the self-expression of her identity, delineating responsibility as a respect for interpersonal and cultural difference. Indeed, the reason Levinas so often insists upon the unpleasurable significations of ethics is so that we should not forget how, whether signified in the excess of gifts and goodness or by the unremitting rigor of trauma and obsession, responsibility imposes itself as the meaning of all relationship, quite apart from the other's worthiness as an object of esteem. The ethical relation does not begin from a premise of mutuality or equality, in which a valued interlocutor gives as good as she gets.

Instead, ethics is for Levinas inscribed within the hypothetical scenario of injustice, which is always just vestigially historical enough to remind us of the violences others suffer in the everyday world, in both past and present society. An essay such as "Useless Suffering" (1982), which also provides Levinas's most sustained reflections about the Holocaust, challenges our belief that ethics might be conceived under so-called ordinary circumstances in which the other and self enjoy a relationship of mutuality. Ethics cannot begin from such a supposition, Levinas implies, precisely because the precepts of bourgeois normality are far from normative. The Holocaust traces the extreme deformation of Western society's liberal, progressive ethos, reminding us that, even if Nazi violence was in some sense culturally atavistic, it exploited the techniques of modernity and built its ideological antisemitism upon, in Levinas's phrase, a "hatred of the other man" endemic to the structures of nationalism, self-interest, and sameness from which our constructs of rights are also derived.[40] So, too, Levinas's persistent use of figures of destitution and his direct allusions to Third World poverty are meant to remind us how typical the deformative condition of violence and of oppressively inequivalent socioeconomic structures were throughout the late twentieth century, continuing now also into the early twenty-first. Just as ethics inspires what we might call the metaphysical necessity of critique, so the facticity of injustice—of any condition in which the other suffers extreme violence, political degradation, or economic deprivation—characterizes the necessary sociality of all such critique. Given under the sign of mourning, of unease, of bad conscience, dedicated to the memory of the victim or based in a reception of the stranger who has priority even over the neighbor, ethical responsibility, I argue, begins from the fact of injustice.

Nevertheless, the memory of injustice I chart here is taken up through largely unarticulated assumptions within Levinas's work and elaborated thereafter through theoretical principles with far wider and more practical implications. By focusing throughout on the especially violent or unpleasurable dimensions of Levinas's ethicofigural language, I expound the peculiar intersection between ethics and the history of injustice (with the Holocaust looming for Levinas as for much of late-twentieth-century democratic culture as the paradigmatic example of historical injustice) even as I elaborate what memory means when bound ethically by and to that about which it cannot speak positively. At one level, then, this book intervenes once more in the debate waged between advocates of history and the proponents of memory, but, rather than foreseeing a simple way out of the impasse, I seek to situate Levinas as though he addressed the suspicions we have about both history and memory, posing ethics as a challenge to each realm. To speak finally of what I wish here to call "vigilant memory" as an implicit Levinasian concept, we must formulate a construct of remembrance consequent upon a radical revaluation of memory itself, one newly dedicated to injustice and to a vigilance in relation to the other that resists many of the cultural representations commonly standing for our memory.

In the first chapter I elicit the figure of mourning as a significant sign of ethics in the Levinasian canon. Arguing that the anxiety about the death of the other is the corollary formulation of the mournful emphasis of relationship, I trace the increasingly recurrent status of this premise in Levinas's later philosophical writings. My second chapter expands this mournful framework into a more specific reading of Levinas's reclamation and revision of the Nietzschean bad conscience, which is made to function as a sign both of history and of our ethical responsibility in and for history. For the most part the first two chapters are offered as sympathetic, if also critical, elaborations of Levinasian ethics, whereas chapters 3 and 4, while still espousing the potential value of Levinasian ethics to our contemporary political thought, proceed much more dialectically—at times conceding points to important critiques (such as Badiou's) of Levinas's work, at times raising new lines of critique, and at other times bringing Levinas into conversation with contemporary cultural, political, and philosophical positions in need of rethinking.

In keeping with the stronger element of critique directed at Levinas in the second half of the book, wherein I chart Levinas's sometimes confused articulation of the status of the victim and the typology of stranger versus neighbor, I try to discern in chapters 3 and 4 and in my afterword a productive, overtly political horizon for what are at the very least sites of ethical sensitivity in Levinas's work. So, in chapter 3 I offer a dialectical reading of the implicit status of the victim in Levinasian ethics, tracing Levinas's own implication in a cultural language of rationality that would begin from the supposition of agency and impose the requirement of sacrifice on those who seem incapable of willful actions in time. Ultimately, even as I admit the contemporary suspicion of the so-called cultural reverence for victims into this debate, I suggest that, despite Levinas's own complicity with a strain of martyrological thought, his metaphoric transpositions of the subject-positions of victims can call us to account for our cultural avoidance of the victim. In the fourth chapter I read the tension between the figure of the stranger and the figure of the neighbor in Levinasian philosophy, first showing how Levinas's increasing use of the neighbor in his late writings might superficially bring us back to familiar ground and reaffirm certain cultural notions of identity (perhaps as part of a nationalist project such as Zionism). Yet even the purported familiarity of the neighbor undergoes a striking estrangement in Levinas, so that just as the neighbor's nearness connotes the violence he might do or which might be done to him, a potential for violent alienation haunts every cultural project of identity.

In liberal society we prefer to imagine responsibility as part of the social contract, as that which is perceived in its generalized form as truth and applied to the local situation, and our constructs of rights commonly depend upon the cultural notion of an *I* identified with its freedom, made seemingly transparent via its basis in the knowledge and pragmatic possibility of its cultural milieu. Implicitly throughout this book and more directly in my afterword I take up the question of responsibility in light of the modern demystification of morality as a production of cultural power and identity-positions and of the questions posed to identity-based politics about its apparent complicity in the basic structural inequalities of liberal society. Asking to what degree our responsibility for others within and without our own society might be delimited and even attenuated by the wisdoms of identity politics, I am inquiring as to what remains of the *ought* insofar as it refers us to the sufferings of others. Although contemporary theories of identity seek to demystify the generalized conditions of knowledge and to revise freedom in the name of the contextual heritage by and through which any *I* speaks, even so identity continues to be measured in such a cultural hermeneutics by its ownmost capabilities. By contrast, ethics is for Levinas a sign of an incapability preoccupying every self, of the extent to which a subject is dedicated in responsibility even to that which she cannot as yet understand or do anything about in the immediate context. Levinas's emphasis on the absolute anteriority of ethics should not be understood, then, as a temporal, quasi-hierarchical principle of causation, such that ethics (as, say, individual relation) precedes or preempts sociohistorical interpretation. Rather, ethics arises within, if not quite from, a determinative context; it comes to us through the filter of historically realized conditions by which we would take account of it, even if none of these finally exhausts ethical meaning.

CHAPTER ONE

Ethics as Unquieted Memory

I think that *the Human* consists precisely in opening oneself to the
death of the other, in being preoccupied with his or her death.

Emmanuel Levinas

While avowing little positive content, mourning nevertheless functions throughout Levinas's canon as an internal rhetoric of his discourse as well as a sign of rhetorical imperatives denoting and inflecting his descriptions of ethics. To speak as he
does of the other's significance as though it were not only tested but attested to by
the event of death is to intuit a social realm whence memory takes its cues and by
which it takes hold of its imperatives. It is to speak of memory itself as mournful.
Specifically, by contrasting a mode of immemorial memory to a historical hermeneutic explicitly rooted in the perspective of history's victors and survivors, Levinas distinguishes memory from the progressive flow of knowledge in which it is located and
according to which it would become nothing but the past, or what Giorgio Agamben
calls the inalterable "so it was" of history; and in so doing he also discerns a radical
alterity in memory such that it is structurally, and not just intentionally, attentive to
the moment of another's death.

For Levinas the death of the other is that paramount example of vulnerability by
which every ordinary relationship is marked, and mourning is in turn a vulnerability before the other who may come to harm or a vigilance on behalf of another even
after she has suffered her final fate. In such susceptibility to the other Levinas discerns
a mode of ethical valuation. Yet it is only fair to ask whether susceptibility can by
itself ever be meaningful. Susceptibility seems a kind of emptiness, a lack of content

in self to be filled up from the outside. Exactly to what and to whom is a mourner susceptible?—to merely hallucinatory manifestations from the past, to ghosts such as the inscrutable armored figure who is supposed to be Hamlet's father, to those forever silenced voices of the many victims of interpersonal or political violences in history? Mourning, as I have previously argued in *The Ethics of Mourning* (2004), may well seem meaningful precisely in its resistance to symbolic, socially constructed meanings and may even be driven fundamentally by objections that seem tantamount to the ethical perception of injustice. Yet there is always a question at the far end of our mourning, imperfectly expressed though nevertheless persistent: what are we to make of a discourse of objections that remains, finally, without any object? Precisely those things to which a mourner can no longer sensibly refer are those upon which her mourning insists as centrally significant, as though a course of unrealizable action were demanded by the persistence of reference within mourning. As grief adheres to a sensibility completely interior to its own experience, it always raises the question of its relevance, even as the one who stands outside of mourning, no longer or not yet immersed in grief's sensibility, asks, *Just what is all of this for?* Feeling ourselves under suspicion from those who stand safely beyond mourning's immediate reach, and wanting to find practical implications for mourning's seemingly impossible praxis, we may turn either to memory or to history as seemingly reliable frames of reference, as though mourning demanded always that the past be recalled. Indeed, in making us turn again to the past, mourning serves as a determining motive for our imaginative or intellectual relation to history, justifying itself (if but tautologically) by giving the appearance of necessity to our social structures of remembrance.

On the surface, then, mourning implies that one might still hold in memory what one once held dear in actuality. Such a posture could last hypothetically as long as a single person's entire lifetime; but, insofar as it is a response to a particular occasion, based in the particularity of the one who remembers, mourning could not exceed such a term. To mourn for what you never had or for what did not personally affect you already stretches and generalizes the construct of mourning to a point where the affective intensity upon which mourning depends becomes implausible. By just such an overextension in time, mournful memory brings us into the realm of history, inspired by traces of affective significance that made an event and the persons characterized by it memorable. And a mournful history, if indeed we might speak of such a thing, would function as a paradoxical bridge concept, reminding us of the conflicted priorities of memory's always locatable motivations and history's generalized construct, while intimating a hypothetical place where they might meet. Already the mournfulness of history might seem fundamentally conservative, seeking to preserve what has been lost and presuming a collective unity or personal integrity upon which the loss was inscribed. Indeed, since mourning arises most persuasively on a seemingly personal scale, able to be shared and even to become again collective only insofar as each grieving person claims to have an immediate relation to the loss about which he or she or we speak, mourning might coincide with memory by the positive connotation of possessiveness that is at the core of all socially conservative discourse.

What I want to suggest, however, is that for Levinas mourning is a discursive mode referring to an excess in all remembrance, to an exteriority that arises as greater than any historiographical or cultural ordering of our knowledge, and yet is not reducible to the priority of the private, parochial, or simply communal interest. Mourning begins seemingly from within the situation of public (read also: historical) language, prepared to find any generalized construct of loss unpersuasive with regard to this latest, newest grievance. Were mourning to begin as already reconciled to public modes, finding no tension between the present occasion of loss and those abstract, even ritualized social forms by which the loss must be rationalized, it would altogether lack the sense of crisis, indeed of grievous resistance, by which we intuit the value of what has been lost to the mourner. Even the mourner's necessary realism cannot mitigate, at least not right away, the poignancy of loss. Moreover, in mourning every claim to possess the other is already betrayed by what reality reveals, and so as an attitude without content, mourning characterizes a speaker who has forever lost the content of which she would speak. Inflecting memory toward an attitude of vigilance, mourning seems divided between the concentrating, conservative tendency of memory (to reduce the world to a manageable scale, as it were, to those possessions and possessable persons one already holds, once held, or might still hold dear) and the interruptive force by which any loss is set apart from, even as it exists within, the always impressive, regathering social order.

In this sense, then, the persuasiveness of mourning intimates a rupture in the public sphere as the realm of generalizable knowledge or of socially enactable behavior, and gives rise to a further suspicion, produced on the other side of grief but experienced even from within it, that our grief may in both socio-structural and pragmatic terms be tantamount to its uselessness.[1] Is the disruptive force of mourning nothing more than such an unenactable, finally useless demand? And, if so, how could mourning ever return us to historical, public meanings without betraying in advance its raison d'être? Already there is an emphasis here such that mourning would remain distinct from any system of morality attempting to reorder the disordered, overwhelming phenomenon of grief and to contain the apparent arbitrariness of loss by way of its systemic meaningfulness or by fitting it back within a set of dutiful obligations. And here also is the clue, I wish to maintain, to mourning's abiding public significance. For, even as mourning begins as though it came properly from the sensibility of individual consciousness, it already projects ethics beyond the immediate, experiential scenario, beyond also the parochial imperatives of communalism, and opens the subject through what affects her to the wider political realm of responsibility.

This proposition, explored more fully in the pages that follow, does not put to rest the problem of historical allusiveness that also troubles mourning's ethical meaning, since, by seemingly privileging affect within the sphere of intimate relations (even if one emphasizes the interruptive rather than conservative significances of such affect), mourning might thereby only occlude the larger referents of the historical moment. For instance, if the Holocaust constitutes a significant, though not absolutely determinate, influence on the Levinasian project, the restrictive emphasis he gives to the face-to-face relationship might elucidate a single, or multiply individuated, referent for loss that would be less than representative of the full force of Holocaust history. There is here a problem both of metonymic proportion (can we truly say that a singular death is representative of large-scale suffering and atrocity?) as well as of reference (can we really say that the loss for which one mourns pertains to history if we fail to indicate the historical significance of the other or the political importance of the injustice she has suffered in the greater flow of historical events?). Although the Holocaust provides an implicit context for the extreme significations and emergency scenarios that describe ethics in the Levinasian project, Levinas remains explicitly dissatisfied with any historicized explanation of ethics precisely because history as such—which is to say, as answer or as the true light of knowledge—must reduce ethics only to its seemingly inevitable results in time. We cannot proceed as though a hypothetically alternate perspective or a radically alterior consciousness were not also implicit in every historical event and were not absolutely as meaningful, if only in the negative sense of what was lost or violated, as our prevalent historical view. Based in the assumptions that history is always also political and that any event ordinarily obtains its meaning based on documentation drawn from the victors and survivors, Levinasian ethics, in its mournful valences, challenges the obvious results of history as though hypothetically from within the event itself and yet exterior to it at the same time—which is to say, from the perspective of an other who suffers an event's consequences without benefit.

In this chapter, then, I position Levinas's work against the model of Heideggerian anxiety in order to remark especially on his objections to the limiting sociality of the constructs of care and usefulness, arguing that Heidegger is never for Levinas entirely to be separated from his own historical implication in Nazism, though neither is his philosophy to be simply dismissed as the product of an obviously moribund ideology. Functioning much more representatively, as an authentic voice of Western culture, Heidegger serves as an allegorical metonymy in Levinas's work—for the totalistic reach of knowledge, for the indifference of history's productiveness, for an inattentiveness to the other. By aligning ethics with the emotive resonances of a mourning irreconciled to the oppressive results of history, Levinas disrupts the hegemony of Heideggerian subjective care; and he does so, specifically, by refusing the privileged perspective of the survivor as the ground for mournful consciousness. Resisting the continuities of survival, Levinasian memory is, according to the mournful, revisionary connotation I here emphasize, an attentive openness to other historical and political meanings, a vigilance that would mirror the basic posture of vulnerability Levinas locates at the center of ethics. Memory, which proceeds from the other, must persistently distinguish the one who dies from the history to which she might be lost.

In Levinas's descriptions of mourning, including perhaps most significantly his readings of the *Phaedo* in a series of lectures given at the Sorbonne in 1976, there emerges a distinct view of that imaginative vulnerability crucial to ethics. As Levinas deftly enfolds mournful proof texts (from the Bible, from Plato) as well as anecdotally mournful postures into his account of the impossible responsibility structuring ethics and perhaps language itself, he is ever mournful for, if by his own terms not quite mindful of, a history not to be mended by mere political emendations. In its mournful vigilance ethics attends to death's fundamental injustice, the character of which becomes most evident in the politically perpetrated unjust death. Against those who perceive in ethics only an evasion of or reduction in the scope of politics and historical causation, which would promote illusory practices whereby a subject might limit the referents of her responsibility rather than focus on the structural dimensions of oppression or injustice in her society, Levinas helps us to see that the apparent individuality of the ethical relation is in reality an infinitely extensive structure of responsibility for others who are here now as well as for those who are remote in time or place. This responsibility is what politics begins from. In its mournfulness responsibility extends always beyond the moment of its particular instantiation, responding to every historical occasion of responsibility as though it only increased the burden of the subject's also necessarily political responsibility for others.

FACING DEATH

In Heidegger's philosophy we confront the most famous twentieth-century formulation of death and its relationship to meaningful human existence. Giving a lecture in March 1987 on Heidegger, entitled "Dying For . . . ," Levinas paid tribute to the permanence of the Heideggerian project and addressed himself, specifically, to the matter of how and to what extent Heidegger turns us toward ethics.[2] Once Heidegger had expounded the verbal and adverbial qualities of Being (*Dasein*), Levinas argues, he effectively revised the objective view of man as "a property or conjunction of properties." Since all things mean to the degree that they are *zuhanden* (ready to hand) and since the order of things already implies and assumes other people, the common world of human relations signifies in Heidegger the very possibility of work. According to this structure of commonality in which a being is situated and through which the purposiveness of work is signified, there is already a care for the other enfolded in a being's care for itself. Death exists not at the center of this possibility of caring but, rather, at the end of all possibility, as that which must be preempted by our humanity. In short, real human possibility always clings to an ontological meaning of which it is both proof and symptom. When a being checks itself on the horizon of death and finds meaning, according to that famous phrase, in *being-toward-death*, death bestows a concreteness on existence, giving shape to the being's concern—specifically, in the care for another, which is practically a care for her food, drink, clothing, health, and shelter, for how she lives in the world. On this front, however, Levinas queries Heidegger's implicit definition of ethics: does death mark the end of possibility such that our concern, which makes existence meaningful, must remain concentrated on the things of this world? By such a logic, Levinas fears, the "the death of the other" might never signify to the survivor anything more than "funerary behavior and emotions, and memories" (D 215). Since the care for persons can be signified only according to practical claims and the expressive possibility of work, Heideggerian concern must necessarily fail to imagine a responsibility for the other greater than that which can be expressed through conceptions of usefulness and material possibility.

One cannot help but hear in Levinas's protest of Heidegger's views on death an anticipation of the more particular complaint Levinas voiced in the brief essay "As If Consenting to Horror" (1988),[3] in which he took account of Heidegger's Nazism and reckoned his precursor's ultimate failing to have been a retrospective failure of conscience—which is to say, a failure to accuse himself publicly after the war and to offer a formal statement of regret for his political positions.[4] Although it is altogether possible that Heidegger failed to consider the implications of his philosophical project in Nazi ideology and to understand fully even as late as 1936 the movement to which he had lent his good name, nevertheless he consented to his own complicity with Nazism by choosing not to respond to the atrocities in retrospect once the full scale of genocide was known, during the years following the war. This is a striking objection precisely because it is such a mournful and seemingly useless one: what Levinas requires of Heidegger, we might well argue, is precisely "funerary behavior and emotions, and memories," a mere statement of responsibility for what has already passed, for that which he can actively do nothing about. Yet to have admitted even this much would mean professing a form of historical consciousness in which ethical regret had real significance. Such a response would have challenged the orthodoxy of the view (apparently held by Heidegger) in which history seems a kind of fatalism, nothing more nor less than what has indeed already been realized.

In the absence of any statement of regret, Heidegger involves himself all over again in the history of politically perpetrated injustices as one who too casually accepts, even in retrospect, the cultural practice of murder and genocide that characterized Nazi society. Or, in more general terms, it would seem that the philosophical project of apprehending death on the horizon of subjectivity lends itself to a real history that involves a moral and ideological failing with regard to the other. Since the alterity of the other may vanish with her—which is to say, precisely at the point of her *annihilation* (that ambiguous Heideggerian threshold)—Levinas demands that we consider what it means to surrender the significance of the other to her death.[5] By mournfully reversing the Heideggerian notion that the literal demise of the other results in the demise of her significance, Levinas identifies the very ground ethics must seek to recover. Any philosophical system of thought resigned to the death of the other, he thus supposes, not only cooperates with a Western cultural ideology that fails in its ethical vigilance on behalf of the other but also remains complicit, at least potentially, with horribly persistent ideologies such as Nazism premised on the rejection of alterity at every level.

Lest my reading of Levinas reading Heidegger start to partake too much of Levinas's own revisionism (which is to say, of those elements of misprision Jacques Derrida has observed in Levinas's response to Heidegger), it is worth noting that Heidegger himself worried about the political ramifications of our conceptualization of death.[6] Sharing something of Freud's sense of the delicate balance between will and repression, of the dialectical relation between civilization and its discontents, even of the tumultuous relation between the aggressive expressionism of humanism and the existential material from which it lives, Heidegger on several occasions hinted that the attempt to master death contributes to the cultural production of death. The point is nicely made by David Krell when he aphoristically summarizes the tenor of Heidegger's thought on death under the motto "Let death be." Sympathetically adopting the Heideggerian view, Krell worries that the "subtlety of conceptual manipulation and violence in the handling of death are proportionally related, the one increasing in step with the other."[7] According to Krell, the movement toward a mastery of death distorts our humanity in its wake, and an entire history of metaphysical wrestling with death only lends itself to cultural modes of death obsession, which can bear no life-affirming fruit. Levinas, in reading Heidegger, comes out in a very different place, finding that there is a much greater degree of metaphysical virility in Heidegger's thought than Krell, for example, concedes and that, even when Heidegger's sentiments about death seem pacific, they are colored historically by a species of dangerous resignation.

By contrast with Heidegger, Levinas argues that, despite our every attempt to contain death within symbolic structures, the interruptive significance of death is inescapable. Denying that the material facts of annihilation should function as a pronouncement on the other's value, Levinas speaks, as though troubled by the failure of the dead to maintain a place in the world, of an ethical subject not yet outside of mourning who refuses the stoical leanings of Heidegger or the therapeutic detachment recommended by Freud. In the Freudian scheme the work of mourning must be described from the privileged perspective of one who is beyond the event of loss in both time and place—which is to say, from a *survivor's perspective*.[8] Yet even in Freud's account, mourning, prior to the moment in which an ego passes beyond its original attachment, seems hardly distinguishable from melancholia. It is only because mourning cedes to necessity, because it can be judged by virtue of where it arrives, that Freud is able to exempt mourning from pathology. According to the remoteness to be achieved by any successful work of mourning, a mourner in the Freudian account views the lost object from the detached perspective of retrospection or distances the past, in the broader terms of the cultural work of commemoration, in order to understand it.[9]

From an early point in his career Levinas was resistant to the commemorative dimension of both representational and historiographical discourses, supposing in *Totality and Infinity* (1961), for example, that they are obtained at the expense of ethics.[10] In a language imbued with the sentiments of mourning, Levinas consistently disparages history because it is equivalent to the perspective of the survivors who "interpret, that is, utilize the works of the dead" and, as they practice their violent historiographies, also "appropriate the works of dead wills to themselves" (*TI* 228). Like the psychoanalytic therapist or successful Freudian mourner who views grief through the historical lens of an overarching social economy—that is, from a posture of remoteness in which the lost other becomes an object interchangeable with other esteemed objects, suited to the determinative ideas and passions of the ego— the historian necessarily sides with collective representation against any singular attachment. In order to conceive of history's opposition to the dead works and dead wills of those who become in retrospect figures of the past, Levinas initially describes a gap that opens between the will expressed in a work and the work's "destination . . . to a history that [an] I cannot foresee" (*TI* 227). The intention that dies in any work corresponds quite literally to the *fate* of heroic intention, in the sense that any hero "finds himself playing a role in a drama exceeding his heroic intentions" and thus finds that his "sovereign will" has been foiled (*TI* 226, 227). For Levinas the idea of *fatum* signals what must become of any work. It is the fate of the work to be alienated from the self and appropriated by a foreign will or a set of foreign wills. Since fate is also the idea the historian forms of a work, which is necessarily alienated from the will of its producer, *fatum* stands for a historian's retrospective attribution of an order inherent in the work, as if it had been from the start expressive of its cultural regime, a function of the ruling world of ideas. As such, it is always counterpoised to an interiority expressed in and by the work.

MOURNING THE OTHER WHO DIES

Although the Holocaust is not put forward directly in *Totality and Infinity* as a referential ground for Levinas's philosophical discussion of fate, when the hypothesis of heroic intention modulates into the realm of the survivor's perspective it is plausible to hear some resonance drawn from the new valences of meaning brought to bear on the term *survivor* in the years after World War II. For Levinas survival is, like the fate described by heroism, a matter accounted for in time, from beyond the ethical moment of which it speaks. On this note Levinas's account of interiority, with its vestigially heroic significations, might be productively compared to two works that come well after *Totality and Infinity*—Terrence Des Pres's *The Survivor: An Anatomy of Life in the Death Camps* (1976) and Tzvetan Todorov's *Facing the Extreme: Moral Life in the Concentration Camps* (1991).[11] In his influential study of Holocaust testimony Des Pres set out to challenge the prevalent view, developed in the decades after the war through the application of psychoanalytic categories, that survivors whose asocial behaviors endured beyond an appropriately temporary period of suffering could be deemed, by evidence of their prolonged fixation on the past, to have fallen prey to a pathological attachment to their suffering. And if this were not enough, psychoanalysts such as Bruno Bettelheim had also discerned an aspect of pathology in many survivors' original passivity in the face of persecution. Interpreting such judgments as part of a long-standing cultural preference for heroic confrontations with fate, Des Pres not only explicated the language of Holocaust survivors themselves so as to elaborate an ethic of endurance contrapuntally demystifying Western paradigms of heroic capability so often linked to ethics, but also argued that the extreme circumstances of the concentration and death camps converted endurance itself—the excruciating literality of survival—into its own ethic.

Yet, though Des Pres's admirable revaluation of survival made an enduring contribution to the study of Holocaust testimony, he also tends throughout *The Survivor* to associate an ethic of survival with modes of late-twentieth-century existential consciousness that slightly bewilder, even perhaps belittle, the historical parameters of his own argument. As survival becomes a lens through which to view history, Des Pres concentrates especially on those rhetorical tropes within testimony that convey the remarkable dignity of Holocaust survivors even against the oppressive evidence of their lives in the camps, and thus, in his historiographical preference for the survivor's perspective (as opposed, say, to the victim's), he returns the act of survival to the reign of culture, almost as though, despite his direct challenge to the Western legacy of heroism, survival offered itself as a substitute heroism.[12] For his part Todorov advocates a posture of antiheroism that gets similarly reconstituted in terms of a quasi-heroic survival.[13] Explicitly associating heroism with the idealistic adherence to absolutes, Todorov contrasts this posture to what he calls "ordinary virtues," such as dignity and caring, which are enacted with pragmatic rigor in the face of necessity and have little or nothing to do with abstractions based in cultural, ideological, or nationalist identity. History, as Todorov sees it, extends itself by means of the same ideological and abstract imperatives through which it has always been driven, except that now we must seek the persistence of virtues on a smaller scale.

For instance, as he searches for ordinary virtues in the Warsaw ghetto uprising enacted by desperate Jews in 1943, Todorov contrasts their motivation to the heroic rationale informing the Warsaw rising spurred by the Polish resistance movement in 1944. The difference, he insists, is that the Jews responded to a situation of ultimate exigency, unmotivated by an ideologically informed self-conception according to which their actions might be consummated by the historical consciousness of future generations. Yet these ghetto fighters, in standing for virtues that could not possibly triumph, also performed actions that were exemplary within history and partook implicitly of heroic sentiments in their belief that individual life might be productively sacrificed for collective, abstract meanings. What Todorov emphasizes by enfolding this apparent counterexample within the rubric of Western heroic consciousness is how hard it is to perceive virtue as aligned merely with immediate exigency. By revising the scale of intentionality informing virtuous actions, and by preferring smaller-scale motives to grand, idealistic cultural narratives for virtue, he adheres to a postmodern humanism, ever suspicious that ideology always falsifies reality, even as he also refuses to exempt our modes of historical consciousness, informed by corrective contemporary historiographies, from basic ideational patterns of thought. "History ultimately triumphs over remembering," he asserts, "and history needs heroes" (24).

As also for Levinas, memory signifies in Todorov as a resistance to a quasi-Hegelian, historical flow of meaning within which it must necessarily be included. Nevertheless, Todorov's pragmatic humanism inspires him to offer a calculus of ordinary virtues that could remain intact even in the totalitarian ethos, even in the Nazi or Soviet concentration camps, which he interprets as concentrated epitomes of all totalitarianism. As a result, Todorov might well be charged with conflating the camps with totalitarianism and discerning the ordinary means of resistance possible even within an extremely oppressive state apparatus as a lens for reading the hyper-thin remnant of agency left to victims and survivors of the Nazi camps. His interpretive method leaves him open to a variety of historicist and theoretical objections, not least of which is that he veers, not unlike Foucault or even Badiou, between a radically postmodern appreciation of the radical contingency of history by which normative ideals are rendered obsolete, universalizing assertions to the effect that human dignity still matters in the moment of exigency and must impress itself upon the rest of us as valuable afterward. Underlying those matters of conscience that persist even for the oppressed subject who faces extremity is the perception of choice as a constitutive element in the revisionary order of ordinary virtue, as though choice, effectively preserving the center of our conventional models for moral decision making, remained a recognizable, translatable category whether or not the political context for the freely exercised conscience had been taken away.

Such a commitment to the performance of virtue on a voluntary, if also albeit greatly reduced, scale is precisely what Levinas rejects in his own revisioning of ethics. Insistently separating the ethical meaning that inheres in the situation of extremity from the intentional understanding of the one who undergoes such an experience, Levinas finds that atrocity and all forms of extreme suffering cancel not so much virtue as the entire interpretive rubric by which virtue is traditionally accounted for. To celebrate the newly exemplary heroics of survival or the ordinary virtues that contribute to survival, to choose the strategy of either Des Pres or Todorov, is to indulge a compensatory system of morality, as if the ethical perceptions and choices of those within the camps might make up for the agentive roles they could not play in history. To the extent that Levinas invokes the specter of heroism within the situation of extremity, he includes the surviving perspective within, rather than exempting it from, the trajectory of heroic history, since neither proves adequate to the meaning of ethics. Survival in *Totality and Infinity* is framed both generically and philosophically (not yet, as in Levinas's later writings, by way of direct reference to Holocaust survivors); and, as Levinas implicitly enfolds the survivor's perspective into the situation of *interiority*, such an interiority necessarily contests its absorption into a cultural regime of foreign wills and into the remotely objectifying narratives of historians and also implicitly contests a cultural politics coinciding with the philosophical acceptance of death.

Still, even this contestation, with its operative idiom of battle, is for Levinas as futile as it is heroic in connotation. A hero's fate is always more powerful than the contrary will traced within heroism. All conventionally heroic portraits of courage in the face of death assert an impossible independence of the will, which insofar as it resolves the tension between interiority and predominant cultural paradigms would finally cultivate the self's acceptance of its own death, as though the self could apprehend itself as if it were its own possession. Through an illusory autonomy, the will would refuse consent to those who oppose it and yet find that it still "gives satisfaction to the foreign will in spite of itself, by the result of its behavior, precisely by its *work*" (*TI* 230).[14] The corporeality of the will means it is already entangled in the world through its interaction with other wills and its power to give or withhold itself, always subject to "the usurpation carried out by the conquerors, that is, by the survivors" (*TI* 228). There is no necessary reason why the will as a history of resistance to its opponents should endure as a significance within history, since the historian retrospectively sets the terms for what it has meant to survive or not to survive.

In *Totality and Infinity* Levinas invoked the paradoxical influence of the survivor long before what several contemporary critics have since referred to as the international "rise of the survivor" or that period described by Alain Finkielkraut during which French Jews began to reinterpret their metaphorical place in the post-1945 national consciousness of France. Already in 1961, with prescient suspicion of the cultural motives that over the next two decades would partly inform the survivor's elevation to the status of a cultural icon, Levinas lodged an implicit complaint about the way survivors could be too readily absorbed back into revisedly triumphal historiographies and enfolded in the widely fashionable *myth of the resistance* so consistently deployed in postwar France as a trope for misreading much of the country's collaborationist history.[15] In this era French historiography had hardly begun to dissent from its nationalist imperatives, and survivors were more consistently imagined as political resistors than as arbitrarily victimized Jews. In his dissent from this cultural logic Levinas specifically exempts memory (associated in *Totality and Infinity* with interiority) from the conventional praxis of history and develops a distinction between the memory of the one who dies and the memory of the survivor. Much as a historian requires conceptual and temporal distance to understand the other who has died and thereafter comprehends the other as a function of a life that has commencement and end as points elucidated in universal time, a survivor is bound to his retrospective view. But "death which for the survivor is an end," Levinas insists, must "be not only this end" (*TI* 55).[16] By suspending the survivor's mode of retrospection and the historian's narratives of a self apprehended as an accomplishment of birth or nature, memory suggests, instead, a realm "where what is no longer possible historically remains always possible" (*TI* 55).[17] Although we may well suspect that such a realization of impossibility articulates merely a wishful reversal, uttered, as it were, from the hypothetical position of the victim against the predominant typology of surviving, by much this same reversal any sympathetic survivor would speak for the one whose perspective is no longer possible. In this way Levinas arrives at the self-contradiction of all mournfulness: to speak for the other who dies is to return her impossible perspective to the idiom, now revised or reimagined, of practical possibility.

TO WHOM DO OUR FUNERARY EMOTIONS REFER?

The only vantage point, then, from which what is no longer possible could be realized as a resistance to history is the impossible perspective of an interiority standing to be lost in history. Levinas names this impossibility itself "memory"—memory as an inversion of historical time that is tantamount to an interiority refusing the historical fate according to which it would become "nothing but the past" or "a pure loss figuring in an alien accounting system" (*TI* 56). The mournful imperative within Levinasian ethics casts itself forward by means of an impossibility implicitly characterizing all testimonial speech insofar as it would remain absolutely centered upon those who have suffered unjust deaths. We are by now so familiar with this paradoxical condition of Holocaust testimony as to be almost unable to honor its truly contradictory resistance even to paradox. As Primo Levi insisted in *The Drowned and the Saved* (1986), every survivor was preoccupied by the inadequacy of his own testimony precisely because the true witnesses to the camps were those who perished there, those who in succumbing to genocide became submerged within their own precipitous inhumanity, never to reemerge. More recently, Giorgio Agamben has attempted to give ontological validity to the rift that characterizes the survivor's testimony, as it speaks simultaneously for a historical condition and about the ontological realm of our inhumanity, giving evidence of the de-subjectifying tendency that necessarily codetermines the possibility of subjectification within language.[18] For Agamben the inhuman gaze of the true witnesses—those who were the *Muselmänner*, or nonpersons, of the camps—presides over the act of testimony and forever recalls the biopolitical terror of the camps as part of the already realized limit to our historical humanity. It is precisely by means of what the survivor cannot say—in other words, by means of Primo Levi's exemplary preoccupation with those whose voices were historically submerged and rendered inhuman—that testimony obtains its universalized relevance for its audience.

In response to Agamben we might ask whether a historical event that achieved the utter deformation of human existence should come to stand hereafter for the political condition of our existence. Or we might wonder whether the victims of the "experiment of the camps" should be abandoned to a fate in which they signify primarily as a sign of the relative success of Nazism, of the degree to which the Nazis, having irrevocably exposed the biopolitical underpinnings of the Western nation-state, have since determined the entire order of culture as incapable of separating achieved humanity (*bios*) from its animal codetermination (*zoē*).[19] Why might particular historical victims continue to have bearing upon our cultural memory for reasons other than that they have effectively spurred a conceptual shift in our ontological paradigms? This is already in a sense a Levinasian question. For in Levinas it is quite as though the other who has died, whether she be imagined as a victim of the extermination camps or of the politics of famine in Africa, could refuse the meaninglessness of her own death—a stance which is obviously not realistic.

Although critical of arguments from pathos, Levinas himself falls into pathos when he insists upon interiority's refusal, in what he calls the "death agony," to be measured as a loss for the survivor or as a sudden absence within philosophical meaning: "Dying is agony because in dying a being does not come to an end while coming to an end; he has no more time, that is, can no longer wend his way anywhere, but thus he goes where one cannot go, suffocates—how much longer . . ." (*TI* 56). The other who dies is thus significant in his radical suffering, separated from the historical time of beginnings and ends, an interruption, as it were, of historical teleology. From the perspective of the other who dies, we might receive testimony of the experience of death, if the act of testimony were not already implicated in the survivor's voice and thus already looking beyond the moment of death. Here lies the meaning Levinas gives to the muteness of the shades during Ulysses's journey to the underworld: since the dead cannot report anything that is not properly a memory belonging to the knowable realm of the real world, the shades are not—cannot possibly be—forthcoming. The other who dies announces a time fundamentally separate from the time of those who survive him, a secrecy at the heart of interiority. Interiority itself is the wish not to become comprehensible to history. Although the primacy of history demands the sacrifice of interiority to history, interiority is always that which resists its own sacrifice in history. By this trajectory the interiority of which Levinas speaks—which implicitly recalls Nietzsche's suggestion that interiority is realized in history through those institutions of remembrance inflicted upon a suffering humanity—is interchangeable with the function of memory interpreted as an inversion of historical time, and this interiority can never be a future possibility simply added to the end of old possibilities.[20]

There is, then, in memory's service to impossibility a radical wishfulness, perhaps best glimpsed in the essay "Dying For . . ." when Levinas directly challenges, in a passage cited earlier, Heidegger's emphasis on ineffectual "funerary behavior." To the extent that emotion and memory would conjoin in such behavior by concentrating only on the aorist quality of the past—the past as completed action and as finally determined meaning—each term seems circumscribed by its opposing term, producing funerary behavior that entirely forecloses the anterior significance of the other. By rereading the ethical connotations and subjective emphasis of emotion, however, Levinas argues for the other as the one who begets the movement of *e-motion*, just as she also occasions the requirements of memory. Thus the valences of mournful remembrance must shift. Any sentiment or act of memory defining the other through a recognized and fixed emotional determination has already surrendered the force of the other's alterity. As a critic of a certain species of memory— specifically, of remembrances filtered through the lens of either the survivor or historian—Levinas objects to memory's reifications, to our ideological tendency to make the other an artifact or souvenir, indeed, to the entire commemorative facility of modern Western culture signified, for example, by the endless proliferation of monuments and museums. All recollective memory gives itself too easily to fixed ideas of the past, interpretable only according to a cultural logic advocating the acceptance of death, allowing the other who has died to become nothing but past.

By the Levinasian construction, in contrast, memory in its mournful connotations, functioning as what I am here calling "vigilant memory," sets itself apart from the continuity of survival and history to serve as an ethical resistance inscribed within our knowledge in all its utilitarian or commemorative forms. This point is neatly reinforced by a prooftext Levinas opposes to the Heideggerian view of death, the friendship tableau of 2 Samuel in which the prophet weeps for the deaths of Saul and Jonathan in battle: "Saul and Jonathan were lovely and pleasant in their lives, and in their death they were not divided; they were swifter than eagles, they were stronger than lions" (2 Sam. 1:23). Levinas reads this biblical verse with an imaginative vigor that seems more literary critical than strictly exegetical, discerning ethical meanings that reside not in any religious purpose but in a strictly a-theistic, mortal conception of death. Refusing to unite Saul and Jonathan through the hypothesis of another life, the biblical text offers, instead, an impossibly poetic extension of the lived unity of their lives. Undivided by death, enfolded in a moment of mutual dying, Saul and Jonathan seem elegists to one another, signifying for and before one another, vigilantly refusing to surrender each other, as if even in death, Levinas speculates, "all relationship to the other person were not undone" (D 215). Levinas's perception of their continued relationship is not merely metaphorical, producing, say, the illusion that they were stronger than death and could never be vanquished by it. As the biblical text speaks of a love beyond the animal effort and intensity of ordinary human desire, of a love altogether exceeding effort and distinct from either character's genuine capabilities, Saul and Jonathan live only in the meaning of their dedication to each other. Their dedication as one-for-the-other gives meaning to their humanity precisely in this "worry over the death of the other . . . before care for self" (D 216). Such dedication undoes the finality of the past by opposing the other's death as completed event; yet it is not, of course, the events of the past that can finally be undone—indeed, horror, death, and injustice continue to demand acknowledgment as facts. Rather, it must be our relation to these facts of the past that gets altered by ethical testimony. To imagine death only as the limit of lived possibility and to recollect the past as that which is entirely irrevocable would be to submit oneself to death as to a judgment. It would be to ignore the central meaning of death as the ultimate harm that may come to another, as the injustice always waiting to be imposed upon the other, always threatening to cancel the meaning of her existence, an injustice that no mere wishing will sufficiently oppose.

Highlighting Levinas's obvious implication in mourning is, however, only half my point. Although his mournful exegesis of 2 Samuel attempts to free the other from a survivor's interpretive will, mourning's wishfulness is not simply determinative. For Levinas brings all the rigor of his anti-idealism to bear on the mournfulness that inflects and inspires ethics. Against the commonsensical conclusion that the community of the living must bestow meaning upon the dead, he argues, instead, that the other who dies assigns meaning unto the self—the other's expressiveness seeming no longer annihilated in death but referred, as it were, to the radical unknown of death as a departure. Emphasizing the self's fundamental inexperience with regard to death, Levinas insists that mournful memory, in responding to the death of another, is necessarily dedicated to an alterity. This is neither an act of imaginative solidarity nor simply a function of metaphoric reversal. It would be all too easy to move from the particularity embodied in the death of the other to general claims about the psychic life, as if memory enacted a universalizing solidarity dependent upon imaginative mediation, the self always participating vicariously in the fate of the other, as existentialists propose, through dread of its similar fate. Similarly, it would be misleading to emphasize Levinas's rhetorically quick reversals of subject-positions within the interlocutive situation as though this movement predicted a practical imaginative exchange. Such reversals of subject-positionality might call for psychologizing explanations, accounting for the secondary position of the other who dies through the psychic disposition of the one who subjectively undergoes the event of loss. But we cannot interpret the alterior time of dying as a mere projection of a subject's inner life onto the impossible position occupied by the other who dies precisely because the mournfulness of Levinasian memory dictates an unassumable positionality, by which memory is perpetuated and by which it also interrogates the past, without arriving at definite answers.

READING GRIEF'S EXCESS IN THE *PHAEDO*

On the topic of death Levinas's references are more scattered than coherent, especially in the early work. In the many section, chapter, or unit titles in *Totality and Infinity* and *Otherwise than Being* (1974), "death" is never employed as an organizing concept or thematically central thought, nor is it ever a central topic of discussion for more than a few paragraphs at a time. Yet, when death is mentioned, it is immediately yoked onto the ethical relation, not as a contradiction of the possibility of ethics but as the very proof of ethics. The two primary variations on this rhetorical technique are the claim, first, that an ego becomes responsible for another at his own peril and at the risk of death and, second, that the other is the one for whom I am responsible as though I were ultimately responsible for his death. Much as Levinas's use of the conceits of unpleasure became especially prevalent in the years immediately prior to *Otherwise than Being* and in the decade and a half after its publication, his references specifically to the death of the other also proliferate during the latter portion of his career. Shortly after publishing his second major philosophical monograph, during the academic year 1975–76 Levinas gave a lecture course at the Sorbonne on the topic of "Death and Time."[21] That series of lectures did much to assemble and clarify Levinas's philosophical thoughts on death while also bringing to the surface a more overtly elegiac emphasis in the Levinasian project.

In his first three lectures for the course Levinas elaborates the importance of the individual death and attempts to deconstruct the philosophical attitude toward death by treating an archetypal scene in which the original philosopher of Western culture contemplates the meaning of his death. At several key moments in these early lectures Levinas refers to Plato's *Phaedo* and specifically therein to the famous death of Socrates. Oddly, Levinas's references concentrate much less on the philosophical matter of Plato's text (which is to say, on the content of Socrates's thoughts on death) than on the dramatic frame of a dialogue devoted largely to questions of mourning. As a consequence of this slightly skewed emphasis, Levinas offers a reading against the grain of Plato's text. For, although the rhetorical trajectory of the *Phaedo* sides with Socrates's effort to renounce sorrow and embrace his own death (the very attitude that led Herbert Marcuse to implicate the Socratic mindset in what he called a cultural ideology of death), Levinas recalls the "scene of mourning" rather than the consoling content of Socrates's speeches. A double narrative frame encompasses the mourning scene in which Socrates argues finally for death as the true aim of the philosophical life. In the most external frame Echecrates provides a reason for the story's transmission in demanding from Phaedo, who was among those in attendance during Socrates's final moments, an account of the famous philosopher's death. As soon as Phaedo begins to tell his story, he in turn establishes a second frame (returned to, briefly, at the end of the dialogue) pertaining to the mournful mindset of the friends who await Socrates's death with him. Himself disinclined to pity—though, he admits, it is only a "natural" response "when . . . present at a scene of mourning"—Phaedo divulges that Socrates's friends were sometimes laughing and sometimes weeping, especially one of them, Apollodorus. With regard to the friend who has laughed and wept more abundantly than the rest, Phaedo adds a qualifying remark, "you know this man and his manner [*tropon autou*]," apparently judging Apollodorus's emotional excess to be symptomatic of a character flaw (P 204–5).[22] Yet Phaedo also confesses his own agitation, thereby implicating himself, perhaps with some reservation, in the spectacle of ostentatious mourning. A second example of excess soon follows when Xanthippe appears, saying "the kind of thing that women always do say," lamenting that this will be the last time Socrates will see his friends (P 209). Appearing but briefly in her role as gender stereotype, she is escorted from the prison, wailing and beating her breast, never to benefit from Socrates's reasonable discourse about why he not only accepts but embraces his death.[23]

Although Plato means to cast suspicion on such mournful sentiments, they are nevertheless inexorably planted in our memory. Ostensibly, the question of mourning subsides once Socrates begins to offer his wisdom as the central content of this dialogue. Yet, much as the constantly failing disciples of Mark's gospel witness the empty tomb with fear and trembling rather than full remembrance of Jesus's words about the redemptive dimension of his own death (16:8), Socrates's friends will again lapse into mourning as he dies at the end of the *Phaedo*. The teacher figure has espoused a rhetoric of transcendence equating the mournful mind with a perspective too attached to the world and the body's pleasures, but those who receive his words fail quite measurably to take them to heart. Mourning may be the sign of a philosophical failure in Plato's text, yet even as such it organizes the Socratic attitude by what it must overcome.

Two scenes become especially significant insofar as they demonstrate Socrates's arguments for the transumption of mourning while simultaneously charting mourning's resistant persuasiveness. First, there is the scene in which Socrates alludes to having once tried to write poetry in order to interpret a dream in which he'd been told to make music. Implicitly interpreting music as metonym for any vocation leading to harmonious achievements, Socrates admits that he needed confirmation that he'd chosen the right music in life—which is to say, philosophy over the more conventional music of poetry. After reaffirming the vocational superiority of philosophy, Socrates asks that word be sent to Evenus that he should soon follow Socrates if he is indeed a true philosopher, for a philosopher, although he may not kill himself, does "desire to follow after the dying" (*ethelein d'an tōi apothnēiskonti ton philosophon epesthai*) (P 214–15). What are we to make of this phrase "to follow after the dying"? It has to be understood initially, I think, as a figure of mourning, as though by an imaginative act Evenus would overidentify with the soon to be dead Socrates and indulge a melancholic death wish. Even as Plato's dialogue takes its cue from Socrates's own adamant refusal to psychologize the behavior of mourning, Socrates maintains that to study philosophy is to study dying and being dead. The philosopher who devotes himself properly to matters of the soul quickly discovers the body to be a hindrance that limits him to seeing and hearing inaccurately, forever deceiving the soul in its quest to perceive the true essence of a thing. Since the philosopher longs to exercise the faculty of reason uninhibited by the body and to intuit pure knowledge, which can only be achieved when we are dead, he lives by practicing dying, by desiring that moment when the soul shall part from the body. Death is a state the philosopher has been eager for his entire life.

By advocating a philosophical attitude toward one's own death, Socrates would contain the rhetorical figure of mourning he has just deployed, translating the seemingly literal possibility of following after the one who dies into a stoical posture. At the pinnacle of his argument for the philosophical attitude toward death, Socrates summons yet another oddly anecdotal proof, again indebted to a question of mourning: "When human loves or wives or sons have died, many men have willingly gone to the other world led by the hope of seeing there those whom they longed for, and of being with them; and shall he who is really in love with wisdom and has a firm belief that he can find it nowhere else than in the other world grieve when he dies and not be glad to go there?" (P 235). It is unclear just who Socrates has in mind when he speaks of the many who have gone willingly to the other world to follow those "whom they have longed for." Certainly, Orpheus is a likely referent, and thus the behavior Socrates describes may be either poetical or pathological. Although one may sympathize with Orpheus's desire to retrieve Eurydice, one knows at the same time that Orpheus's exceptional action, by which he succeeds in expressing his passion and bringing the beloved again to light, only proves the rule that such pursuit is impossible. Then, too, even Orpheus has followed the beloved only so that he may return with her, following the one who dies without succumbing to the philosophical desire to die. As Socrates implicitly approves an identification with the dead that would lead the survivor to surrender the pleasures of living, and even invokes such cases as if they were frequent, it is entirely plausible for us to conjecture that his portrayal of a psychological willingness to follow the dead may be largely owing to his own proximity to death. Yet to describe such a response as if it were a normative impulse, to have employed a conceit dependent upon the temperament of mourning in service of his own rhetorically self-serving refutation of mourning, already suggests a breakdown in the figurative logic of the *Phaedo* that is more than incidental.

Just as Socrates's figures of mourning exert an internally contradictory, even subversive influence on his arguments against grief, a connotation of excess gets carried over into the continuing argument of Plato's dialogue. A crucial point is reached when Socrates insists that "when you see a man troubled because he is going to die," you can be sure he is "not a lover of wisdom but a lover of the body" (P 236–37). The rhetorical technique of deflected self-reference is unmistakable here: in exorcising a grief he feels for a life soon to be abandoned, Socrates's figurative remembrance of a man who is troubled by his own dying may recall his own hypothetically poorer self. Disparaging the limitations of the aggrieved man by neologistically referring to him as a "lover of the body" (*tis philosōmatos*) rather than a "lover of wisdom" (*philosophos*), Socrates's rhetoric is, if perhaps not strained, certainly labored. The too bodily oriented figure proves a troublingly resistant opponent, and Socrates's turn to ad hominem argument oddly accuses the man of being at fault because of who he is—which is to say, someone less than a philosopher. (Might this also be the tone behind Phaedo's characterization of the excessively grieving Apollodorus?) In other words, the *philosomatic* temptation, here figured as the potential to grieve for oneself in advance, revisits the pathos of mourning wherein the affective response to the death of the other must depend upon a somatic history of longing, love, and desire. Simultaneously considering the temporally absurd possibility of grieving *after* one's own death ("Shall he who is really in love with wisdom . . . grieve when he dies"?), the entire scene highlights the slightly absurd emphasis placed on grief from the start of Plato's dialogue. For surely what is most conspicuous about the scene depicted in the *Phaedo* is that Socrates's friends have begun to mourn for him prematurely. If Apollodorus, Xanthippe, and the hypothetically grieving philosomatic man all seem ridiculously excessive, it is because their actions have slipped forward in time, enacting mourning's demand for the other in the present, even before the event of loss.

Such mournful prolepsis reveals, however, the basic ethical structure of grief, which desires to preserve what it cannot possibly preserve. And thus we come to Levinas's reading of the *Phaedo*. For the frame of the Platonic text, which reflects the dramatic emphasis of mourning itself, intimates for Levinas the ethically difficult claim that pertains to all mourning. Signifying as greater than the projective play by which a mourner interprets any particular instance of death to be a manifestation of his own fate (or, a function of a survivor's sentiments), the death of the other has the structure of a drama enacting a "departure toward the unknown, a departure without return":

> Death—as the death of the other [*autrui*]—cannot be separated from this dramatic character; it is emotion *par excellence*, affection or being affected *par excellence*. It is in this sense that we see, in the *Phaedo*, at the beginning and the end, the evocation of the death of Socrates. Beside those who find in this death every reason to hope, certain among them (e.g., Apollodorus, "the women") weep more than they should; they weep without measure: as if humanity were not consumed or exhausted by measurement, as if there were an excess in death. It is a simple passage, a simple departure—and yet a source of emotion contrary to every effort at consolation. (DT 9)

Whether "emotion" is made roughly synonymous with "excess" here is not quite clear, but the term gets valorized by Levinas apart from its fate within the Socratic scheme, as the question posed by mourning endures beyond such philosophical answers. On the hither side of death's departure there is the mourner, who remains a witness to an absence entirely predicated upon, yet also interpreting, the priority of relationship. According to this emotional drama an anti-consolatory insistence runs alongside and competes with every philosophical interpretation of death, as though Levinas here encouraged a disobedient reading of the *Phaedo* while finding (almost deconstructively) the obvious markers of such dissent already evident in Plato's text.

Even the lapse into pathos, which Socrates denounces precisely because it falls outside of philosophical argument, exerts its influence on Levinas's mournful revaluation. In Plato's text Phaedo and the others can no longer restrain their tears once Socrates has taken the poison. Fully entering at this point into a structure of mourning with which he appears to have been already complicitous, Phaedo confesses that "in spite of myself my tears rolled down in floods, so that I wrapped my face in my cloak and wept for myself; for it was not for him that I wept, but for my own misfortune in being deprived of such a friend." He is embarrassed by his grief not because it might be discomfiting to Socrates but because the tears give him away, against his better judgment and against the very lesson he has been taught, as being unable to hold to his teacher's words. Still alive as his friends weep, Socrates can do nothing but rebuke their tears ("What conduct is this, you strange men! . . . Keep quiet and be brave") until they regain their composure (P 401). Thus, as the philosopher's apparent self-determination fails to determine the meaning of his own death, the friends catch sight of an important ethical ambiguity. Merely by failing to abide by their teacher's own philosophic acceptance of death, by proving unable to abide a heroic attitude, they testify to death's dramatic power and enact, if only ironically, a mode of witnessing to the other that is inspired by fear for his death.

To perceive in Plato's highly literary scene an existential truth owing more to the dramatic event of death than to the dramatic conceit of Plato's text may be to perform a slightly naïve, perhaps even antirhetorical, exegesis. Yet this is what Levinas by and large does. Whether Levinas's underestimation of Plato's rhetoric results from a commitment to devaluing the ethical possibilities of literature and rhetoric or whether Levinas believes that death exercises a literally subversive influence on every attempt to represent or contain it, the dramatic weeping of Socrates's friends attests to an aspect of humanity greater than mere psychic need, in excess of both the philosophical resoluteness and hypothetically transcendent meaning Socrates would derive through death. This resistant surplus of humanity seems the agnate term to death's fundamental excess. As Levinas says, "Death is a scandal, a crisis, even in the *Phaedo*." The dramatic frame of the *Phaedo* has been fully interpolated by the dramatic nature of death. A short while later in the lecture Levinas observes the absence of Plato from the scene of mourning: "In the *Phaedo*, one character is missing: Plato. He does not take part therein; he has abstained. This adds a supplementary ambiguity" (DT 14). It is as though the supplement, here unmistakably deconstructive in connotation, must refer to what Plato himself leaves out of the text, having been inspired by what the text cannot adequately account for.[24] This supplementary ambiguity pertains most directly to Plato's own attitude toward mourning: his abstention from self-dramatization implicates him in death's dramatic exceeding of philosophical consolation and suggests an author compromised by his affective relation to the other of whom he speaks, as yet unable to see how mourning could ever procure solace or be reconciled to desire.

In the third lecture from the Sorbonne course, Levinas refers yet once more to the *Phaedo*, and this time he marks his resistant reading even more overtly:

> This irreducibility of the emotional shows itself even in the Socratic effort made in the
> *Phaedo*, a dialogue that tends to recognize in death the very splendor of being. . . . Even

there, however, the approach of the dying Socrates does not lose its affective resonance, whereas the recognition, in the process of dying, of this announcement of being
(Socrates will finally be visible in death) would be the rational discourse of knowledge
and theory. This is the whole intent of the *Phaedo*: theory is stronger than the anxiety
over death. But even in this dialogue there is the *excess* of emotion. Apollodorus weeps
more than the others; he weeps beyond measure—and they must send the women
away. (DT 18)

Implicitly recalling his emphasis in the first lecture on an "excess" in death itself,
Levinas now appeals directly to the so-called emotional excess of Apollodorus and
the women, who are at least superficially caricatured figures of mourning. Working
back to recall an interrelation between emotion and the motivating excess of death,
Levinas argues that the ontological status of emotion, as an exception to intentionality, pertains to a question death generates in order that our relationship with infinity or time might be produced. Death demands a structure of signification proceeding toward that which is, ironically, beyond expectation or intention, as though
signification itself were linked to such excess. What Levinas gleans from the *Phaedo*
is the limit of any ontological conception of death or any philosophical conception
in which death bestows meaning on existence, and it is always just such a normatively drawn limit that grief necessarily trespasses, if only for a while.

The idea that grief is an excess has corollaries in Christian theology, wherein
grief quickly runs toward a pathology challenging theodicy and the very order of
a world ordained by its metaphysical premises, as well as in the history of literary
mourning, in which any expression of grief may tend toward excessive grief, if only
because grief is already useless, already excessive precisely in the sense that it can do
nothing for the dead.[25] Yet this capacity to weep for another, even to weep theatri-
cally for a fate not immediately determined by personal relationship, necessarily
bears (again, if only in an ironic sense) on the question of responsibility. Under any
regime of knowledge in which "theory is stronger than the anxiety over death" and
in which Socrates's refutations of grief might become authoritative, the mourner
who "weeps more than the others" will be excessive insofar as she breaks with rationality's attempt to quell the "affective resonance" of death. But she thereby bolsters
an ethics that must, by definition, be unsettling. Like grief's excess in the *Phaedo*,
which cannot be suppressed even by Socrates's wisdom, mournful responsibility
pursues the one who fails to perceive it just as persistently as it discovers the one who
deflects responsibility onto other persons. Insofar as the emotive relation to the death
of the other corresponds to the facticity of a signifying excess, humanity might be
defined by what exceeds all systems of being, according to the excessive fact of the

other who already objects to a world too well ordered by our conceptual knowledge. As the mournful perception of ethical responsibility comes fully into view through Levinas's struggles to wrest death's meaning from the horizon of a subjectivity anxious about its own mortality back onto a relational structure that finds its "eminent meaning in the death of others," his account of memory's impossible perspective within history gets fully intertwined with grief's ethically oriented excess so as to intimate the surprisingly necessary imbrication of ethics and mourning (DT 58).

THE DEATH OF EVERY OTHER

When in the *Phaedo* Socrates speaks originally for all Western philosophy, as though he were already invested with the full authority of a subsequent tradition, he is the archetypal philosopher who in Levinas's view would "recognize in death the very splendor of being" and thus anticipate Heidegger's formidable interpretation of death. His own dying would suggest to Socrates, as though he already spoke for the very possibility of which each being is capable, his paradoxical power over it: to be toward death is to be out ahead of oneself so as to glimpse the ownmost possibility of which each being must take charge.[26] As early as the 1947 essay "Time and the Other," Levinas had perceived the deceptive trajectory of Heideggerian virility asserted in the face of death and insisted that the Heideggerian subject necessarily fails in its capability, if only because death—and here Levinas's revisionary insistence comes terribly close to reiterating what Heidegger also admitted—is the event "in relation to which the subject is no longer a subject" (TO 70).[27] At least in part, this basic incapacity in relation to death emphasized by Levinas is, as Jacques Derrida and Tina Chanter have argued with regard to much of Levinas's thought, already Heideggerian. Levinas's distinguishing emphasis over against Heidegger (which Derrida does not entirely permit him) is based, however, in a secondary incapacity pertaining to death, based, that is, in that alterity denoted by death from which Heideggerian being too readily withdraws.

Although death is an alterity unassimilable to subjectivity and resistant to the schematics of knowledge, it is not simply that which is unknown, since that would imply a subjective consciousness that might one day expand to include the consciousness of death. Rather, death is, more definitively, that which can never be known: "Death is the impossibility of having a project. This approach of death indicates that we are in relation with something that is absolutely other, something bearing alterity not as a provisional determination we can assimilate through enjoyment, but as something whose very existence is made of alterity" (TO 74). In its aspect of unknowability, death announces a failure in the cultural project of identification

(TO 55).[28] Yet since everyone's death but my own occurs as an event in the world, the resiliently Heideggerian subject, observing that the public dimension of death must refer each being to its own fate, interprets the death of another as always also proving the *not yet* reality of one's own death. Standing against the incapacitating function of death, the Heideggerian subject immerses itself in the facticity of the everyday world and in the renewable project of subjectivity, as though in flight from death.[29] In reply, Levinas emphasizes a more radical incapacity that preoccupies even the ontological view of death—namely, the signifying otherness of death as based in the other person's death rather than my own. As long as my view of death pertains to my own finitude, the death of another person will seem merely to prove the rule of finitude, calling for an assertion of identity in the face of that which threatens it. By instead reordering the very terms of our cultural preoccupation with death, Levinas insists that the event of death interprets the final unavailability of the other as a negative proof of her alterity: death is by definition that which I cannot know and also the ultimate state in which an other is unavailable to me. Moreover, insofar as the other's death marks an irreconcilable resistance to the self's existential *pouvoir,* one must respond to it as though it were a statement in the interrogative mood: "is there not a more interrogative question behind this question, such that death, despite its certitude, would not be reduced to the question, or the alternative between to be and not to be? . . . Does death not have its eminent meaning in the death of others, where it signifies 'by way of' an event that cannot be reduced to its being?" (DT 58). Much as death supposes an incompletion of being that remains a question for the self, the other poses an ethical resistance that can hardly be accounted for as just an obstruction of knowledge.

It is by this very interrogative structure of signification, underlying the possibility of cognition before it has been codified, that the positive content of the face-to-face relation can be said to give rise to ethics. The Heideggerian anguish over death might well reveal a being's finitude, but Levinas suggests that the "good conscience of being" would nevertheless remain "intact in that finitude" (PD 166).[30] There is a positive content behind every interrogation of good conscience, the positive content which is the other herself and my responsibility for her. In this sense the other who dies yields a meaning proper to ethics itself. By preventing the resumption of identity as well as identity's most basic premises, the death of the other articulates a question at the heart of ethics: *Can I be fully myself while another suffers or dies?*

When Levinas refers identity to the other, who comes before every attempt to contain the world through representation, he already supposes that such an opposition—of, say, my own fullness versus another's deficiency through suffering—distorts the sincerity of ethical relation. In *Otherwise than Being* he therefore defines subjectivity as preeminently given over to responsibility, made meaningful by a structure of signification according to which the subject is already for-the-other apart from any conscious formulation of its obligations. Much in the same vein, the Sorbonne lectures of 1975–76 foreground a configuration of mournful emotion and memory's resistant relation to historical knowledge. Although he often focuses on the affective response to the death of the other, we must understand *affect* (despite several surprising appeals to pathos in his lecture course) as having about as much to do with our ordinary conception of pathos as we are able to forget. Unlike the heaviness of conventionally imaginative pathos, in which identity falls back upon itself under the weight of a saddening experience, the affect inspired by the other's death prompts a movement in self, an *e-motion* within identity. This movement within identity is structured according to a crucial rupture in identity, as though critique might emerge in response to those assertions or self-statements emanating from a subject's identifiable positionality not after the fact but from within culture, as a question already inhering in identity's purported facticity. In dislocating the coherence of identity, the emotional response articulates the subject as that which has been questioned by the event of death:

> Will not the inquietude of emotion itself become the question that in the proximity of death will be precisely at its origin? Emotion as a de-ference of death, which is to say, emotion as a question that does not assume, in the posing of the question, the elements of its own response. This is a question that grafts itself onto that most profound relation to infinity which is time (time as the relation to infinity); an emotional relation to the death of the other; a fear or courage but also, beyond compassion for or solidarity with the other, a responsibility for him in the unknown. Still, this is an unknown not aimed at or seen in a manner that may be objectivized or thematized, but which must rather be taken in as an aspect of that inquietude that interrogates the inconvertible question of response—an anxiety in which the response reduces to the responsibility of the questioning or of the one who questions. (DT 17; my modified trans.)

In choosing the slightly more obscure English word *inquietude* as a seemingly literal transcription of the French *inquiétude*, I have deliberately opted against the more familiar term *disquietude* employed by Bettina Bergo in translating this text. My distinction here depends mostly on a connotation not consistently sustained by the conventional English usage of the two words. Whereas to dis-quiet suggests a disruption in a former, inherited, or given state of quietude and also assumes a prior restfulness in identity, *inquietude* perhaps connotes a state of emotion rivaling quietude more originally, as if identity were to proceed as much from a state of unrest as from a simpler, edenic calm. In point of fact, Levinas wants to blur the line between the two connotations: the death of the other is disquieting in the sense that it questions the suppositions of identity by which the self ordinarily lives, but the inquietude it provokes also refers us back to the origin (or *naissance*) of the question, to an anterior state of being in which we are already in relation. As the death of the other prompts an affective movement in the self underlying all responsiveness, the form of our response also refers us to an "inconvertible question" in the sense that we must remain open to and interrogated by an exteriority. In other words, our response is ethical precisely to the extent that it is not conceptually predetermined. By intimating the capacity to be moved apart from our intentions or preconceptions, our emotional relation to the death of the other describes a state of receptivity far surpassing the self's practical capability in the world.

That ethics should depend upon an intersection between inquietude and emotion is far from an obvious point. It was Heidegger who had pronounced anxiety the source of affectivity, tracing the dread felt before the death of another to the basic threat of mortality weighing upon us all, but there is in Heidegger, as I have already suggested, always a recuperation in the face of impossibility.[31] By contrast, Levinas supposes that inquietude is a relation to an exteriority always in question and never fully answered. Already, even apart from the particular requirements of the ethical relation, sensibility is opened, much as Rosalyn Diprose has also emphasized with regard to the connotations of the Good in Levinasian ethics, toward the signifying structure of language by way of its capacity to be disturbed.[32] Mourning interprets this affective aspect of experiential existence as though it were inherently inscribed by relational significance: in mourning's turn to face even that which is no longer there, it already supposes a structure of relationship, preventing (if only hypothetically) our retreat into an empirical description of the dead as though they were objects to be fitted into a representational scheme. Inspired by an emotive responsiveness, memory is less the work of representation than a movement provoked by exteriority, by an other who is not strictly subject to ideation or to the mournful survivor's perceptions.

Nevertheless, if the inquietude occasioned by the death of the other expresses the ethical relation as a structural reality for each person, there is also, for Levinas, a personally subjective resonance to the survivor's response, so that "non-indifference toward the death of the other" denoted by the structural reality of relationship is characterized implicitly by the individualized mournful attitude (*EN* 202).[33] So, too, when Levinas speaks of the immemorial dimension of the ethical relation, he elicits the manner in which the self pursues its indebtedness to the face of the other as if it wished to grasp the other and turn relationship into a mode of knowledge but never could. In a 1982 conversation with Christian Chabanis, Levinas privileges the death of the other as an event definitive of what it means to be human, even perhaps as an individually humanizing event: "But for the survivor, there is in the death of the other his or her disappearance, and the extreme loneliness of that disappearance. I think that *the Human* consists precisely in opening oneself to the death of the other, in being preoccupied with his or her death. What I am saying here may seem like a pious thought, but I am persuaded that around the death of my neighbour what I have been calling the humanity of man is manifested" (PD 157–58). Despite Levinas's previous distrust of the survivor's perspective, the emphasis here seems less on any subjective capability in the survivor than on the vulnerability of a survivor who steadfastly mourns those she has survived. Whatever else "being preoccupied" with the death of the other might connote, it refers us to a difficult, subjective praxis of remembrance. Depending upon that which is both exterior and absent, memory is implicated from the start in an affective response to absence, defined in the unquieting effect of the other's disappearance. Memory, by this mournful valence, is a vigilance long before it achieves any ideational content, and as such vigilance always unquiets the commemorative reach of our remembrance.

According to Michel de Certeau, memory "works when something affects it" and remembers an object "only when it has disappeared," so it is, properly speaking, a "sense of the other" that lives anew in an act of memory.[34] For de Certeau remembrance is a transvaluation of the past into the present, an inscription of the other onto the elusive moment of the contemporary mind. It is not hard to see how such a logic would render the death of the other the ultimate test of memory's capability. Yet the problem, as Levinas helps us view it, is that a survivor's realized memory competes directly with her obligations to a seemingly obsolete form of relationship, locating her capability within a set of permanent concepts or principles as yet invulnerable to the loss of the other, achieved in a present tense tantamount to the rights of the vanquisher. It is only through the paradox of an ethics that does not require any recollective representation of the absent other that we begin to see how the inadequacy of memory before the event of death signifies an alternate mode of memory—derived as memory's vigilance—to be valued apart from its practical or historical capabilities.

By this very self-critical, even self-contradictory valuation of memory, Levinas arrives at what he frequently calls the *immemorial* aspect of the ethical relation. This immemorial memory of the other traces a debt to the other, one that can never be paid and can also never be equated to a history of the relationship. The other obligates before she enters history and after she departs from the realm of the historical event—or, as Derrida phrases it in the future present, "She will have obligated," by which he suggests that the obligation ordinarily perceived as past has not yet been met or fulfilled.[35] The immemorial quality of Levinasian memory supposes a critique of all commemorative resolutions of the past, which necessarily betray the other's reality for the survivor's. What Levinas insists upon with considerable consistency from the early to the later work is a remembrance reverting to the time of the other—not as a stultifying nostalgia that renders the present finally empty of significance but rather as a question signifying in inquietude that has effectively rended present time and challenged identity with the many obligations that remain unmet by already posited capabilities. The necessarily incompleted past defines ethics as always opening toward the other in a relation never to be finally accomplished. To put the matter another way, we could say that mourning performs a dislocation within memory, what Levinas also refers to as a de-posing of identity. Mourning encourages a connotation in which memory stands aside from the reifications of retrospective knowledge and withstands the pressures of representation, and it is precisely this possibility of a memory standing against the conventions of memory that marks responsibility as only imperfectly defeated by the death of the other.

THE UNIVERSAL RELEVANCE OF THE UNJUST DEATH

Reading Plato's *Phaedo*, one might almost forget that Socrates is executed by the state. By contrast, Xenophon's account of Socrates's death in *The Memoriabilia* keeps the protest of an unjust death closer to the surface, and yet, in vehemently objecting to the state's actions against an innocent, as Søren Kierkegaard observed in *The Concept of Irony* (1841), Xenophon characterizes Socrates as so entirely unobjectionable, indeed unphilosophical, that one has difficulty imagining how the state ever came to be offended by him.[36] Kierkegaard's account of Xenophon's uninspiring Socrates cooperates with a larger rubric in which Kierkegaard also opposes philosophy and history as though they marked the difference between the arrival at profound, inner, or transcendent truth and merely superficial explanations of phenomena. In order to maintain the prestige of philosophy, Kierkegaard must uphold heroic remembrance of an absolutely unique Socrates, and thus Kierkegaard's cautioning against being "infatuated by the charms of the particular" (10–11), which are associated with history, fully complements his intuition of history's capacity to find even the exceptional individual relatively unremarkable. Nothing dates Kierkegaard so quickly for his contemporary readers so much as this refusal to concede to history anything that philosophy might yet render in the less evident, more meaningful, even Socratically ironic light of transcendent truth.

In Levinas, of course, history is not separable from philosophy by such means, since both are as readily implicated in the cultural preference for the heroic consciousness of victors. If this implication requires us to see history, as was Kierkegaard's wont, through an inverted lens whereby those least rewarded in the immediate context lay claim to the most enduring significance, any technique of ironically preferring those who were vanquished or unrealized—which is evident in Kierkegaard but also in Levinas—must promote an inversion of value by which the historical person, say, as one who is being murdered by the state, might yet appear greater than what vanquishes him. The question we must then pose is whether a mournful appreciation for the defeated, especially for those whose defeat signals the oppressive, unjust wills exercised against them in history, must turn preeminently on such an unrealistic revaluation. And at least in part our answer to this question must be yes: according to realism, history always proceeds without those who are not already obviously included in its progressive unfolding. Even though Hegel proposed a way to reconcile a transcendent ideational structure to those phenomena articulated by immanent historical knowledge, he could not imagine (except perhaps in his examination of the unquieted consciousness of the bondsman from the "Lordship and Bondage" section of the *Phenomenology*) what might become of those who were never self-consciously positioned within history's forward momentum. Mourning in Levinas's work, serving as both a trope for and a mode of memory, returns us, as it were, specifically to the site of an unhistorical perspective, as to that cultural place from which ethics has begun to revalue in advance our conventional historical measures of cultural and political achievements.

My point here is that, although Levinas seemingly cooperates with the Platonic tendency to abstract Socrates's story from its specifiable historical context, his revaluation of the story's affective dimensions marks the fact of historical injustice as inevitable matter for the ethical relation, perhaps even as the fundamental core of all ethical thought. If I have avoided the temptation to name Levinas as the referent of his generically philosophical, mournful subject—which is to say, as though his biographical profile might help us to read him, not unlike the way he reads the character of Socrates in the *Phaedo*, as someone whose implication in grief qualifies in advance each of the philosophical or ethical positions he adopts—such deliberate neglect on my part establishes my own theoretical positionality vis-à-vis Levinas's. By refusing to impose Levinas's own personal history and cultural situatedness as contingently determined explanation of his conflation of mourning and ethics, I run the risk of replicating certain ahistoricist propensities of Levinas's thought, but I incur this risk deliberately, in order to reinforce the point that in Levinas the other's particularity, while serving as the fundamental datum of ethics, is not easily reconciled to the particularisms of sociohistorical event, of cultural identity, of individual or group histories. Levinas's persistent concern for the other who is failed by our cultural categories for identity, a concern which is apparent both figuratively within his descriptions of the ethical relation and thematically in his generalized, even vague statements about injustice, draws our attention to the shortcoming of all straightforward inversions of power (the strategy of siding uncritically with the minority group versus the majority) as well as of most oppositional assessments of oppression (those strategies of resistance that, in an almost Hegelian fashion, deploy their resistant labor within an already constituted system and thus mirror the cultural terms of the powerful parties against whom they struggle): that ethics might become simply an uncritical preference for the oppressed, who might thereafter mythically construe in themselves a self-righteousness immune—say, from within a future position of power—to the very deformative tactics of power by which they, the oppressed, presently suffer. In Levinas ethics is dedicated to the haunting ramifications of responsibility structuring even the ethical consciousness of the oppressed group, such that the persecuted are frequently imagined as though they were responsible even for their persecutors. The memory of injustice always exercises this influence upon the corrective action of social justice, calling suffering toward a greater responsibility even beyond what it initially offers in solidarity. The realism of such an ethical theory, I would contend, is that it absolutely refuses utopianism and any construct of justice that would hypothesize a perfectible future equality. It refuses such habits of thought because they tend to reinforce the illusory assertion that current social systems (say, capitalism or communism) have already approximated the conditions of equality and tend to reify extant social constructs of justice as already good enough, when by the plain facts—of an immensely oppressed Third World, of an international working class enduring economic conditions that are degrading, of those who are altogether disfranchised even within liberal societies, or of nation-states' recurring propensity for genocide—they are not.

In one sense, then, Levinas's advocacy of the other's particularism stands against the Western tradition of upholding universal dictates, of asserting generalized moral principles that are good for all occasions and all times, and of congratulating ourselves for the elaborate systems of rights we have already put in place—all of which might characterize the very same culturally hegemonic propensity Alain Badiou associates with human rights discourse. Yet Levinas's critique of universalizing philosophy from the standpoint of that always neglected datum that is the other person in his degradation or in her suffering does not simply overthrow the future of all ethical universalism. Rather, as I noted in my introduction, the very possibility of universalism persists in and is even perhaps sustained by what it occludes. What universally binds all of us is the requirement to turn to that which disproves the adequacy of our current political system and the conceptual universals of justice by which we would legitimate it.

Insofar as responsibility turns us from our reliance upon already established identity as from any attempt to regulate other people by what already supports our self-
conception, we must be turned also to remembrance of those who cannot be regulated by Western law and its system of rights precisely because they were never
included in its central functionings. The other's experience of violence and systemically orchestrated oppression exposes extant norms for justice as contradictory—
beneficial to some, harmful to others. In Levinas responsibility necessarily refers
the chauvinism of all cultural identity to the other side of history, to those we
have neglected, systemically excluded, and either directly or structurally harmed.
Broadly speaking, then, we might identify three revisedly universalizing aspects of
the Levinasian project that emerge as a consequence of his mournful focus on the
unjust death:

1. A first aim is to disjoin the other's particularism for each responsible subject
    from a cultural definition of the other as a person, neighbor, or co-nationalist
    about whom one has knowledge. Insisting on the signification of a responsi-
    bility that arises through suffering or in the event of death, even perhaps a
    suffering that occurs at the hands of one for whom a subject is nevertheless
    responsible, Levinas refuses to associate the ethical terms of responsibility
    with the established cultural characteristics by which the other person might
    be defined. In death the other is as unknowable as the fate that befalls him,
    and yet the subject finds in this encounter, which is precisely an encounter
    with alterity and unknowingness, the very meaning of her responsibility.
    Thus, in an essay such as "Dying For . . ." the speculative exegesis on Saul and
    Jonathan takes us beyond a conception of relationship as care for the other
    based upon work and what human beings accomplish together and overturns
    self-reflexive cultural identity by way of the ultimately unfortunate event: for,
    even as the death of the other demonstrates an alterity that will not reduce to
    self-knowledge, it simultaneously demands that the subject venture beyond
    self-concern. Upon an ethical subject so postured, Levinas inscribes inqui-
    etude as the vocation of ethics, as an affective movement in the subject occa-
    sioned by the crisis or potential crisis that may befall the other who signifies the
    subject's responsibilities. The inquietude provoked by the death of the other or
    by the potential scenario of the other's death is the very sign of ethics. As he
    elsewhere phrases it, "the death of the other has priority over yours, and over
    your life" (PD 164). Or, again in "Dying For . . . ," when he refers to this atti-
    tude as "dying for the other," the other's death generates the very meaning of
    "love in its responsibility for one's fellowman" (D 216). To be preoccupied with

the death of the other, even if there is in this preoccupation a quasi-sacrificial connotation, is to discern the constitutive sense in which responsibility must be inconvenient, arriving from beyond expectation, as well as that sense in which responsibility becomes universal precisely insofar as it is still unrealized.

2. Relatedly, in Levinas's Sorbonne lectures he charges the unjust death itself (as my reading of Levinas reading the *Phaedo* makes clear) with a social dimension that situates each subject within range of a responsibility for the others to whom harm comes. Conjoining the philosophical problem of death forever to the basic problem of ethics, Levinas presumes that every subject exists in some socio-structural relation to injustice. To come upon the possibility of the other's death in his everyday vulnerability or to perceive in her death, once it arrives, an injustice against which ethics must be forever, if imperfectly, vigilant means that a subject is universal only by way of her responsibilities. For Levinas an injustice inheres, at least potentially, in every death. If for this reason alone, the other's death is always possibly, perhaps even characteristically, apprehended under the hypothesis of murder. By extension, the temptation to murder underlies the sociality of the ethical relation and is inscribed, as it were, on the face of the other, who signifies in his exposure to harm, in her irremissible vulnerability to murder, and paradoxically in the very command that comes from the face—"Thou shalt not kill." In works such as "Freedom and Command" (1953) and *Totality and Infinity* Levinas conceives of ethics as preoccupying the possibility of murder, so that an "(im)possibility of murder," as Jill Robbins phrases it, "inhabits the language relation to the other at its origin" (64).[37] Much of the risk Levinas incurs with his figurative use of murder he incurs deliberately. Through his quasi-fictional deployment of the murderer as someone who in Cain-like fashion cannot altogether forgo those responsibilities he incurred prior to his act of murder and his attempted murder of ethical meaningfulness, Levinas characterizes the situation of death— which is not a subsiding into nothingness but a contested otherness, an alterity with which subjectivity always struggles—as the threshold for every construct of just relations.[38] Figuring death as an opponent, Levinas supposes that death threatens us from beyond with a dangerous otherness, as though in its radically transcendent alterity there were already a malevolence that "strikes me in an evil design or in a judgment of justice" (*TI* 234).[39]

It is quite as though any possibility of natural death has been subsumed by the prospect of violent death, and if we were to object, for example, that Levinas's perceptions of death have somehow been deformed by his biographical experience and the historical circumstances of the Holocaust, we

would also have to bear in mind that his argument runs from the philosophical fact of death directly toward such historical possibility. Which is to say,
when Levinas claims that death approaches "as fear of someone," or when he
argues that, in facing death as that which is against me, the *I* glimpses the possibility of a murder "inseparable from the essence of death," he insists that
death's severe opposition to ethical possibility is conjoined to an all too real
history of murder and atrocity (*TI* 234). The hypothetical, even quasi-mythi-
cal scenario of murder takes historical form; it is the universal of responsibility moving into history, into the context of a social particularity that for all
its contingent circumstances will not diminish, in any sense, the socio-structural signification by which every subject who is put in touch with the historical realization of murder and the abiding possibility of further violence is
made responsible. "Murder, at the origin of death," Levinas says, "reveals a
cruel world, but one to the scale of human relations" (*TI* 236).

Such a conflation of death with the socially determined situation of injustice may blur the historical distinction between those unjust deaths perpetrated by human beings and the natural and necessary fact of death, but it still
speaks an ethical truth: death is not only the ultimate injustice that may be
done to the other, it is the condition according to which the body of the other
is given over to a radical vulnerability in every moment of its being. Thus, the
death of the other is the very occasion—prior to the event of death as in the
moment of death's arrival, and even after death has been perpetrated—of any
ethical valuation of the other. Almost from the start Levinas had conceived of
violent death both as a murderous restriction on the ethical possibility of subjectivity and as a fate threatening every other with whom the self may come
into relation. By so often alternating subject-positions in his analysis of violence—by moving from the hypothetical perspective of the victim to that of a
subject who would do violence or murder to another—Levinas inscribes the
act of violence upon the life of the other as a situational inevitability. The
statement "the Other is the sole being I can wish to kill" is coupled with its
reverse corollary (*TI* 198), which is that the face as a site of defenselessness
suggests the way in which every face I encounter is exposed to death.[40] Yet,
according to these ethical crossings of positionality, each subject in history is
already surrendered, Levinas supposes, to her responsibility for the other in
and through time, as if there lurks always in each social situation a potential
for any subject to do violence to the other with whom she is in relation or to
suffer violence at another's hands. It is as if ethics were meant to perceive in
every instance of the other's suffering the possibility of his death, which might

result from the interpersonal event of violence or from the wider sphere of systemically orchestrated political actions, such as oppression or atrocity, inflicted
on the other. However pessimistic this may seem as a vision of society—no
matter how much this seems a vision traumatically haunted by the Holocaust—
Levinas's refusal to treat extraordinary violence as an atavistic regression from
modern civilization forces us to read murder not as aberrant but as a constitutive possibility of all human relations.

3. The other universalizing emphasis of the Levinasian project pertains to
Levinas's interpretation of a history of injustice by which we are all bound. By
interpreting the devastations of the Nazi era (1933–45) through the seemingly
singular, often dehistoricized and generalized situation of ethical particularity, Levinas casts the Holocaust as a submerged historical referent for the face-
to-face relation of ethics. To be in relation to another is also to be forever in
relationship to the history of atrocity, which occupies the present moment
in potentiality and memory. Of course, it would be possible to read Levinas's
insistence on the absolute anteriority of the other to all forms of knowledge,
and thus also of ethics to history, politics, ontology, or phenomenology, as an
elaborate rhetorical stratagem for preempting the Holocaust as a determinative influence on his own project. For Levinas does not follow someone such
as Maurice Blanchot, his close friend and intellectual collaborator, in supposing an epochal rift occasioned by the Holocaust in the liberal humanist
conventions of Western culture. Instead, Levinas discerns the preconditions
for annihilative violence in Western culture's neglect of its own most valuable
insights (the Hebrew Bible, Plato, Descartes, Kierkegaard, Buber, all intimate
to some extent the respect for alterity Levinas also advocates). In all of this he
seems to imagine the signifying structures of ethics as though they preceded
and must also survive, however precariously, the extremity of the Holocaust,
even while the possibility of ethics has come to be characterized by this historical, supremely unethical event.

Unlike Todorov, Levinas does not seek to preserve an identity constructed
upon its capacity for virtue or upon the specific contents of individualized
morality in the situation of extremity. Instead, he proceeds as though the very
meaning of ethics must already have anticipated and designated a responsibility for the worst that could be done in history either to an individual person
or, through the political actions of states, to many persons. Ethics as such
must signify apart from the intention or deliberative choices it elaborates
within the flow of historical consciousness, assigning obligation to the subject
and glimpsing the very condition of the subject's humanity and her meaning-

ful existence in the primordial fact of responsibility for another person. A subject assumes the meaning of her own entry into consciousness only by way of the significations of responsibility, by having been defined as a subject in a passive rather than active attitude, by having been subjected to the other in the extended moment of his historical existence. If there is, then, in the very structure of Levinasian responsibility a peculiar quality of mournfulness, such mournfulness seems not only inflected by the author's Holocaust consciousness (as is the case with regard to his explicit critique of Heidegger's Nazism) but also characterized by it, as though the meaning of the Holocaust were made to seem universally abiding within the ethical possibility that befalls each subject in time hereafter. The Holocaust, in this sense, becomes a universal referent for historical injustice, predicting the necessity to assume responsibility for all socially determined injustices. As such, mourning is also a mode of historical consciousness, turning especially on the memory of the Holocaust's victims or on the oppressed of the Third World or on those who are ordinarily forsaken by the normative structures of the liberal society, none of whom can be located either on the side of history's progress or inside the transcendent truths of philosophical knowledge. As the literally forgotten matter of liberal progress, as people whom the liberation theologian Gustavo Gutiérrez once referred to as the "souvenirs of history," these others are witnesses to the other side or underside of history's meaning. In the particularity of their suffering they can no more be gloriously transvalued by metaphysical presuppositions than they can be left behind by the conclusions we might prefer to draw about ourselves from our Western models of history.

THE HOLOCAUST—NOT JUST ANYBODY'S INJUSTICE

In closing this chapter, I want to emphasize the historical dimensions of Levinasian ethics even within its ostensible turns against the conventions of historiography and to suggest how in particular the memory of injustice foregrounds the intersection between ethics and politics in his project. No matter how we construe the memory of injustice, we should concede in advance that there is already a counter-argument prepared for us. As Alain Finkielkraut perceived in *The Imaginary Jew* (1980)—in terms at least partly indebted to Levinas but also anticipatory of his subsequent musings on the Holocaust and the hypothetical usefulness of suffering—those who refuse to forget are besieged by a cultural suspicion that demands to know how the past may prove useful to the future.[41] For Finkielkraut even those Jews who defend their acts of Holocaust memory as a way of retaining a "link with their vanished culture" are

forced to rationalize memory as "nothing but a form of vigilance," assigning themselves the culturally useful role of being guardians against the possibility that such a
past might again return (53). Such vigilance of memory is, for Finkielkraut, already
in disservice to those who must be remembered in their own right and not for their
service to a nation-state all too happy to forget them. Memory is the last refuge of the
victim's meaningfulness, and if it is relinquished even briefly or offered nominally to
the future its ground will disappear entirely, subsumed by a narcissistically self-referential modernity—which is "in love with itself" and which will not even notice this
final disappearance (54). Finkielkraut's posture is mournful to the extreme, very much
in a vein I have associated with Levinas. When Finkielkraut supposes that history can
be emptied of its onwardly directed vision and concentrated on an eclipsed culture,
he provides us with a possible answer to the question of what it might mean for mourning to be historical or for history to become mournful, but the difference between
Levinas and Finkielkraut, I would maintain, is implicitly a political one: for, as Levinas insists that ethics attend both to others who are the victims of historical injustices
and to those undergoing political acts of erasure in the present, he positions mournfulness as a belated vigilance on behalf of the dead that is simultaneously a sign of
the ethical responsibilities incurred in present time.

In the past, either more primitively or more rudimentarily, history seemed a
praxis in which historical consciousness, or the narratives supporting historical consciousness, remained inseparable from the actual events to which such consciousness referred. Certain strains of contemporary historiography (one thinks of Pierre
Nora or Michel de Certeau in France or in the United States of Hayden White and
Dominick LaCapra) have theorized such an intersection as constitutive of all historical praxis, so that any history must also be a narrative of allusiveness in the almost
literary sense that potentially obscure references are made meaningful only via their
location in narrative.[42] Speaking generally, self-reflexive historical consciousness
suggests that what history still refers to (what our historians are able to deem worthy
of transcribing as though it were also permanent matter) is in large part what we can
remember. At its origin history spoke of events on a much wider scale, aspiring
toward a certain kind of objectivity, worrying that any individual apprehension of an
event could not adequately explain it in its entirety. Nevertheless, history's narrativization had always provided a bridge—between, on the one hand, subjective
understanding as attuned to what is immediately experiential and, on the other, our
historical forms of knowledge, which require remoteness and a seemingly objective
detachment reflecting the greater scale of events being recorded.[43]

With the empiricist revolution in history, suddenly a scientific, investigative logic
limited the scope of what could be presumed according to prior knowledge, so much

of which now seemed overly metaphysical in its suppositions. Forced to focus only on what could be deduced from documentary standards of evidence, empiricist history, as the latest aspiration to objectivity, involved a reduction in the scope of objectivity. For objectivity itself now depended upon any historian's immediate subjective capacity to explain the evidence before her without depending on principles of causation (say, the method of the history of ideas) that could no longer be confirmed one way or another. Clearly, what the new methodology also permitted was the possibility that historians could record events as if they were distinct from their explanations, which is to say, as if events were not yet incorporated, and need never be, into a narrative teleology enfolding history once more into lived memory. Empiricist history's disjuncture from a prior conception of history as approximate, generalized memory is not unrelated to the status Derrida attributes to writing itself, which evolves practically as the consequence of a forgetting.[44] In a world dependent upon writing, the quality of memory—which is, by definition, associated with what can be again orally transmitted—is eroded, made to seem insubstantial or metaphysical. Under the rubric of empiricism history coincides with the prestige of writing, a bias that is revealed, for example, in the long-standing reluctance of Holocaust historians to admit nondocumentary evidence such as oral testimony to the privileged center of research priorities. At the most naïve level such a hermeneutical orientation might mistake the authority of documentation for sincerity, as though written documents were utterly reliable, as though perpetrators of crimes could not create deceptive paper trails that would have to be, at some later point, supplemented or counteracted by skeptical modes of history perhaps based in part on testimony by those who were without the authority or means to record their experiences in history.

Insofar as the question of mourning pertains to history, it might suggest not only the real facticity of the absent perspectives in our normative histories but, perhaps more basically, the paucity of the evidence before us, whether archival or materialist, for judging the meanings of historical events. To recover the limited perspective of certain voices omitted from the archetypal narratives of Western history would be, however, to correct history only by way of certain overly confident strains of memory, as though some of the once neglected facets of individual or collective memory might be recovered and history thereby restored to its proper place in culture with our capacity for historical consciousness greatly recuperated. A significant problem in determining just what should constitute history (which texts, which evidence, which perspectives?) arises from our scale of reference. Now more than ever, when the praxis of the historians seems to have permanently parted ways with historical consciousness as it is lived in culture, history denotes a frame of reference exceeding memory. In an age when what can be recorded far surpasses what can be remembered—indeed, if one follows Jean-François Lyotard, when what can be accounted as information within a society far surpasses the capacity of most people to understand the technological or political processes by which the state of knowledge has been reached—any emphasis on memory can seem vaguely nostalgic.[45] If so, perhaps all we can mean by mournful history is this lost capacity of memory, a mourning even for what memory can no longer retrieve.

Perhaps the question of mourning is better understood, then, as a challenge to history, as that which searches out the failure of history's credibility. An intersection between mourning and history makes clear a relation already also supposed by memory's mournful premises—that history as such is always about who gets to remember, and what gets remembered is predictable according to just *who*, according to a set of identifiable voluntary and socially assigned affinities, remembers. At least one strain of contemporary history, perceiving the limits of the historiographical conventions of objectivity, has taken this route. Inspired especially by Foucault's techniques of subversion as well as his elucidation of the cultural regimes of knowledge with which such techniques are necessarily complicit, intellectual movements such as New Historicism, cultural materialism, and postcolonialism have all favored a hermeneutic that seeks to recover points of resistance set within and occluded by traditional formulations of historical knowledge. By such methods an alternative history gets written in the margins of dominant historical textuality or set alongside imperialistic, totalizing historical narratives, quite as though history could be altered by referring to contingent, conflictual, or seemingly arbitrary or anarchic nodal points within our ordering sociopolitical narratives. Already implicit here is a fantasy of devolution I would call mournful. Revising our view of the past by looking again at its occluded voices and its officially suppressed identities, our newer histories retrieve other meanings from the past than those that have thus far been deployed in legitimating contemporary structures of sociopolitical power. On the whole, any methodology advocating a challenge to history from its purported margins will tend to invest a degree of hope in a competitive vying for power, a capacity allotted to those newly speaking from the margins of world history. Yet, as attested by the preparedness of capitalist economy to deform internationalist, postcolonial, and transnationalist discourses into the cooperative language of globalization, all such vying may already conform to Hobbesian, Nietzschean, or Darwinian principles largely evolved as modes of complicitous dissent within the predominant competitive paradigms of Western nationalist, capitalist culture.

Among the other most prominent late-twentieth-century challenges to history are the historical discourses that attempted to respond to the Holocaust and to the wide-ranging theories of French poststructuralism, neither of which (as I suggested in the introduction) should be reduced simply to being a symptom of the other. Never-theless, poststructuralism inclines toward a theory of perpetual crisis that has great relevance to certain emphases in Holocaust Studies. Especially under the influence of Derrida's deconstructive techniques, which supposed that Western systems of knowledge were constantly presuming centers of authority that could not be vali-dated except insofar as they were already taken for granted by texts forever valoriz-ing the very ideas they were attempting to challenge, poststructuralism perceived history as a mode of ideologically constructed, officially sanctioned memory that could not resist its own ontological habits of conformity—even when its modes, based in science, seemed to be separate from the institutional sponsors of, say, lib-eral nationalist ideology. For Derrida the necessarily self-authorizing gestures of tex-tuality, dependent as they are upon a construct of presence roughly tantamount to the text's overreaching principle of authority, already meant that the center of cul-ture was never as secure as it supposed itself to be.

The Holocaust is only rarely invoked as a ground by Derrida for his linguistic skepticism, yet his radical turns against the mythical confidences of representation have seemed to some commentators to be marked by his own Jewishness as also by a post-Holocaust consciousness. The affinity, as I see it, pertains to what Derrida frames as a divide between representation and the metaphysical presences it would obtain and what Holocaust historiography perceives as a rupture in the very capac-ity of representation, most often pointing to a crisis in the efficacy of knowledge. As Lawrence Langer frames the problem, for example, the Holocaust would forever cast into doubt not only the metaphysical groundings of discourse but the humanis-tic enterprise of culture.[46] As an event occurring apparently at the very heart of West-ern culture, the Holocaust challenges the historical purposefulness of all knowl-edge, disrupting the teleological momentum of culture as idealistically expressed by Hegel but also more or less adhered to by all liberal democratic citizens of the West-ern nation-states, even unto the contemporary moment. Thus, the turn against the metaphysical, humanist foundations of representation is also a turn against the nar-rativization of history in a progressive trajectory. Even a purportedly empiricist his-torian such as Berel Lang, who prefers the firsthand evidence of documents and tes-timony to the transparently representational and therefore imaginatively remote procedures of literature, indulges antinarratological fantasies when it comes to this subject, as he speculates that the only proper historical form for treating the Holo-caust might be the crude history of the annals, a listing of events entirely indepen-dent of the necessarily interpretive techniques of narrativization.

What the hasty abridgment of poststructuralist methodology and post-Holocaust sensibility uncovers is their common apprehension of their own post-ness, of our having arrived at a point in time when our confidence in culture gets forever cast into the mythic past. By such a logic the Holocaust introduces a faultline in history, as though its relatively singular eruption means that all the edifices of culture, before and after the event of disaster, have been built foolishly upon ground that can no longer hold. Posed thus as an interruption of history insofar as history might be reconciled to the conventions of memory, the Holocaust supposes the demise of basic humanist conceptions, whether they rely upon implicitly religious premises or upon the demystifying secularism of Enlightenment culture, on which contemporary historical praxis continues to be based.

Most relevant here is that poststructuralist claim, explicitly articulated by Maurice Blanchot and Lyotard on the European scene and on the American scene by Geoffrey Hartman, that the Holocaust is a historical event enacting an interruption in the metaphysical, ontological, and phenomenological precepts of Western thought. Blanchot seems especially pertinent, since in *The Writing of the Disaster* he tries to imagine an *écriture* that has been forever altered by what it cannot name and yet can never escape. For Blanchot the incomprehensibility of the historical event of disaster exercises a determinative influence apprehended only through the measurelessness of the event itself. Only the most surprising of paradoxes can convey a history in which what is offered to the subject as a resource for consciousness altogether annihilates the progressive flow of historical knowledge: "The holocaust, the *absolute* event of history—which is a date in history—that utter-burn where all history took fire, where the movement of Meaning was swallowed up, where the gift, which knows nothing of forgiving or consent, shattered without *giving* place to anything that can be affirmed, that can be denied—gift of very passivity, gift of what cannot be given. How can it be preserved, even by thought? How can thought be made the keeper of the holocaust where all was lost, including guardian thought?"[47] The erasure of history by the "utter-burn" of the Holocaust means that history has become contentless, unable to produce even the thought that survives it. Yet in the aftermath of disaster all of us "who have known only partially, or from a distance" about this great interruption of history are addressed by it, called to become watchful with regard to that which we can no longer see and could never really have seen. Blanchot's terms of perception are impersonal, nondescript, and generalized enough to be associated with the sphere of historical knowledge for which they are constantly being interchanged. Even to give the name of ethics to such a mode of consciousness seems presumptuous, since the vigilance that has been provoked in any single witness is for an indeterminate, already devastating event. Blanchot's subject exists in history as an attempt to answer for what cannot be answered for, as a perspective from within or after the event seeming almost as unassumable as history itself. As is also true for Hartman, if perhaps less so for Lyotard, there are vestiges of humanistic hope informing Blanchot's perception of crisis: the metaphysical, mythic, or archetypal justification for our actions has now forever eluded us, but still we turn to the place of devolution as if what we witnessed there made it the only site upon which our renewed commitment to culture could be constructed.[48]

The influence of Levinas upon Blanchot, and vice versa, has been observed by not a few commentators, and certainly there is much in Blanchot's formulation that cooperates with Levinasian ethics.[49] Most obviously, Blanchot intimates the futility of any moral system that would divulge a set of ordinary moral criteria to delineate a post-Holocaust identity commensurate with the scale of historical suffering it will have glimpsed. As I have already suggested, Levinas might well agree with Blanchot's implicit proscription against conventional history as well as his explicit defiance of the ordinary scales of moral knowledge, yet Levinas also sets about discerning structures of ethical signification that inhere even in the seemingly forever rended enterprise of Western culture. If such a project seems on the surface more conservative in its relation to traditional structures of meaning, there are elements of greater historical specificity (since Blanchot's quasi-apocalyptic formulation never quite brings us back to practical social structures) in Levinas's multiple formulations, by which we are constantly referred to the materiality of existence, or the very structure of sensibility, as determinative of ethical meaning.[50]

Be that as it may, we cannot turn in our mournfulness from conventional histories to the province of memory in order to answer simply for the history of injustice concealed by our histories. For, insofar as mourning also coincides with the apparent obsolescence of memory, any attempt to speak of a mournful history must be paradoxically dependent on memory's limits. Ahead of time we know that memory—as the reductive version of an event, as that which marks a capacity to delimit history even while the scientific dimensions of historical method remain virtually unlimitable—encourages a mode of referentiality already too esoteric fully to stand in for historical significance. If history's credibility is made to depend on limiting history (again) to the reach of memory or, specifically, to what is still within reach of an individual or group to recollect as experience or approximate experience, history must finally confess its own implication in what theories of memory more readily admit: the fact that every representation of the past is a remembrance colored by bias, perhaps by grievance or by a will to power, and informed by an ideological positionality frequently accounted for as though it were synonymous with the politics of identity. But even were we to be contented with this rough equation of history to the willful politics of collective memory, this is hardly an ethical solution in the Levinasian sense. To acknowledge the historian's work as a mournful recovery of what has been lost to memory might mean construing the coexistence of history and memory as a conversion of the former to the latter, foreseeing a praxis of history, along the lines of what Finkielkraut imagined, to be conducted largely as a mode of reverent memory.

Ethical vigilance, or what I have called "vigilant memory," must be distinguished from this prospect. For the shortcomings of mourning, as with ethics, is a tendency to distill the socially determined responsibility to an individualized essence, with the result that either or both together come to be characterized by an exceptionalism that might altogether forsake insight into the systemic parameters determining injustice. Just as ethics may treat the phenomenon of the widow or orphan or the victims of a tsunami in Sri Lanka as aberrant events requiring extraordinary charity but not necessarily political change, mourning may degenerate to a set of presumptions referring only to what the mourner already took for granted, even insofar as those presumptions are part of collectively constructed identity. Mourning so easily falls into self-indulgence because what aggrieves the mourner most particularly is his own violated sense of justice, her loss of ideological advantage. In the wake of 9/11 the quality of American mourning frequently fell back upon nationalistic imperatives, and comparison was often made to Pearl Harbor as though the proper analogy to such an event were the one other historical violation of American sovereignty in more than a century. In each case what was assaulted at least in part was a sense of imperialistic invulnerability, which effected an apparent trauma at least to the presumption of vulnerability. This was not just anybody's vulnerability, it was ours. If it were just anybody's suffering, political indifference might be a plausible response. The fact that it was our own made mourning seem requisite behavior. Already within this logic there is inscribed a predictable recalcitrance, which arose specifically in response to efforts by Noam Chomsky or Gore Vidal to make Americans perceive their own sufferings under terrorism in structural correspondence to other people's experiences of terrorist violence, even perhaps in analogy to the sufferings of people in countries damaged by those state-terrorist violences enacted by the United States. Proceeding along similar lines, the film 11'09"01—September 11—which symbolized an internationalist perspective by featuring eleven filmmakers from different countries who explored the mournful response to 9/11 in eleven separate eleven-minute segments that often put the event in explicit analogy to political injustices suffered commonly by oppressed and terrorized peoples in their own countries, in some cases as the direct result of the United States' foreign policy—met with a grudging response.

I invoke these examples of the restrictive, conservative, or nationalistic turn mourning can take because, according to the political horizon I have tried to sketch in this chapter for the mournfulness of Levinasian ethics, it matters greatly whether we can move beyond the self-referential position—*this is not just anybody's suffering, it's ours*—to conceive of the structural interrelations and explicit political relations by which every occasion of extreme violence, especially those enacted by us, would involve an overcoming of indifference such that we could say in response to the suffering of others, *this is not just anybody's responsibility, it's ours.* In Levinas's turn against the formal conventions of historical knowledge, there is a fundamental ambiguity between political knowledge and the unadmitted facts of history. Yet his parallel commitment to the unrelenting significances of history, especially insofar as history is also always this history of having harmed others, suggests a political horizon for ethics that cannot rest in communal, ethnic, or nationalist self-concern. The strongest influence of the Holocaust is felt, in this respect, with regard to the inarticulateness that necessarily imbues any effort to speak of genocide, whether from within the experience of suffering as a victim or from without as one who witnesses to, turns from, or critically looks into the center of atrocity. Mourning is at the center of this interruption, denoting the intensity of ethical particularity as a peculiarly universal obligation, quite as though the wrong done to the other could eternally accuse historical consciousness for its necessarily generalized descriptions, for always remitting its vigilance with regard to the past event of violence as though it were also the sign of an immediate yielding to present injustice. To describe a mode of discourse that pertains to the impossible vocation of speaking for the lost others in history, if not directly by way of their recoverable or representable perspectives— this is to envision an ethical attentiveness always alert to what we are either by convention or cultural indifference often unprepared to revisit.

CHAPTER TWO

The Unpleasure of Conscience

I have not done anything and I have always been under accusation . . .

Emmanuel Levinas, Otherwise than Being

Much of the task of the preceding chapter was to argue for the mournful connotations of Levinasian ethics not as owing to sorrowful, historical contingencies in the
author's life, but rather as a sign of a necessarily ethical stance. In philosophical
terms this means that ethics becomes characterized by an apparently irreconcilable,
even incommensurate, divide between the self's ethically structured meaning and
the practical functionings of an everyday *I*, which might ordinarily understand itself
by the cognitive sense it is able to make of the predictably historical world. There is
a distinct possibility, then, that mourning might become an ethical sign foreseeing
only a supremely unenactable horizon, as though the real meaning of responsibility
were to signify, at least from within the realm of practical politics, as irresponsibility.
The danger of such an ethics — as Gillian Rose argues, for example, in *The Broken
Middle* (1992) — resides in its failure to conceive of any effective realm of mediation
wherein we might discern our responsibilities and thereby consider which of them
demand that we alter or reconstruct prevailing political and legal conditions.[1] Including Levinas in the general antinomian proclivity of poststructuralist thought, Rose
describes Levinasian ethics in its postmodern valence as aspiring to nothing more
practical than an interruptive function. Ever suspicious of representation's capacity
to translate the force of ethical signification into normative obligations, distrustful
even of all mediation, Levinas cannot help us imagine, she fears, how ethics could
ever be returned, unless perhaps as the pure exception, to politics.

Rose provides reasonable ground on which to suspect postmodern ethics' apparent refusal of rational normativity. If the radically transcendent other by definition eludes every attempt to apprehend her, how could she possibly demand that we respond practically to that social structure within which we all find our responsibilities? And how could she ever impose herself except as a kind of generous, transcendent violence? According to Bettina Bergo, the divide Rose intuits in Levinas between the pre-thematic structure and the thematic content of ethics, as well as between the ethical realm and the political, has a prestigious philosophical precedent, since it develops that same contradictory distinction Kant draws between reason's transcendent freedom and practical reason as deployed in the name of historically contingent duties.[2] What the Hegelian dialectic proposed, instead, was a structure for maintaining the interactive play between the formal necessity of systemic thought and the individual instance of consciousness, such that the historical trajectory of consciousness might not only demonstrate the forward implication of subjectivity's apparently limited perception in a meaningful totality but bespeak the very possibility of reconciling the permanently formal dimension of transcendent thought with factical, contingent existence.[3] Where would we be, Hegel asks implicitly, without such a reconciliation of the disparate aspects of our consciousness?

The short answer is: on the threshold of bad conscience. In Hegel consciousness is characteristically divided by two modes of understanding, and, insofar as it cannot effect their reconciliation, it degenerates into a state of unhappy consciousness. According to Judith Butler in *The Psychic Life of Power* (1997), a peculiar ambivalence presides over the drama of psychic subjection permeating Hegelian dialectic.[4] By this insight the unhappy consciousness might seem uniquely positioned to challenge the workings of dialectic even as it serves also as a triggering mechanism for the dialectic. Reading the connection between the famous "Lordship and Bondage" section (178–96) and the subsequent section on "The Unhappy Consciousness" (197–228) in the *Phenomenology*, Butler perceives a double displacement operative in Hegelian subjection. In Hegel's famous allegory for the dialectic, the bondsman's labor substitutes for the lord's and brings about a functional disavowal of body, since the lord has in effect said to the bondsman, "you be my body for me, but do not let me know that the body you are is my body" (*PLP* 35). What the bondsman produces under such a condition is already not his own, so that any attempt to claim ownership of his labor results only in an ambiguous signature, at once the bondsman's and also the lord's. Nevertheless, this proves to be the very occasion upon which the bondsman's self-recognition is constituted, since "the very forfeiture of the signature" means that the bondsman's subjectivity becomes fearful, specifically, about his situational loss of control (*PLP* 39). This redoubled burden placed upon labor generates in turn the perpetually self-sacrificing structure of the bondsman's subjectivity: all that he produces is simultaneously erased, allowing the threat of death, which the lord's logic of social domination had sought to supplant, to reemerge as that which might altogether undo the bondsman's labor.

According to this double displacement, then, the unhappy consciousness is that state of mind established by the necessarily compromised status of subjectivity. What's more, as the realm of the ethical gets established, the crisis posed to the bondsman's already displaced labor is further displaced by his achievement of a corresponding psychic subjection. Rationalizing his subjectivity, the bondsman adopts what Hegel describes as an attitude of stubborn self-righteousness, in which the bondsman not only experiences his subordination to ordering norms as beneficial but treats his own subjection as synonymous with the meaning of his subjectivity. As though compromise could be interpreted in the bondsman's own terms, the realm of the ethical deflects fear and the loss of control, maintaining subjectivity apart from the natural law of impermanence as well as, consequentially and less fortunately, from the transcendent function of Spirit by which every bondsman's labor might become again his own. Butler reads the fundamental ambivalence of Hegelian dialectic forward into Foucault's hypotheses about the imperfect function of power, which even while enacting the social drama of subjection also generates a resistant energy within subjection.[5] For my part I am here reading the structure of unhappy consciousness forward through Nietzsche and Freud, each of whom also features largely in Butler's philosophical history of psychic subjection, into Levinas.

Butler's Foucauldian assessment of the subject's cultural state of subjection may be especially relevant to Levinas's later work. In *Otherwise than Being* (1974) he explores the grammatically accusative assignation of subjectivity as having determined every subject by way of a structurally exterior responsibility, and then in his 1980s writings he unapologetically reclaims the figure of bad conscience as a preeminent meaning of ethics. Whereas the horizon of poststructuralist thought inspired by Nietzsche and realized most concretely by Foucault has depended on a distrust of the structural inequivalences of social power and has sought to expose the determinative influence of power upon all subjective desire, and thereby to demystify the social structures by which we all are subjectively bound, Levinas refers the social drama of inequivalence to a quasi-etiological source in the other person, as if the confining, binding influence of power were already a distortion of that which properly foregrounds us as responsible subjects. As in Foucault, there is in Levinas an ethical plot of resistance to power insofar as it aligns with the normative function of knowledge or representation, but subjectivity's resistance to, say, the order of knowledge depends explicitly, and paradoxically, upon its sub-jected relation to exteriority.

Notably, in Hegel it is the structural inequivalence between the bondsman and lord, as also between his perception of his labor and his real achievement (which is to say, between the subjective and objective realms), that nevertheless inspires the movement of a subjective overcoming that cooperates with the systemic trajectory of consciousness. Within such a progressive systemics the unhappy consciousness denotes a peculiarly historical dimension of consciousness insofar as it poses a hypothetical resistance to the dialectic, and especially marks those epochs, such as Christianity and Romanticism, in which the unreconciled dimension of human existence becomes especially pronounced. Further back, in epochal terms, there is the problem of Judaism. Hegel does not treat Judaism directly in the *Phenomenology*, but Jean Wahl, one of Levinas's most revered teachers, had emphasized in *Le Malheur de la conscience dans la philosophie de Hegel* (1951) the special status of Abraham, the paradigmatic Jew, as an original for the Hegelian unhappy consciousness. Inasmuch as Wahl gave the unhappy consciousness renewed currency in postwar France, and there are also no doubt traces of Wahl's influential elaboration of Hegel in Levinas's own surprisingly appreciative revaluation of the bad conscience, at least some of Levinas's revisionary relation to Hegel might therefore be imagined as a response to the figure of the Jew—whom Hegel calls recalcitrant and whom Levinas imagines as resistant—within systemic philosophy.[6] It is even possible that Levinas's self-positioning in his confessional writings recapitulates the figure of the Jew who will cooperate with neither the forwardness of Hegelianism nor the assimilative universalism of Western culture. But if this is so, I wish to emphasize that such implicit positionality has far less to do with a confessional than with a hypothetically philosophical function. It is, in other words, a position within language, an alterity that is transferable to others who are also alterior to philosophical normativity.

Of course, the position commonly attributed to the Jew by Christian theology and also by much post-Enlightenment, residually Christianizing secularism is that of being a recalcitrant particularist, someone unwilling to lend himself to quasi-Pauline universalisms in which there is neither Greek nor Jew, in which humanity might hold all beliefs in common so long as those views cooperate with an ascendant system. In a published talk, "Israel and Universalism" (1958), first collected in *Difficult Freedom* (1963), Levinas responded to a lecture by a Catholic priest who had sought to anchor the cultural construct of universalism in what the three great monotheistic religions share. Discerning in the priest's ecumenism a residue of the basic Christian hypothesis that Judaism equals obsolescence, and speaking as a representative Jew, Levinas reminded his audience that "we reject, as you know, the honour of being a relic."[7] In the later published talk "Hegel and the Jews" (1971), reprinted in a second edition of *Difficult Freedom* (1976), Levinas further troubled the horizon of Hegelianism, as a metonymy for the project of Western philosophy, by emphasizing the memory of what it proposes leaving behind every time it subsumes an obsolete mode of consciousness within the progressive flow of Spirit. Hypothesizing that Judaism is for Hegel the negation of Spirit, an antithetical position moving backward against the teleology of historical consciousness, Levinas highlights the problematic status of Abraham, who, in concentrating on his own self-preservation, functions as a contradiction to nature and fulfills for Hegel a tragic destiny, albeit one toward which Hegel is not altogether unsympathetic. Although Levinas's siding with an Abraham who will not yield himself to universalism is not specifically designated in such terms, Abraham's noncooperation with predominant moral and philosophical meaning seems, especially in light of Wahl's remarks, to prefigure Levinas's more pronounced turn against the workings of consciousness and the norms of good conscience.

As a purportedly unredeemed, tragic Abraham remains, according to Hegel's terms, less than spiritual in his bestial focus, he recalls the inadequately forgotten origin of the unhappy consciousness, which always depends upon a double forgetting—of the lord's body in the bondsman's labor, and of the bondsman's impermanent labor in the normative form for subjectivity which is ethics itself. A revaluation of the unhappy consciousness proceeding by the terms set for it by Hegel might have emphasized a particularism wishing to exempt itself from the dictates of universalizing culture, as though Levinas as Jew were to remain always other to the rule of Western philosophical sameness. Yet this is precisely the interpretive choice Levinas does not make. If for Hegel ethics is always both compromise and portent, a score settled with an unsettling inequivalence presiding over consciousness, Levinas, by contrast, refers us to that which is beyond a subject's project, both anterior to and beyond the workings of the progressive system of Western knowledge. He does not perceive the resistance of ethics simply in a mode of particularism withdrawing from politics insofar as politics is always about systems. The particularity of the other must be repeatedly and collectively reckoned; it creates the demand for an accounting of the system via that which it excludes or forsakes. Ethics is never merely the aberrant, exceptional relation to politics, an act of exempting self or other from a system so as to be kept forever apart from its implications.

To render the problem posed by the unhappy consciousness largely in Hegelian terms—as Robert Bernasconi, Bettina Bergo, and even Rose have done in their readings of Levinas—already supposes that ethics must remain scandalous to politics, forever assigning meanings that are, in pragmatic secularist terms, also impossible, unenactable, only ever useless. By perceiving ahead of time a separation between ethics and politics and dedicating ourselves to reconciling the transcendent, formal significations of ethics to the contingent world of politics and historically enacted power, we might proceed as though the matter of ethics were inherently ahistorical and its responsibilities either altogether ideal or falsely universalized rationalizations of those people, things, and ideas we already hold dear. As I suggested in my introduction, Alain Badiou has accused Levinasian ethics of just such an irrelevance, one that vacillates between ideological complicity with reified cultural identities and pragmatic uselessness. Such a demystified account of Levinas is necessarily indebted to Nietzsche's famous critique of morality, if also evidently to Badiou's own commitment to the reconstructed Hegelianism of the Marxist dialectic. Although I wish to emphasize the background importance of the Hegelian unhappy consciousness for the Nietzschean bad conscience, Nietzsche even more so than Hegel, I want to argue, cast a long shadow over the reach of Levinasian ethics. Nietzsche introduces a more precisely historicized social critique, according to which ethics is always an act of running away from history, at least from any rigorous, systemic analysis of the functioning of power, self-interest, or desire within history. Levinas revisits precisely this boundary-driven notion of ethics in order to offer us, again if only figuratively, an ethics that is inevitably historical, even as it resists the manifest or predominant content of so much mainstream, nationalist, Western history. In this sense Nietzsche, whose critique has become virtually synonymous with our understanding of bad conscience, provides the ground for much of what Levinas surprisingly reclaims for ethics through the figure of bad conscience Nietzsche so lamented.

There may finally be an impasse between Nietzsche's devaluation of morality and Levinas's reclamation of ethics as the ground for all philosophizing, yet we cannot proceed as though Levinas had simply overlooked or evaded Nietzsche, thus failing to take any account of the very shortcomings Badiou attributes to ethics. There is a far greater response to the Nietzschean critique in Levinas than Badiou's suspicion might suggest—a presence of Nietzsche in Levinasian ethics that might seem all the more alarming to Rose insofar as it attests, by one trajectory, to postmodern ethics' project of destabilizing both the law and the moral norms of culture. In making the journey from Nietzsche to Levinas, the bad conscience remains dependent upon Nietzsche's complex analysis of the structural inequivalences operative within the history of moral systems, and yet it also comes to signify a self governed by a disproportion between agentive capabilities and its real responsibilities in the world such that, for Levinas, the self can only be said to be responsible by way of its dedication to that which is absolutely beyond its imaginative or practical dominion. According to Levinas's peculiar reclamation of bad conscience, then, a subject's unease has an ethical meaning that pertains explicitly to her responsibility for another insofar as that is always signified as a relation of disproportion—with the other either signifying through an excessive claim never to be dismissed or standing for a surplus of suffering from which the subject can never be exempted.

From an early point in his career Levinas could employ the phrase "good conscience" with rigorous irony, only fully adopting the bad conscience as a central trope for ethics in the years after *Otherwise than Being,* in the essays of the 1980s. In supposing the self's own sufficiency, the good conscience was already that figure for a complicity unaware of its contradictions. By the terms of the previous chapter the good conscience might characterize a mourning readily squared with nationalistic outrage at what *those* others have done to us, whereas the bad conscience would inspire a mourning that explores, in retrospect but also as a figure for presently recurring responsibilities, its implication in or perpetration of others' sufferings. What I want to suggest here is not only that the construct of ethics as mourning becomes more or less interchangeable with Levinas's reclamation of the bad conscience but also that the bad conscience is Levinas's way of giving a more definite historical shape to the burden of mournful subjectivity. According to the framework for responsibility I have established through the memory of the unjust death, the mournful bad conscience is that which, even as it would turn away from what it has done directly or indirectly or perhaps not done in any obvious sense, must yet work out its ethical meaning as a function of such neglected attentions. Rendering ethics susceptible to difficult, extreme, or even catastrophic history and thus to a mode of mournfully connoted historical memory that opens, as it were, to the unpleasurable significations of ethical obligation, Levinas implies that our history of failed responsibilities signifies ethics as greater than and prior to our sense of agency, particularly as that which is denoted even in our mistaken apprehensions or failed applications of obligation. This is by no means to excuse political indifference, but rather to raise the stakes of politics and to extend its parameters with regard to those for whom any of us may be responsible.

IS SORRY REALLY THE HARDEST WORD?

In discerning a hatefulness at the heart of Levinasian ethics, Paul Ricoeur pointedly ignores those descriptive terms through which Levinas produces the relation to the other as the very measure of the good, a relation aspiring toward the infinite and signifying as generosity itself.[8] This is not altogether surprising, since any phenomenological account of moral responsibility such as Ricoeur's must maintain a reciprocity between the moral subject and the objects of its responsibility. It matters little, in fact, whether Levinas's ethical descriptions emphasize an excessively generous goodness or, on the contrary, the persecuting intensity of responsibilities altogether anterior to reason and voluntary choice—in either case, they fail Ricoeur's most basic standard by refusing to posit a moral subject who becomes conscientious precisely by becoming adequate to her responsibilities. Paradoxically, in *Otherwise than Being* Levinas's most severe statements about ethical responsibility coincide with the renewed centrality he gives to the subject as the ground for the ethical relation, and yet the result, from Ricoeur's perspective, is that the very possibility of subjectivity—what Richard A. Cohen calls the lure of self-esteem[9]—might be forever devastated. The disagreement here is not just a matter of philosophical priorities (although it is also that); it is rooted in history. In this respect, as he implicitly accuses Levinas of perpetuating the nexus between morality and bad conscience, the hatefulness Ricoeur attributes to Levinasian ethics would draw its force from Nietzsche's critique of the methods and systems by which morality obligates its subjects to its codes, all those fearful, punishing reminders of obligation concealing an originary basis in relations of power.[10]

If one upholds the Nietzschean critique of morality, it is hard to decide whose language for ethics seems more naïve, Ricoeur's or Levinas's. To maintain a reciprocity between the responsible subject and its objects, Ricoeur ignores the cruder economics Nietzsche had discerned behind all morality. In the contractual relationship, which soon became legal obligation, a creditor bound his debtor through the threat of pain, thus instilling a memory of duty as recompense in the debtor.[11] In this originally economic social transaction, and in the specter of pain associated with it, Nietzsche discovers the beginnings of moral concepts such as guilt, conscience, and duty. Thus, from a Nietzschean perspective, when Ricoeur speaks of moral reciprocity without having mentioned the genealogical derivation of morality as an economic transaction preserved through cruel means, he might be charged with reverting to a morality altogether innocent of the modern demystification of morality. For his part, when Levinas recovers—most dramatically in essays such as "The Bad Conscience and the Inexorable" (1981), "Nonintentional Consciousness" (1983), and "From the One to the Other: Transcendence and Time" (1983, modified 1989)—a language of ethical severity, which retrieves among other figures the conceit of bad conscience, he concedes more to the Nietzschean critique than is immediately apparent.[12] Granting that Nietzsche is right in perceiving an unmendable inequivalence informing all ethical relationship, Levinas revalues the ethical connotations of such an imbalance, as though it were more original even than the moral practices, political interpretations, or applications of power in history through which morality has been construed. Since idioms of inequality, power, and even violence remember the very situation from which ethics speaks, there is an unpleasure, or an excess, pertaining to the very facticity of the other. To denote ethics through an originary, forceful alterity is to dissent from Nietzsche's strictly political genealogy of morality, but it is also to share with Nietzsche a pervasive suspicion of the ordinary benevolences according to which a moral subject might be supposed to perform her duties.

The bad conscience is so much part of our reality, I want to maintain, that it functions within subjectivity at an almost instinctual level, often rejected out of hand by consciousness or codified out of existence by morality and politics. We might look to Nietzsche to absolve us, as though our complicity in structures of power could be reinterpreted through an expression of will, yet our naggingly misfortunate conscience is persistent. Between le mauvaise conscience and le malheur de la conscience there is a fundamental relation, for the misgivings of ordinary conscientiousness always refer to a potentially unhappy, misfortunate condition in which we are not only less than equal to a comprehensive view of our obligation but also inadequate to the signifying force of every potential responsibility. Such is the case of a woman who responds to an acquaintance's story of misfortune by saying matter-of-factly, yet also sincerely, "I'm sorry." Perhaps the acquaintance finds this response puzzling and so replies: "But why? You didn't do anything," at which point an awkwardness ensues. The woman did not mean for her sorry to confess ultimate responsibility for having caused his misfortune, but by taking her at her word, the acquaintance altogether demystifies a statement of bad conscience and assures her that as long as she did not cause his misfortune she need not apologize for it. The probability of further awkwardness, the likelihood that she is not greatly consoled by these words of absolution, holds still a further significance. For she did not say she was sorry wishing to be absolved of her responsibility any more than she quite intended to insert herself into the position of primary agent. Her instinct was to take some responsibility, if only through language, if only because a story of misfortune had been imparted, demanding distribution of its unpleasure. Functioning even at this merely casual level, as a speech mannerism so habitual that saying "sorry" seems a social grace that is yet, for all its stiff formality, still better than saying nothing, her confession of responsibility bears only a vestigial relation to the rigors of bad conscience. But it bears a relation all the same.

Saying "I'm sorry" after listening to a Holocaust survivor or to a Guatemalan compañera whose sons and husband were murdered by death squads hardly seems adequate and may even seem wholly inappropriate, yet there is a fundamental sense in which, apart from the reparative actions one might take to steer a future course toward justice, such minimally trite words may be all one has to offer. A simple statement of regret for misfortune or for social injustice—whether one has caused the suffering, merely facilitated it, or witnessed it by accident, perhaps by being told the story afterward—can also be a kind of political statement. It is just such a statement that Levinas wished to hear from Heidegger in the years after the Nazi genocide had come fully into historical view. A mournful confession from this great philosopher and intellectual mentor of the part he had played in legitimating Nazism would have given some evidence in him of a bad conscience about the trajectory of genocidal history he could not fully have foreseen or in all probability have intended but for which he was nevertheless, at least in part, responsible.[13] If we were to become truly scrupulous about our implication in political structures, about our participation in the globalized, ideologically orchestrated aspects of economic injustice that inform and pervade our contemporary Western privilege, all of us who were late-twentieth- and early-twenty-first-century citizens might find, in the depths of our simple statements of regret upon hearing of misfortune and in the social awkwardnesses that often ensue, far deeper evidence of our own bad conscience, which necessarily pertains to the misfortune of others. What Levinas required from Heidegger with regard to his conspicuous complicity in a hateful ideology was not in this sense exceptional. By failing to heed his own bad conscience, which as a function of language in Levinas's proto-ontological formulation of ethics all of us must have, Heidegger witnessed to a more general failure (which does not, in Levinas's view, diminish the particularity of his ideologically contemptible omission of conscience). The bad conscience is not only a mode of ideological responsibility, although, as I emphasize later, it has far-reaching implications for ideology; it is also that which discovers responsibility as a requirement particularly obtaining for each of us. The bad conscience is the structuring logic of our intuition and the application of responsibility in history, even for those histories we have not entirely foreseen, have never desired, or cannot fully believe ourselves to have helped bring to pass.

At the limit of the apology, which is to say at that point at which saying "I'm sorry" seems marred in advance by its inadequacy to the situation, we intuit a responsibility to be defined as though any immediately achievable reconciliation would serve only to suppress our sense of obligation. Phrased in these terms, the bad conscience poses a question: can injustice be answered through our sorrow for it? In English the evolved connotation associating *sorrow* with *sorry*, which resulted from the change from *a* to *o* in the Old English root (*sarig*) for *sorry*, permits an original "soreness" informing every declaration of sorriness to get confused with the etymological distress behind *sorrow*. This is an unfortunate conflation, for it exposes if only by accident a pathos of conscience, always turning the moment of purported conscientiousness from the fact of responsibility. To be sorry for another is to claim to be pained by another person's loss. It is even, we might say, again drawing support from etymology, to mistake that person's pain for my own, as though the acquaintance of our hypothetically apologetic woman might have wished to reply: "But why? You didn't suffer my loss." The reason that her being sorry must be inadequate is not just a consequence of an experiential divide whereby she cannot, or should not, convert another person's injury into her own pain but also a function of the damage the utterance of such sorrowful sorries might do to responsibility. When the acquaintance says, instead: "But why? You didn't do anything," such a reply does not necessarily intend to absolve the woman of all responsibility. For even though responsibility comes from the other, the other can never absolve us of our responsibility. Relationship is already obligating. Perhaps, then, what the acquaintance really means to say, or at least unconsciously intuits, is the following: "Aren't you sorry I told you this? I'm taking it back now; I'm letting you off the hook. I shared it with you, but maybe I shouldn't have"—in which case, the supreme awkwardness of the scenario derives from the fact that at some level both the woman and her acquaintance know that responsibility doesn't work that way. It cannot be rescinded.

What I want to suggest is that the bad conscience remains always on the hither side of any reparative statement of regret or any proposal for reconciling loss, and as such it seems a position (contra Nietzsche's speculations about the nurtured, even reified woundedness that structures all bad conscience) only rarely occupied by normative morality. Consider briefly the example of two important American films, Oliver Stone's *Salvador* (1985) and Steven Spielberg's *Schindler's List* (1993), each of which spectacularly constructs conscientiousness as a hypothetical response to the memory of injustice.[14] In Stone's film a journalist-protagonist (played by James Woods) is witness to the United States–funded, brutally paramilitaristic tactics of the right-wing Salvadoran government's suppression in the 1980s of the popular movement in its country. The American journalist's solidarity with a people who are innocently victimized (which is to say, conspicuously depoliticized by the movie) is epitomized by his love affair with a Salvadoran woman, whom he attempts to rescue from history by illegally smuggling her into the United States. In the film's climactic scene of pathos, the bus he and she are traveling on is stopped beyond the U.S. border and, as the woman is pulled from the bus by immigration officials, the journalist exclaims in helpless desperation, "You don't know what it's like in El Salvador. You don't know what it's like there. You have no idea." His excruciating moment of conscientiousness is in effect the American journalist's apology for his own existence in light of what he has seen: if he could deliver a single Salvadoran into the mythic freedom of America, which is altogether unlike "there," he would alleviate his own psychic soreness over the suffering he has witnessed. Symbolically, as they drag the woman from the bus, the American several times tells her he's sorry, even as he futilely denounces the unmoved, impersonal officials. Distilling political conscientiousness into a singular gesture of failed rescue, Stone's film imagines a responsibility that might still be individuated even as it simultaneously suppresses the journalist's, perhaps also the audience's, bad conscience over the role the United States has played in the Salvadoran civil war.

Salvador is certainly not apolitical. It does portray American complicity with General Roberto D'Aubisson and the right-wing Salvadoran regime and was no doubt intended to raise awareness about the plight of the desperately poor and persecuted in Latin America. But by film's end the protagonist, in his pained, good-conscience intervention, can be said to remember only the contrast between American freedom and the brutal politics of El Salvador. His conversion of conscience corresponds finally to a conversion experience he would offer a single Salvadoran woman. For, once smuggled over the border, she would become a de facto American; she would escape totalitarian brutality to find democratic freedom. The journalist can offer her nothing better than our way of life, and the pain he feels finally over his inability to do even this much for a single Salvadoran ultimately deflects attention from the systemic causes that might be evoked by a sustained posture of bad conscience. And it also largely forgoes questions, for example, about international economic policies by which Western nation-states regulate the politics of the Third World and, more specifically, about foreign and military Cold War policies the United States encouraged, covertly deployed, or forcefully enacted in Central America as a response to the perceived threat of nondemocratic—by which we really mean anticapitalistic—social and political movements.[15]

An even more pronouncedly sorrowful sorriness occurs in the climactic scene of *Schindler's List*, wherein Oskar Schindler, having delivered his Jews to freedom and kindly overseen their final hours in a forced labor camp, prepares to flee as a war criminal from the Allied forces. Prior to this, the film has already developed its conversion narrative, according to which the opportunistic Schindler, as a result of having witnessed directly the brutality enacted upon the Jews, comes to be stricken by an ironic conscientiousness, played out through the back-and-forth negotiating between Schindler (Liam Neeson) and Itzhak Stern (Ben Kingsley), as though Stern were a modern-day Abraham bargaining with the reluctant conscientiousness of the godlike Schindler. Before Schindler flees as a war criminal, he tearfully falls to his knees to lament the others he might also have rescued ("I could have saved more," he says), so that the force of his conversion is here reiterated, renewedly bound by a terrible sincerity. There is a glimmer of bad conscience at work here, that the film works not so much to contain as to exorcise.[16] As Schindler starts to list the material possessions he might have exchanged for Jews who in coming to work in his factory would have been protected by his providence, the survivors assure him he has done all he could. His bad conscience emerges after the fact to mar Schindler's memory of his own generosity with a counter-memory of his original motive for becoming interested in the lives of these Jews, which was simply to exploit them as cheap labor. Yet the tears of such unmitigated conscientiousness, by which Schindler might remember his own complicity with Nazism, are washed clean by means of a secondary conversion syncretistically blending knees-folded Catholic repentance with a species of martyrological Jewish witness, until the reciprocating tears of those saved Jews who feel bad about Schindler's exorbitantly nagging bad conscience restore him to the good conscience of sentimentality. Just so all scenes of sentimentality suppose the good-enough intention, a good faith desire to alter an injustice, if only through extreme feeling. No longer crying for those he might also have saved, nor implicitly over the memory of those whose fate must be at least partly linked to his own early complicity with Nazism, Schindler is remembered by—and accordingly refits his conscience to—those whose lives he has spared. In effect, the memory of the Schindler Jews (which is also an idealizing memory they hold of Schindler) absolves him of further responsibility, limiting the measure of the hero's conscience to that which he has effectively achieved by intervening on behalf of over a thousand Jews.

In *Schindler's List* the pathos of conscience seems finally unhistorical. The exceptionality of the story offered to us, a story of triumph pulled from amidst the devastating normalcy of the Holocaust, is fulfilled in a pathos realized in reciprocity: Schindler's tears are answered by the tearful eyes of the Schindler Jews who feel sorry for him, who seem every bit as pained by the memory of his afflicted conscience as by the historical significance of what they have suffered. Again here the apparent workings of conscience, depicted as a character's pained response to the memory of injustice, set up the terms for understanding history by deflecting systemic explanation. Still, the eventually suppressed bad conscience flickers momentarily with the demand for systemic accountability, as if Schindler's possessions might testify against him about what it means to have prospered not directly by desiring other people's suffering, but nevertheless explicitly through the workings of a political system that thrived ideologically, if not always practically, upon the disfranchisement, exploitation, and collective murder of an entire people. The bad conscience would seem easiest to trace precisely in the moment its meaning as responsibility is refused. We infer Heidegger's lack of bad conscience about the Holocaust from the glaring absence of any mournful remembrance on his part, and even if we were to suppose that he had been privately pained by his complicity with Nazism, the question of bad conscience turns always upon its public dimension. For, just as Schindler puts his bad conscience on display so that it might be exorcised, we expect the bad conscience to correspond at least in part to public, collective, or systemic account-ability. If conscience can be returned simply to the realm of individually deter-mined, directly caused, or intentionally motivated actions—as in the fantasy of Spielberg's Schindler that each material possession stands for an unrescued Jew—there is already a diminution of the naggingly unpleasurable, implicitly systemic connotation according to which we are responsible for our participation in ideolog-ical structures.

UNPLEASURE, REVISITED

Already in my readings of *Salvador* and *Schindler's List* I have proceeded toward a connotation of bad conscience seeming far more Levinasian than Nietzschean. What Nietzsche would emphasize with regard to either of these cases, no doubt, is the substitutive role morality plays vis-à-vis genuine action. Arriving only after the fact, all the bad conscience can do is remind us of what we could not do originally, while perhaps serving also to make us overly circumspect in the realm of culture, even when we should be bold. Does the bad conscience ever anticipate truly pro-ductive action, or does it, restricting real agency, focus only on what was not done properly or what should not be done? Negative moral sentiments such as guilt and regret define, in Nietzsche's view, a failure of moral motivation, but they also simul-taneously describe an imbalance between the subject's historical intentions, agency, and actions and any objective, external, or collective standard by which they might be measured. In the traditional moral scheme of responsibility, in both its meta-physical and utilitarian genealogies, the imbalance informing guilt stands always to be exorcised through an extrinsic, often collective act (such as scapegoating or ritual purification, punishment or public repentance) that exonerates the subject of her failure to measure up to the external ideal or collective standard of morality. In short, religious or moral piety replaces human inadequacy. Over time, Nietzsche contends explicitly, as culture became more and more attached to the institutions of morality and likewise dependent upon the memory of restrictive obligations, it came quickly to disguise the real genealogical imbalance precipitating moral sen-timents such as guilt or regret and to conceal the cultural resources of genuine political agency.

In *On the Genealogy of Morals* (1887) everything depends on whether social forms are instituted with injury as the governing principle or from a condition of power in which injuries are merely the incidental consequence of a powerful, for-getful expressiveness.[17] In their varied effects, violence and cruelty are vehicles of memory, inscribing memory in the mind of the promissory debtor of that which he must either repay in kind or agree to forfeit by allowing a substitute violence to be enacted against his person or property.[18] No point is more important to Nietzsche than this: justice is distinct from the codified transactions or punishments that have evolved into morality. Justice does not develop from memory as debt and punishment, nor from the cruder psychological response of resentment. Originating in the Hellenic world as social transactions conducted among those of similar social standing, justice is ideationally based in a supposition of equivalence, enacted between parties who have never been severely indebted to one another and do not therefore require an economically derived language of obligation to adhere to their commitments. Any memory of pain would be absent from this equation, since the *just* person is always someone capable of forgetting injuries.[19] For its part morality is largely a social institution competing with and intervening in the progress of justice. Unlike the true beginnings of justice, the interrelated histories of morality, memory, and punishment depend on a relation to unpleasure, as Nietzsche traces the morality of Western culture to the simple, unpleasurable fact of human vulnerability—which is to say, the fact that human beings can be injured. The Nietzschean critique has the odd effect of bringing the relation to unpleasure more overtly to the fore in the critical analysis of our institutions of justice and morality while at the same time aiming to undo the forcefulness of unpleasurable memory by which, he hypothesizes, our regulatory cultural systems have long been perpetuated.[20]

One might characterize Nietzsche's entire genealogical project as an attempt to chart not only morality's complex internalization of basic, natural elements of hurt but also its consequent overestimation of hurt itself. Appropriating Kant's term for an obligation apprehended through the subject's failure of moral agency, Nietzsche redefines the "bad conscience" as a moral institution evolved under the sign of a historical ambiguity—that is, developing from the moment when a group of human beings is suddenly unable to indulge the ordinary and quite natural human capacity to attack, persecute, change, or destroy others.[21] The arrival of the bad conscience has been precipitated by a conquering race's or state's imposition of its will, power, and creativity upon another larger group of people who were all but formless (at least according to the quasi-imperialist terms Nietzsche employs) before they were conquered. Since this happens all at once, the bad conscience is in effect traumatic, arriving through "a leap, a compulsion, an ineluctable disaster which precluded all struggle and even all *ressentiment*" (GM 86). To have all of the natural energy that would have been directed aggressively toward others turned suddenly upon oneself and one's collective group leads to a fundamental unease with the human capacity for creative, willful actions. The bad conscience arrives suddenly in the weaker party, displacing a capacity for externally directed actions. In this way a specter of unpleasure presides over the bad conscience, which we may underestimate on "account of its initial painfulness and ugliness" (GM 87).

Among those who have been forced to redirect their aggressive instincts and actions upon themselves, there is always an overestimation of hurt. Such a hypothesis testifies to the irremissible inequivalence that structures conscience. Indeed, much of the Nietzschean account presumes, even as it also naturalizes, this precipitating state of inequivalence. By choosing in effect to hurt themselves, people disguise their structural disadvantage and rename their weakness as moral superiority. According to Nietzsche, morality hones this capacity for feeling wounded. It is the moral person who esteems her hurt or remains attached to her unpleasure as if it were that aspect of self in which she is most fundamentally herself. In yielding sovereignty to moral institutions that define obligation as other and greater than the self, each individual in society forsakes a horizon of sovereignty that might articulate the true meaning of individuality—namely, a capacity for self-determining obligation, or the right to make promises and the ability also to fulfill them. By Nietzsche's demystificatory terms responsibility is that which can never be fulfilled by the individual, and through our moral institutions we inherit almost unbearable responsibilities, much as those initially disadvantaged parties of social and legal transactions did when they promised from a position of debt rather than one of reciprocal exchange. Which is to say, we also promise (as they did more literally) to surrender something of ourselves if and when we are unable to fulfill our obligations. All of morality, as derived through the Jewish and Christian legacy, relies upon the bad conscience as that institution through which we embrace a radical critique of the self's possibilities, a critique exposing the subject as a plot of nothing more than self-contradiction, nothing less than self-contempt.

Following precisely these lines, Levinas's use of the term *bad conscience* offers itself as a revisioning of Nietzsche. By revaluing the very antinomies—expressive freedom versus obligation, reciprocity versus indebtedness, sovereignty versus incapability—upon which Nietzsche had based his demystifying genealogy of morality, Levinas inherits and revalues the oppressive connotation of bad conscience. Ethics, he insists, cannot avert its signification as a debt of responsibility never to be fulfilled. Whereas Nietzsche as Freud after him (the harmony between the two is neatly explored by Judith Butler) had focused on the psychologically oppressive ramifications of responsibility and the manner in which social institutions of conscience produce a stultifying conformity in individuals, Levinas reclaims responsibility even in its unpleasurable excess as the signifying structure of self, as the irremissible fact of sociality from which all of our constructs of moral obligation and cultural identity are derived.[22] At the center of the signifying enterprise of responsibility, Levinas elaborates a paradoxical revaluation of unpleasure as the very sign of ethics.

By giving emphasis to the now heavily Freudian term *unpleasure* in my discussion of *On the Genealogy of Morals*, I have meant to suggest how aptly the phrase describes Nietzsche's terms for the founding conceits of moral conscience but also how likely it is that Freud's own account of unpleasure is dependent on Nietzsche. Unpleasure is not simply a state of lack but a positive phenomenon, corresponding in Freud to an excitation of the mind, even as pleasure denotes the diminution of disruptive energies.[23] Unpleasure, Freud supposes, is primordially the phenomenon of the mind interrupted from the "principle of constancy," which is the very foundation of the pleasure principle.[24] Neither Nietzsche nor Freud imagines that the world, or more precisely the world of the mind, could be entirely free of life's unpleasure, since a naturalistic or realistic view of the human person must admit the phenomenality of unpleasure. In conceding an interrelation between the memory of pain and the historical development of human interiority, and emphasizing the adverse, far-reaching psychological significations of the painful genealogy of cultural memory, Nietzsche implicitly defines unpleasure, somewhat tautologically, as that which is detrimental to the self. Freudian theory carries over this precise ambiguity, and we should never underestimate the extent to which, for Freud, all cultural progress must be founded upon that which is necessarily detrimental to self— namely, the psychic mechanism of repression through which the self is made to function within collective meaning.

What Freud calls unpleasure is also backward looking, as if the self were forever in conflict not only with its past of instinctive desires but with much of its abandoned history, which has been imaginatively intertwined with forsaken desires. The most conspicuous figure for unpleasure, which has received much attention since the early 1990s, is the trauma, which Freud took up in *Beyond the Pleasure Principle* as if it were a challenge to his entire project. Contemporary trauma theorists such as Cathy Caruth have picked up on Freud's speculative bewilderment before the trauma and argued that the phenomenality of trauma marks the place where history returns to consciousness involuntarily and, as it were, unremembered.[25] What I would choose to emphasize—as a way of preempting the debate about whether the trauma is an adequate figure for history—is that, by forcibly disrupting the ordinary flow of identity, traumatic unpleasure becomes a sign of (perhaps only a trope for) extrinsic social and historical determinations, in short, a sign of the ethical force of such events. Bringing to mind evidence of a real world that will not cooperate with a private plot of identity, unpleasure demands and institutes the critique of subjectivity within a history larger than its own will and pleasure. For all the criticisms recently brought to bear on trauma theory, what has been largely overlooked in current debates is that trauma so often functions (in Caruth, for example) as a figure for ethics. If trauma is perhaps not the hermeneutical key some have held it to be, it nevertheless figuratively addresses the crucial problem of how individual obligation might yet occur for that which one does not consciously intend in the moment or remember afterward. Indeed, one should not altogether discount the fact that much of Caruth's own language about the trauma's technique of making us responsible for histories we do not specifically remember (which she derives from other poststructuralist influences) owes an implicit debt to Levinas's characteristic formulation of responsibility, which supposes that the *I* cannot become meaningful except through its relation to alterity.[26]

For his part Levinas elaborates a self's capacity to become unpleasurable to itself as though such a capacity—or should we say incapacity?—were in strange proportion to an extrinsic claim, namely, the historical fact of alterity being exercised upon it. At the point where ethics would meet history, ethics is already a responsibility for the other in history or, more specifically, an implicit responsibility for those who are others to or alienated from the conventions of history. Because there is always a certain unreliability to the moral subject, the responsibility of the moral subject means that it finds itself already assigned to relationship and meaning, obligated well beyond its ordinary capability. The parallel here to the Nietzschean problem of obligation is conspicuous, except that the subject's aversion to its own will has been read in reverse—as though it were instead a reversion to an ethical condition before will. Inheriting Nietzschean critique, Levinas transumes it in order to bring us back strangely to the necessity of the subject and to suggest that it is the structure of responsibility that locates a subject in history.[27] Through the irremissibility of its responsibilities a subject itself proves uncancelable and irreplaceable.[28] As opposed to the Nietzschean view, Levinas imagines that subjectivity is not diminished under the sign of suffering but, rather, expanded by having been called out of itself to be for-the-other.

By this model there is a structural inequivalence between the subject and its other—which alternates for Levinas between the apparent power the subject has over another when she arrives as the beggar, the orphan, or the widow and the power she has over the subject when her alterity takes the subject hostage to her claim. Such inequivalence functions as a kind of motivating force for the moral subject.

So, when Levinas describes the construct of relationship as one of *commandment* and *obedience*, the Kantian overtones of a morality referred beyond itself are pushed to a new extreme:

> A categorical imperative: without regard—so to speak—for any freely taken decision that would "justify" the responsibility; without regard for any *alibi*. An immemorial past, signified without ever having been present, signified on the basis of responsibility "for the other," in which obedience is the mode proper for listening to the commandment. Harkening to a commandment that is therefore not the recall of some prior generous dispositions toward the other man, which, forgotten or secret, belong to the constitution of the *ego*, and are awakened as an *a priori* by the face of the other. This hearing of a commandment as already obedience is not a decision emerging from a deliberation—be it dialectical—disclosing itself in the face of the other, the prescription deriving its necessity from a theoretical conclusion. A commandment whose power no longer signifies a force greater than mine. The commandment here does not proceed from a force. It comes—in the guise of the face of the other—as the renunciation of coercion, as the renunciation of its force and of all omnipotence. . . . It is the heteronomy of an irrecusable authority—despite the necessities of being and its imperturbable routine, concerned with its own being. This is precisely the whole novelty of an ethics whose disobedience and transgression do not refute authority and goodness, and which, impotent but sovereign, returns in bad conscience. (DR 172)[29]

I quote this passage from "Diachrony and Representation" (1985) at some length in order to emphasize the flow of Levinas's figurative language, which works here as an inverted *apophasis* (the rhetorical figure whereby a speaker mentions something by claiming not to mention it), seeming almost to inspire the paradoxical meaning of the bad conscience as the evident and yet unstated symptom of the subject's most basic responsibility. After Levinas mentions the Kantian "categorical imperative," each of his subsequent repetitions of *commandment* and *obedience* charts a figurative regression from ideational content, until the other is characterized ultimately by a "disobedience" that unmakes and unmasks the reciprocal premise of obligation, a disobedience that refers us to a mode of obedience existing before its institution and anterior to any manifest response the subject has to another person. In this sense, a belatedness presides over every response to the other's commandment: an *I* responds not to the content of a present declaration but to an immemorial obligation that conceptual commemoration would serve only to distort.[30] Using the bad conscience here to emphasize the distance between ethical signification and our renderings of ethics as a matter of selected, selective obligations filtered through the idealistic trappings of Western liberal discourse, Levinas negates the benevolent presuppositions of morality ("some prior generous dispositions toward the other man") to suggest that responsibility always survives the event of "disobedience and transgression."[31]

Conceived only categorically, obligation would overlook the atypical, situational particularity within which the subject understands the moment of her responsibility. It is as though there were a denial of responsibility inherent in every act of knowing, which involves a "suppression of the singular, through generalization" (*OTB* 87). Thus, as Levinas proceeds by way of a radical revision of Kant, he vastly extends the authority of that which is extrinsic to the subject.[32] A subject finds not only that it is ordered from beyond itself but that it exists apart from any capacity to reconcile itself, by way of will or intention, to extrinsic imperative force or to what Kant describes as the dictates of moral reason.[33] Responsibility occurs because the subject is motivated by that which is outside of it, even characteristically by that which accuses the subject of being inadequate to the task of responsibility. For Levinas the subject is "from the first in the accusative form (or under accusation!)," so that ethics becomes synonymous with the entire realm of signification, and he insists on this in order that we should avoid the mistaken impression that a particular accusation arises, as it would in most social contract or liberal legal theory, only after the failing of an original premise of reciprocity (*OTB* 53). The other finds the self (and the self finds itself through the other) not in its nominal proceedings but in the accusative case upon which it is initially constructed.

According to this hypothetical etiology of responsibility, in which the *I* is summoned as someone irreplaceable insofar as it is responsible, a peculiar inversion of identity occurs in passivity: a subject surpasses its economically confining attachment to reciprocity only by being already signified in its responsibility. In a certain sense, then, Ricoeur is right to call this an ethics of "irrelation," for, as Levinas himself says: "By way of the substitution for others, the oneself escapes the *relation* [*le Soi-meme échappe à la* relation]. At the extremity of passivity, the oneself escapes the passivity or the inevitable limitation that terms within relation undergo: within responsibility's incomparable relation (*la relation incomparable de la responsabilité*),the other no longer limits the same, it is supported by that which it limits" (*AQE* 146, my trans.; refer to *OTB* 115).[34] Even as ethics escapes relation in the economic sense of a systemic, internally regulated set of limitations, "responsibility's incomparable relation" reinstitutes relation by supposing it at another level.

If according to Nietzsche the disproportion between parties is the historical specter of morality, Levinas extends this insight, until it runs against the grain of Nietzsche's own skepticism, until the motivation for ethics is disproportion itself. It is the asymmetry of the ethical relation that moves a subject. Or, to phrase this in the mournful terms of the last chapter, it is the literality of *e-motion* that corresponds to an inquietude within consciousness. Thus disturbed, subjectivity is nevertheless an arrival at a plain fact—that no one else can stand in the place of my responsibility. Moreover, according to this structure of signification, in which self is by definition for-the-other, a subject must absolutely adhere to its difficult vocation, even though its responsibility is also greater than any subjective capacity. In Levinas an inability always haunts ethics, as though responsibility hovered ambiguously, somewhat mournfully, between neglected actions and those actions that were literally impossible because the subject had not yet conceived of what to do or had been absent from the scene in which she might have acted: "I have not done anything and I have always been under accusation—persecuted" (OTB 114). Always pushed unpleasurably beyond what it can immediately fulfill, implicated in the fate and misfortune of others such that simply saying "I'm sorry" seems as absolutely inadequate as it is at times necessary, the subject necessarily answers for a history of failures and for memories of injustice it cannot, or will not, remember as its own doings.

THE BAD CONSCIENCE IN HISTORY

As I have previously suggested (in chap. 1), the line we draw from ethics to history, or from history to ethics, is by no means a straightforward or uncontroversial one. History, which is always a narrative account that a group offers of itself and of the set of specific and abstract materials through which an era or event is understood, is not simply in the Levinasian view the ground upon which ethical responsibilities themselves are provisionally constructed. A historical view of the ethical scenario does not render the particular claim of the ethical relationship merely relative to a given moment (as, say, Nietzsche or Foucault might lead us to describe the particular set of power relations informing our statements of values), nor, conversely, can it make the specifically local perception of obligation universally valid (as though the universalism of knowledge might remain intact if one proceeded carefully from the particular to the generalized event, rather than through already generalized abstractions). Although one can speak, as Nietzsche does, of morality as the systemically realized practices and unrealized ideas about ourselves in history, which are susceptible to changes in power over time, such a description necessarily fails to account for claims that have been made upon us and yet not answered for.

When Nietzsche intuits the bad conscience as the emanation of a contract never entered into explicitly by parties who are nevertheless bound by it, he has glimpsed a meaning of ethics Levinas wishes to uphold as part of its preeminent significance. Since we really do act in time as though we were inspired by such imaginary debts, and since our capacity to appease the particular perception of a debt will not cancel the signification of an indebtedness that figures the very possibility of relationship, Levinas supposes that it is only the transcendent calling of ethics (which is apart from and absolutely prior to the thematic expression of any deity, religious doctrine, or metaphysical dogma) that allows us to perceive the inadequacy of all historical measurings of incurred obligation. In other words, it is not history that is determinative of ethics; if anything, ethics is determinative of history, impressive even beyond history's realized form as causal narrative or normative state of knowledge. Ethics intimates what history still requires. Seemingly suspicious of the potential for history to function as a substitute ontology and reminding us that in and of itself history absolves no one, Levinas ultimately imbricates history with ethics in such a way that ethics speaks to what is immemorial in history as well as to the future of what history only imperfectly expresses about human relationship.

In Levinas's project the space in which ethics takes place seems a relatively undetermined province, a condition not yet inscribed by historical necessity or the political positionings of identity. In the essay "No Identity" (1970), for example, Levinas offers his most direct account of this intersection between the phenomenological openness of sensibility and the ethical signification of the subject as that which is prior to and apart from identity.[35] The original openness begetting ethics is not an openness to others constituted through universal reason nor an openness along the lines of Kant's third analogy of experience. Neither is it consciousness opening to the presence of essence, as Heidegger would suggest. Rather, Levinas emphasizes the vulnerability of sensibility as a capacity to be wounded, an openness that is "the skin exposed to wounds and outrage." In declining the passivity of sensibility, Levinas describes an "aptitude, which every being in its 'natural pride' would be ashamed to admit, 'to be beaten,' 'to receive blows.'" As he further imagines the "unendurable and harsh consent" enlivening such a "passivity . . . strangely despite itself," Levinas presumes his own version of a pseudo-ontological ground, upon which the motivations and actions of an ego are necessarily derived in all *sincerity* (NI 146). Quite frequently, in this essay and elsewhere, Levinas speaks of that ground as the structural directness of the face-to-face encounter, which requires a sincerity, or "frankness," that "exposes [a self]—even to wounds" (NI 147). Ethical sincerity does not designate the choice to abide by an obligation or to represent oneself straightforwardly or even to do what is best by the other, all of which are familiar moral philosophical connotations. Denoted only as an inability to get out of the way of the other, Levinasian sincerity entails an absence of choice, the impossibility of beginning from any point other than the self as a site of vulnerability already signified as being for-the-other. As soon as one joins sincerity to intention (as in most of our ordinary uses of the term), one introduces a symbolism that deflects the ethical meaning of the other. All representation, Levinas supposes, serves a conceptual realm of meaning that contains, deflects, and at times suppresses the ethical content from which it lives. Nevertheless, the return, or rather the persistence, of those vulnerabilities seemingly deflected by representation is unremitting.

It is most centrally the figure of the bad conscience, I wish to contend, that gives historical emphasis to the nexus of unpleasure and sincerity constituting any subject's place in language and culture. Since Levinas rarely traces the logical trajectory of his descriptive terms or his designating tropes for ethics (if there is a philosophical distinction, for example, between sensibility and knowledge, no such distinction is evident between the signifying function of the other's goodness and those forceful significations of unpleasure associated with the other), any such claim must be made in part as a matter of inference. Yet, as Levinas turns during the latter half of his career to the figure of the bad conscience while also turning with greater regularity to the Holocaust, he opposes Nietzsche's suggestion that the bad conscience is the very manifestation of a subject's insincerity, a sign of the subject's endeavor to shift the ground of obligation from those historically determinative contractual relations of debt toward the abstract good of duties that are simultaneously chosen. Levinas brings to the bad conscience—while also suggesting that the bad conscience brings this state of things about—a fuller historical connotation. The bad conscience is the sign of an ambiguous threshold between the vulnerable openness of responsibility that accuses any self and the defensive attempt to delimit a self and protect it from connotations of responsibility that might disrupt its well-being. As such, the bad conscience brings to mind (in a way that a figure such as sincerity never could) the connotation of identity as that which has turned from the history of its ethical responsibilities. By bridging the more general unpleasure of ethics and those unpleasurable facts of history through which we are reminded of our responsibilities, the figure of the bad conscience increases the burden of self-accusation, supposing that the self's inadequacy to its responsibility is not strictly a matter of the signifying excess through which one enters into relationship with the other, but is also that which is made evident in the historical event of a failed responsibility.

By this account, the bad conscience states an irrevocable condition of ethics that Levinas so often emphasizes—the sense that responsibility is anterior to any conceptual representation of the other as well as to any formulation of an intention toward her. This is much the point of the later essay "Nonintentional Consciousness," in which Levinas positions his thought against the background of Husserlian intentionality, beginning with the basic ambiguity between thought and the thing it thinks as articulated by the Husserlian project. There is operative in Husserl's phenomenology "a privilege of the theoretical, a privilege of representation, of knowing;

and, hence, of the ontological meaning of being"; and Levinas's concern is that, according to this scheme, there could be no relation to the other not positioned along the horizon of theoretical thought as part of the good conscience that inheres in our traditions of representation (NC 124).[36] Levinas's particular worry here, I wish to suggest, is a historical one—specifically, a question about what happens when theoretical thought becomes complicit, perhaps necessarily so, with a politics that denies the other as the legitimating ground for actions taken by the self or a corporate political body. Since the entire tradition of philosophy—and Husserl provides for Levinas only the latest instance of this tendency—upholds the privilege of consciousness "as a modality of the voluntary," it tends to treat the resistance offered to representation and the "consciousness of mental activity" only as that which has not yet come to light (NC 127). According to this basic theoretical schema, nonintentional thought is merely, as it were, a symptomatic defect, a state of not yet knowing something that proper reflection may one day draw forward and articulate. Revaluing the tenor of nonintentionality, Levinas suggests that one who is "without intentions, without aims, without the protective mask of the character contemplating himself in the mirror of the world, self-assured and affirming himself" is yet signified by this modality as by a positive presence (NC 129).

This is in fact the very place where Levinas introduces the bad conscience in this essay, describing it as a reversion from intentionality, as that which interrogates the identity of one who is invested in the world and its representations:

> In its nonintentionality, on the hither side of all will, before all wrong-doing, in its non-intentional identification, the identity draws back from the eventual insistence that may be involved in identification's return to self. Bad conscience or timidity: accused without culpability and responsible for its very presence. Reserve of the non-invested, the non-justified, the "stranger in the earth," in the words of the Psalmist, the stateless or homeless person, who dares not enter. The interiority of the mental is perhaps originally this. Not in the world, but in question. In reference to which—in memory of which—the self that already puts itself forward and affirms itself, or confirms itself, in the world and in being, remains ambiguous enough—or enigmatic enough—to recognize itself, in Pascal's terms, as being hateful in the very manifestation of its emphatic identity of ipseity—in language, in saying "I." (NC 129)

Nietzsche had suggested that the painfulness of morality and the delusive, abstracting formulations of obligation—while creating us as irresponsible to our wills—have forced us to live the interior lives that we do. By speculating in Nietzschean fashion that the "interiority of the mental" has come "perhaps originally" from the bad conscience, and by intimating a prehistory of interiority drawn into question before it ever attained its "eventual insistence" in the world, before it ever returned to itself abstracted, codified, and justified by morality, Levinas confronts Nietzsche's definition of morality as a veiled history of power, here bringing the fuller connotations of historical memory to bear on the bad conscience.

How ought we to understand the paradoxical interrogative force of the bad conscience "in reference to which—in memory of which" the self already offers itself to the world? Strictly speaking, this would be a memory of that which cannot be remembered, a scheme of reference dependent on the nonintentional sphere and its significations. Yet even the preceding descriptive metaphors in which Levinas refers to those who are not invested in the world because the world has not offered them a home (those conspicuous strangers I will have more to say about in chap. 4) suggest that this memorable, yet unremembered, point of reference has a larger sociohistorical connotation. It is quite as if the self could remember beforehand the others whom it would neglect. The historical claims I am making for Levinas's language may seem at times more like the accidental consequences of metaphor, but, as Kenneth Burke (and Nietzsche before him) so often insisted, there are no mere metaphors in language: rather, metaphor preserves the historical sediments of our evolving language. Levinas's metaphors—of estrangement, of statelessness, of homelessness—bring with them the vestiges of history. On one level Levinas recalls the biblical imperatives of Jewish thought that dictate responsiveness to those who are others within and without the community; on another he recalls the long and more recently catastrophic history of Jewish estrangement from the world. As Levinas invokes the historical specters of injustice and suffering for which the self and the social constructs it inhabits are largely responsible, it is not hard to discern here a suppressed allusion to the Holocaust entangled with the plight of the Third World poor. Drawing upon memory of severe cases of exile, of inhospitality suffered among the nations, and of the facticity of persecution, Levinas arrives at the full interrogative force of what it means for the self—as we recall again Ricoeur's concern about Levinasian ethics—to be "hateful" (NC 129). In short, a self's hatefulness is the historical weight of what the self has endured at the hands of others but also what the others have endured as the result of particular subjects' conspicuous failings or violences. In the bad conscience of our interiority, in our sense of having been already accused before we or the others have perpetrated what we stand ready to be accused of, history is still to come—yet already we know its worst results.

In this passage, having distilled systemic violence into the individualistic scenario, Levinas forges an intersection between the self's hatefulness and the mournfully, murderously inclined fate of the self as subject. The self's apparent loathing pertains to its own possibility, and such a reversion from the self's intentions depends on

Levinas's persistent use of the Cain and Abel story as a prooftext for the self's willful, intentional life. It is remarkable how deeply inscribed the archetypal murderous situation is, especially in *Totality and Infinity*, upon Levinas's account of how the face is encountered. Frequently cited in the first half of his career, before he had explicitly reclaimed the bad conscience as such, the Genesis story prefigures Levinas's later accounts of the bad conscience, reminding us always of the extent to which responsibility is signified even in the remission of intention. In Genesis 4 the ethic "Thou shalt not kill" exists implicitly, though perhaps mythically, prior to the cultural prohibitions of Mosaic law. There is some question about whether the story is to be read as enacting the rationale for this commandment or whether the commandment is already assumed by the moral logic of the story. Whether or not Cain ought to have known the commandment beforehand, his belated expression of conscience—asking only after the fact, "Am I my brother's keeper?"—arrives as an ironic expression of guilt; yet nowhere in the story is it clear that the ethic of being the keeper of one's brother was already in place. The problem of reading Cain's intention within the Genesis story thus turns us, more particularly, to the difficulty of determining how well his implicit intentions can be read as proportional to a state of moral knowledge.

In *Altered Reading* (1999) Jill Robbins astutely observes that many modern interpretations of the famous Genesis text take us to verses 4:3–7 immediately prior to the murder, with the hope of finding there an intention.[37] But there is a notable gap in the original text between this scene, in which God rejects Cain's sacrifice, and the immediately subsequent scene, in which Cain murders his brother. In the transitional verse during which Cain speaks to his brother, the Hebrew text says only, "And Cain said to Abel his brother . . . ," and then leaves out the words that were spoken, if indeed any were spoken. Midrashic readings as well as some of the most prominent translations often provide the missing phrase, "Let us go outside," almost as if the interpretive tradition were confessing that it had to seek the motive outside the text itself. Commenting on André Neher's reading of the text, Robbins intriguingly suggests that "it is as if the textual gap or lacuna in its materiality were the very cause of the murder that the episode recounts," an ironically apt reflection on the tradition's demand for an intention that would serve as a principle of causation in this text (71).[38] What I would add is this: that same textual gap doubly signifies the paradoxical fact that a murderous intention must fail to coincide with its intended object and also that intention as such evades a greater responsibility signified by the text. If Cain were to announce his intention, even through the oblique statement of an intent to go outside, intention and action would meet in narratological terms as though Cain's responsibility for his brother had been fulfilled, albeit negatively, by the act of murder. Most commentators (and I take it that this is also Robbins's assumption) proceed as if the scene in which Cain's sacrifice is rejected provides a motivating conflict, which is eventually fulfilled in his act of violent vindication. In brief, Cain displaces his contention with God into an assault on his brother.[39] Yet such an interpretive line would also presume that Cain, unless he is to be deemed a moral child, apprehends God's requirements: in his brooding silence he would act in full understanding of principles he freely chooses to oppose, altogether in bad faith with regard to the moral expectations that have been placed upon him.

What the Genesis text most likely espouses is a moral logic of a subtler, more extensive variety. For, when Cain answers God's query as to the whereabouts of Abel with the evasive reply, "Am I my brother's keeper?" his nonanswer holds the place of the originally absent or inadequate intention, only retrospectively accounting for his failure to answer for a moral crime that had not yet been formally proscribed. Cain's reply is so startling in part because his evasion pronounces a responsibility not only greater than the question of legal proscription but in excess of his self-understanding (recall that for Nietzsche the bad conscience is always also in bad faith about the self's motives). If Cain were to lie directly about his actions, his concealment of his crime would imply that his renegade, but also implicitly natural, violence needs containment. Still, it is only in the crudest of criminal actions that a subject admits to himself in advance that his actions constitute an abrogation of a discernible set of cultural obligations, such that his criminal actions—and not his scruples—would express his will and subjectivity. So, too, with social institutions: a code of morality, even when in conflict with the self-interest of privileged agents, does not necessarily disguise and, by disguising, describe the entire field of motivations through which social institutions and their immediate beneficiaries chart a course of sociopolitical action. Nietzsche's tendency to read the bad conscience as though it were interchangeable with bad faith has the odd effect of underestimating the formidability of ideology, which cannot be (well, perhaps it can, but it shouldn't be) understood simply as a mode of false consciousness exposed, thanks to skeptical genealogies, to the better light of truthfulness. Indeed, the inconsistency of the Nietzschean voice, which alternates between a rigorous demystifying hermeneutics and a facile politics of willful expressionism, is at least in part encapsulated by this too easy conflation of bad conscience and bad faith.

In attempting to undo Nietzsche's conflation of the moral history of the bad conscience with the bad faith expressions of morality throughout history, Levinas appears to concede the prevalence of the latter (since the institutions of morality, like the institutions of philosophy, are deeply compromised realities), without, however, forsaking the entire history of morality. The bad conscience possesses for

Levinas a quality of straightforwardness (as a directly designated responsibility) and at the same time an obliquity (as a response to a responsibility perceived only via the indirection or failure of an agent's moral actions). In other words, the bad conscience always witnesses to the concealed meaning of responsibility. Insofar as it is oblique, insofar as it proceeds toward its responsibilities evasively and belatedly, the bad conscience suggests a dimension of responsibility not adequately met by legal proscriptions or by intentions confined to the established system of moral thought. Thus, when Cain defines himself via the very principle of meaning he overtly disavows, his reply to God epitomizes this Levinasian connotation of bad conscience. A responsibility he will not own announces itself as an unease within identity, as if Cain were deconstructing his own identity: *Am I no more than one who watches over my brother? Am I none other than the one who is defined by this responsibility?* It matters greatly whether Cain has improperly conceived of his obligation to his brother or has in fact omitted his brother from the horizon of his self-definition. Even if we cannot imagine a Cain who experiences his bad conscience in such a way that he might remember his moral transgression (a Cain who would have known full well that he did wrong when he murdered his brother)—even if we permit Cain the slightest space of good conscience in which he acts only as a literal-minded moral subject, prompted by involuntary and, in Nietzschean terms, naturally aggressive instincts, yet ignorant of what is wrong until he has been expressly told not to do it— his responsibility for his brother nevertheless befalls him as that which might be brutally deflected in any given historical moment but never permanently evaded. In this sense, the responsibility Cain accidentally pronounces through his act is more historical than the terms of his own historical consciousness, more ethical than his conscience.

In all of this, the Genesis text also proceeds by forging an intersection of the bad conscience with mourning. What Cain's ambiguous admission of responsibility imposes is a hypothetical vigilance on behalf of the now dead brother, almost as if his keeping watch over the brother's disappeared body could signify retrospectively an ability to keep Abel from harm at those murderer's hands that were his own.[40] Lest this seem too strange a reading, I would remind the reader that the very function of the story in both the Jewish and Christian communities of interpretation— as a parable not only forbidding violence but positively compelling an ideal of communal responsibility—depends upon such a logic. As this story sets up a moral standard, it relies upon an intersection between murder and responsibility, in which murder constitutes a scene casting responsibility as simultaneously forgotten and inevitable. According to Levinas's figurative use of murder, so highly dependent as it is on the story of Cain and Abel, the question of responsibility within the murderous scenario is read in reverse: our neglect of the other, the failing of our attention, may at any moment prove murderous.

By this very logic the bad conscience is also oddly cast as a figure of mourning. The moral subject's regretful belatedness—in which he comes to consciousness after the fact of murder—brings about vigilance. Perhaps even more significantly, the bad conscience develops a horizon for sociality in which the others who come to harm at a distance from my intention still remain my responsibility. Expressing the facticity of responsibility as a discomfiture in the subject, even over that which I have not done, a specter of murder hovering over the death of the other interprets responsibility as if it were always also about the scandal of unpleasurable memory, such that the harm befalling the other at anyone's hands were the consequence of my own intentions. Already Levinas presumes that the posture of mournfulness in its fullest ethical connotation is characterized by an aspect of bad conscience. But, according to a move made by Genesis 4:1–16, which Levinas seems only too willing to follow, the badly conscientious Cain, who was the murderer of his brother, is made also to stand as the one who is responsible for him in memory and according to the cultural memory of others who must preserve him even in his guiltiness. God demands Cain's responsibility by way of an act of remembrance, which is to say, through a gesture of mourning: "Where is your brother Abel?" (Gen. 4:9). In this sense Cain's most evident failure in the story (since the murder itself is not represented) is his failure of vigilant memory, his inability to mourn or to remember. Every attempt in cultural history to interpret this story as imposing a vigilance against our own murderous impulses, be they private or social, extends just such a peculiarly mournful logic in which the sign of forgetfulness has been transposed onto the act of murder itself.

In the next chapter I will turn explicitly to the problem of what it means for the responsible subject to be cast, even hypothetically, as the one who does another harm. What I would emphasize here is the strangeness of Levinas's figurative adoption of the story of murder, as Levinas implicitly charts a wider social rubric for murderousness and positions murder as though it were a foundational anxiety of ethics. In a certain sense, with regard to the Genesis text, we might say the only way for the murderer's story to become the story of humanity's original social crime (with the transgression in Eden standing as the preliminary metaphysical crime) is for us to recapitulate the specter of forgetting and neglect that allows the other to come to harm. The story of Cain and Abel is one without witness: there is only the murderer and his victim, this uniquely interpersonal crime altogether lacking the structure of sociality or third-party intervention that makes every crime, at least in potentiality, also a matter of social permission. In the absence of a witness who has not perpetrated the crime, the story inserts Cain's hypothetically mournful conscientiousness, which remains altogether unrealized insofar as Cain rejects an ethical care for his brother that he, even after the fact, might have conceptually assumed. In the mournful remembrance of murder proceeding beyond this text, Levinas attributes to every responsible *I* an intuition of itself as if it "were depriving someone of his living space, as if I were expelling or murdering someone" (PD 164). Since the specter of murder preoccupies all sociality and may even be paradigmatic of the social, at its ethical core sociality must also refer us to a vigilance on behalf of the other who dies, of the one who comes to harm—even if perhaps by my hands or by my ideological complicity, and yet apart from my intention.[41]

THE BAD CONSCIENCE AND THE HOLOCAUST

Once Levinas admits violence to the center of any consideration of ethics, the rational wish to locate responsibility in the straightforward aspect of intentionality, in the deliberative time before an act or in a hypothesis of self-determined virtue that ascribes justice to oneself, seems inadequate. It is worth considering how the place Levinas gives to violence compares, say, to a more directly moral philosophical accounting of moral fault within a bad political system. To construe the possibilities of morality in the face of totalitarianism and atrocity might be to proceed as though the conspiring circumstances of history exercised little determinative influence on those who were, in a crucial sense, as much subjects as agents of the history they endure. In *Moral Responsibility in the Holocaust* (1999) David H. Jones addresses the question directly, arguing that even in the midst of a "bad political culture," in which the effect of socialization might make acceptable what is morally wrong by the standards of liberal democratic culture, we can arrive at an ordinary verdict of moral blameworthiness with regard to, say, actions such as participating in hateful ideologies or killing Jews, since ethics always survives by means other than strict ideological socialization.[42] Any exemption from moral blameworthiness (which is not the same thing as the function of blame under the law) would entail a significant diminution in one of the three conditions necessary for moral action: (1) the capacity to recognize what is morally right or wrong; (2) the ability to deliberate a course of action and consider alternative actions; and (3) the relative political freedom to act in accordance with what one knows to be right and in consistency with one's deliberations.[43] What Jones decides is that, even if there were individuals who were socialized by Nazi ideology so as not to recognize killing Jews as morally wrong, substantial evidence suggests that within Nazified German culture various individuals demonstrated the capacity to resist (most notably those who explicitly dissented from

Nazi ideology but also those who, despite antisemitic attitudes, chose to rescue Jews). Thus, in Jones's view, the explanatory hypothesis of socialization hardly exhausts moral agency. In studying the Holocaust, he decides, we must treat history not merely as the anonymously cumulative effect of material conditions and cultural attitudes but as the set of specific ethical recognitions, deliberations, and actions that fell to those who participated in the Nazi genocide, either by directly perpetrating crimes or by passively accepting their culture's deeply antisemitic ideology and its genocidal consequences.

I offer this brief account of Jones's moral philosophical exploration of blameworthiness from within the historical moment of the Holocaust in order to set it apart from Levinas's approach to the intersection of ethics and the Holocaust. Jones chooses a set of intentions that can be directly tied to actions and the hypotheses of deliberation that must have preceded them. It is rather telling, in this respect, that he concentrates on those who acted conspicuously in the historical moment, on the perpetrators rather than on their victims, and in doing so also partakes of a Western cultural preference for equating morality with perceptible agency. What one has to imagine for this to work is sincere perpetrators, who, even if led by their ideology to misunderstand their obligations, have always also possessed, at least implicitly, the capacity to have chosen better actions. There must be a proportion, according to Jones, not only between intention and action but also between deliberation and morality, such that the one who violates the most evident moral contracts of liberal society is never far removed from a capability to enact those contracts faithfully, even while such a one is caught in the throes of fascist ideology. Although Jones's reconstruction of ethical deliberation is hardly Nietzschean, it does partake of at least one Nietzschean presupposition: the question of proportion governing moral responsibility must be located within the will to act and thus, rather conspicuously, with those who made the consequential moral choices that determined Holocaust history. For Nietzsche, however, the fact that morality built itself up by veiling cruder social relationships of power, only to be advanced through the increasingly mixed significations of Christendom, puts moral obligation at odds with those genuine instincts based in our will-to-power. What is perhaps most remarkable, if one adopts a Nietzschean long view of moral history, is how completely morality achieves a transvaluation of the practical positions of the political sphere of power and how consistently moral philosophy insists on the real agency of moral thought as if it were commensurate with political will.[44]

In one sense, then, Levinas begins like Jones, albeit less directly, from the crisis posed to ethical meaning after Auschwitz. Unlike Jones, however, he refuses to return ethics to a dependence on intention. In each case, with regard to Jones's explicit reconstruction of the individualist parameters of responsibility and also with regard to Levinas's figurative turns to a violent history read as though it were a lens through which to view ethics, there is the strong possibility that ethics might transform history into the merely personal, immediate, or naïvely universalized yet individualistic situation of an ethical encounter, reducing the extensive scope of history and the tremendous scale of suffering that belong to the Holocaust so as to render the incommensurate experience comprehensible.[45] From a Levinasian perspective such a hazard is risked especially by those, such as Jones or Todorov, who would approach the Holocaust via normative applications of moral philosophy, as if the categories of virtue had remained—or at least had the capacity to remain—relatively intact under the extreme conditions of the Nazi totalitarian state. It is precisely Levinas's point that responsibility in its basic structural significance, which runs parallel to the meaning it derives through the history of injustice, must exceed the individualist scale. Supposing intention to be a relation of proportion between the subject and the events for which she is responsible as well as the acts she initiates, Levinas defines responsibility as arising not only anterior to but also against the properties of intention. In a conventional moral philosophical account, disproportion gets raised as if it were that which prevented the intention from fulfilling itself in action or the obligation from correctly expressing a subject's capacity in its immediate circumstances— which is to say, as though disproportion were that which obstructed motivation.

If history begins in a sense at the point where the individual act does not provide an exhaustive explanation—and the opposite point is, after all, the basic lie Nietzsche accuses morality of perpetuating against history and realpolitik—ethics in the Levinasian sense takes up the question of responsibility from the place where it cannot be obviously assumed. Although Levinas is critical of history writing for being already implicated in the play of subjective freedom and totalizing systems, it seems clear to me that Levinas's surprising revaluation of the structural inequivalence that begets ethics is meant to acknowledge the point (and there is no more Nietzschean point than this) that history is precisely a history of the implication of reason (read also: Western political culture, religion, philosophy, and morality) in violence. Violence, or the systemic fact of injustice, occurs at the center of the social structure through which good conscientiousness, as coinciding with cultural norms, would be legitimated. One can only be just in proportion to the social reality of justice, and thus the very facticity of violence already compromises conscience. Ethics, in starting also from the place in which the other's murder is pragmatically possible, even socially acceptable, yet still in no way a measure of her significance, must refer us to the one who suffers whether by a remote set of intentions or as the consequence of a systemic order within which every *I* must locate its own responsibility. Any attempt to preserve one's good conscience as a citizen during the moment in which another suffers or dies—that is, by turning away from the memory of injustice—necessarily represses that very place or perspective via which social structures might be deemed ethical.

It is for this reason that Levinas's later ethicofigurative vocabulary involves another surprising trope (besides the figure of murder) for bad conscience. As a revisionary evolution of his former distrust of the survivor's perspective in *Totality and Infinity*, Levinas turns to the conceit of *survivor's guilt*, unmistakably borrowing it from Holocaust studies and memoirs. In its earliest usage, as a term employed by psychoanalysts such as Eli Cohen and Bruno Bettelheim, "survivor's guilt" seemed largely an aberration of conscience, in which survivors of the Holocaust felt guilty for having survived in the place of countless others who died at the hands of the Nazis.[46] As Levinas freely adopts the notion of survivor's guilt and extends the survivor's apprehension of guilt beyond the situation of those who experienced the trauma of Nazi concentration and death camps, he is surprisingly unrelenting in upholding the moral precision of the survivor's feelings of guilt. In the 1975–76 Sorbonne lectures on "Death and Time," Levinas refers to the survivor as if he were structurally or historically guilty of the death of the other and further characterizes each responsible subject as a Cain-like survivor, even if he has committed no crime or cannot recognize the harm she has caused: "We should think of all the murder there is in death: every death is a murder, is premature, and there is the responsibility of the survivor" (DT 72). Implicated in the fate that befalls an other seemingly beyond the purview of her intentions, the responsible subject interprets a culpability pronounced by the other's death as though this were the very fact of ethical relation. In "my deference to someone who no longer responds," there is, Levinas asserts, "already a culpability—the culpability of the survivor" (DT 12).

To exist for oneself is to appropriate the world as experience, and it is also to usurp the place of the other who has exerted a claim on me prior to anything I might do for myself. But the ethical relation is always a direct challenge to this act of usurpation. Thus, at the heart of Levinasian ethics there is a structural turn from usurpation to substitution. Responsibility denotes the relation in which one lives for the other and so depends upon a signifying structure of me-for-the-other in which usurpation gives way to an ethical substitution. There is undoubtedly a connotation of sacrifice here (which I explicate in greater detail in chap. 3), and it leads to some extraordinary ethicofigural arguments, as, for example, when Levinas speaks of a subject who becomes responsible for the other who persecutes him. To my present point, however, there is the simpler fact that the death of the other exerts a special signifying pressure on the meaning of all responsibility. In historical terms Levinas's reclamation of a seemingly pathological, even excruciating, mode of conscientiousness means that his ethics correlates with an admiration for the extreme humanity of those who were victims in their own right but could yet feel responsible for the lives of others who were finally, even fatally, vulnerable.

In this light Giorgio Agamben's argument in *Remnants of Auschwitz* (1999) stands in noteworthy contrast to the Levinasian position. I turn here to Agamben to consider both his strategic evasion of Levinas and his also conspicuous dependence on Primo Levi, whose philosophically framed, yet spare, testimonial writings oddly complement my reading of Levinasian ethics. In the process of explicating Levi's articulation of the survivor's painful sense of living in the place of another, Agamben revisits a dispute between Bettelheim and Terrence Des Pres over what, if anything, a survivor's experience might be referred to in order to obtain its meaningfulness. Des Pres (whose apology for the survivor I briefly addressed in the last chapter) objects to Bettelheim's definition of the survivor as the one who was finally rendered incapable of feeling guilty for his own survival, thrust by history into a state of pathological childlikeness. Des Pres discerns, instead, a fundamental dignity, an attitude of extreme care for one's body and thus for life, in the very act of survival itself. According to Agamben's neatly imbricating account of these two opposing positions, Bettelheim and Des Pres each end up accusing the other of an ethics of heroism, this symmetry of their counter-charges leading Agamben to interpret the entire dispute as proof of the final impossibility of any living being's attempt to separate guilt from innocence.[47] All of which serves as evidence of the persistent phenomenon of unmastered shame. Building also upon the construct of survivor's guilt, Agamben decides that the phenomenality of such shame is owing to the fact that the camps are symptomatic of a biopolitics wherein the ordinary interplay between subjectification and desubjectification—which involves a necessary interaction not only between *zoē* (biological existence) and *bios* (spiritual, cultural existence) but also between the inhuman and the human—was realized in a social order that introduced the nonhuman permanently into socially constructed being.

For Agamben shame preoccupies every act of testimony, and every act of testimony is an act of speaking in lieu of, indeed on behalf of, another who is the hypothetically pure subject of testimony—namely, that other who is the infamous *Muselmann* of the camps. As beings who lost all sense of what made their lives humanly meaningful and wandered the camps already marked for death, the *Muselmänner* were, in Agamben's terms, beings who having lost the capacity for communication exemplified the relative success of the Nazis' biopolitical ideology. As such they were also the nonsurviving remnant of the camps' truly unique historical legacy. In the shadow person of the *Muselmann*, the inhuman was realized. As Agamben says, the category of the inhuman forever denotes the possibility of gazing upon (here

Agamben borrows one of Levi's conceits) the Gorgon gaze of the *Muselmann*, that anti-face (*antiprosopon*) of the inhuman, and this impossible act of seeing calls to us, as an act of "apostrophe from which human beings cannot turn away," through the act of testimony (*RA* 54).[48] Every act of testimony refers to a split in our being, the survivor's shame recalling every subject's own desubjectification, the supreme potential for which has been historically marked and shaped by the experience of the *Muselmänner*. Testimony in this sense is ontological but not ethical. Agamben's commitment to reading testimony through a Foucauldian hermeneutics as part of the universalizing structures of biopolitically determined being also means, as he explicitly remarks, that we must accept the Nietzschean critique as having established a point of no return for ethics, and Auschwitz as having posed at the same time a "decisive rupture" in the very terms of Nietzscheanism—specifically, the supposition that by our willing it the past might be overcome (*RA* 99).[49]

For the most part Agamben seems eager here to forsake the discourse of responsibility, which gets associated by him with the tragic posture of guilt. According to a Hegelian analysis of the Greek hero, as Agamben emphasizes, tragic consciousness is characterized by the contradiction wherein an "apparently innocent subject [assumes] unconditionally objective guilt" (*RA* 96). But the capacity for this posture, so frequently adopted in bad faith by Nazi perpetrators such as Eichmann, renders the Greek hero, who had survived even the Nietzschean critique, newly obsolete. Offering a dictum that echoes Adorno, if seemingly more modestly, Agamben says simply, "After Auschwitz, it is not possible to use a tragic paradigm in ethics" (*RA* 99). The apparent modesty of this claim disguises its insinuating implication, which is that Auschwitz, as apprehended in the irretrievable, desubjectifying degradation of the *Muselmann*, makes scandalous any notion that a subject might be responsible objectively, generally, or even perhaps systemically for that which it has not done. Whether or not Agamben has Levinas specifically in mind at this moment, the Levinasian recuperation of the bad conscience is fully implicated in the uneasy bargain Agamben negotiates between a post-Nietzschean ethics (which forces us to abandon forever the construct of guilt) and Auschwitz (which demands that we give up the spirit of voluntariness by which we were supposed to have given up our guilt). Thus, the scandal of the voluntary upon which the Levinasian reformulation of ethics turns is also invoked by Agamben, but instead to remind us of testimony's radical reformulation of the condition of language, which now must speak of the human as though it has been both violated and redefined by the intrusion of the *Muselmann*'s inhumanity.

Agamben's nonencounter with Levinas on this point occurs in part through his brief mention of another great post-Holocaust critic of Nietzscheanism, Jean Améry.

Agamben cites Améry's revisionary return to Nietzsche only to decide that, even if the surviving victim may be tempted to answer Nietzsche via a "simple restoration of the morality of resentment," this is not an option (*RA* 100). As he defends Levi before Améry's caricaturing charge that Levi is "the forgiver," Agamben slightly caricatures Améry's own position as though upholding the resentment of the victim necessarily amounted to the advocation of revenge. Again preferring Levi, Agamben discerns in his countryman a "new, unprecedented ontological consistency of what has taken place," which also contains within it a criticism of Nietzscheanism — specifically, that we cannot will the return of Auschwitz because "it has never ceased to take place; it is always already repeating itself" (*RA* 101). Although Agamben's formulation resembles the mystificatory mechanism by which trauma theory similarly declares the eternal return of the undesirable history, there is a crucial difference: for Agamben the mechanism of return occurs not through the psychic apparatus but, rather, through a permanently shameful aspect of ontology realized in the political realm that now forever orders consciousness.

Notably, the distinction Agamben makes between a victim's righteous anger and a victim's testimony to the altered reality of human existence turns at a crucial point on an invocation of Levinas's discussion of shame in *On Evasion* (1935). In order to reject Améry's explicitly negative humanism, in which the inhumanity of history would be opposed by a sustained vigilance from the perspective of victimized humanity (a position canonized in the American context, albeit in slightly different terms, by Lawrence Langer), Agamben invokes the early Levinas, at a point in his career when he was breaking with the project of Husserlian phenomenology (which in Levinas's account had wrongly tried to bind thought to its intentional, theoretical form) by foregrounding the rift in consciousness that legitimated Heideggerian ontology. In *On Evasion* Levinas adopts the ontological critique of knowledge to speak of the shamefulness of the existent's nudity, by which he means not merely the naked material body but, rather, the expansive, eternal force of being (*Dasein*) to which an individual existent is always unoriginally referred. As Levinas says in the final line Agamben cites from the 1935 text, "What shame discovers is the Being that *discovers* itself" (*RA* 105). If shame arises from our presence before ourselves, or what we might call, in Judith Butler's idiom, the necessary ontological subjection of the existent to that which precedes it in existence, the Levinasian project is cued by an escape (or *évasion*) from being, which simultaneously preoccupies this apparently necessary structure of ontology.

In Heidegger this existentially motivated escape, which is inspired by an occasion of subjective insufficiency, means that the existent must legitimate a concern for itself in the principle of *Dasein*, taking refuge in what it is derived from, as though in its eternal function *Dasein* were not just a principle but the nonhumanly ordered dimension of our humanity. In Levinas there is perhaps a greater aspect of self-hesitation on the part of the existent upon finding itself, as Agamben aptly paraphrases Levinas, "consigned to something that cannot be assumed" (*RA* 105), whereas Heidegger discovers the ownmost possibility of self in its reclamation of its impersonal resources. Embracing a reformulated (though still somewhat Heideggerian) ontology, Agamben turns the structure of shame toward the specific drama of desubjectification: "It is as if our consciousness collapsed and, seeking to flee in all directions, were simultaneously summoned by an irrefutable order to be present at its own defacement, at the expropriation of what is most its own. In shame, the subject thus has no other content than its own desubjectification; it becomes witness to its own disorder, its own oblivion as a subject" (*RA* 106). In the place of *Dasein*, Agamben inserts the radically inhuman, a new ontological imperative that is supremely without content. The difference from Levinas's solution (even in an early 1935 work that merely anticipates his larger ethical project) is remarkable. Indeed, Levinas's longer post-1945 view of shame as an ethical sentiment is by all appearances deliberately underestimated by Agamben. Insisting that what cannot be assumed according to the drama of shame is not only or even primarily that which is external, Agamben fails to trace the horizon of Levinasian thought, both for the ways it might resemble his own solution (most obviously, with regard to Levinas's subsequent discussions of *il y a*, that anonymous, terrifyingly negative force that haunts any positive ontology) and for the ways it might challenge his perhaps too easy turn from the principle of exteriority.

Although in this early text Levinas merely invokes the multiplicity of beings, gesturing at an intersubjective level of existence that might refer us beyond the all-pervasive structure of Heideggerian ontology, already there is an intimation of the answer Levinas would give, once his philosophy had been forever altered by post-1945 memory, to the supposition that in shame we fall back terrifyingly and avoidantly upon the existence by which we are preordered or find, in Agamben's terms, that we have no content other than our own desubjectification. For Levinas would eventually suppose, through his revaluation of the bad conscience, that the content of shame is primordially the other, before whose suffering or death the subject is commanded, completely given over to the external insofar as it is ethical, even if the ethical should prove to be that which is outside being, knowledge, or political justice as it has thus far been conceived. Oddly, by his invocation of Levinas on shame, Agamben would emphasize his intent to admit the nonperson of the *Muselmann* into the discussion so as to prove the altered order of existence, or the historically realized function of desubjectification within language, brought about by the Holocaust. Yet in referring us only to an early, pre-Holocaust text, in which Levinas had not yet developed his trenchant ethical critique of Heideggerian ontology, Agamben deployed a strategic evasion, which might also account for his underestimation of the ethical, even guilty function of Levi's own testimonial writings.

On the far side of post-1945 memory we find Levinas's most direct declaration of survivor's guilt as a determining figure for the bad conscience occurring in "Diachrony and Representation" (1985), in which he describes the phenomenology of sociality as a consequence of an implicit ethical command not to remain indifferent to the evidence of the other's dying—"not to let the other die alone; that is, an order to answer for the life of the other man, at the risk of becoming an accomplice to that death." Already there is confusion here with regard to the ethical subject's posture. In entering into the responsibility by which it is already structured, a subject risks her own complicity (the possibility of "becoming an accomplice") in bringing about the other's death. Levinas continues:

> The alterity of the other is the extreme point of the "thou shalt not kill" and, in me, the fear of all the violence and usurpation that my existing, despite the innocence of its intentions, risks committing. The risk of occupying—from the moment of the *Da* of my *Dasein*—the place of an other and thus, on the concrete level, of exiling him, of condemning him to a miserable condition in some "third" or "fourth" world, of bringing him death. Thus an unlimited responsibility emerges in this fear for the other, a responsibility with which one is never done, which does not cease with the neighbor's utmost extremity—despite the merciless and realistic expression of the doctor, "condemning" a patient—even if the responsibility comes to nothing more at that time— as we powerlessly face the death of the other—than saying "here I am," or—*in the shame of surviving*—than pondering the memory of one's wrongdoings. Despite all the modern denunciations of the inefficacy and facileness of a "bad conscience"! (DR 169; my emph.)

Even for Levinas this is an unusually dense and allusive passage, which oddly conflates Holocaust memory and the archetypal story of murder. It includes a contentious dig at Nietzsche (as the father of those who have demystified the bad conscience and made its scrupulosity seem facile) as well as perhaps the most overt and contrary reference to the techniques of psychoanalytic therapy to be found in Levinas's canon. It is not a stretch to imagine that the doctors who here condemn patients should be imagined as psychoanalysts studying the so-called pathology of Holocaust victims, among them prominent historical figures such as Cohen and Bettelheim who for Levinas seem of a kind with the satirically portrayed character in Cynthia Ozick's "Rosa" (1986), a medical scholar who writes the survivor-heroine to solicit her participation in a study so that he can assess her "survivor syndroming," the ugliness of his jargon a mirror for his objectifying callousness.[50] Like Ozick, Levinas sides unapologetically with the pathology, and useless suffering, of victims, but he also discerns a moral worth pertaining especially to their undeservedly bad conscience.

As survivors claim responsibility for more than they could ever have been practically responsible for, Levinas nods to the "shame of surviving" in terms that seem either proleptically borrowed from Levi's essay "Shame" (1986) or indicative of the debt Levi may have owed to Levinasian categories:

> It was not possible for us nor did we want to become islands; the just (*i giusti*) among us, neither more nor less numerous than in any other human group, felt remorse, shame, and pain for the misdeeds that others and not they had committed, and in which they felt involved, because they sensed that what had happened around them and in their presence, and in them, was irrevocable. Never again could it be cleansed; it would prove that man, the human species—we, in short—had the potential to construct an infinite enormity of pain, and that pain is the only force created from nothing, without cost and without effort. It is enough not to see, not to listen, not to act. (Sh 86)[51]

In Agamben's reading of Levi such sentiments dedicate testimony to incorporating our historically realized inhumanity into the sphere of subjectivity, forever recalling those whom we might wish unremembered into the faltering horizon of humanity. As I have suggested, his solution proposes a re-ontologization of the subject, since altered by the violent providences of history. Indeed, according to his demystificatory explication of the social function of the "state of the exception," by which a nation-state announces a purportedly temporary abrogation of law and thereby exposes the fundamental premise of power, or bare sovereignty, through which the law is instituted and perpetually legitimated, Agamben reads Auschwitz as the complementary result of the Nazis' experiment in creating a biopolitically ordered state. Significantly, the state of exception through which the Nazis consolidated their power was never lifted, and it thus functions as more than a ruling conceit. As a consequence, Auschwitz becomes nothing less than the place in which the state of exception "coincides perfectly with the rule," the extreme situation rendered paradigmatic (RA 49).

I do not wish to underestimate Agamben as a perceptive exegete of Levi. Much of Levi's conclusion aptly squares with Agamben's point that Levi, insofar as he focuses on what the human species has constructed in Auschwitz, implicitly recounts the biopolitical project of the camps. Yet the presiding conscientiousness, indeed the entire structure of thought by which Levi imagines speaking on behalf of the others as an act of taking responsibility for their pain, is supremely Levinasian. The ethics of Levi's emphasis are unmistakable: it was the just (*i giusti*) among the prisoners who felt this shameful responsibility for others. There is every danger that the vestige of voluntariness in the attitude of the just might recapitulate the posture of self-righteousness Hegel associates with the unhappy consciousness, or that state of mind by which the subject apparently regulates its own necessary renunciation of its material, bodily existence, and Agamben is surely right to disavow any attempt to interpret Auschwitz through the Nietzschean solution of hyper-voluntariness, as though we could choose even our adversity in construing ourselves as meaningful subjects. In Levinas's revaluation of the bad conscience, it is precisely such a remnant structure of intentionalism that gets overthrown: the bad conscience proceeds from the outside, not as the contradictory external force of the notion of Spirit (Hegel) or as the masked function of power (Nietzsche) but as the forceful expression of the other. How different is Levi's solution? In the passage quoted above, the just assume an attitude of receptivity, even of passivity in relation to the suffering of others. The attitude of justice is not so much that which they have assigned to themselves in order to conceive of themselves, through the logic of virtue, as just. The just here resemble that paradoxical, indeed martyrological dimension of the Jewish myth of the just man, which Andre Schwarz-Bart so effectively deployed in his important Holocaust novel, *The Last of the Just* (1959). It is very much the same emphasis Levinas gives to the construct of election, as when in "Israel and Universalism" (1958) he revises the construct of the chosen people to speak of "exceptional duties" rather than "exceptional rights" or when in his more overtly philosophical writings he deploys election as a trope for responsibility.

Shame is in the Levi text the highest of ethical sentiments, a remorse for other people's misdeeds. It denotes humanity as a responsibility for all that is potentially and in reality enacted against our fellow human beings, even in the situation in which the specifically causal determinations of suffering are being politically enacted also against a responsible subject. Such shame necessarily refers us to the structural dimension of responsibility. Levi's passage is imbued with a Levinasian sense of what it means to become enfolded in another's suffering, a process of ethical complication, of becoming an accomplice in such a way that one assumes the hypothetical posture of being the cause of the injustice another suffers. When such an attitude is imposed from the outside—say, by bystanders who judge the victims according to ordinary moral categories and expect them to be responsible for themselves or their own family and community so as to suppress the causal responsibility the bystander himself must assume—a dangerous apoliticism might attach to Levi's, or Levinas's, position. But the fundamental point of each author is that another's suffering inspires, even requires, responsibility. Someone has to take responsibility for this situation however it came to pass, and if one is a witness to the event of oppression, through direct contact with other victims or only through an imaginative proximity to them, then a responsibility for the other's oppression, even a hypothetically causal responsibility for it, falls upon the subject who is by this largely involuntary act of receptivity defined as responsible.

In the passage already cited from "Diachrony and Representation," what seems superficially oddest about Levinas's ethical logic is his move to make the two conceits for the bad conscience — the murderer and the one who witnesses death or survives murder — uncannily interchangeable. When Levinas cites the biblical commandment not to kill, he deploys Exodus 20:13 as an interpretive intervention much as biblical commentaries, both Jewish and Christian, have often done, and thus supplies Cain with his missing intention. By the time he arrives at the statement "Here I am," the murderer's confession is already a figure (along the lines of the conceit of murderous responsibility explicated earlier) for a subject's answerability for the other, quite apart from whether or not the subject has directly perpetrated a murder. According to Levinas's figurative logic, which here extracts the statement as ethical edict from its context in the story, the burden of the murderer's guilty conscience carries over into the everyday fear of taking the place of the other, of being somehow preferred by fate. Yet this everyday ethical anxiety is also imbued with the extraordinary connotation of the Holocaust survivor, of the one who can feel relentless guilt for the others because they died in such close proximity, in an intimacy in which one's own survival often meant, according to the perverse economics of the concentration and death camps, that another had in fact died. Indeed, Levi invokes the same Genesis text to almost exactly the same ends in "Shame." At a central moment in the essay, shortly before the passage already cited, Levi asks of himself as survivor, "Are you ashamed because you are alive in place of another?" (Sh 81), and then proceeds to chart a series of guilty acts he did not commit, such as his failure to accept positions of special favor or to steal another's bread, only to demonstrate that, despite the lack of "obvious transgressions," he cannot completely obtain the posture of good conscience. Even though certain acts were not committed, they cannot be excluded from the meaning of his survival. And on such a note Levi entertains the hypothesis of his own quasi-murderous survival: "It is no more than a supposition, indeed the shadow of a suspicion: that each man is his brother's Cain, that each one of us (but this time I say 'us' in a much vaster, indeed, universal sense) has usurped his neighbor's place and lived in his stead" (Sh 81–82). Much as Agamben generalizes about the altered ontological reality of humanity after Auschwitz, Levi appeals to a universal construct of responsibility that is entirely predicated — as, I argued in the last chapter, it also is for Levinas—on the facticity of the unjust death. This cannot be a responsibility particular only to the survivors, to their unfortunate proximity. Their experience is to have been witness to the disturbing undercurrent of all responsibility, as Levi's vestigially humanistic universalism comes to seem not unlike Levinas's own anti-ideational humanism, a humanism derived through and on behalf of the other man or woman. After speaking of the perverse election that he, an atheist Jew, had to endure, Levi offers his perhaps most Levinasian formulation: "I might be alive in the place of another, at the expense of another; I might have usurped, that is, in fact, killed" (Sh 82). In the world from which Levi testifies, the transposition of killing onto survival cannot be termed metaphoric in the ordinary sense, for the crossing over of these terms is far too historically determined.

So, too, in "Diachrony and Representation" Levinas strangely configures "violence and usurpation," as if the violence done by perpetrators to victims were always also to be construed as part of the rubric of intentionality and nonintentionality by which the one who witnesses such violence must, like Levi, define his own responsibility. This specter of usurpation, however, is not to be confessed, as in Nietzsche or Freud, as a primal aggressivity by which we are all defined. It is, rather, the vestigial form of our intentionality, defined by acts we have not ourselves directly intended. Accordingly, Levinas's survivor recollects not only his usurping survival but his own "wrongdoings," much as Levi recounts the survivor's extraordinary pains for the other's "misdeeds"—as though all those moments in which we are less than ethically vigilant on behalf of the others amounted to our complicity in social structures that have organized and given permission to their sufferings in the world. In Levinas, as also in Levi, the event of responsibility, which is in effect tantamount to the fact of another's suffering, implicitly requires a systemic understanding: that we should understand the structures by which we survive, always potentially in the place of a neighbor near or far.

If in Levi the interchangeability of violence and surviving can never quite seem metaphoric, in Levinas, we must insist, it is just that. Although Levinas presumes a great intimacy with Holocaust history (implicitly enfolding his own much less gruesome history as a survivor into this account), his appropriation of the primal scene of the camp as a conceit for ethics means that the terms of comparison have relaxed just enough—which is to say, have again separated in such a way as to be not absolutely determined by history—to be again called metaphoric. It is this metaphoric space, within which the subject must venture imaginatively toward the other in her history of suffering and in her susceptibility to death, that permits the bad conscience to arise as a figure for ethics. For metaphor and ethics share the presumption of some remoteness from history as from necessity. Even in Levi's text the narrator's capacity for ethical reflection on what he is witnessing depends on his imaginative ability to project his own consciousness into the future as one who remembers the significance of what he is witnessing for the world that will survive it. What Levi's projection and Levinas's relentlessly vigilant retrospection suggest is that ethics itself relies upon an imaginative separation from history in order that the subject might again insert himself into history with a fuller awareness of his complicity, with the possibility of agency newly presented. What this also suggests (in contrast to the universal moralizings of Todorov or Jones), however, is that if ethics is to remain historical it must give up its propensity for exemption from context, for imagining the event as a perfectly rational enactment of intention or an instance of pure morality.

CODA

For Levinas the bad conscience is the adverse of the simplifying fantasy of rationality, and as such it reintroduces a relation to history precisely as a disruption between intention and result, between identity and one's utmost concerns.[52] Returning us briefly to "Nonintentional Consciousness," in which Levinas atypically permits his philosophical elaboration of the bad conscience to intersect with his more historically minded concerns, I draw attention to an oddly confessional moment in which Levinas offers a rationale for his own project as a break, specifically, with the Husserlian phenomenological project, suggesting in a parenthetical aside a more historical determination for his project: "That is the reason (but also because of the events that took place from 1933 to 1945, events that conceptual knowledge has been able neither to avoid nor understand) why my reflection deviates from the last positions of Husserl's transcendental philosophy, or at least from its formulations" (NC 124). Announcing his project as historically altered by Nazism and giving the Holocaust a status it does not quite hold in his early work, as it precariously approximates the status of causal signifier, Levinas suggests that the Holocaust must turn us to ethics, as ethics must turn us to the remembrance of our complicity in such history. This articulation of a historical, even epochal, rationale for his philosophical project cannot be taken as the final word on Levinasian ethics, for it must be read as part of a digressive, essayistic style through which Levinas attempts to draw for his readers some of the practical implications and considerations of his thought. Undoubtedly, it is connected to Levinas's most overt meditation on the Holocaust in the essay "Useless Suffering" from the previous year. There too Levinas speaks directly of Auschwitz as canceling the metaphysical justification of suffering through theodicy and argues that it is the "unjustifiable character of suffering in the other" or the "pain of the other" that brings the self as a responsible being into existence: "Accusing oneself in suffering is undoubtedly the very turning back of the *I* to itself. It is perhaps thus that the for-the-other—the most upright relation to the other—is the most profound adventure of subjectivity, its ultimate intimacy" (US 98, 99).[53] The nod to the Nietzschean bad conscience is unmistakable as Levinas traces that very structure Judith Butler so astutely describes as the "double recoil of the bad conscience" both in Nietzsche and also in Freud. Levinas starts from there, but the act of self-accusation is not a subjection in service of an ideational structure so much as a consciousness of an irrevocable interrelation that structures our existence. To the extent that we are inclined to agree with Levi or with Levinas that the very definition of our humanity might rely upon such extreme instances of memory, we must read the bad conscience as if it had always (at least by way of the anachronistic transpositions of Levinas's mournful consciousness) pointed toward the Holocaust.

If the Holocaust seems the greatest historical instantiation of bad conscience in Levinas, he has insisted that the useless suffering of genocide's victims be given meaning by reading suffering not as useful or necessary to history's progress but as the necessary moment from which our ethical responsiveness arises. Against the moral models offered by Jones or Todorov, Levinas does not give us an ethical vocabulary in which it would be possible to imagine the individual's perception of his responsibilities within history and thereby to judge how well a subject has fulfilled his capacity for morality. Instead he calls us to shift our definition of what morality requires in light of history's extremity. Since the historical claim of the Holocaust seems too great for personalized accounts of morality, and since collective identity provides no surer ground for responsible lament, the Levinasian bad conscience becomes the measure of a responsibility for history that a singular self could never fully perceive or enact. Ultimately, the responsibility to lament such history must be paradoxically signified by an unease with, even a regret about, one's limited apprehension of what one has been responsible for.

CHAPTER THREE

Where There Are No Victorious Victims

Should a human imagination be able to conceive of the possibility
that it is being willed out of existence, not for something it has done
or been, but only because of its existence? An imagination which
fully anticipated this possibility would, it seems, be that of the agent,
not of the victim.

Berel Lang, Act and Idea in the Nazi Genocide

One of the fallacies of Western democratic culture is the belief that its fundamental premises are more or less realized by extant social conditions and need only
be applied, again, to the latest scenario requiring correction. So, for example, when
we talk of rights being denied to a particular party by a state or social institution (say,
through prolonged economic deprivation or as the result of an act of violence or
organized social discrimination), there is an implicit assumption that the right has
been intact prior to the contemporary violation. Our language of rights, with its basis
in liberal social contract theory, proceeds from the presumption of a free society,
whose members have the minimal capacity for rational inquiry and the requisite talent for moral deliberation that together enable genuine political agency. Although
in reality what the liberal society calls rights are more like privileges held by the relatively few, the question democracy always poses to the capitalist economy upon
which it depends is how far we can extend the parameters of privilege before the benefits of the already privileged are significantly diminished. Most often we insist that
what we call freedom already exists for the majority—in which case, those outside of
freedom's immediate purview are there not because of any measurable fault in the

premises of democratic culture, but rather because of a misapplication (one perhaps of their own doing and presumably also correctable) of our principled premises.

A commitment to progressive rationality requires that the victim's experience be treated either as so exceptional that it comes to seem absolutely aberrant or as redeemable according to the longer trajectory of rationality and justice (in other words, as merely a temporary condition). Recently a host of critics has arisen to attack what they see as a mounting late-twentieth- and now early-twenty-first-century cultural esteem for the victim—the splintering effects of multiculturalism, identity politics, or theories of ethnic particularism all seemingly dependent on nurtured historical grievances. Such suspicion directed toward the aggrieved has found a corroborating vocabulary in contemporary slang, as the term *victim*—in phrases such as "she's such a victim" or "stop playing the victim"—has taken on an impossibly contradictory valence, as though victims were always also agents, stupidly failing to foresee their extreme suffering and thereby perhaps permitting it and then, of course, dwelling on it ("don't dwell" is another contemporary colloquialism symptomatic of a broadening cultural disdain for the victim). It is with respect to their hypothetically long view that victims are deemed most threatening. By refusing to forget, or at least not to talk about, their experiences, victims contribute to a cultural politics in which the memory of injustice prevents the resumption of those already extant categories of equality, justice, or freedom by which the liberal society would perpetuate itself with straightforward confidence.

In the early 1990s a number of books attempted a recovery of an American character fallen into decline in inverse ratio to the alleged cultural ascendancy of victims. Shelby Steele's *Content of Our Character* (1990), Joseph Amato's *Victims and Values* (1990), and especially Charles J. Sykes's *Nation of Victims: The Decay of the American Character* (1992), all argued—with competing degrees of generalizing and moralizing haste—that America had regressed to a resentful, litigious, egotistic, whining, even adolescent society.[1] This was because victim politics, which in Steele's phrase were "grounded too deeply in the entitlement derived from past injustice," had gained the day. As Sykes framed the problem, America's characteristic compassion had been exhausted by the rising passions of self-declaring victims: "What was once conferred compassionately is now demanded by self-proclaimed victims in tones that seem increasingly shrill and meanspirited."[2] To support his rejection of victims' plaintiveness, Sykes reverted with confident naïveté to declarations of good conscience, supposing that Americans appropriately exercise compassion where it is truly necessary. Sykes no doubt would find his thesis affirmed by the American response to the tsunami in Southeast Asia in early 2005, which the American media used as an occasion to reinforce the cultural conceit of American benevolence—as, for example, when Bill O'Reilly staged on *The O'Reilly Factor* a debate with a for-gone conclusion on the topic of whether the United States was the world's most gen-erous country or when Arnold Schwarzenegger, in an appearance on *The Tonight Show*, ecstatically cited American charitable giving as an excuse to forget about "the bad things," such as the war in Iraq, and remember that "America is the most gen-erous country in the world."[3] Given that Americans are so compassionate in the face of natural disaster, the problem might be, at least in Sykes's terms, that nowadays too many people falsely interpret inconvenience as injustice, muddying the ordinarily clear waters of conscience. Sykes is not worried by what one would have thought to be the obvious objection to overextending the category of *victim*, that we might cause real victims to go unrecognized or unrepaired. Instead, as he slides blithely from examples of whining litigants to the therapeutic tactics by which adversity fos-ters the dream of happiness and then to readings of an array of revolutionary and resistant ideologies, including certain aspects of Civil Rights discourse and William Ryan's famous sociological treatise *Blaming the Victim* (1971), Sykes quickly reveals his own aversion to the very category of the victim. Tracing victimism to collec-tivist discourses accounting for social injustices as varied as the racial oppression of African Americans and the systemic disfranchisement of women, Sykes treats the ille-gitimate complaints of some victims as symptomatic of his general misgiving about all victims.

For many of its most severe critics the Holocaust has similarly contributed to a cultural esteem of the victim. So, for example, in *The Holocaust in American Life* (1999) Peter Novick ponders the ascendancy of "the Holocaust" in American cul-ture, finding the fact that it has been far more commonly recalled after 1970 than in its immediate aftermath to be indicative of an ideological, rather than soundly his-toriographical, momentum.[4] Not unlike Steele, Amato, and Sykes, Novick remarks upon an "important background condition," specifically, the rise of "victim culture," a phenomenon for which the memory of the Holocaust, though perhaps not directly responsible, was at least a catalyst (8). Overstating the degree to which the esteemed victim has become a cultural norm, Novick simultaneously underestimates the tremendous ambivalence that has accompanied Americans' apparent willingness to give lip service to Holocaust victims and other victims of significant social injustice. By discerning a teleological direction for all Holocaust memory in American culture that cooperates in his view with currently entrenched commitments to identity poli-tics, Novick overlooks the varying, indeed often inconsistent, ideological uses of the Holocaust in American cultural history.

So often leveraged for debates about late-twentieth-century culture and society, the Holocaust functioned throughout much of the 1960s as a trope for imaginative transpositions of oppressed subjectivity from group to group (say, from Jews to blacks) while also signifying within the strictures of Cold War rhetoric the imminent threat of totalitarian states, from the Soviet Union to Third World countries such as Cuba or Guatemala. Increasingly after the mid-1970s, however, it obtained meaning according to its own exceptionality from all comparison to other social modes of oppression.[5] As such, it was positioned as though it were a unique aberration in the progressive history of the liberal society, a perspective that Novick accuses of being simply unhistorical even as it also masks specific cultural uses to which the Holocaust is put in our contemporary political moment. For those who interpret the Holocaust as a radical rupture in the progressive project of the Enlightenment, however, the Holocaust marks the failure of a political heritage. As a sign of discontinuity, it forbids too-ready analogies between historically disparate circumstances of suffering while simultaneously challenging our continued confidence in the language of rights so fundamental to democratic discourse. What Jean-François Lyotard calls "the differend" describes just such an irreconcilable grievance within liberal, rationalist discourse.[6] Befalling the victim in a proportion beyond ordinary moral measure, beyond the reach of legal and civil remedy, the differend is an ethical claim realized as an incommensurability within experience.

Along with Maurice Blanchot's *The Writing of the Disaster* (1980), Lyotard's *The Differend* (1983) has been a crucial text for legitimating a poststructuralist critique of Enlightenment rationality specifically informed by post-Holocaust sensibility, as though the overwhelming meaning of the Holocaust resided in the disruption it imposes upon all quasi-Hegelian, progressive narratives for democratic culture. Even as poststructuralism sought to expose the deep complicity of democratic, post-Enlightenment culture in fundamentally oppressive, totalizing, sometimes proto-totalitarian social structures, the Holocaust obtained an aura of exceptionalism, with its victims described as irreproachable, as though any attempt to interpret them again from the standpoint of normative structures and social categories were a betrayal effectively reenacting their original, historical experience of victimization. With the Holocaust serving as the paradigmatically disastrous event, Blanchot describes the *disaster* as a nonexperiential un-knowing, which instantiates a fundamental opposition between the victim and rationality. By this mournful hermeneutic the victim's perspective would be the only perspective from which we can speak of the Holocaust, even if, or perhaps precisely because, it signifies the defeat of knowledge; or again, as Blanchot asks, "How can thought be made the keeper of the holocaust where all was lost, including guardian thought? In the mortal intensity, the fleeing silence of the countless cry."[7] Testing our confidence in rationality as that which defends us against and even perhaps prevents the horror that devastates meaning,

Blanchot figures rationality as a purportedly "guardian thought" simultaneously eluding its most basic cultural function.[8] In Blanchot's view rationality attempts, feebly, to recollect what it failed to anticipate. Yet the event of the disaster so surprises us as to fall out of causal syntax, reverting to a literality unredeemed by abstract thought, putting a strain on language measured in part by Blanchot's strangely disjunctive figurative conjunctions—the imperfect oxymoron of "fleeing silence," or the numerically awry epithet "countless cry" that describes it. By qualifying the singular, more forceful cry, which is concretized in its particularity, with the infinite and implicitly plural epithet "countless," Blanchot suggests the ways in which the disaster already eludes knowledge via an experiential multiplication graduating toward a numerically sublime proportion. The countless cry is impossibly allegorical in the sense that it would stand as an experience needing to be accounted for, yet never simply countable.[9]

We have many strategies for expressing what is not properly speakable. Any theoretical discourse committed to revising the conditions of rational understanding so as to take better account of uncounted or uncountable experiences of suffering stumbles not only upon the contradictory evidence of its own eloquence but upon a greater paradox as well: if the inadequacy we now perceive in our capacity to convey suffering is owing to a particular historical event that brought about the crisis in representation's efficacy, there still must exist (at least hypothetically) a language in which such experience could have been or might yet be spoken. In speaking of the victim's fleeing silence and countless cry, Blanchot helps give phrase to what has been often and as variously stated in relation to the Holocaust—that our failure to master the past may emerge, paradoxically, as the only appropriate ethic of representation when it comes to speaking or writing about the Holocaust. To designate silence as its own language, even while simultaneously acknowledging ordinary language's failure and the impossibility of fully explicating the ethical and psychological depths of suffering, is to give special place to the victim's perspective as a crux for any meaningfulness to be obtained from disastrous events.[10]

In this chapter I want to test certain premises that would devolve from an ethics grounded in the victim's perspective. If the Holocaust can be said to have occasioned a further revolution in our ideas about who and what a victim is, it is nevertheless also true that our cultural conceptions of the victim determine how we think about events such as the Holocaust and in what terms such an injustice is best accounted. It seems only too obvious that extreme violence and social injustice cannot be theorized without some reference to the victims by which such phenomena are measured. Just as there can be no truly victimless crime, it would make no sense to speak of injustice without reference to victims. Yet this is consistently what most theories of justice try to do, at least insofar as they try to reconcile their grievances with already extant, normalized sociopolitical structures.[11] Then, too, quite as though the social symptom already proved the premise, victims themselves are often dismissed as irrational, not only according to common social prejudices but by many of the legitimating structures of our society. Victims, inasmuch as they speak still from within the perspective of grievance, are frequently deemed in both legal and common parlance to be unreliable witnesses. Having been robbed of the capacity to serve as the origin of their own fate, having been cast outside the structure within which a subject proceeds from deliberation to action, that very structure so fundamental to our rational narrative for progressive society, the victim is assessed as one who cannot speak about what happened to her and simultaneously adhere to the core of rational thought. All witnessing to the fate of the victim, even when it does not come directly from her mouth, even if it is not based in his experiential testimony, incurs the risk of irrationality. To remain too long on the side of the victim is to risk losing one's faith in the narrative of rationality itself. Any theory of political, social, or ethical injustice turns upon a contradiction inherent in the concept of injustice itself. Yet, insofar as injustice is not merely the violation of a formerly established state of justice, it disrupts status quo constructs of justice and refers us to relations of imbalance or instances of social woundedness every bit as fundamental to our culture as the hypothesis of liberal progressiveness. In this sense, a victim of injustice can never be fully accounted for within the field of rationality. Accordingly, our efforts to recuperate the victim to the narrative of rationality are always also about bringing her back into the fold of culture and recruiting for her an agency absent from the historical experience of victimization. In the face of such a task, rationality itself may seem revisionary or simply wishful.

What the ethical philosophy of Levinas suggests with regard to this debate is that our articulation of responsibility need not cancel the victim's deficit nor already suppose a state of balance or impartiality in which grievances have been forever suspended. Whereas Nietzsche gave the lie to the socio-philosophical project of Western morality by referring the occasion of obligation itself to a genealogical history of punishment and willfully exercised power, Levinas criticizes rationality for its refusal to account for powerlessness, for ignoring precisely the excess or deficit within self-consciousness by which a subject is always referred outside of itself to the other person who cannot be contained by the structures of knowledge. In the previous two chapters I have traced the trajectory of Levinas's mournful hermeneutics in order to discern ethics as a mode of unquieted memory and to read the bad conscience as a figure for a radical failure within history that nevertheless determines the future of responsibility and the aspiration of justice. Here I turn to the question of what it means for ethics to be derived as though from a perspective synonymous with vulnerability itself. As I reckon the impulse of our rationality to take account of the countless cry of the victim even while simultaneously describing the victim as, by definition, outside of knowledge, I consider a possibility, partly glimpsed by Levinas, that the present order of rationality might be challenged ethically as well as politically in the name of the victim. In discerning this trajectory for a reading of Levinas, I have set myself on a collision course once again with Alain Badiou's critique of Levinas and, more specifically, his general rejection of postmodern ethics' purported infatuation with the victim. Here again, as also with his enfolding of Levinas into the ethics of difference (discussed in my introduction), Badiou's interpretation of Levinasian ethics is characterized by both perspicacity and distortion. By perceiving humanity under its most degraded aspect, with the concentration camps casting themselves forward in our imagination as though they were somehow paradigmatic of society, contemporary ethics can no longer imagine, Badiou laments, the spark of an immortal striving by which human beings aspire to their own humanity and to those cultural constructs by which they might hold themselves in common.[12] In Badiou's terms human rights, the objection to evil, and the language of otherness have all carved out a "victim ethics" that diminishes our perception of what might indeed be remarkable about human beings even within the most degrading circumstances.

Badiou's skepticism about victims and their central place in modern ethics forces us to ask, first of all, whether Levinasian ethics, which rarely uses the direct terminology of the *victim*, ought really be characterized by such a focus on the unremarkable, incapable human being. To this I would answer provisionally that, if we twist Badiou's emphasis only slightly to describe instead what is remarkable about human beings even in their relatively incapable responsibility before the others by whom they are called, we are very much within a Levinasian framework. Notably, however, both Badiou and Levinas answer the possibility of oppressive degradation by way of metaphysical constructs: Badiou's distinctively immortal desire that separates humanity from bestiality; and Levinas's transcendently signified other, who pronounces for every subject a vocation in responsibility greater than her capacity to fulfill it. Although I wish to honor in this chapter the attention Levinas gives to the figure of the victim, and thus implicitly to counter Badiou's suspicion that there is an apolitical, conservative horizon to an ethics framed by concern for the victim, I am concerned nevertheless that Levinas does not escape (any more than Badiou does) the metaphysical trappings of—or, more precisely, the religiously structured framework for—the useful victim.

Ultimately, any ordering of the victim's experience within the field of rationality or, for that matter, within a system of ethics must find a secondary use for victimization, as though a victim's absence of agency did not prevent her from determining history. This ordering mechanism of rationality can be associated with the sociostructural phenomenon of sacrifice, which always depends upon a community's commitment to overcoming the impossible literality and resistant negativity of the victim's experience by locating a principle of causation behind the experience, even when that principle of causation turns out, perhaps necessarily, to be invested in mythical or superstructural patterns of ideology. This structure of secondary use or usefulness—which is the logic of sacrifice itself, the very possibility that a victim qua victim will prove victorious—is ironically that which permits all contemporary reactionary doubts about whether a victim's primary, unintended experience could ever have been as unforeseen, as inopportunistic and devastating, as it appears to have been at first glance. By drawing attention to sacrificial structures influencing even our most conscientious attempts to speak in the name of Holocaust victims, as to the impact of the implicit figure of the victim upon Levinasian ethics, I wish to elucidate the necessarily ideological components of ethical theory while emphasizing the heuristic difficulty of bringing into the light of memory the injustice done to a victim when such memory ought not to be validated by the terms of its cultural usefulness.

ACCOUNTABILITY IN THE NAME OF THE VICTIM

Nietzsche made explicit a supposition at least as old as Hellenic culture itself, the idea that justice was a social equation involving equal parties. In effect, justice is privilege, the particular privilege of socially codified power. According to our moral systems and legal codes, to be a victim is to succumb to an aberrant circumstance, falling from equivalence into inequivalence but always with the possibility of regaining one's proper privilege. If those who are aggrieved are deemed constitutionally, even Darwinistically, weak in their disposition, they can claim power only by masking their inherent inability to enact genuinely strong willfulness. If one is a victim of more than temporary contingency—say, if one is a woman who suffers the consequences of sexual abuse or a Mexican border worker who endures the bare life of severe economic exploitation—one might have little hope that the conventions of justice will compensate for one's particular grievance, for the simple reason that one is not simply an equal among equals. Still, we are told repeatedly from within the prevailing social logic, often as though victims had a long history of getting what they want from the rest of us, that to be a victim is either a matter of temporary consequence or a permanent social condition of little matter, even perhaps a seemingly natural condition. Every attempt to find justice for victims is limited in advance by the fact that it depends, seemingly, upon one of these two self-canceling definitions, or perhaps some admixture of the two.

At least one result of the discrepancy between the state of justice and the condition of being a victim is the persistent attempt within the project of progressive rationality to convert the victim's fate into something more manageable or the victim into someone involved in agentive considerations that qualify her experience of victimization. From the standpoint of social contract theory and of the basic philosophical premises supporting the liberal nation-state, the requirement that we convert victimization to a mode of thought consistent with rationality and that we incorporate the victim's suffering within the pragmatic, phenomenological trajectory of social experience is as absolutely necessary as our belief that justice is an already realized, relatively stable condition. Only the victim says otherwise. When Berel Lang speculates, in the passage cited as an epigraph to this chapter, about the conditions under which a victim might conceive of an intentional structure of thought aiming at her demise, he draws attention to the basic exceptionality of the victim's experience within the order of rationality. Lang refuses the temptation to convert victims into agents, which is so often performed by imagining how a victim might have anticipated her fate and acted so as to avoid it. And yet already in the succinct antinomy *victim/agent* there is a relational premise, for Lang pursues his moral philosophical account of the Holocaust in the name of the victim, yet according to the ideas and actions of those who have perpetrated genocide. Throughout *Act and Idea in the Nazi Genocide* (1990) Lang puts forward a rigorous reclamatory apology of responsibility as historical answerability for actions and thus explores a correlation between act and idea that need not depend as much upon a perpetrator's obvious foreknowledge of his actions as upon the ideational structure implicit in his executed agency.[13]

A victim is, by definition, someone who inhabits a condition of exceptionality within any mode of rational reckoning. In plainest logic the victim is someone without intention because, even were the victim to foresee what will happen to him, insofar as the event cannot be altered by his will, what he sees might just as well be nothing. At the same time, this apparent absence of intentionality provokes a crisis in rationality, so that (at least by one prominent cultural logic) the problem of victimization pertains to a simple deficit of knowledge, almost as though the hypothesis of a victim's knowledge might replace the deficit in intentionality. All debates about what victims of the Nazi genocide knew of their fate beforehand revisit this crisis, often forsaking an emphasis on the structural determinations of victimization so as to imagine what the hypothetically intentional, conceived-ahead-of-time parameters of the victim's experience might have been. Any intentional relation the victim might adopt with regard to what befalls him, though it seems experientially meaningful, remains structurally without consequence. Whether what a victim believes about the future turns out to be true or false, every victim of violence participates in a kind of delusory knowledge—as this theme gets played out repeatedly in testimony and fictional work about the Holocaust—by which an inevitable end might be forestalled but not avoided. Nevertheless, by the same terms our suppositions about a victim's foreknowledge have already begun the work of converting her into an approximate agent of the event and, by attributing to her a rational perception of her situation as victim, making her also responsible for what happens to her.

It is just such a logic that Lang refuses when he altogether exempts Holocaust victims from a mode of knowledge commensurate with genuine responsibility. As he insists upon the disproportionality between suffering and intention that inheres in a victim's experience and turns from there to a consideration of the actions of genuine agents, it is almost as if the utter absence of determinative rationality in a victim's experience were reflected or mimicked in the perpetrator's abbreviated deliberations about the crimes he commits. Moreover, the categorical construct of *victim*— the simple fact that there is a victim of an act—provides evidence of an accountability residing with the one who has inflicted harm upon another person. Not to locate responsibility in the perpetrator who has brought about the victim's fate seems a secondary insult to the victim, and thus we measure the accountability of a perpetrator in the name of the victim.

By this logic there is an interrelation between victim and perpetrator operative in Lang's methodology that is not altogether inconsistent with the predominant cultural logic, if only because the victim's exemption from responsibility demands that a perpetrator be completely answerable for the crime. This interrelation, what we might also call a *configuration* of victim and perpetrator, becomes especially pronounced in the supposition that there might be a necessary proportion between the damage done to a victim and the culpability of the one who inflicted it. Neither the rationalizing dimension of ideology nor the bureaucratic obfuscation of causal agency provides escape from culpability, since any action performed by an agent who is subjectively attached to the system already participates in its consequences. Lang, distrusting the diminution of political agency implicit in overly sociological explanations of evil, typically attaches responsibility to the hypothetical, individuated perpetrator, and behind his distrust is a memory of the refuge perpetrators took retrospectively in the mystified workings of the genocidal system, through which their participation in ideology was made to seem involuntary, their actions within a totalitarian state having never properly been their own.[14]

Central to Lang's argument is his own conflicted evaluation of the function of ideology, which is at once suspect in that it casts a rationalizing, falsifying veil over individual answerability and simultaneously necessary in that it preserves the space of intention even within actions that might superficially disguise the intentions behind them. When an agent of genocide requires nothing from the victim except her destruction, he acts on a principle that is "categorical and nonutilitarian," permitting the appeal to principle (we might just as well say *ideology*) to override moral deliberation (AING 15).[15] Ideological principle may serve as an agent's substitute motivation, as Nazi language-rules only further obscured the relation between idea and act, yet, according to Lang's pragmatic humanism, even if the Nazis' language fails to provide a transparent account of intentionality, it cannot be accounted for simply as false consciousness or an inability to perceive right and wrong.[16] Not only does Lang here trouble the especially modern equation of evil with ideological false consciousness, he implicitly opposes a long-standing sociological emphasis in Holocaust Studies, running most prominently from Raul Hilberg and Hannah Arendt to Zygmunt Bauman, that would account for the systemic perpetration of extreme violence primarily through the sociopolitical climate and structures that legitimate violence.[17] The example of the paper-pusher in the office of deportations or of the bureaucrat who made the trains run on time (regardless of whether they were filled with soldiers heading to the front, vacationing German citizens, or Jews robbed of citizenship and ultimately their lives) has become almost a Holocaust commonplace.

Taking up the Arendt/Hilberg theory of the unremarkable perpetrator, Lang specifically intervened in the 1980s debate between intentionalist and functionalist Holocaust historians (no longer the controversy it once was) by reading acts, even those that seem to be generated or facilitated by social structures and ideology, as standing necessarily for a set of proximate intentions. In the intentionalist framework the increasing oppression of the Jews under Hitler's regime bore a logical coherence that was almost strictly teleological, whereas for the functionalists there would appear to have been far less cooperation among the principal Nazi ideologues or coherence among their plans than the genocidal results might seem to indicate. As intentionalists (according to the terms of functionalist critique) smoothed over the rough spots in the historical progression of the Nazi oppression by putting too much emphasis on Hitler and a few higher-ups as authors of genocide, they revealed a crucial aspect of any philosophical or political theory of intention, which must presume that historical actions proceed from, and so can be traced back to, recognizable intentions formed by particular persons, collective groups, or even nation-states.[18] Lang distills much of this debate to what he takes to be its moral philosophical core, pertaining to a correspondence between action and intention. Deeming it a mistake to view intention only as a mental "act" or idea conceived chronologically prior to an action, Lang suggests that, in this crude form, intentionalism supposes a narrative logic linking simply conceived ideas with executed actions—a relation of one-to-one causation—that the greater portion of our moral decision making simply will not fulfill.

Intention, Lang supposes, occurs rather as an aspect of the act itself, so that evidence of a deliberative intention preceding the act (such as documentary evidence of an order from Hitler to exterminate the Jews) need not be produced for there to be intention in it. The intelligibility of the decision and the evidence of the act as purposive should be enough to prove intention. Commenting on the patterns of concealment evident in the Nazis' representation of their genocidal intentions (both in their representations to themselves in internal government documents and in their communications with the German and international publics), as well as in their subsequent efforts to obliterate the traces of the death camps, Lang argues that such efforts must reflect a consciousness of guilt rather than a mere "calculation of prudence," in which case it is only sensible to conclude that concealment indicates an awareness in the perpetrators of a moral contradiction between the so-called principle they were serving and the acts they were perpetrating. In the Nazis' strategic use of torture and in the rhetoric of dehumanization aimed at their victims, there is an excess giving the lie to any purported suspension of moral perception. These behaviors, Lang insists, are "only intelligible on the premise that the victims are not essentially dissimilar from the perpetrators and that something much more morally complex than self-defense is at issue" (*AING* 21). In short, they depend upon a misrecognized interrelation between perpetrators and victims already intimating, since the agent is thereby conscious of perpetrating an act that has a victim, extant moral categories.

On moral philosophical grounds Lang is contending throughout *Act and Idea in the Nazi Genocide* with the long-standing Platonic thesis that no one does evil knowingly. For, if one perceives evil as a consequence of imperfect knowledge, one must conclude either that those who have perpetrated evil did not know any better or that they were not rational beings.[19] In Lang's account the construct of guilt indicates the Nazis' capacity for moral knowledge of their actions. In a retrospective relation to their own acts, there can be no hypothetical diminution of the Nazis' criminality under the rubric of ideology, nor can their wrongs be attributed to inadequate knowledge or a flawed understanding of the good. Unlike the Levinasian bad conscience, which presumes a never to be recuperated imbalance and even assigns obligation to those who bear no direct responsibility for events, Lang's construct of guilt restores the relation between knowledge and moral deliberation, as though it were standing in for a mode of conscience that, while consistently available to the perpetrators, failed to prevent their violence. In the charge of guilt there is always an imaginative holding of the agent to his humanity. To put Adolf Eichmann on trial is to insist upon his responsibility for events directly consequent upon his intentions, converting a vast system of oppression and genocide into a narrative of individual, criminal responsibility while demanding, if only via prosecutorial questioning, that he retrospectively hold himself accountable for what he has done and perhaps reclaim, as Hamlet anxiously intuited Claudius might be doing when he knelt to pray, a portion of his own humanity by belatedly admitting his responsibility.

If such a conversion of the ideologically, socially determined human being into a narratively constructed agent of personal responsibility is fundamental to the procedures of moral philosophy, it is perhaps just as powerfully linked to the procedures of Western aesthetics. Often the apparently avant-garde work of art only serves to reinforce this cultural commitment to interpreting ideology as a matter of personal choice and decision, so that even a film as deliberatively deformative of ordinary viewing expectations as Claude Lanzmann's *Shoah* (1985) reveals its latent investment in humanistic constructs of responsibility. Throughout *Shoah* Lanzmann presents us with scenes that he obviously intends as refutations of the Platonic thesis, rendering the evasions of perpetrators and bystanders transparent. For Lanzmann, even more overtly than for Lang, the capacity for interpretation is not simply a belated intelligence in his audience; it is a capacity not only to know but also to distinguish right and wrong, which has resided all along with the perpetrators and bystanders. If Lanzmann and Lang both counter Plato by insisting that the gap between knowledge and moral agency typically functions as an evasion of responsibility within the present-tense possibility of moral action, each also allows for a retrospective filling in of that gap—Lang by finding that, even when action accrues through seemingly accidental intentions, intention is concealed within action, coalescing as a realized or implicit guilt in the perpetrator's consciousness; and Lanzmann by making his film the medium for recuperating knowledge through remembered actions in which choosing was always implicit. Despite Lanzmann's public advocation of seeing the Holocaust as an absolutely incommensurable event and his rhetorically fashioned stance of contrariness in relation to all cultural techniques for accommodating its disastrous significance, his judgmental posture in relation to perpetrators and bystanders argues for a correlation of intention and result that would make the Holocaust, even as its exceptionality seemingly withstands ordinary forms of historical knowledge, a consequence of individual intentions and thus a hypothetically foreseeable event.

The hazard of Lang's and Lanzmann's respective techniques of holding the perpetrators responsible is that the victim might seem properly defined as an intention, or retrospective thought, of the agent. If we ask what Lanzmann would have made of gushingly remorseful perpetrators and bystanders, who admit their failings much as Lear on the heath imaginatively recounts his own tyranny, who might even remember their victims vigilantly, forever begging forgiveness, we have to speculate that he would not have filmed such scenes precisely because, even if subjectively sincere, they would seem preposterous, exploitative, indeed pornographic to him; yet, as *Shoah* taunts us, through its severely interrogative format, with the unfulfilled prospect of answerability, our imaginations are at least partly dedicated to a desire for just such tawdry confessions of sins. For his part, as Lang also demands an account-ability on the part of the perpetrator that might stand for historical understanding, he implicitly ratifies a construct of rationality in which the perpetrator stands answer-able in proportion to his restored knowledge about the right and wrong of his actions, and as a consequence of which the victim might be rendered dependent upon her fate of being a received datum in the consciousness of the perpetrator. What is most remarkable about this coincidence between Lang and Lanzmann, which turns on the historical coincidence between the victim's fate and the ones who brought it about, is that the attempt to speak as though from the irreplaceable per-spective of the victim should force us toward a point of resolution that resides, as it were, within the perpetrator's moral consciousness.

A similar problem is glimpsed in Jean Améry's importantly contentious essay "Resentments" (1966), which offers perhaps the most strident defense of the victim's unresolved suffering in the mainstream of Holocaust Studies. Revising the construct of *ressentiment*, which Nietzsche pathologizes as a state of mind belonging to those who are denied genuine modes of action, Améry deems it a morally rigorous per-spective, an act of resistance offered to an original, already accomplished violence. Belatedly, it also suggests the possibility of holding out against the too forgetful sta-tus quo.[20] Yet, as he proceeds to distinguish resentment from revenge, Améry uncan-nily configures the victim's subjectivity with the perpetrator's, supposing the moral purpose of legal punishment to be that of making the crime "become a moral real-ity for the criminal."[21] What Améry wishes, perhaps only in retrospective plaintive-ness, is that the SS-man who stands before a firing squad will arrive at a moral moment in which he obtains for the first time a capacity to identify with the victim: "When SS-man Wajs stood before the firing squad, he experienced the moral truth of his crimes. At that moment, he was with *me* — and I was no longer alone with the shovel handle [the instrument Wajs had used to beat Améry]. I would like to believe that at the instant of his execution he wanted exactly as much as I to turn back time, to undo what had been done" (70). For moral order to be restored, Améry appears to say, the victim's perspective must be encountered by those who have perpetrated the act of victimization. Yet, is it really the perpetrator's place, we might well ask, to occupy, even in guilt, the place of his victim? A fantasy of reciprocity emerges in Améry by which he supposes a necessary relation, if only after the fact, between the perpetrator and victim, much as contemporary victimologists similarly seek to investigate a perpetrator's gaze for sociological clues that might not only explain his actions but also establish a relation between a victim's characteristics and the perpetrator's choice of victim. Any hypothesized reciprocity between the two parties of victim and perpetrator, I want to insist, comes dangerously close to appropriating the victim once more to a perpetrator's originally appropriative act of violence. To complete any victim's plaintive cry, especially by grounding our answer to it in the perpetrator's reply, may betray the very principle of ethics by which every complaint against injustice is inspired.

NOT JUST ANY VICTIM

The *victim*, of course, is in sociohistorical terms already a compromised category. Our use of the term within the context of the Nazi genocide is in a basic sense every bit as problematic, and for largely the same reasons, as choosing the term *Holocaust* to designate the events of 1941–45. Each term implies, in a genealogical sense, either divine necessity or a socially redemptive act. Each gets passed down to us through the religious practice of sacrifice, according to which violence is not only retrospectively ordained as though by necessity but additionally plotted for the benefit of the community. In the theory of René Girard the victim marks the transition from the chaotic state of mimetic rivalry based on an apparently animalistic, limitless proclivity for violence in all human beings to the cooperative functioning of human community based also, albeit now in contained form, in an act of violence. Already within the terminology, whether or not we accept Girard's overall reading of religious system or of the constitutive force of violence within the construct of communal unity, there is a necessary slippage in our conception of contemporary victims, who will even in not obviously sacrificial contexts necessarily recall the historical origins of the victim as the one upon whom violence is enacted to serve the social system. In this original connotative sense victims are for the community, even good for the community. There is, however, even within this supposition of purported efficacy already an element of misgiving: for, according to Girard's theory, no matter what particular reasons are given for the choice, the victim has been selected more or less arbitrarily. When the community interprets its own collectively binding violence, proceeding "in the unshakable conviction that it has found the one and only cause of its trouble," it only acts as though there were providence in its choices.[22] It is this latter mode of mythic or ideological knowledge, in which a community's founding acts are concealed to itself, that prevails in the religious lineage of the victim and makes it hard for us, even from within a modern disenchanted worldview, to discern the fundamental arbitrariness that designates as victims some instead of others who might just as well, or as dubiously, have been chosen.

Of course, we now commonly believe, as a matter of convention and of collo-quial connotation, in the innocence of some of those who become victims, per-ceiving in this concession an apparent progress, much as our heightened cultural awareness of the technique of scapegoating, or what Girard calls the "victimage mechanism," also marks an advance of sorts. Originally, in Girard's view, responsi-bility for violence was thrust upon the victim himself, who was hypothesized to be the cause of an externally or internally violent threat to the community. Although the history of religion allows us to catch glimpses of the phenomenon of the inno-cent, ritually ordained victim who had not committed any crime, who perhaps lacked even sexual knowledge of other persons, the innocence of ritually designated surrogate victims nevertheless carried a vestigial remembrance of the arbitrariness by which all victims were originally chosen. What I wish to emphasize is that any morally evaluative question about a victim's innocence performs an insufficient break with the basic structural logic by which victims facilitate the workings of the social system. Indeed, I would contend that the tenuous hypothesis of innocence, even as it revisits the element of arbitrariness behind all victimization, simultane-ously cooperates with the social logic that declares most victims to be useful.

From an anthropological perspective the victim's function remains purposeful throughout history, perhaps until quite recently. Always in the Girardian hypothesis there is a proportion between the violence suffered by the victim and the violence or misfortune he might otherwise bring to the community, which not only translates into what I have termed the configuration of victim and perpetrator but also serves to interpret the victim as a symptom of communal agency. To extend Girard's terms into the context of contemporary criminology or to apply them to the questions raised by Lang, we might say that, at the level of an individually enacted violence, the victim signifies—to whatever extent she or he is encoded within a systemic ide-ology for which each agent remains answerable—from within the function of a per-petrator's intention. Over time the hypothesis of a victim's responsibility for the vio-lence inflicted upon him, of its usefulness from the perpetrator's or community's perspective, was converted into an intentional attitude. Thus, in modern parlance victims became responsible for the violence done to them insofar as they had failed to get out of the way of it, and, insofar as they fail to get out of the way of violence, they must implicitly have intended it. In this sense there is a basic redundancy in William Ryan's famous phrase "blaming the victim"—first, because victims have always been historically those who are blamed and, second, because even within Ryan's modern objection to our habit of blaming others for their socially determined misfortunes there is a carryover, corroborated by the late-twentieth-century American attitudes to which Ryan objects, of an original contempt for ritual victims, who were often subjected before slaughter to elaborate humiliation.[23]

Eventually, if we are to break with the original signification of the victim that persists within contemporary cultural logic, we will have to move beyond innocence to an emphasis on the fundamental uselessness of the victim. Even if violence continues to be defined as productive of sociality or as ineradicable from humanity in our natural and communal existence, our ethically inflected sense of social history might refuse narratives of rational causality imposed upon victims insofar as they are subjects both of malevolent and purportedly benevolent power.[24] Although Lang's exclusion of Holocaust victims from the plane of intentional responsibility effectively absolves them of any necessary relation to the perpetrator's construct of usefulness, such a procedure of exemption remains ethically problematic, since it recapitulates the honorific cultural code of the innocent victim and thereby unwittingly concedes, in structural terms, not just a natural but also a cultural rule of violence. Influenced by the sociological premises of victimology in arguing for a moral responsibility centered inescapably in a perpetrator's intentions, Lang gives perhaps too much credibility to distinctions perpetrators regularly make with regard to their victims, and even allows "that there may be differences among wrongdoers in respect to the measure of humanity they acknowledge in the persons of their victims." Yet in genocide, he argues, agents act toward victims in a way "that demonstrates that they have no claims as persons," which means that they can do nothing—as opposed to most other victims of violence?—to be exempted from the category under which they are perceived (AING 19).[25] This phrasing seems to me unfortunate.

Lang might have established much the same point by saying that, although the violence perpetrated in genocide is ideological, it refuses to permit the victim any space of ideological cooperation or any capacity to avert violence. By claiming, instead, that the reason for genocidal violence has no basis in "personal interest, gain, or inclination," Lang accepts the basic premise of social usefulness behind the category of victim and mystificatorily sets apart some victims from the others who suffer interpersonal, even systemic violences, whose victimization might be evaluated and qualified (again perhaps by way of the emergent sociological terms of victimology) along normative, even hypothetically reciprocal, lines.[26] The categorical exemption of Holocaust victims—who are exempted from ordinary victimization precisely by not being able on any terms to exempt themselves from the violence done to them— necessarily falls into the trap of supposing that victims of violence might well in other cases, just not in this one, be complicitous with either their sacrificial fates within the community or their hypothetical usefulness to the perpetrator.[27]

Clearly, Lang is responding to a history of dubious interpretations of the Holocaust in which victims were held accountable for what befell them, blamed sometimes for going like sheep to the slaughter or for being either too apolitical or political in the wrong way. In reasoning that there is nothing the Holocaust victim did to make himself a victim or might have done to avoid becoming one, Lang preserves for Holocaust victims the very connotation that Badiou finds to be so detrimental to modern ethics. For Badiou when it comes to those who endured the degradation of the camps, whose suffering was equated to the "animal substructure" of existence, "victim" is perhaps the least interesting thing to be said about them. With incendiary verve Badiou claims that just as man as executioner exists in "animal abjection," there is little more we might say about victims, and that, if their torturers can treat human beings like animals "destined for the slaughterhouse," it is because the "victims have indeed become such animals." Regarding those who survive such degradation, Badiou emphasizes their extraordinary effort not to coincide with "the identity of the victim," an effort that is dependent on a sense in themselves of something other than mortal or animal existence, indeed on a spirit of immortality Badiou wants to reclaim as the horizon of our self-definition and ethical existence (E 11). By desperately trying to locate a principle by which victims might be exempted from victimization and hold themselves to this side of humanity, Badiou concedes the most fundamental dimension of our cultural distrust of victims. Indeed, Badiou insists that if we are to interpret the situation of victim in cultural terms at all, we will have to discover what sets a particular victim apart from the politically effectuated fate of being returned to mere animality.

No doubt Lang's exemption of Holocaust victims from any construct of philosophical rationality in which they would preserve their dignity by means of some extraordinary, and at least partly successful, exertion is meant to avoid a falsely heroic assessment of suffering. Yet he nevertheless makes a crucial concession to the cultural logic (represented here by Badiou) expecting victims to have enough rational wherewithal to salvage their own humanity from the midst of its ruin. By declaring Holocaust victims to be uniquely victimized in the sense that they alone could do nothing to exempt themselves from victimization, Lang preserves, at least for all other victims whose bad fortune does not coincide with the Holocaust, a theory of agency that constrictively limits the phenomenology of victimization; and, by further asserting the victim's nonparticipation in her fate as a relative truth, he implicates his critique, I wish to suggest, in the veiledly sacrificial logic of so much of conventional rational inquiry. On the whole I side with Lang's vigilant defense of the victim's nonparticipation in the voluntary presumptions of morality, with this one important qualification. Surely the absence of agency Lang ascribes to Holocaust victims is attributable—at the experiential level of interpersonal violence and at a vaster systemic level in the case of other institutionalized forms of violence—to victims of violence in general. Any declaration of the innocence of some victims, as opposed to others, already partakes of a cultural logic that implicitly perceives sacrificial structures as necessary and may additionally rely on metaphysical premises of original innocence that have the function of condemning those who, though they suffer violence at others' hands, are not innocent enough to merit our sustained objection to the violence done to them. In other words, Lang's distinction saves over for the victim of genocide an innocence of and about any precipitating responsibility for the violence done to her that ought be applied to victims of violence in general or not at all.

LEVINAS AND THE QUESTION OF VICTIM-SUBJECTIVITY

Although our efforts to respond to atrocity by bringing rational inquiry back into balance with moral accountability may seem an understandable, perhaps even a necessary practice (required for the pragmatic implementation of norms), it often leads to a distortion of the victim's perspective. With this concern in mind I return to Levinas. By suggesting that knowledge, intentionality, and agency are inadequate to the anterior facticity of responsibility, Levinas contests rationality's dominion over morality, imagining an ethical space that might more properly be called the victim's own. Much of Levinas's description of the ethical relation, I have maintained, is owing to the Holocaust, and his theorization of a subjectivity standing not so much upon self-knowledge as upon perpetual passivity can even be read, at least in part, as an attempt to recover the subject-positionality of the historical victim. According to the latent figurative status of the victim in Levinas's account of subjectivity, rationality's persistent effort to consider the victim through the lens of agency is challenged in advance, if on no other grounds than this: such a commitment seemingly conflates victims and perpetrators by making them part of a decipherable social equation. Conceiving subjectivity as given over to an unstated command that is prior even to rationality, Levinas suggests a trajectory in which reason itself must be unaligned with our narratives for agency, beginning instead from critique, from the challenge of exteriority, from a radical passivity akin to a victim's absence of self-determinative possibility.

I do not depend on Levinas simply to correct Lang (much of Lang's pragmatic philosophical consequentialism could just as well serve as a corrective to Levinas's often impractical, idealist phrasings) but rather to deepen the problem of the victim's status within rationality. Levinas's sensitivity on this front seems to me distinctive but certainly not irreproachable. Although along the way he deeply qualifies the cultural tendency to interpret a victim's fate as though it were part of rationality's vocation, he also includes himself, perhaps inevitably, in a cultural tendency to configure victims and perpetrators. When Levinas says frequently that suffering for another is to have charge of him or that the meaning of subjectivity is the substitutive connotation of one-for-the-other, he turns the hypothetical victim, who is the subject in pure passivity, toward an ethical meaning, implicitly reinscribing upon the victim a social function. A technique of conversion, even a premise of usefulness, necessarily sustains such a rhetorical trajectory. Even though the signifying force of ethics is supposed to be absolutely anterior to socially realized forms of responsibility for the historical events upon which obligations are tested, ethics is also necessarily a site of sociality, so that the line between what ethics determines and what it is determined by is hard to preserve.

The background of the Holocaust victim is relevant here, and the double bind by which I have characterized Lang's account of the Holocaust victim may have a special bearing upon our account of Levinasian ethics. For, if Lang's moral philosophical explication of the question of agency within the context of the Holocaust details a history of failed responsibility to be examined under the premise that consciousness of their moral wrong or failure remained available at least to the perpetrators, Levinas accuses the Western philosophical tradition of a general moral failure, with the Holocaust serving as both his most poignant example and quite plausibly the culminating proof of that failure. Did philosophy do enough to avert the social trajectory—as we consider, for instance, Hegel's implicit antisemitism or Heidegger's complicity with Nazism—that led to the Holocaust? According to Levinas, philosophical knowledge, by running parallel to the cultural logic predicated upon violence, gets implicated in historical violence and fails the vocation of responsibility. Lang's supposition is that a perpetrator's knowledge qua intention might somehow stand, if only by its deeply negative meaning, as the only adequate term for moral responsibility—an answer, as it were, to the victim's cry.[28] Yet already for Levinas cognition as a mode of seeing and possession is a reduction of responsibility, a process of selectively admitting, even violently claiming for oneself, the anterior fact of relationship. It is the spuriousness of all such readily knowledgeable claims to be adequate to responsibility that Levinas calls into question via those particular failures of responsibility witnessed in the Holocaust. Undoing the harmony of knowledge and moral act, Levinas supposes that the meaning of ethics always precedes the rational, deliberative choice to act rightly or wrongly.

Ethics in the Levinasian connotation entirely disrupts the intentional sequence of idea and act; it is the gap between representation and the other to whom we respond, an *inadequation* in the terms of responsibility and intention, of responsibility and act. Whereas Lang revises the chronological ordering of idea and act to suggest that intention may be an aspect of the act itself, Levinas theorizes an a-chronology in which ethics arises anterior to the intentionally performed action, always also surpassing the event of knowledge. Not only does the other come to be signified in her noncooperation with intention and desire, but she will be paradoxically encountered according to the play between the figurative poles of perpetrator and victim, a trajectory predicted by the dedication of *Otherwise than Being* (1974): "To the memory of those who were closest among the six million assassinated by the National Socialists, and of the millions on millions of all confessions and all nations, victims of the same hatred of the other man, the same anti-semitism." Following upon the dedication, Levinas incorporates that explicit memory of the Holocaust's victims in the paradoxical turns of his argument, as, for example, when he speaks of the other who signifies simultaneously as generosity and violence: "Here the blow of the affection makes an impact, traumatically, in a past more profound than all that I can reassemble by memory, by historiography, all that I can dominate by the a priori—in a time before the beginning" (*OTB* 88). Leveraging the figurative force of trauma so as to signify the inability of knowledge to appropriate the demand of responsibility, Levinas, like Lang, filters intentionality through the figure of the perpetrator and then criticizes any such intentional flow by bringing the agent of violence up short of his power over the other. An other who always escapes and surpasses the encounter, as well as any aim of the agent, reveals the inadequacies of our conscious formulations of relationship. Thus, by a supremely anti-Hegelian formulation, not only are the perpetrator's intentions inadequate to his responsibility for the victim prior to any action he might take against her, but the victim also remains inadequate to her own subjective formulations (say, when she conceptualizes her resistance to or cooperation with violence) and finds herself instead signified by ethical relationship as by the very violence that may be done to her. This last move is perhaps the most surprising and, certainly from the perspective of moral philosophy (not to mention, say, a feminist politics), the most troubling. As such it provides an impetus for much of the critical reading that follows.

Levinas describes what I want to call the *cultural attitude of violence*, which necessarily turns on the question of perpetration. A perpetrator's attitude matters ethically in the sense that an agent's intention is never transparent and must be inferred from the cultural positions he occupies and the history of actions expanding, revising, or creating those positions. Imagining an ethics not naïvely set against patterns

of cultural violence, since such resistance is as often evasive as it is critical of violence, Levinas interprets ethics as within, if also before, the violences that give
expression to its necessity.[29] The problem quickly becomes whether ethics' necessity can ever be separated from the seemingly necessary rule of violence in culture.
Does ethics require the violence to which it would object? Or, to put it more cau-
tiously, can ethics be defined only under the duress of violence?

Strictly speaking, Levinas's answer to these two versions of the same question is
no—as, for example, in *Totality and Infinity* (1961) and *Difficult Freedom* (1963)
he argues that the face of the other declares the *impossibility* of murder. Attributing
to the face a transcendent value, exceptional within representation and culture,
Levinas describes in "Ethics and Spirit" (1952) the paradoxical consequence of the
face's significance: "The Other is the only being that one can be tempted to kill. This
temptation to murder and this impossibility of murder constitute the very vision of
the face. To see a face is already to hear, 'You shall not kill. . . .'"[30] And yet (as Jill
Robbins emphasizes) the ethical force of the face does involve at least this one command, borrowed from language. In this singular utterance the otherwise transcendently signified face succumbs to history, wherein violence is not merely a metaphysical potentiality within language but an event attached specifically to the
agentive hypothesis of subjectivity—which is to say also, part of a will that gets concretized in a perpetrator's actions. In this sense our query as to whether or not ethics
arises from the occasion of violence seems an irrelevant speculation precisely because
it is an ahistorical one. Even in that original allegory of violent sociality—the story
of Cain's murder of Abel—the face is necessarily, if also impossibly, inscribed in
relationships that have been historically realized through violence. While Levinas
allows murder to signify a capability or agency located in history against the meaning of ethics, he also argues conversely that, if murder is a face's relentless, historical matter of course, ethics begins from the face, in the historical context of the violence that may be done to the other.

Much as Lang conceives the genocidal intention morally on the lesser scale of
murder, Levinas's figurative description of the ethical relation in the context of
murderous intention employs a similarly synecdochal stratagem that already supposes an alignment of history and violence apparently determined by the conceit of
perpetrated violence.[31] It is from this direction—or misdirection—that in an essay
such as "Freedom and Command" (1953) we find the concern of subjectivity imagined along the lines of a perpetrator's, or murderer's, intentional gaze: "Violence is
a way of acting on every being and every freedom by approaching it from an indirect
angle" (FC 19).[32] Violence in its etymological connotation of willfulness belongs
especially to the perpetrator, and so the ethical signification of the other arises before,

though also in the midst of, violence as a critique of the perpetrator's intentionality. Performing what Robbins describes as a mistake against the face, violence avoids the real signification of the ethical relation, the straightforwardness (*droiture*) of the face-to-face encounter. Violence in this connotation is the relation of not facing.[33] In other words, ethics would appear to arise as though it were signified by a perpetrator's act of losing sight of ethical meaning, as a variation on the motif of bad conscience given such prominence in Levinas's later work.

Thus, the conceit of murder, according to Levinas's account in *Totality and Infinity*, shows us ethics as what Robbins calls an "intentionality in reverse" (67), the other functioning as an implicit intention against or before my intentions, be they murderous or generous.[34] As a seemingly accidental connotation of an intentionality arising in the act or figure of violence, the other proves her alterity as an exception to the claim of violence. For this reason Levinas speaks of the face of the other as a non-phenomenon, signified in a proximity of which I become conscious necessarily in error: "My reaction misses a present which is already the past of itself" (*OTB* 88). The other's proximity sets her apart from "a conjunction in cognition and intentionality in which subject and object enter," and Levinas finds a figure for the other in the tenderness of the skin, saying that this tenderness of the skin "is the very gap between approach and approached, a disparity, a non-intentionality, a non-teleology." This critique of intentionality, which involves "a defecting of the intentional correlation of disclosure," occurs via the interplay of the other and the subject, as an interstice in language inscribed upon every formal realization of intention (*OTB* 90). In moving from the individual to a collective scale, such a defection becomes oddly a kind of allegory for history.

Even if asserting the impossibility of murder amounts to a correction of violence, it also means, quite obviously, renouncing the evidence of history. Thus, in its mournful valence ethics opposes history by perhaps all too transparently attempting to spare the other the violence he suffers in history, as though Levinas concluded that, as long as murder does not become finally meaningful, its status as realized historical event might be doubted. Insisting upon the mistake of murder, Levinas declares that the alterity of the other can never be contained or appropriated by the violence enacted against him, since "murder exercises a power over what escapes power" (*TI* 198).[35] At first glance such a logic seems cartoonish (the declaration of the character who after being shot at claims, "You missed me," and drinks a glass of water, only to have the water run fountain-like through the bullet holes in his body), or, if less comical, nevertheless a transparently wishful revisionism by which the impossibility of murder corresponds with the metaphoric transcendence of the face, which eludes in its significance alone any action by which it would be possessed or destroyed. In this way an unrealism foregrounds ethics. But what defense could such super-ethical meanings provide against systemic injustice, genocide, or the Nazi ideological war against memory and evidence? And, according to the critique of ethics offered by history and its particular violences, could ethics ever avoid becoming an escape from history? Still, we will miss the point if we wonder only how the violence done to the victim is to be stopped before it happens or if we are dedicated to a no less wishful hypothesis in which the perpetrator can be retrospectively returned to moral intentionality in order to be turned toward moral responsibility. Much as Berel Lang declared that in genocide "the victim is no longer, except in an accidental physical sense, a person at all" (*AING* 20), Levinas addresses the evident historical possibility of such a cancellation of the person by placing ethics in a merely accidental relation to intention and to historically realized actions, as he imagines that the humanity of the other, whose vulnerability signifies ethics, must by definition be saved over from both the murderous intention and the physical assault on his being.

From the standpoint of a practical ethics the danger here is that by such imaginative maneuvering we might simultaneously un-write the objective plight of the victim. Thus, Levinas insists upon a coincidence of the victim's fate and ethical meaning, which is arrived at in the situation of practical defenselessness—not only in historical connotation but by the very principle that assigns him a value greater than his historically determined being. Characterizing the other in the literality of his defenselessness, in *vulnerability*, *nakedness* (or the exposure of skin), *poverty* (or destituteness), *hunger*, and *suffering*, Levinas imagines an other who is unprotected to the point of dehumanization, without even the solace of what Blanchot calls the "guardian thought" of rationality. Whereas such historically realized conditions might appear to invent potentially recognizable, if often falsifying similarities between a victim and perpetrator, Levinas supposes that to recognize similarities even in retrospect would be to appropriate the radical difference of victims, and so he implicitly deploys the opposition *victim/perpetrator* as an uncompromised antinomy likened to the gap of alterity itself, which inspires ethics, which perceives in conditions such as *persecution* and *torture* and *trauma* figurative signifiers of the ethical relation. This is a crucial point: for Levinas the other qua victim signifies from within the moment of his inhumanity, his inhumanity both an extension of his vulnerability and the occasion of another subject's responsibility.

Ultimately, what surprises us in Levinas is his inversion of a more familiar aspect of our moral culture—that the perpetrator should remain the locus of the responsibility for the victim—in order to claim exactly the opposite, that a victim is often the locus of responsibility for a perpetrator. If responsibility arises as a trauma or through persecution or through a passivity akin to being taken hostage, its only proper center is the victim, which leads to a surprising formulation whereby "passivity deserves the epithet of complete or absolute only if the persecuted one is liable to answer for the persecutor" (*OTB* 111). Even more disturbing perhaps than Levinas's willingness to render the suffering of the subject qua victim ethically purposeful in this way is that, within his presentation of the face-to-face relation under the figurative auspices of the perpetrator and victim, Levinas frequently confuses and inverts historical subject positions, as though it were the victim who had to accept responsibility also for the historical event, as though it were possible to attribute to Levinas the belief, as Philippe Nemo in fact does, that "the Jew is culpable for Auschwitz" (196).[36] About such an interpretive formulation we must at least concede that it paraphrases, perhaps slightly in caricature, the paradoxical status of the victim within Levinasian ethics. To the extent that the scandal of the victim attaches to her passivity—and this is the reason why she must be so often redefined in culture via an imaginative hypothesis of knowledge or resistance—Levinas rejects the straightforward scandalousness of passivity, arguing implicitly that the victim is a sign of ethics just as passivity is ethics' proper mode. Such a passivity does not, by Levinas's account, make one vulnerable to violence so much as it presumes that the other already vulnerably endures the reality of violence. Although ethics is not undertaken directly as a principle of witness, as a vocation of martyrdom, as sacrifice in any conventional sense, the cultural influence of sacrificial logic is at least residually traced in such a formulation, and never more so within Levinas's canon than in his discussion of *substitution* as the conceit for responsibility.

JUST WHO SUBSTITUTES FOR ANOTHER?

The 1968 essay "Substitution," based on a 1967 lecture, is commonly understood to mark a turning point in the Levinasian project, preparing the way for the larger argument of *Otherwise than Being*. We could focus the shifting emphasis of the Levinasian project upon several different nodal points, but most remarkable for my present purposes is Levinas's paradoxical deconstruction in the period from 1967 to 1974 of the responsible ego as an identity even while he simultaneously offered a fuller articulation of the subject as the locus for responsibility. As Levinas frequently declares, the subject is by definition a site of responsibility and thus only meaningful within language according to that to which it is given over in advance—in a phrase, in its obsessive dedication to the other through the signifying structure of one-for-the-other. The essay "Substitution" constituted a first run at ideas Levinas would soon more fully elaborate, but as such it also provided a cornerstone for the set of ideas I have previously described as an ethics of unpleasure. According to the connotation Levinas gives to *substitution*, ethics is characterized at least in part from the perspective of a victim, someone who incurs the risk we would ordinarily associate with sacrifice and yet does not become a sign of violence itself, someone who refuses the honor of having her fate rationalized as though the identity of the victim and the violence she has suffered were mutually conditions of ethical purposefulness. What may also surprise us about Levinas's formulation, especially given the emergent Judaic typology of his philosophical language during the latter half of his career, is the manner in which he deploys the Christ figure as an archetypal victim in this seminal essay's rhetorical tapestry, employing a Christological conceit thereafter to be investigated and extended in *Otherwise than Being*.

In giving emphasis to a Christian typology operative in Levinas's work, I am not proposing that the Jewish biblical sources of Levinas's quasi-sacrificial notion of substitution should be ignored. Much work has already been done to trace Levinas's philosophical thought to eminent Jewish sources; more remains to be done analyzing not only the productive impact of Jewish tradition upon his ethics but also the detrimental consequences of certain unexamined modes of Jewish religious thought in Levinas's work.[37] I concentrate my discussion of Levinas's implication in the sacrificial structure of religious thought, however, on his relation to Christian typology because, in the first place, I assume the necessary imbrication of Jewish and Christian religiosity within the cultural context of a Christianized, still Christianizing West never quite free of its original supersessionist designs on Judaism; and because, in the second, by demonstrating Levinas's complicity with certain aspects of Christian sacrificial logic I hope to make the liability of his religious conceits more evident and further emphasize the inherent problems of all martyrological constructs whether inherited through Judaism or Christianity. My argument, although it overlaps at a few significant points with Philippe Nemo's dialogic critique of Levinas, runs counter to Nemo's explicit goal of showing how much Levinasian ethics owes its profundity to the surprising contention, inspired by Christ, that a human being should repair the damage he has not done. Nemo also holds that Levinas approaches this radical formulation, but argues that he brings his ethics up short of the truly generous reparation of Christ's sacrifice. On both points Nemo's logic is obviously Christianizing. Yet Nemo's apparent sympathy for Levinas's work may also indicate that, insofar as Levinasian ethics intuits the particular of responsibility within the situation of violence or evil, it retains something close to a sacrificial logic that Nemo, according to his own revisionary relation to redemptive eschatology, must approve.

Nemo's sympathetic critique of Levinas emerged in response to Levinas's review of Nemo's *Job and the Excess of Evil* (1978), in the form of an essay entitled "Transcendence and Evil" (1978) first published in *Le Nouveau Commerce*. Nemo's book is relevant to my discussion not least of all for its opening gambit that his commentary is not about evil as "social injustice, the suffering of prisoners in camps, the suffering of whole peoples immolated in modern wars" (1), but, rather, about the individuality of suffering. In turning from the Holocaust, he also turns more precisely from interpretations of injustice purporting to analyze the phenomenon of widespread suffering through the norms of collectivist, poststructuralist thought, which by emphasizing the generic aspect of existence treat the human person as anonymously subjected to often oppressive social principles.[38] Instead, Nemo focuses on the element of excess in each individual's anxious experience of evil, such that an individual discovers that, Job-like, she has been singled out for suffering, as if by that which is entirely outside herself and yet possesses additionally the quality of an intention. Most important, in the response to such evil, in the fact of our being horrified by evil, Nemo discerns the possibility of our aligning with the Good. Only the excess or beatitude of the Good can compete with evil's excess, and thus evil's transcendent dimension demands that the Good be generated as greater than the mere opposite of evil, as a supervening, entirely generous, yet individuated transcendence.

In "Transcendence and Evil," imitating the first step of a deconstructive critique, Levinas produces a commentary that mostly recapitulates Nemo's original text, although already through Levinas's own peculiar philosophical lens. For the most part Levinas but gestures, after declaring that he will not suggest "improvements" to Nemo, at a contradiction that might render Nemo's argument finally unsustainable. In Nemo's insight that God's reprimand of Job, "Where were you?" might impose itself as a "record of truancy" by which Job (as the representative man) would be made responsible even for what was not his work and thus stand within a "solidarity" and "responsibility for everything and for everyone," Levinas discerns the influence of his own philosophy (or, at the very least, "an idea which is familiar and dear to us" [TE 180]).[39] By way of commentary, Levinas gives a supplementary emphasis to the relation between "the evil suffered by another person" and that which "afflicts me in the evil that pursues me," assuming that Nemo's individuated anxiety cannot reliably apprehend responsibility for the victim except by being breached, or broken in upon, by the relational dimension of sociality (TE 181). According to the interruptive forcefulness of the "Good which is not pleasant," Levinas specifically refutes the compensatory, counterbalancing logic of Nemo's argument, in which evil would find itself rivaled by the Good as though by recuperative design, as though it were especially and only God who could recognize and judge the experiential quality of the evil humanity endures (TE 181–82). By contrast, Levinas insists upon an anti-redemptive plot for responsibility, and a few years later he would extend his critical dialogue with Nemo's postmodern Christianity, acknowledging a debt to Nemo in a highly significant footnote on the figure of Job, in the essay "Useless Suffering" (1982).

Nemo also responded to Levinas in an appendix titled "To Pursue the Dialogue with Levinas," which accompanied Levinas's review essay in the 1998 English edition of the book on Job. In that short essay Nemo explicitly takes up the question of the Christological dimensions of his own method and proposes a mode of reading that might pass beyond dogmatic religiosity in order to secure—via the insights of a secular rationalism he at one point upholds by way of reference to Girard's anthropological, demystificatory hermeneutic—the truthfulness of the Christ story apart from the predisposition of biblical faith. Nemo's method, like Girard's, is never quite free of Christianized bias, and yet he conducts his argument as though it were. Arguing for a resemblance between his own work and Levinas's at the level of ethical sensibility and yet quarreling specifically with Levinas's refusal to locate the Good in any pleasurable or salvific plot, Nemo insists that, while Levinas allows for the paradoxical sense in which the particular human being may be inadequate to her responsibility, he also defines ethics as though there can be no remission from this situation. Acknowledging thereafter Levinas's criticism of him for having failed to put the other's suffering in the foreground, Nemo retorts that for his part Levinas has failed to understand how a subject's suffering, whether in the situation of the persecuted Holocaust victim or of the symbolic Jew bound by a Law not freely contracted, might be a "burden that has become too heavy" (197). This unmistakably Pauline gesture accuses Levinas of having overextended responsibility so much so that it might approximate punishment, of altogether failing to allow for the point at which responsibility might relinquish its vigilance and rely on a mediation that supplements the subject's own efforts.[40] Although Levinas and Nemo both owe an obvious debt to the sacrificial logics of Judaism and Christianity, respectively, Nemo worries, with the self-assurance of the Christian who assumes that redemption already precedes him, that the hyper-responsible subject of Levinasian ethics, who otherwise adopts the wider vocation of the human being under Christian kerygma, will fail to see her way clear to a productive vision of sociality by failing to have foreseen the necessary lapsing of evil or suffering.

In both Nemo and Levinas responsibility remains in a crucial sense under the sign of sacrifice, which runs more or less continuously from Judaism to Christianity, or even vice versa. Without eliding the difference between Jewish and Christian martyrologies, I assume—with Daniel Boyarin, for instance—their necessary imbrication within Western culture. According to Boyarin, the theological figure of the martyr elaborated by Judaism in a post-Christ world depended historically on a complicated intertextual hermeneutics by which Jewish martyrological stories were developed alongside narratives about Christian sacrificial victims or triumphantly self-sacrificing martyrs, and at least until the fourth century the borders between the two religions were "so fuzzy" as to make distinguishing one from the other extremely difficult.[41] In this light any turn to the Jewish martyr or victim must also work from within the Christianized context of the West, cued perhaps by nothing less than a cultural anxiety, such as the one Levinas gives voice to in "Hegel and the Jews" (1971), about being swallowed up by even the most generously inclusive versions of Christian typology. According to the allegorical procedures of Christian exegesis, so many of the central figures of the Hebrew Bible, such as Abraham, Job, Jonah, and the suffering servant, came to be viewed (through the better light of Christianity) as ancestral in a purely antecedent sense. At least some of Levinas's highly respectful disagreement with Nemo is based, then, upon Nemo's overly Christianized view of Job's suffering, as Levinas objects in largely philosophical terms to an exegesis that yields Job forward to the redemptive plot Christianity imposed upon all suffering; and, even as Levinas professes a reluctance to improve upon Nemo, he gives notice that he will not imitate a Christianized hermeneutic whereby one gains the upper hand by appearing to have superseded one's interlocutor through a superior mode of belief, if not necessarily of argument.

Despite the obvious evidence for Levinas's resistance to Christian typology, I am arguing that Levinas does nevertheless in a highly sustained manner draw upon the figure of Christ in imagining the substitutive vocation of ethics. Unlike Nemo who finds Levinas's ethical thought at its best to be close in spirit to the Sermon on the Mount promulgated by the Matthean Jesus, I locate this structural imbrication as an allusive pattern within Levinas's text, and I do not assume that the effect of resemblance is to move Levinas closer in any positive sense to the structure of Christian thought. Levinas's allusions to Christ do, however, suggest a more complex, ambivalent, and potentially compromised relation between Levinas's thought and the Christian paradigm of victimization, and, if there is more than just resemblance here, the allusiveness may trace a revisionary complaint that, even as it revisits Christian sacrificial structure, provides us with a refined critical lens for viewing the enduring cultural appeal of sacrifice. But we must admit simultaneously that, insofar as Levinasian thought remains embedded in what it criticizes and gets drawn back within the orbit of Christianity and the apparent cultural prestige of the paramount sacrificial victim, such resemblance may have the effect of reinforcing Levinas's complicity with the cultural logic of sacrifice. As I have already argued with regard to Lang, the cultural logic of sacrifice is the ground for all ethical arguments for exemption, so that even those places where Levinas might locate ethical exemptions obtained through suffering can never quite elude the problematic political consequences of a cultural logic already steeped in the privileges of exemption. In this sense, Levinas's occasional strategy of exempting Israel or Jewish thought from pragmatic political analysis—say, in those instances in which Levinas compares Israel to the figure of the suffering servant—becomes less sustainable not only ideologically but, as I hope to show, ethically.[42] And his contradictory estimations of Christ as victim become a sign of the difficulty that befalls almost every interpretation of the victim.

The victim is implicit early on in the 1968 essay "Substitution" when Levinas, attempting to define a subject's ethical obsession as based in the other's proximity, starts to imagine how consciousness might be structured other than through freedom. Whether freedom is understood to emanate from a phenomenological, existentialist, or simply liberal rubric, it always supposes an ego who chooses her own actions, inheriting and including exteriority only to the extent that she is able to do so—which is also to say, only after exteriority has already been intuited. For instance, existentialism had discerned responsibility as that which must be embraced other than as dutiful obligation but only after an individual has fitted herself to a course of self-transcendence and imagined, perhaps for the first time, others as truly equal individuals projected along the same course. Against the heroic emphasis of the existentialist project, Levinas insists that the meaning of the subject resides in passivity. Speculating about how best to articulate a subject's relation to an exteriority it cannot assume by choice, Levinas asks, "How can there be in consciousness an undergoing, or a Passion, whose 'active' source would not in any way fall into consciousness?"[43] Lest we miss the Christological note here, Levinas continues in the very next paragraph to speak of "the Passion" as "absolute in that it takes hold without any a priori" and then further associates it with the signifying force of persecution, asking how "such a Passion" might obtain a place in time and consciousness (S 82). The answer to this last query is not Christianity's too simple answer—on a cross, in about 33 A.D. Still, though Christ is never directly mentioned in the essay—and I am certainly not implying that Levinas ought to be read as a Catholic manqué (although the fact that his wife and daughter were hidden during World War II by Catholic nuns probably inspired an aspect of gratefulness in his use of Christian imagery, and the Catholic hierarchy's subsequent approval of much of Levinas's work would seem to suggest that the philosopher's quasi-Catholic language was not entirely lost on Christian audiences)—the invocation of Christ's anguish is unmistakable. Indeed, for Levinas the Catholic focus on Christ's anguish, though it frequently veers (from a Jewish perspective) toward the twin heretical practices of idolatry and iconography, nevertheless discerns the fate of every subject as having been already dedicated, in his or her suffering, on behalf of others.

The task of the essay "Substitution," then, is to define subjectivity apart from the social trajectory of identity, as prior to the retentive, reflective capacities of subjective consciousness. In Levinas's terms there is thus a recurrence in oneself, akin to a contraction, a materiality of self which is yet distinct from Maurice Merleau-Ponty's existentialist emphasis on embodiedness. This sacrificial quality, inscribed as the recurrence of subjectivity, carries with it further echoes of the Christ myth. It is hard to say just how much significance we ought to attach to Levinas's description of a subject "ill at ease in [its] skin" or "immolated without taking leave of itself" (S 86), but the vestiges of sacrificial myth seem (indeed, are meant to seem) inescapable. Such mock-sacrificial language contributes to Levinas's exposition of the subject's passive unfolding into responsibility and of the extraordinary nature of all responsibility. Since the responsible subject is "accused of what it did not do," defined from without by a "persecuting accusation," Levinas assumes and adopts the crucial paradox whereby Christ's passion proves meaningful only because he is not someone who, as a matter of personal history, can possibly deserve what happens to him (S 88).

From the historico-sociological perspective, if we grant even reluctant credence to René Girard's interpretation of the gospels, the originality of an otherwise so obviously unoriginal story of human sacrifice derives from the fact the Christ myth insists upon the absolute innocence of its paradigmatically redemptive victim. Girard's privileging of the Christ story at least implicitly partakes of a Catholic supersessionist reading of Judaism, and it also leads him to underestimate the anti-Judaic dimensions of the original gospel texts, an oversight made only more conspicuous when Girard dismissed anxieties about the antisemitism of Mel Gibson's film *The Passion of the Christ* (2004) as all but irrelevant to the film's meaning.[44] Although Girard has spoken of the Job story and the lore of Isaiah's suffering servant as anticipatory of the gospels in their dedication to the innocence of sacrificial victims, even in these progressive Hebrew texts, he supposes, religious logic requires that the seeming innocence of the victim also be a sign of relative culpability. Job is redeemed because he submits not just to God's authority but to the knowledge of his relative guilt. Lacking God's glory, Job is guilty, if only by contrast to divinity.[45] Only according to the schizophrenic subject-positionality of the Christ myth, by which the audience perceives the sacrificial victim from the outside as a sign of its own sinfulness (a logic more or less consistent with myth) and imaginatively presumes the perfected innocence of the singular victim (a logic of redemptive exoneration), does the victim's absolute innocence factor as part of his social significance.

I will return to the problematic social implications of Christ's innocence shortly, but for now I wish to emphasize simply that Christ assumes responsibility for the sins of others by a metaphoric extension or application of his innocence. According to the

Christian paschal mystery Christ redeems humanity's sin, conquering death as the one who alone does not deserve to die and as the one who according to Catholic theology was conceived free from the taint of original sin. Neither of these two theological principles is highly significant in Levinas's revisionary appropriation of the Christ myth, except by its absence. Perhaps fearing that his ethical logic has become too intertwined with the language of Christian soteriology, Levinas shortly hereafter insists that by suffering he does not mean "humiliating oneself" and does not refer to the "magical power of atonement" (S 90). His qualification notwithstanding, Levinas has nevertheless carried over a central mechanism of the Christ myth—specifically, its notion of Christ's limitless responsibility, as one who bears the burden of all humanity's sinfulness and makes himself responsible for it by way of a substitution: namely, Christ-for-the-others. Having described a de-Christologized subject who bears the weight of the world, "answerable for everything and for everyone" (S 90), Levinas closes his essay by reemphasizing the link between the responsible subject's passivity and the conceit of the Passion, which he has earlier referred to as the "passivity of the Passion of the self," incessantly substituting for others (S 91). Describing a subject who is hostage for others, Levinas implicitly alludes to the Christian theology of the hostage and its appropriation of the political eschatology of Isaiah's suffering servant for use in an otherworldly soteriological plot. Yet, insofar as Christ is, to borrow Calvin's locution, *ransomed* for humanity, a substitute for the truly culpable one whose sins he expiates, he must also be responsible for his persecutors, much in the way Levinas describes the ethical subject as "substitutable for the persecutor" (S 94).[46]

Again, in thus far tracing implicitly Christological conceits from a cornerstone essay in Levinas's canon, I have not aimed toward Christianizing, or even theologizing, Levinas's philosophy. The occasions upon which Levinas speaks directly against Christianity should be enough to prevent any misunderstanding on this point. Yet, as should be at least partially evident in his dialogue with Nemo and also obvious in lectures and interviews Levinas gave throughout the 1970s and 1980s, he fashioned himself an advocate of Judeo-Christian dialogue, which in a post-Holocaust era Christians had finally begun to undertake in a truly interlocutive spirit; and his apparent striving for the grounds of cooperativeness generated at least a few extraordinary examples of ecumenical conflation. In a 1985 interview with Myriam Anissimov, for instance, Levinas gratefully recalls Blanchot's reverence for Israel and then declares that the "*shoah*—the passion of Israel in the sense in which one speaks of the passion of Christ—is the moment when humanity began to bleed through the wounds of Israel."[47] As in the 1968 essay, the invocation of Christological language refers Levinasian ethics to a Christian cultural context, but it seems odd that Levinas does not greatly trouble his own use of Christological conceit.

As he intermittently incorporates the language of the Passion throughout "Substitution," alluding to the Christ myth as if it provided a textural density without ever obtaining the status of a fully interlocutive text, there is a seeming innocence to Levinas's use of metaphor on this front. Left largely unaddressed are the problems such obviously religious borrowings (what is more, borrowings from another religion) bring upon Levinas's work. Quite plausibly, Levinas wished to draw upon the mutual prestige of the Jewish and Christian traditions to counterbalance contemporary formulations of "unconditional freedom" (S 90), as well as Hobbesian-inspired theories about the self-interested antagonisms informing reason's sovereignty: "It is through the condition of being a hostage that there can be pity, compassion, pardon, and proximity in the world—even the little there is, even the simple 'after you sir.' All the transfers of sentiment which theorists of original war and egoism use to explain the birth of generosity (it isn't clear, however, that there was war at the beginning; before wars there were altars) could not take root in the ego were it not, in its entire being, or rather its entire nonbeing, subjected not to a category, as in the case of matter, but to an unlimited accusative, that is to say, persecution, self, hostage, already substituted for others" (S 91). If Hobbes is the target here, this is nonetheless an astonishing passage, if only for the offhand remark that casual politeness is genealogically indebted to a historical possibility that any one of us could be taken hostage by a person who passes through the door ahead of us. Even more poignant is the parenthetical speculation about the originality of altars, reflecting the author's stunningly naïve investment (at least on this particular occasion) in the mythic coverings of the Hebraic and Christian scriptures. Even if one reads a story such as the binding of Isaac as resisting the social practice of human sacrifice and attempting to divest the requirements of violence from religious praxis, the biblical story is already steeped in the historical consciousness that altars are indeed places of violence (one gets to the ram by passing over the innocent human victim not without at least spilling some blood, if only from a substitutive animal victim). To suppose that the altar itself has not also been a site for discerning basic historical incompatibilities with foreigners is to remain uninstructed by the sociology of religion, as though the famous scene from 1 Samuel 5 (in which the covenant is placed alongside the idol Dagon, with the pagan false god repeatedly tumbling to the ground while no one is looking) were not also meant as a parable confessing the element of social antagonism that defines any altar or temple as the locus for national spirit.[48]

There is a further problem attaching to Levinas's implicitly Christological borrowings—specifically, the plot of salvific economy, within which the victim's suffering is both a necessity and an effective expiation. Let me summarize the Christian soteriological economy as briefly as I can by way of reference to Karl Barth, among the most esteemed of the Reformed tradition's twentieth-century theologians, whose relatively high Christology serves for my purpose as a bridge between Catholic sacrificial logic and the Protestant theory of justification. In the fourth volume of the *Church Dogmatics*, entitled *The Doctrine of Reconciliation* (1953), Barth presumes that the righteousness of God must be realized in the posture of judgment, thus corresponding to the "wrong of man, to man as a wrongdoer."[49] An original logic of punishment seems as unavoidable as it is persistent in the plot of redemption, so that God's justice is based on the dual suppositions that man as a wrongdoer should die and that it is God's will that man should yet be maintained (by God) in death. Into the very place of the man who should be responsible for his own sinfulness Jesus enters benevolently, performing an act that Barth describes as "the self-substitution of God for us sinful men" (*DR* 550). Christ's substitution is at the center of the theology of incarnation, crucifixion, and resurrection, yet Barth neatly summarizes the economic logic by which Jesus is the necessary sacrificial object, the only one who could perform an act of expiation precisely because he occupies the subject-position of judge, still pursuing God's case against humankind, even as he also conducts the case of the judged on their behalf: "In order that He may be for them what they cannot be for themselves—an active subject and a passive object in that conflict" (*DR* 551). We cannot overestimate the importance of this supplemental extravagance in the redemptive scheme: an ordinary victim, someone who as a human being is necessarily also a wrongdoer, is inadequate to the narrative logic of sacrificial redemption precisely because he cannot stand properly as an advocate on his own behalf.

According to Barth's musing, all human beings "had to suffer this, but they could not suffer it," since if any one of them had been made to suffer singularly the judgment of God, he could not have also suffered it for the others, and, furthermore, "even if they were willing and able to do so, how could they who have given offence, suffering merely what they have deserved, banish the offence from the world by their death, even their eternal death?" (*DR* 553). God's judgment is purportedly such that any human being must succumb to it, as within a relation of absolute inequivalence, able to bear up under it only so long as God chooses not to enact what genuine justice requires. The economic requirements of divine justice are too severe for humanity. And thus it follows that anyone who would stand accused by God must necessarily suffer punishment and the fate of a victim as the only possible result. In other words, the absolute inequivalence between human being and God requires the victim position. Because the ordinary human victim could do nothing to recuperate his obvious ontological disadvantage, Jesus Christ acts as the substitute who can doubly withstand judgment because, in the first place, he has not deserved his fate and because, more significantly for Barth, he is himself a participant in divine right-

eousness, hypothetically capable of contesting God as an equal party and yet yielding himself, in the place of properly condemned humanity, to the results of sin,
which are judgment and death.[50]

What I wish to emphasize here is that Christ is at once a singularly pure victim
(since he is perfectly innocent of any wrong for which he suffers) and not a victim
at all (since he participates in the principle of judgment by which he himself is
judged). From a purely sociological standpoint, putting aside the speculation about
what God's justice would require, I would suggest that any redemptive theology
must always seek to overcome the scandal of the victim, as one who dies and suffers
undeservedly. The divinely invested Jesus Christ, who proceeds from God and takes
both God's part and humanity's, restores the aspect of agency seemingly absent in
the moment of crucifixion, and the excruciating cries of the dying Markan or
Matthean Jesus quoting Psalm 22 ("My God, my God, why hast thou forsaken me?")
are finally subsumed by his theologically presumptive knowledge as well as by his
active participation in his own fate (Mark 15:34 and Matt. 27:46, KJV). Seeing Jesus
Christ as Judge restores the illusion of agency in his victimlike fate: just who substitutes for the others is an absolutely just being—in other words, not just anyone but
only a just one. By "act[ing] passively," as Barth phrases it, Christ takes upon himself a set of meanings in which the significance of his innocence coincides with his
humiliation, "the act of His lowly obedience" (DR 555). Yet this spectral agency, the
premise of a theological action that is paradoxically passive, also revises the fate of
all victims, who though no longer required to be victims by God's righteousness
remain signs of a justice that contradicts the very hypothesis of their innocence.
Once the perfectly innocent victim has been crucified, the innocence of all victims
seems either exceptional or incidental, since this truest of all victims acted in the
midst of—indeed, as an expression of—his apparent passivity.

The reason I have digressed briefly to offer this reading of the Christian salvific
economy is because Levinas's allusive invocation of the Passion and thus also of
Christ's substitutive responsibility must carry over at least in part (even were it to
remain entirely unacknowledged) the implicitly sociological economy in which
the victim assumes a seemingly central place only to be, effectively, displaced.
Though the continuity between the conceit of the Passion and an ethic of sacrifice
proceeds unchecked in "Substitution," Levinas pauses once, near the end, to prevent the perception that he is advocating sacrifice as a principle: "To say that the
soul should sacrifice itself for others would be to preach human sacrifice" (S 94).
Most likely, Levinas's hesitation here is informed by a tradition of both Christian
and Jewish martyrology, which gradually conflated the witness to truth with the violence done to the ones who bear such witness. Yet, in an essay otherwise harmo-

nizing a Christological conceit with the author's interpretation of suffering subjectivity, such qualification seems almost feeble. Whether or not Levinas shortly thereafter began to think better of having offered an apology for sacrifice inflected by Christological overtones is impossible to determine. What is apparent is that, in revising the essay for inclusion in his major 1974 monograph, he takes fuller account of the implications of his conceit, showing greater critical consciousness about the limits of sacrificial language, even as he carries over the essay's presiding spirit of sacrifice. As the Christological language takes on additional layers in *Otherwise than Being*, the Christ myth operates nearer to the surface of his main argument and is also subjected to a thoroughgoing, skeptical investigation, what we might call a critical revisioning of Levinas's own prior use of it. In attempting to undo our confidence in the Christological answer to victimization, Levinas deflates the aura of theological necessity or salvific economy that sanctions the sociopolitical history of victimization.

Perhaps it should not surprise us that Levinas would attempt to deploy a de-Christologized Christ as a paradigm for ethics. Nineteenth- and early-twentieth-century New Testament scholarship, followed laggingly by much Protestant theology and even more reluctantly by mainstream Catholicism, had long attempted to separate the historical Jesus from the Christ myth, believing that a rational, post-Enlightenment era had finally and forever overthrown magical thinking.[51] Skeptically supposing that the primitive Christian community could not tell the difference between the historicity of Jesus's life and its own mythic investment in its theological meaning, scholars such as Rudolf Bultmann placed central importance on the sayings and teachings of Jesus, separating the ethical purport of the gospels from that content dedicated to a crude religiosity.[52] For the most part this scholarship conducted itself independently of the severely antireligious, modern sensibility of a figure such as Nietzsche, but the "death of God" theology of the middle-twentieth-century represented a convergence of the Nietzschean line of philosophical critique and the religious revisioning of Protestant theology. When Levinas refers to the "death of God" late in the fourth chapter of *Otherwise than Being*, the reference is most obviously understood as a reference to Nietzsche, but it is every bit as likely that he has in mind the death-of-God theology's paradoxical revaluing of the gospels through the lens of contemporary skepticisms about revelatory religion.[53] Like the death-of-God theologians, Levinas treats the demise of doctrinal transcendence as an opportunity, supposing that the "death of God perhaps signifies only the possibility to reduce every value arousing an impulse to an impulse arousing a value" (*OTB* 123). As I suggested in the previous chapter, Levinas consistently revalues Nietzsche's own genealogical revaluation of morality, suggesting that the exposure

of morality's origin in the relation of power and the devastation of its logical authority only serve to discover a still more anterior aspect of ethics, that which precedes
the articulation and codifications of moral values. Levinas's firm commitment to a
de-transcendentalizing hermeneutic is further evident, for instance, in his revisioning of Buber's I-Thou paradigm, which both preceded and ran contemporary to the
death-of-God theology, similarly owing a tremendous debt to the influence of existentialism. Insofar as Levinas preserves the signifying force of a transcendence escaping ordinary knowledge, he owes more to Buber than he sometimes wishes to admit,
but for Levinas a clarifying distinction separates him from his obvious precursor: for
the ethical relation is already, without reference to a divine paradigm, indebted to a
quasi-transcendental dimension—specifically, to the face of the other as it eludes
the form of its own revelation.

Although Levinas's de-transcendentalizing hermeneutic positions him along the
foreseeable horizon of other de-Christologizing discourses, unlike many progressive
revaluers of Christianity Levinas does not separate the man Jesus from the Christ
figure by preferring his ethical teachings to his violent, sacrificial death. If anything,
Levinas proceeds surprisingly along opposite lines, almost never quoting Jesus unless
to show him implicitly as a derivative prophet authoritatively plagiarizing the Jewish
traditions he inherits. As Levinas concentrates, instead, on the figure of a crucified
Christ, quite as though his passion were of far greater significance than anything
Jesus might say about it ahead of time or afterward, what is finally most remarkable
about the revisionary incorporation of "Substitution" into the central chapter of
Otherwise than Being is that Levinas here extends rather than diminishes the Christological conceit. One of the chapter's predominant tropes for a subject's unintentional assumption of responsibility is *incarnation*. Describing the recurrence in self,
steeped in passivity and suffering, Levinas refers to its "exposure to wounds and out-
rages," implicitly alluding not only to the spectacle of the crucifixion but to the techniques of theological rationalization according to which such extreme suffering seems
providential: "the oneself is provoked as irreplaceable, as devoted to the others, without being able to resign [*comme voué, sans démission possible aux autres*], and thus
as incarnated in order to offer itself [*comme incarné pour le 's'offrir'*], to suffer and to
give" (*OTB* 105; *AQE* 134). Incarnation as Levinas means it is hardly a metaphor for
embodiedness in the sense that Husserl or Merleau-Ponty might mean it.[54] Levinas
has adopted the rhetoric of necessity that propels any Christian theology of incarnation; and when he speaks thusly of the oneself as having been left without any possibility of resigning its mission (without the choice, to approximate Levinas's usage
in French, of *de-missioning*), he further remembers the spiritual agony of Christ in
Gethsemane, who had speculatively proposed resigning his mission before remem-

bering that he had no choice in the matter ("Yet not my will but yours" [Matt. 26:39, REB]). Christ's achievement of spiritual resignation qua acceptance depends entirely on his spectral wish to resign from sacrifice, his mission having now been imbricated with his *démission*, forever a sign of a responsibility that is not voluntary.

What Gethsemane anticipates is the inevitability of Christ's excruciating death, dramatizing for the audience our human objections, here voiced by the man Jesus, to such a redemptive scheme but so as to give final, theological approval to the design and its result.[55] Enhancing the incarnational drama, Levinas's use of the word "démission" casts an unmistakably theological, mock-missionary aura over his entire scenario, as though the ethical subject were as preoccupying of scriptural meanings as preoccupied by them. The trope of incarnation reinforces the metaphoric play upon the Passion in *Otherwise than Being*. Referring elsewhere to recurrence itself and to the self's ipseity as "incarnation," Levinas disavows a biological reading of incarnation, claiming that the "corporeality" of which he speaks already submits to a higher structure and thus to a connotation of dispossession by which the self, though not simply alienated from its intentions, is nevertheless dedicated to what has not been of its own doing (*OTB* 109). According to Levinas, the very meaning of an incarnated subject is its passivity, an "incarnated passivity" that individuates the subject as unique according to the responsibility it might assume (*OTB* 112). Just as Christ was the only one who could stand in for the others, Levinas gives this as the vocation of every responsible subject—to be the only one who is, at this moment, responsible for the others.

At least part of what Levinas might gain through his paradoxical revisioning of incarnationist Christian theology, I wish to suggest, is the prospect of humanity's undergoing responsibility not as an alienation of originary, natural freedom, but rather as an affirmation of the inherent vocation of subjectivity. This trajectory develops from the fundamental problem of ethics as he had conceived it in *Totality and Infinity*—specifically, the problem of how alterity can present itself to the sameness of being without being converted into a sign or a temporarily alienated thought of interiority, the very conversion Hegelian philosophy renders inevitable. The "form of incarnation" counters such alienation to suggest, instead, "being-in-one's-skin, having-the-other-in-one's-skin," as though incarnational subjectivity not only produced the paradoxical connotation of being ill at ease in one's own skin but were to derive from such ill-at-eased-ness the insight of ethics (*OTB* 115). At the very least, then, I am proposing, it must strike us as peculiar that Levinas saw fit to answer his own metaphoric appropriation of Christology in the 1968 essay by expanding the tropological range and value of Christological conceit. Yet this expansion, which functions finally as a kind of rhetorical overextension, also serves to bring the problem of sacrifice to the fore in the Christ story, urging us ultimately to revalue the terms of sacrificial structure.

VICTIM OF CIRCUMSTANCES

In mythic stories, according to Girard, victims of violence are produced by a structure of mimetic desire and a social mechanism of scapegoating about which the myth itself remains firmly unaware. Part of the way we know we're on the threshold of nonmythic storytelling is that the scapegoating mechanism comes to the surface and gets thematically manifested in the work, as though particular revelatory texts in history were capable of performing the therapeutic work of remembrance much as Freud had imagined it. Any story still thoroughly under the spell of myth will be unable to recognize or name the scapegoat as such. Girard usually supposes that Old Testament stories remain mythic. But the gospel texts—which Christian theology nevertheless consistently misreads—reveal a progress away from myth. For not only do the gospels name the scapegoat by speaking explicitly of the lamb of God, but, insofar as they refuse to perceive the scapegoat as guilty—in other words, by insisting upon the victim as an innocent—they allow the scapegoat to emerge as a theme. If we were to give a slightly different emphasis to Girard's formulation, we might say that by projecting a horizon in which the innocent victim, functioning suddenly as a subjective reality, continues to occupy the position of guilty object, the gospel texts allow for a structuralist demystification of the cultural logic of sacrifice. Much as Freud imagined the repression of desire to be fundamental to the progress of society, scapegoating is in Girard's view a constitutive element of culture. Although we cannot altogether overthrow its efficacy as a cultural logic, we can hope to see the social requirement of scapegoating clearly and thus to limit its chaotic, collectively unconscious manifestations.

Girard's confidence that the Christ story really intimates a thematic exposition of the scapegoating mechanism is probably not shared by Levinas, who is more skeptical about the story's social conscientiousness and yet perhaps naïvely invested, too, in its fundamental sacrificial principles. Girard proclaims the uniqueness of the Passion story (even more clearly than the stories of Job or the suffering servant) to have resided in its cultural-historical discernment of the violent rejection of the victim internal to all sacrificial social narratives, whereas Levinas imagines, paradoxically, that the victim's subject-position should be occupied not so much as a point of resistance to socially perpetrated violence but as an imaginative hypothesis of ethical meaning inhering within all socially perpetrated violences. What the story of the Passion would impart, quite distinct from the superficial theological meanings attached to it or the ethical teachings offered by the hero upon whom it is centered, is the lesson of the responsible subject. Christian theological elaborations of the Passion, Levinas suggests, must consistently overlook this central point. Only a de-Christologized Christ, who is no longer the historically singular Christ but rather the ethically unique subject for whom he stands, perhaps the kind of figure Hazel Motes imagines as the center of a "Church of Christ Without Christ" in Flannery O'Connor's religiously absurdist novel *Wise Blood* (1952), can impart these strictly ethical meanings.

There are additional hints in the fourth chapter of *Otherwise than Being* that Levinas is engaging, with skeptical and even quasi-heretical facility, key debates in the history of Christology. Even a cursory knowledge of patristics would return us to the constitutive debate of Christology—how to reconcile the being of Jesus as flesh with the providential, divine meaning that is supposed to inhere in his person. As J.N.D. Kelly perceives, the propensity for one-sided solutions developed early in Christian apologetics, casting its influence over the future of subsequently orthodox, thoroughly ambiguous solutions that purported to affirm what the gospels had already proposed—that Jesus was both of the flesh and of the spirit.[56] Among the early heretical formulations the Ebionites represented a school of thought, affiliated with a Judaizing strain of Christianity, that cast doubt upon Jesus's divinity, whereas the Docetists doubted that Christ's carnal embodiedness and thus also his sufferings were real. The Docetic influence can be perceived in a theology, attuned to the currents of Gnosticism, that interpreted Christ's body as phantasmal, and such heretic emphasis gave way thereafter to what Kelly calls "Spirit-Christology," in which the incarnation was accounted for by explaining that Jesus Christ was the preexistent Son of God who had united himself with human nature. Subsequent Church fathers gave great emphasis to the aspect of Jesus's preexistence as the Logos of God, so that the Word was named as the presiding principle in the person of Jesus and his life deemed a realized form of the preexistent Logos. When Tertullian asked more explicitly how it was possible for two divergent substances to coexist in the person of Jesus, he came up with the conceit of a Jesus Christ who clothes himself in the flesh, and this strange conceit of Christ's having worn his flesh like a garment persisted in the patristic theology of such figures as Novation and Clement. The subsequent variations on this idea were many, but the hint of heresy or Docetism lingered even into the work of Origen and Marcion, who suggested that Jesus did not precisely have a human soul but was, rather, the Word incarnate.

If Levinas's metaphoric language can be said to reflect certain aspects of the patristic debates—and obviously I mean to imply that it does more than just reflect them—he appears to interpret all Christology as if it tended toward the Docetist rejection of Jesus's real humanity. Any explicitly theological formulation runs parallel to the cultural problem of all logical or logos-based representation, which for Levinas is always to be contrasted to a subject who is defined ethically, prior to rationalizing doctrinal articulations of her significance as a being. Responsibility as the fundamental orientation of the subject is anterior to the "logos of response," and Levinas insists, perhaps alluding to the schizophrenic retentiveness of Trinitarian theologies with their three-in-one structure, that the oneself does not resolve itself on "the ideal pole of an identification across the multiplicity of psychic silhouettes kerygmatically proclaimed to be the same by virtue of a mysterious schematism of discourse" (*OTB* 102, 104). The ostensible opposition here is to post-Hegelian, Husserlian phenomenology, but, according to his figurative language, Levinas accuses Hegelian dialectic—not merely coincidentally, if we recall his complaint in "Hegel and the Jews"—of resolving its multiplicities by theological, indeed kerygmatic, imperatives. The notion of kergymatic proclamation brings with it Pauline connotations, much as the "mysterious schematism of discourse" recalls the Hellenizing tendency in Christian theology, a trajectory of belief approved by way of Platonically logical structures emphasizing oneness or sameness.[57] Insofar as the obsessive, passive, and suffering subject stands within language, however, Levinas will not allow the Christianized logos to have the final say, quite as though he refused to let the Passion be sufficiently accounted for by referring Christ's fate back to his preexistent status as the Logos. In this sense Levinas's de-Christologized Christ is also, at least in part, a de-Hellenized one.

As a counterpart to his persistent turning against logos, Levinas deploys a smattering of slightly heretical Christological phrases in order to maintain the ethical subject as a persistent source of controversy within rational discourse. Neither systemic nor even entirely consistent, these brief allusions nevertheless emphasize the involuntary positionality and recursive plight of the ethical subject, who like Christ is someone whose responsibility does not proceed directly from his own initiative— "a creature, but an orphan by birth or an atheist no doubt ignorant of its Creator" (*OTB* 105). Such an explicitly antitheological formulation seems aimed to suppress the metaphorical inheritance of Levinas's Christological conceit, altogether canceling the theology of preexistent originality through which the Passion had been rationalized in history. A short while later Levinas takes on the dramaturgical emphasis of certain strains of incarnational theology, contrasting the uniqueness of the subject derived in and through its responsibility to a language of generality, which would interpret the Passion within the order of ontology. Still speaking of the subject, Levinas reminds us, "it is first a non-quiddity, no one, clothed with purely

borrowed being, which masks its nameless singularity by conferring on it a role"
(*OTB* 106). The analogy here to the Gnostic tendency in patristic Christology is
imperfect: alluding to the conceit whereby Jesus puts on human flesh as though
donning a garment, Levinas recasts a theology in which Christ is merely role-play-
ing as though it were akin to the situation of a subject who takes on borrowed being
to disguise his anonymity and singularity. Indeed, if we read the metaphor in the
other direction, for what it says not about Levinas's ethics but about the Christological myth from which it is borrowed, we hear an accusation of Christian theology for
forgetting that the victim's fundamental plight is an event of anonymity—an experience of naked destitution against which the providence of a name, even if one is
hypothetically named a Son of God, provides no protection.

When Girard, for his part, opposes the revelatory thematic of the gospel to myth,
he presumes an aspect of naming more social than personal in its significance.
Although resistant myth sees suddenly, as it were, from the perspective of the victim,
nothing fundamentally changes with regard to the victim's situation. She is unable
to avoid the violence that befalls her. Oddly on this front, Girard fails to take account
of the extent to which Christ as the paradigmatic victim appears in the gospel to pronounce his own fate as scapegoat and so actively participates in the social spectacle
of his victimization, a principle of voluntary martyrdom which Christian theology
has ever since rationalized and reified. Surely it is not hard to argue that as myth the
gospel texts merely reform the social mechanism of scapegoating and solicit the victim's voluntary embrace of sacrifice in order to overcome the potential crisis in
mythic confidence. From a sociological standpoint what might seem most significant is that Christ enters into the myth from outside its socially determinative structures, and the gospels' schizophrenic account of who it is that requires the sacrifice
of this victim (is it God, the Romans, the Jews, or Jesus himself?) suggests a crisis in
the sacrificial structure. When Matthew depicts a Jesus who deliberates in Gethsemane and then sees that his death is required, the victim's pattern of thought has
become theological in the sense that he thinks from an ontological perspective that
must ultimately overlook the violence of the historical moment by foreseeing resurrection and a larger scheme of theological redemption. What Levinas achieves,
then, by concentrating on an unredemptive, fully incarnated suffering, is a view of
ethics as persistently occupying the subject-position of the victim, almost as if Christianity (even in the high Catholic liturgical remembrance of the Passion) could not
truly abide the memory of the violence it has systematically required.

Perhaps more than any other text, Matthew's gospel seems the implicit antecedent for Levinas's strange revisioning of Christology. There is at least one explicit

allusion to the Matthew text (specifically, to Matt. 8:20) to which I'll return in a moment, although Levinas more commonly alludes to the Hebrew scriptures even while offering his quasi-Christological articulation of the subject's responsibility. Thus, Levinas approvingly cites Lamentations 3:30 in a subsection on "Self" in *Otherwise than Being*, remembering the verse implicitly against its future appropriation by Matthew and Luke: "'To tend the cheek to the smiter and to be filled with shame,' to demand suffering in the suffering undergone (without producing the act that would be the exposing of the other cheek) is not to draw from suffering some kind of magical redemptive virtue" (*OTB* 111). In a footnote Levinas gives the reference to Lamentations but fails to gloss the gospel text alluded to in parentheses, a verse in which Jesus first caricatures Old Testament ethics as advocating the eye for the eye and tooth for tooth and then recommends, instead, a course of radical passivity, indeed a passivity that gets flipped over into agency: "But I say to you, Do not resist an evildoer. But if anyone strikes you on the right cheek, turn the other also; and if anyone wants to sue you and take your coat, give your cloak as well, and if anyone forces you to go one mile, go also the second mile. Give to everyone who begs from you, and do not refuse anyone who wants to borrow from you" (Matt. 5:39–42, NRSV). The line between an ethics of humility bound up in self-humiliation and a praxis of self-relinquishing so radical as to be purely for the benefit of the other is hard to discern here. Levinas's implicit objection to the evangelist's appropriation of Lamentations pertains clearly to the enthusiasm for suffering that Jesus encourages and, in the long historical view, to the Christian tradition's transformation of self-sacrifice into a codified virtue magically benefiting the one who embraces it.

What Levinas supposes is that suffering is no longer quite suffering once it has been freely chosen. Suffering must be that which is undergone as coming from the others in such a way as to be for them—an "absolute patience only if by this from-the-other is already for-the-other" (*OTB* 111). Still, much as Matthew has deliberately but poorly remembered the Hebrew scriptures throughout his gospel in order to underestimate his final indebtedness to Jewish ethics, Levinas here abbreviates the spirit and context of the Matthew text, which does not merely advocate masochistic virtue but interprets the relinquishing of will as though it inherently inclined by the force of conversion into an almost involuntary generosity. True, Matthew's Jesus advocates a specific course of action, which would, according to Levinas's philosophical terms, already transform the relation of ethics into discursive knowledge, but there is also more than a trace of Matthean generosity in Levinas's own interpretation of suffering's ethically connoted shame.

The other most famous biblical reference to smited cheeks occurs in the Book of Job:

> They have gaped at me with their mouths;
>> they have struck me insolently on the cheek;
>> they mass themselves together against me.
> God gives me up to the ungodly,
>> and casts me into the hands of the wicked.   (Job 16:10–11, NRSV)

It is not hard to imagine how Christians interpreted such a passage through a hermeneutic of allegorical typology, reading Isaiah's suffering servant as predictive of Jesus Christ's Passion.[58] Although Levinas does not make such a connection explicit in *Otherwise than Being* and does not actually refer to this text, by placing Job amidst the leitmotif of Christological imagery he deploys in the fourth chapter he has alluded with deft obscurity to a tradition of reading Job as a proto-Christ. The use Levinas makes of Job addresses the hypothesis of a victim's innocence, which according to the logic of the Book of Job would depend upon a mode of reason steeped in freedom, according to which it is only what one recognizes as responsibility that can be held against one as a moral failing: "as though I had witnessed the creation of the world, and as though I could only have been in charge of a world that would have issued out of my free will. These are presumptions of philosophers, presumptions of idealists! Or evasions of irresponsible ones. This is what Scripture reproaches Job for. He would have known how to explain his miseries if they could have devolved from his faults!" (*OTB* 122). All Job's protestations against the claims of bad conscience cannot withstand his irrevocable responsibility for what he has not directly done. The fate of Job signifies a demystification of all innocent victims. Never quite as innocent as he imagines himself, the victim is responsible for far more than he could have intuited or foreseen, yet he is also never as conveniently guilty as the social logic of scapegoating supposes him to be. As precursor and countertext to the Passion narrative, the Book of Job testifies to the impossibility of any victim's innocence functioning as an exception to the social rationale that justifies his fate. In other words, a singular victim, even one as noteworthy as Job, cannot exempt himself from all other examples of victimization.

Levinas's technique of counter-reading the Christological overtones of suffering, by listening again to the Hebraic archetypes upon which the gospel text draws, is subtle. Yet this hermeneutic is reinforced by the use Levinas also makes of Jonah, who is famously remembered by Matthew's Jesus as a Christological antetype. When the Pharisees ask Jesus for a sign to confirm his authority, Jesus accuses them of being, literally and figuratively, in bad faith: "An evil and adulterous generation asks for a sign, but no sign will be given to it except the sign of the prophet Jonah. For just as Jonah was three days and three nights in the belly of the sea monster, so for three days and three nights the Son of Man will be in the heart of the earth. The people of Nineveh will rise up at the judgment with this generation and condemn it, because they repented at the proclamation of Jonah, and see, something greater than Jonah is here!" (Matt. 12: 39–41, NRSV). According to the extraordinary allegorical reach of this passage, the sign of Jonah, which involves the preposterous scenario of being swallowed by a whale and later spat up safely on shore (perhaps a little wet, frightened, and humbled, with a few gastric fluids to be wiped off), is made to prophesy the even more fantastically providential rebirth of Jesus from the grave. Imaginatively resurrecting the dead of Nineveh in order to condemn his audience for their lack of perspicacity, Jesus in effect taunts the Pharisees with their own historically unique belief in the resurrection of the body, interpreting an entire history of ethical failures as though it were distilled in their inability to recognize his Christological significance.[59]

Although Levinas never treats the Christological appropriation of Jonah directly, it can be assumed as part of the background when he offers a highly divergent, though nonetheless allegorical, view of the prophet: "The impossibility of escaping God, the adventure of Jonas, indicates that God is at least here not a value among values. . . . The impossibility of escaping God lies in the depths of myself as a self, as an absolute passivity. This passivity is not only the possibility of death in being, the possibility of impossibility. It is an impossibility prior to that possibility, the impossibility of slipping away, absolute susceptibility, gravity without any frivolity. It is the birth of a meaning in the obtuseness of being, of a 'being able to die' subject to sacrifice" (*OTB* 128). Levinas's interpretation, though exegetically sound as a reading of the Book of Jonah, inherits the gospel's interpretive insistence on the tale as an allegory for death and rebirth, discovering even a hint of voluntarism (what it means to be able to die) in the prophet's attitude toward death. In the Hebrew text, Jonah of course is adamantly involuntary about his vocation all the way until tale's end, perceiving his election as nothing less than a curse guaranteeing that, as judge, he will also function as a scapegoat for people's wrongdoings, the one upon whom they deflect their anger for having been called to responsibility. For his part, Levinas, in treating the Christological revisioning of this story as though it had forever infected the story's original meaning, can only arrive at Jonah as a sign of sacrifice by imagining the birth of a vaguely voluntaristic ethical meaning within the story's sacrificial structure. In other words, even as Levinas's evocation of sacrifice ostensibly turns from Christian typology, it simultaneously turns yet once more upon the fortunate connotations of sacrifice.

There is no mistaking the fact that for Levinas Jonah's story is primarily about the inescapability of responsibility, about the involuntarism and passivity through which all ethical meaning is generated. As a precursive countertext to the Passion story, Jonah helps us recognize the specifically ethical assignation that inheres in Christ's passivity, despite all theological attempts to imbue his passivity with the form of action. The Christian interpretive mode (which I've articulated through Karl Barth's theology but which is already implicit in the evangelists' representation of Jesus as one who foresees and freely chooses his death) overcomes the uncomfortable dimension of passivity in the name of theological purposefulness. This, for Levinas, is one of the centrally troubling legacies of Christian theology: its imbrication of passivity and hypothetical agency. In response to the presumptiveness of all Western theories based on such a legacy, Levinas refers to an anarchy in responsibility, as though ethics could begin from nothing, positioned "beyond the normal play of action and passion in which the identity of a being is maintained" (*OTB* 114). Attempting to dismantle the conceptual stability that aligns a moral subject with the possibility of action, Levinas deploys redundant formulations such as "passivity undergone" (which means, roughly, a suffering that is suffered) in order to enact a separation between action and passivity.

Nevertheless, I want to emphasize that, even as he apparently upholds the oppositional meaning of *passivity/action*, Levinas several times slips back into an ambiguity necessarily informing this antinomy, his language determined by his implication in the sacrificial logic of his prooftexts—as, for example, when he rejects the mystical conjoining of passivity and activity (of which Christ is the archetypal example) and yet insists that, within "the possibility of every sacrifice for the other, activity and passivity coincide [*se confondent*]," or, which is to say more accurately, become confounded or intermingled (*OTB* 115; *AQE* 146). Against a possibility that sacrifice might be simply rejected by means of a critique presuming new conditions for the interrelation of unequal parties, Levinas admits the persistence of sacrifice within the possibility of ethics. The emphasis he puts on the confounding of activity and passivity registers Levinas's plausible objections to the imprecision involved in sacrificial memory's forsaking of the victim's absence of agency, yet it also suggests—since *con-fondre* is literally to dissolve substances and mix them—the degree to which all activity necessarily dissolves and simultaneously reverts to the signifying mode of passivity. A little further on Levinas insists that "substitution is not an act" but, rather, a "passivity inconvertible into an act" (as if the dissolving could not also work in the other direction), and at least part of his point is that passivity has quite literally preoccupied the possibility of every pragmatic action, as though the act of substitution were already a belated interpretation of that vocation anteriorly assigned to every self (*OTB* 117).

As the overall force of the fourth chapter of *Otherwise than Being* is directed toward a reconception of what he describes as the "passivity-activity alternative," Levinas finally alludes directly, although still not by citation, to Matthew's gospel, asserting that "the persecuted one is expelled from his place and has only himself to himself, has nothing in the world on which to rest his head" (*OTB* 121). In the verse alluded to here, an already prepared-to-be-sacrificed Jesus speaks of the foxes having holes and the birds having nests, whereas "the Son of Man has nowhere to lay his head" (Matt. 8:20, NRSV). Much as Jesus is without a home in the world because his purpose is entirely to be a self dedicated for others, Levinas's allusion construes the ethical subject as irreplaceable in his responsibility, even to the point of absolute weariness. Having previously spoken of the subject's passivity as preventing identity and being "without any rest in itself" (*OTB* 107), Levinas now subordinates this weariness to the ethical relation of "substitution and sacrifice," as though Jesus's own world-weariness intimated not transcendent restlessness so much as the ethical possibility that to don flesh even temporarily (which is not Jesus's unique drama but the mortal condition of every person) were to be exhausted by the requirements of humanity. With a slightly Ebionitic emphasis, Levinas remembers the Passion along the brilliantly heretical trajectory of Martin Scorcese's film *The Last Temptation of Christ* (1988), in which the physical actuality of crucifixion demands that Jesus retrospectively and prospectively take account of himself as a mere man, considering his all-too-human life apart from any theologically transcendent escapism. This is what it means to be incarnated, even if one is supposed to be a Messiah: it is to find one's transcendent significance suddenly trapped within the limited yet illimitable situation of ethics, as though Jesus's proclamation of Psalm 22 on the cross were to interpret his God-forsakenness as a redundant sign of his broken humanity. It is to imagine the sign of Jonah as resistant to its Christological appropriations, a reminder always of the inescapability of responsibility as well as of the suffering, human form it must always assume.

QUESTIONABLY USEFUL SUFFERING

Thus far I have maintained that Levinas's engagement with Christological language functions as both critique and continuance of sacrifice's many signifying modes. In closing this chapter, I draw out this paradox by considering its implications for ethics in its historical connotations. Specifically, I want to ask whether Levinas's attempt to generalize a critical consciousness about what typically becomes of victims in history or about the way in which our culturally determined histories position and rationalize the fate of victims leads him to reinscribe sacrifice as a universal of language itself. To perceive sacrifice not only in the substitutive connotation of responsibility but as part of the very structure of language's signifying capacity might even be to perceive communication itself as sacrifice. Thus, Levinas claims at one point that as "an adventure of a subjectivity . . . different from that of coinciding in consciousness," communication with the other expresses the "gratuity of sacrifice" (*OTB* 120). If this does not quite make a virtue of suffering, it certainly discerns necessity in it. Subjectivity, as located by way of the discursive situation, would seem to bear the aspect of a victim sacrificed for the good of the other.

In concluding the central tenth chapter of *The Scapegoat* (1982), which challenges the nihilism of the contemporary ethos via the gospel text, Girard insists that it matters greatly how a text represents the sacrifice of the victim, "whether from the perspective of the persecutors or the victim" (124). Although their respective readings of the Passion diverge widely, it is hard to imagine Levinas disagreeing here with Girard's commonsensical, structuralist credo—that we ought to take care to decide whether we are reading tracts in support of sacrificial necessity written from the perspective of those who put the other in the position of sacrifice or apologies for the victim that find themselves, inevitably or just normatively, implicated in social structures of violence. Indeed, as in the 1968 Ur-text Levinas acknowledges our professed rejection of sacrifice—"But to say that the other has to sacrifice himself to the others would be to preach human sacrifice!" (*OTB* 126)—by almost mockingly approximating it. The emphatic sincerity of this exclamation (the punctuation is there also in French) seems to translate the line as pure interjection, as a ventriloquistic rendering of a frustrated interlocutor who wants to say, *But, by now, at this late point in the twentieth century, aren't we finally done with sacrifice?* Like Girard, Levinas proposes that, insofar as we continually believe ourselves to be on the other side of sacrifice, even while reaping its biased benefits, we underestimate the extensiveness of its reign.

But unlike Girard, who supports the capacity of certain exceptional texts to thematize the social mechanism in which they perhaps less willingly participate, Levinas does not place his trust in the efficacy of representation: "The oneself cannot form itself; it is already formed with absolute passivity. In this sense it is the victim of a persecution [*victime d'une persécution*] that paralyzes any assumption that could awaken in it, so that it would posit itself *for* itself. This passivity is that of an attachment that has already been made, as something irreversibly past, prior to all memory and to all recall" (*OTB* 104). Although Levinas here names the mechanism with which he is concerned, he can imagine its power being dispelled only by placing the significance of sacrifice beyond the crude forms of violence through which it has been interpreted. Such a move seemingly reverses the Nietzschean demystification of morality and bears at least some resemblance to a phenomenon closely related to morality—

namely, the Christian tendency to spiritualize suffering such that its meanings elude
the severely limited horizon of pain and illuminate instead the prospects of a glori-
ous alleviation. Only Levinas will not embrace the triumphalist fantasy of the better
place as anything but mere utopianism. The here and now is our only place, and,
insofar as it is our place in the sun, as Levinas is fond of saying, citing Pascal, it always
also requires from us an act of usurpation, which is an act of occupying a place another
might have occupied. Even when the subject occupies an unpleasurable place, he
is positioned vis-à-vis the other, articulated through a substitution for the other in
which the subject's suffering locates a responsibility even for what the other might
do as persecutor or what she might suffer as victim. In this respect the persistently
anti-thematizing statements of Levinasian ethics testify to the manner in which
responsibility, assumed in the here and now, has been preceded at every moment by
immemorial signifying structures irreducible in their final meaning to any particular
historical moment.

Our common protest against sacrifice, according to an interjection Levinas imagines for us but never quite answers, is based in the fear that ethics might be derived
from it as regressively coded, in short as a mere lapse into barbarism and supersti-
tion. Failing to answer this charge directly, Levinas lets it stand rather as indicative
of a cultural misunderstanding of the victim who is at the center of sacrifice. With
language again inflected by Holocaust consciousness, Levinas likens the singular
dimension of a subject's responsibility to the historical moment of being held hostage
for the others: "A subject is a hostage" (*OTB* 112). Presumably, history can abuse the
subject's passivity by requiring crude, atavistic sacrifices, yet the sacrificial adventure
at the heart of language cannot altogether be evaded. To the extent that Levinas's
Christologically conceived trope of substitution overthrows a plot of mystification
that relies upon the victim's purported innocence, he remembers innocence as a
sign of uselessness at the heart of suffering. At least this would come to be his emphasis in the 1982 essay "Useless Suffering."

Written during the late phase of his career, after the major 1974 treatise *Otherwise than Being* and as he began more frequently to make direct use of the Holocaust as signifying a crisis in Western culture's epistemological and ontological
frameworks, this essay calls the Holocaust to mind in a more substantive manner
than any other, though not as an event altogether exceptional among a list of other
twentieth-century wars, totalitarianisms, and political atrocities or genocides. Ostensibly proclaiming in this essay an end to theodicy, Levinas offers a quasi-apocalyptic
speculation that the death of God, which Nietzsche had merely pronounced, was
realized historically in the extermination camps, given the "meaning of a quasi-
empirical fact" (US 97). Instantly one thinks of the famously central scene in Elie

Wiesel's *Night* (1958), in which three prisoners, a child central along them, are executed in a grotesquely staged Passion play (scholars have since suspected that the
staging attributed to the Nazis within the text is at least partly the product of Wiesel's
own imaginatively dramatic reconstruction of history). Whether demonstrating the
final end of a particularly Christian version of a God who watchfully presides over
suffering human beings or of a more general end to Jewish, Christian, and all other
theodicies, Wiesel plots a scene of almost unendurable witness, the Nazis having
forced the surviving prisoners to watch the suffering of the slowly executed prisoners and not look away. This inability to look away, which stands as a kind of negative
parable for the mode of remembrance Wiesel requires from his audience, also
brings to an end the prisoners' capacity for ordinary virtues such as compassion.[60]

Or we might turn to a second analogous story, this time a Hasidic tale of the Holocaust also deploying Christ as a figure for the sufferings of the Holocaust victim,
which advances a point similar to that of Wiesel's inset story while also elucidating
the substitutive workings of ethical imagination. In this tale, based on a survivor's
oral testimony about a real historical execution of the Jews of Eisysky, a sixteen-year-
old Jewish boy falls early into the mass grave and survives his execution.[61] Later the
boy climbs out, naked and bloody, seeking refuge at the cottages of obviously preju-
diced, superstitious Catholic peasants who were only recently his neighbors. At the
first door, received only as a Jew whose suffering is absolutely of the historical
moment, he is told to go "back to his grave" and turned away with horror. In desperation he tells an efficient lie as a woman is about to close another door in his face,
pronouncing himself the peasant's own beloved Christ come back from the grave
("Look at me—the blood, the pain, the suffering of the innocent" [55]), whereupon
she admits him and grants him three days of hospitality and concealment. As a parable savaging the compassion of Christians, who suppose themselves to be fashioned
in the memory of Christ, the tale is relentlessly ironic, revealing a fierce logic of
sacrificial displacement, whereby the death of Christ enacts the symbolic end of
Judaism and even predicts the future deaths of Jews forever required to expiate a
crime for which there is no expiation. Perhaps even more basically, however, this
Hasidic tale reflects the ethical contradictoriness of any *act* of compassion, which
depends precisely upon our ability to look away—all hospitality predicated upon the
possibility of refusal even more than refuge. The precedent of the peasant who turns
away the frighteningly persecuted other anticipates—and inscribes meaning upon—
the woman's reluctant hospitality, which is based not in an inability to look away
from the spectacle of suffering but rather in her metaphoric perception of the Jew as
a resurrected Christ. The image of a twentieth-century Jew risen from a mass
grave is overcome only by her expectation of a suffering already marked by its

foreseeable end, by the possibilities of looking beyond the immediacy of this single, historically suffering Jew to the theology of what suffering, in any moment,
means eternally.

For Levinas theology's trespass inheres in the requirements of theodicy. Throughout "Useless Suffering" Christian typology comes under suspicion, but so do Jewish
redemptive narratives and the wider cultural legacy dependent upon the theological revisioning of suffering, which may even be discovered in "watered-down form
at the core of atheist progressivism," too confident in the efficacy of goodness, always
anticipating the triumph over "injustice, war, misery, and illness" (US 96). Against
all such propositions Levinas discerns the potential meaning of suffering from within
the literality of pain, as a historically limited or concentrated experience. Suffering is,
at this level, a refusal of meaning. In an allusion to the gospel of Matthew's sacrificial optimism in verse 11:12 that the violent (those who are signs of violence, whether
victims or perpetrators) *bear away* suffering as by a transcendent logic, Levinas
reminds us that "the unbearable is precisely not borne" (US 91–92). There is yet
another aspect, however, to this literality. By definition, the one who suffers does so
as marked only by adversity, thus bringing to mind the adversary who inflicts suffering or the figure of a perpetrator whose significance for the victim cannot be escaped.
Although our perceptible desire for there to be a conceptual horizon of action, temporarily denied in this particular moment, might imbue passivity with meanings
greater than mere self-cancellation, Levinas insists upon the nonactivity of suffering,
even to the point that it signifies "independently of its conceptual opposition to
activity" (US 92). To imagine suffering as inherently resistant is to falsify it. Again
here, as I mentioned in chapter 1 in connection to Levinas's critical reservations about
the cultural meaning of the survivor's perspective, Levinas's skepticism about resistance may be owing to the cultural myth of the resistance within France.[62] Supposing that the vocabulary of effective resistance lets bystanders and collaborators off the
hook, without ever having to arrive at bad conscience, Levinas implies that, regardless of its possible social connotations and revisionary uses, passivity must be more
passive even than receptivity.

Still, even within such painful suffering there is inscribed a social meaning,
which proceeds along the ethical trajectory of vulnerability I traced in chapter 1:

Is not the evil of suffering—extreme passivity, helplessness, abandonment and solitude—
also the unassumable, whence the possibility of a half opening, and, more precisely,
the half opening that a moan, a cry, a groan or a sigh slips through—the original call
for aid, for curative help, help from the other me whose alterity, whose exteriority
promises salvation? Original opening toward merciful care, the point at which—through

a demand for analgesia, more pressing, more urgent, in the groan, than a demand for consolation or the postponement of death—the anthropological category of the medical, a category that is primordial, irreducible and ethical, imposes itself. For pure suffering, which is intrinsically senseless and condemned to itself with no way out, a beyond appears in the form of the interhuman. (US 93–94)

In this passage, which alludes to Blanchot's "countless cry" in *The Writing of the Disaster* as though it were a vocative command coinciding with the other's pain, Levinas by questioning salvific economy implicitly revisits his critique of Nemo's exegesis of Job. Salvation is no longer an ultimate answer to suffering. It is a demand for responsiveness, for responsibility. Even to speak of a horizon of receptivity, however, is to put the suffering subject in the position, paradoxically, of responding to his own suffering, since suffering's meaningfulness would already presage a reply. The same might be said of any victim's suffering: as soon as it is depicted as immediately answerable, the responsibility for providing such an answer can be cast back upon the one who suffers, as though her suffering merely demonstrated childlike dependency or a regressive rejection of the rites of liberal autonomy and required only a parent's, or society's, tough love to get her to stand again on her own. Such a cultural logic, in which suffering contains by structural necessity its own answer, is the counterpart (if we recall my discussion of Lang earlier) to intentionality's solace, which conjoins deliberation and agency in such a way as to locate a foreknowledge of events that renders the avoidance of her suffering partly a victim's own responsibility.

By either a prospective or retrospective logic, we might perceive an answer that a victim—if she could be just a little more rational and adopt a long (suffering) view of her situation—might provide for herself. The victim connotes that sense in which a self cannot assume itself in responsibility ("it is the victim of a persecution that paralyzes any assumption that could awaken in [the oneself], so that it would posit itself *for* itself" [*OTB* 104]). In other words, only the self that cannot answer for itself can be designated as victimized, and only the connotations of victimization can designate that particular aspect of self, which must be, if there is ever to be responsibility for such suffering, referred without final answer to someone else who encounters the suffering one. Qualifying his own use of persecution as a trope for responsibility such that the persecuted one must bear a surprising responsibility for his persecutor, Levinas hereby declares that any practical or imaginative act of passing political responsibility back onto the subject who suffers denies the interhuman, ethical dimension of all suffering. In this way he speaks paradoxically then of suffering as though it necessarily referred us to inter-ventions from or on behalf of the other, even while it remains, at least potentially, useless.

In all of this the Holocaust serves as both test case and prooftext for Levinas's interpretation of the victim. Near the end of "Useless Suffering" he invokes Emil Fackenheim's attempt to read the Holocaust as indicative of a chasm within both the human and divine order, which would thereby make theodicy roughly as obsolete as our social norms for equating history with rationality. In asserting that the Nazi genocide was without precedent in history, Fackenheim's argument about the lack of historical precedent works on two fronts—with respect, first, to reasons provided by the perpetrators and, second, to the experiential apprehension of suffering by the victims themselves. Insofar as the Holocaust differs from other "actual cases of genocide," Fackenheim supposes this is largely because, in those other cases, "whole peoples have been killed for 'rational' (however horrifying) ends such as power, territory, wealth," but the Nazis' crime was "evil for the sake of evil."[63] In other words, Fackenheim proceeds toward the uniqueness of the Holocaust by classifying its peculiar horror as arising from its motivelessness, from the absolute irrationality of those who perpetrated the crime. Whereas Lang in arguing for the distinctiveness of the Nazi genocide takes seriously the rationalizing function of ideology and then discerns the consciousness of criminal intention necessarily implicit in the Nazis' actions, with the result that perpetrators seem firmly anchored in rationality and responsible for (sometimes concealed) intentions because of what they've done, Fackenheim grants the Nazis a quasi-transcendent, perfectly exceptional contempt for their victims—a seemingly motiveless yet nevertheless forceful motivation. I would suggest that most arguments for the Holocaust's uniqueness—whether the emphasis is placed on the systemic totality of the Nazis' genocidal project, its near success, or on the absolute inflexibility of their categorical terms for defining their genocidal hatred—remain committed to interpreting the uniqueness of the event through the historical traceabilty of the perpetrators' intentions. What Fackenheim supposes is that any reason given for genocide will never be reasonable enough.

What seems peculiar to me, however, is that, even as he exempts the Holocaust from ordinarily rational motivations, Fackenheim implicitly casts other genocides back within reach of reasonability. I am not suggesting that Fackenheim's emphasis on an absence of genuine motivation for Nazi criminality is altogether inaccurate. There is a basic sense in which antisemitism, as what Levinas calls "hatred of the other man," or what Girard would help us read as an ideological, indeed sacrificial, veil cast over the fundamental arbitrariness behind any choice of victim, must remain existentially motiveless. But, then again, so must other forms of social or racial persecution and less identity-based interpersonal violences. If ideology cannot exempt a perpetrator from knowledge of his wrongdoing, nevertheless it often functions, at least in part, as the rationalizing mechanism through which responsibility for injus-

tice is deflected from the subject in her self-perception as agent. For instance, the ideological dimension of capitalism does not consist simply in a belief in the efficiency
of free markets but also in a rationalizing myth that supposes gross inequities in distribution of wealth are not also what is produced by the system, as though the apparent wrong of poverty were not directly the responsibility of those reaping the benefits
of capitalism's preternatural imbalancing of resources, means, and opportunity. The
phenomenon of Nazi irrationality does not seem nearly as aberrant as Fackenheim
would suppose. Rather, it exemplifies the social logic, which is precisely an illogic, of
all persecution. False reasons—at least from the standpoint of sociocultural praxis as
opposed, say, to moral philosophy—are no less reasons for their inaccuracy about the
agent's own motives or the persecuted party's blameworthiness.

Pursuing this last point, Fackenheim proceeds from the perpetrator's unlocatable
motivation to the victims themselves: "Still more incontestably unique than the
crime itself is the situation of the victims." Such a turn from the perpetrator's seeming motivelessness to the victim's perspective is generated by the discursive structure
of rationality, by the remarkably persistent ambiguity of the antinomy *perpetrator/
victim*, according to which the very fact that victims are produced by perpetrators
makes the two positions seem forever imbricated, even inseparable. In Fackenheim's
view, however, the Nazis' victims are uniquely positioned vis-à-vis their perpetrators
because as victims they could do nothing to exempt themselves from their fate: "The
Albigensians died for their faith, believing unto death that God needs martyrs. Negro
Christians have been murdered for their race, able to find comfort in a faith not at
issue. The more than one million Jewish children murdered in the Nazi holocaust
died neither because of their faith, nor despite their faith, nor for reasons unrelated
to the Jewish faith [but] because of the Jewish faith of their great-grandparents [who
brought] up Jewish children" (70; cited as in US 98). If it seems odd that Fackenheim should discern a potentially religious perspective within the social fact of
lynching, we have to remember that his argument devolves from the theological
framework toward the particularity of history. Indeed, it is precisely through the lens
of theological necessity that such former events of suffering must be characterized
as though their victims might find comfort in a plane of intentionality far more
expansive than the narrow, historical circumstances of the violence done to them.
The fissure in history (what Arthur Cohen calls a "tremendum" and Lyotard a "differend") depends upon a temporal schematization in which the present-tense perspective refuses to lapse into the pattern of historical necessity.[64] A similar logic is at
work in Anthony Hecht's Holocaust poem "More Light! More Light!" (1967), in
which a Christian martyr, standing as the archetypal victim who even in extreme
pain can perceive meaningfulness in his suffering personhood, is the precursor to

Hecht's retelling of a story of nihilistic death (borrowed from Eugen Kogon) in which a German soldier forces two Jews and a Pole to become complicitous in their own deaths and the deaths of one another, with the result that they are nihilistically emptied, in the moment of their final victimization, of a vestigial dignity they might yet have clung to.[65] By this technique all rationalizations of suffering participate in the larger perspective of history, deploying a transcendent long-view that overcomes a particular historical moment. For Fackenheim, as for Hecht, history might almost seem until the late twentieth century to have been occupied only by the faithful, by those persons capable of locating their own suffering beyond the historically specific moment of its occurrence, even if they did so by having recourse to a mode of thinking that poet and securalist theologian alike might denounce as delusional or mythical.

Insofar as Fackenheim supposes that, generally speaking, most victims remain within range of intentionality (dedicated perhaps to a purpose that enfolds a particular evil perpetrated against them within a greater historical, teleological project), he also insists that the Holocaust's victims lack such a perspective, uniquely. Thus, his appeal to innocence: the peculiar innocence of Holocaust victims (to reinforce this emphasis, Fackenheim refers metonymically to the one million murdered children, as though only children are exemplarily undeserving of such an awful fate, as though children were not also killed in other genocides) exempts them from a rational structure interlinking perpetrators and victims. In their inability to foresee or recast their suffering through the lens of necessity, capable of turning neither to theodicy or martyrology, Holocaust victims are denoted by a special attribute of innocence. Notably, it is for Fackenheim the ostensibly unique situation of the Jews, insofar as they were absolutely unable to exempt themselves from the political category by which they were grouped and thereby persecuted, that exempts them from the fate suffered by more typical victims. Thus, he develops his hypothesis of innocence: these particular victims were truly undeserving of what happened to them. Yet the counterbalancing point cannot be completely suspended: other victims may have been more deserving of what happened to them, or at least able to place themselves back within a consequential narrative that made their suffering and death stand for their own faith or for the progress of society. Perhaps any argument for uniqueness, based on the experiential difference of the suffering of victims, must partake of just such a sacrificial structure, exempting some rather than others through the argument of innocence.

Levinas cites Fackenheim at length (including all the passages mentioned here), and it is in fact through this Fackenheim excerpt that we arrive at the only direct mention of the "victim" in Levinas's 1982 essay. In making use of Fackenheim, Levinas again seemingly performs a deconstructive, or *clôtural*, reading, imitating Fackenheim's terms in order to differentiate himself, subtly, from them. Thus Levinas initially affirms the appearance of innocence in Holocaust victims, saying that "they represented the human beings least corrupted by the ambiguities of our world, and the million children killed had the innocence of children." Already there may be some qualification here, as the exceptional case of the Holocaust victims is declared "representative" of other human beings and the children's innocence is exposed as a tautological proof (their status as children made equal to innocence). Drawing out Fackenheim's slightly contradictory logic, by which the Holocaust's victims at once did not die the confident death of martyrs and yet must also be remembered through contemporary Jews' belated acts of witness as though they were nevertheless martyrs to the continuity of Jewish identity, Levinas says, "Theirs is the death of martyrs, a death inflicted in the torturers' unceasing destruction of the dignity that belongs to martyrs." The Nazi assault on the dignity of martyrdom does not serve in Levinas, as it does for Fackenheim or Hecht, to prove finally the historical uniqueness of this set of victims. Rather, the example of these victims proves to be Levinas's central example of the "undiluted malignity" of pain, of suffering's inescapable literality. In coming to Fackenheim's own overarching theological premise, which pertains precisely to the "end of theodicy" brought about by what Levinas (again universalizing Fackenheim) calls "this century's inordinate trial," Levinas proceeds to the central point of his own essay, which is to make the nonrevelatory commitment of a theology rejecting theodicy "at the same time and in a more general way reveal the unjustifiable character of suffering in the other, the outrage it would be for me to justify my neighbor's suffering" (US 98).[66]

Perhaps the most immediately irrefutable charge one might bring against Levinas in his use of the Holocaust here and elsewhere is that he universalizes the historicity of the Holocaust victim, either as a metaphor for his descriptions of the ethical situation or as a metonymy for all historical victims. Yet it is crucial to emphasize that such a universalizing tendency does not merely reinforce a stable program of cultural identity but occurs only within the ethical structure of alterity: it is precisely as other that the Holocaust victim gets universalized, the ostensible subject-position of the victim immediately referred to a hypothesis of interpersonal relationship in which the other's suffering must not be reconciled to sacrificial logic. Having perhaps intuited the fuzziness of his own quasi-sacrificial invocations of victims in both "Substitution" and *Otherwise than Being*, Levinas insists more definitively in his 1982 essay that we have no right ever to perceive a sacrificial meaning in another's suffering. As the absolute center of uselessness, the other's suffering can call me as subject to an answerability always inflected by sacrificial connotations, but only insofar as the meaning of my subjectivity is to answer for the other and, specifically, not to make the other answer for me.

Although the Christological conceit is altogether suppressed in "Useless Suffering," the essay remains Levinas's clearest revision of Christ's substitutive vocation, according to which he symbolically replaces humanity and dies so we do not have to. What Levinas perceives in the Christian scheme, as in all redemptive logic, is the requirement of a sacrifice for our benefit, a subjectivity that gains through the sacrifice of others. This is the primary direction of all scapegoating narratives, uncorrected even by Christianity's precarious identification with the victim. For the Christian insistently finds herself the beneficiary of the other's suffering, and thus implicitly, as exemplified by the long history of Christian antisemitism, can put still others into that role in order to serve her own ends. Moreover, as Christianity refers the benefit of sacrifice beyond immediate practical benefit, this structure of deferral guarantees that sacrifice will be ensconced as narrative typology, able to be deployed to legitimate all sorts of practices in the political realm, while it also suggests that its adherents follow a quasi-sacrificial logic (thus the famous complaints of Nietzsche, Marx, and Freud) in their ideational movement beyond immediate reference.

In objecting to the sacrificial benefits of the other's suffering, Levinas makes perhaps his most concrete contribution to a critique of ideological praxis. As I suggested in chapter 1, our confidence in history cannot be upheld naïvely as an inherent corrective to the mythic practices of the past, for even when honed by empiricist method or materialist critique, history remains produced either by the victors or by the claimants to power. Against history as merely a dissembled form of memory, Levinas helps us imagine a history that would proceed rather as the disassembling of memory—to be read, lived, and criticized from the perspective of failed responsibilities, according to those aspects of history altogether falling out of normative historical memory. Only by finding immemorial meanings, by turning to those who in their alterity have been failed in time, by invoking the victim as one whose ethical value and assignation of responsibility cannot be erased even by forms of apparent conscientiousness, can Levinas propose an ethics that refuses, inspired at least here in his 1982 essay by Fackenheim's own wishful insistence, to submit to any scenario in which the Nazis' war on the memory of the victims might have won.

But there is more to this than the facticity of the victim's unassimilable meaningfulness amidst apparent passivity. For Levinas the victim stands as the radical of ethical critique, whereby intentional, representational dimensions of any subject's knowledge are suspended before alterity, implicitly suspending also our teleologically determined, sacrificial recollection of the past—which, in crudest form, would repeat the power the subject qua perpetrator has enacted over the victim in history. Oddly, then, Levinas's apparent de-historicization of victims is in the service of a contrary historicity. Refusing to grant ethical validity to any explanatory narrative that borrows either from intentional or retrospective structures of thought—the one rationalizing suffering as if in advance and the other sacrificing it to the logical flow of history itself—Levinas arrives at the anomalous victim, the one whose de-martyrization runs parallel to a dehistoricizing hermeneutic precisely because history is always also a historiographical, rationalizing account in which victims serve the longer view by being placed usefully within it. Despite all of this, even while insisting upon a thoroughly de-martyrized victim, Levinas does involve himself in metaphoric twistings of the real history of the victim, who in her inability to avoid injustice or violence (whether she has been able to see it coming or not) should be interpreted neither as having chosen it nor having been chosen by it.

And yet what Levinas skirts dangerously close to is an account of ethics in which the conflation of an absence of choice and the fact of being chosen nevertheless for violence, which perfectly describes the victim's fate within the sacrificial narrative fundamental to so much of Western culture, is nevertheless the very meaning of ethics. Insofar as the Holocaust might serve this meaning of ethics, one thinks perhaps of the surprising assertions of Dan Pagis's poem "Written in Pencil in the Sealed Railway-Car," in which an allegorical mother named Eve anticipates her death as she sits beside her son Abel, vigilant even in her last minutes in the memory of another, murderous son, who is perhaps a figure for the Nazis themselves.[67] This focus either on the world that survives her death or upon the figure of the perpetrator as an agent within history suggests a victim who has herself begun to imagine a sacrificial fate within culture. Her dying thoughts interrupted (presumably, as she arrives at the death camp), Eve implores the anonymous, hostile world for which her other son is held largely responsible: "if you see my other son / cain son of man / tell him that I." Not only does this attention to the perpetrator seem quasi-sacrificial, but, according to the poem's absence of punctuation, we are commanded to complete her thought, if only hypothetically, if only thereafter to undo it. One might wish to hear blame or accusation or at least admonition (all sentiments that poets have vicariously placed in the mouths of Holocaust victims), but in the very nature of address there seems to be, instead, an assertion of relationship tending—uncomfortably, I want to suggest—toward forgiveness: . . . *tell him that I . . . forgive him.* Such words cannot be spoken because they belong to a Christianized narrative of sacrificial suffering, one that would redeem the mother's suffering for the good of history (maternity is also a sacrificial figure for Levinas, who responded to critiques offered by Derrida and Simone de Beauvoir that his ethical project was regressively gendered by non-progressively deploying the conceit of maternity in *Otherwise than*

Being as though it signified a quasi-naturalistic "being 'for the other,'" the ultimate sign of vulnerability as ethical meaning [*OTB* 108]). Similarly, the mother's thought lingers in Pagis's poem even as it is undone, newly converted in its silence into a figure of responsibility, a claim on and on behalf of Cain, for whom she assumes responsibility as if the greatest tragedy she suffers were to intuit the wounding of ethics.

For Levinas as for Pagis, victims seem surprisingly responsible for their persecutors, even to the point where the potential slippage in the figuration of victims and perpetrators—that conceptual ambiguity according to which our act of imagining the victim retains at least the fantasy of agency, even the directly responsible agency of a perpetrator—demands a space of subjectivity belonging centrally to the victim proper. By rendering the impossible perspective of Eve as victim, Pagis's seemingly Levinasian poem allegorizes ethics as a relation of incompletion, inscribed within history's realized violences.[68] In her unknowing, the victim is not just a scandal against knowledge. Rather, she denotes responsibility. We are not only responsible for victims in the sense that we should be unable to make their suffering useful. We are responsible, Levinas supposes, from the perspective of the victim, as an extension of those responsibilities terribly assigned to her and to which she might have responded, as an extension of a subjectivity that endures as responsibility even in the midst of the historical defeat of the person on whom it is dependent. Sacrifice is not entirely overwritten in such a connotation. Yet ethics, Levinas argues, must begin from the victims and not from the simplifying, utopian wish that a historical act of victimization had never occurred, for that would be tantamount to wishing that the victims themselves had never been.

CHAPTER FOUR

Of the Others Who Are Stranger than Neighbors

The stranger that sojourneth with you shall be unto you as the homeborn among you, and you shall love him as yourself, because you
were strangers in the land of Egypt.

Leviticus 19:34

It is hard to conceptualize the stranger except as mediated by our cultural relationship to the neighbor. In the moment of our apparent responsibility for them,
strangers seem to become neighbors by drawing near to us so that we may in turn be
friendly, hospitable, or charitable; and, if they do not draw near, then our responsibility may either pass us by or altogether elude articulation. Of course, the conceptual pairing of *stranger/neighbor* also works in the other direction: neighbors can
become estranged, they can even suddenly reconceive neighborliness as a relation
excluding segments of the community. In Jan Gross's historical account *Neighbors*
(2001), which retells the story of the sudden violence waged by a Polish village against
their Jewish neighbors during the Nazi occupation, there is evidence enough to give
us permanent pause about the credentials of neighborliness, as practically lived
proximity, when it comes to inspiring ethics. Although the sociological mechanism
enabling Polish neighbors to treat Jews of the same community in Jedwabne as
inherent strangers and thus, by close etymological and genealogical association, also
as enemies (in Latin, *hostis*, foreign or hostile others) is perhaps too historically lay-
ered to admit of neat summary judgments, there is something in the very principle
of tolerance (as defined, for example, by post–World War I treaties among European
nations dictating policies for the handling of extra-nationals) that already supposes a

historical turning from the other, a return of violence directed against those who may be designated, yet once more, as strangers. Even harboring the stranger in a neighborly fashion does not take us far enough beyond original designations of difference—such as Greek versus Jew, or Catholic versus Jew, or Pole versus Jew—from which tolerance speaks and by which, as political premise, it might revert to its origin as suspended animosity, always with the potential to revoke the cultural ban on violence.

At least one way of conceiving of the Holocaust as a sign of internationalist crisis might be to emphasize the ease with which Western democracies, including the neutral states and Allies, permitted Jewish refugees of Nazi occupied Europe to remain stateless persons, estranged from the claims of citizenship by antagonistic fascist ideologies but also unreclaimed by the rest of the world as the neighbors that an ethics of hospitality, or even a more pragmatic politics of asylum, might have allowed them to become. In the second half of the twentieth century *Auschwitz* was frequently uttered, most famously by Theodor Adorno, by Elie Wiesel, by Jean-François Lyotard, as a historical metonym for *J'accuse*—to be stated, as it were, in the legal and cultural courts of all Western countries not only against the direct perpetrators of genocide but against all who, having done effectively little to prevent or curtail genocide, would still presume upon positive traditions of justice as though the legitimacy of such European traditions and the states upholding them had not been severely impaired by the cumulative legacy of antisemitism, that philosophical crime Levinas calls "hatred of the other man." If in the middle of the twentieth century the Jew became yet again, though more awfully than ever before, a stranger in our midst, one might perhaps decide—as did Jean Paul Sartre and, in much the same hermeneutic tradition, Julia Kristeva—that the challenge posed by the Holocaust, much like the scandals of racism, colonialism, and imperialism, pertains to an anxious stinginess in the self situated within the broader rubric of cultural or national identity.[1] The hostile perception of the other is, by such a logic, always an aggressive, perhaps unconscious, deflection of those qualities a society most anxiously perceives to belong to itself.

Hatred of the other person is, by this logic, a sign of insecurity—even more basically, according to the projective mechanism informing this hermeneutic, a sign of self-hatred. For Sartre in *Anti-semite and Jew* (1946) hatred as veiled self-loathing is perhaps the very sign of the inauthentic existence, confined by bourgeois norms that have become merely symptoms of a conformity allowing neither for the entry of the new nor for what might be called the return of the stranger. And Kristeva in *Strangers to Ourselves* (1989), subscribing to a psychoanalytic sociology and specifically to Freud's valorization of the uncanny as that phenomenon whereby the shock of estrangement denotes what has been previously experienced and then phenomeno-logically subsumed by a culturally disciplined consciousness, interprets the stranger as portending an alienation within identity that would unsettle all of our most basic cultural myths, especially our most vehement nationalist commitments.[2] In either case estrangement objectifies and turns away, in the person of another, a perception of difference that inheres already in the set of identifications that constrict and define culture, and so society might loosen the necessity of this primitive yet persis-tent social logic of estrangement by also admitting its persuasiveness. By finding the stranger in ourselves, by allowing for that sense in which we are also necessarily strangers to ourselves, we might perform a kind of imaginative catharsis, diminish-ing the social horror of the strange in order to espouse a sociality perpetually open, through a genuine politics of welcome, to strangers, refugees, and immigrants of all kinds.

But the events from 1933 to 1945 can also be interpreted at least in part as a les-son about the persistent rejection even by the nonfascist modern nation-states of real political responsibility for foreigners or refugees, even in their moment of extreme persecution and imminent death. Does such a history provide us with an opportu-nity to affirm anew or for the first time what had been rejected? Although it has become increasingly common to insist upon the divide between Jewish heritage and Holocaust heritage, there is little doubt that the Holocaust continues to function, at least in part, as a collective memory that binds, even perhaps fosters, group identity. Much as contemporary discourses of multiculturalism and ethnicity, which develop constructs of identity somewhat independently of the liberal politics of pluralism, often gain authority (if not necessarily a theoretical basis) from the political rejec-tion, repression, and systemic violence perpetrated against minority groups, so Jew-ish identity in the post-Holocaust era drew upon the cultural politics of identity, most obviously in the well-worn historical mandate that postwar Jews must not allow Hitler a posthumous victory.[3] The imperative to remember was already colored by a belief in what was distinctive, indeed implicitly preferable, about Judaism. It was also informed by a technique of remembering inflected by compensatory logic.

In this chapter I want to position Levinas's figurative language pertaining to the *stranger/neighbor* dichotomy against the background of current debates about iden-tity. I do not suppose here, nor have I supposed at any previous point in this book, that Levinas is a standard bearer for an ethics of contemporary culture we might describe as post-Holocaust, post-moral, or postmodern.[4] Rather, by focusing in these pages on the theme of the stranger in Levinas's oeuvre and by drawing out not only metaphorical but also cultural and political connotations attributed to the stranger in works spanning the course of his career, I wish to engage even more overtly the politicized dimension of Levinasian ethics, suggesting connotations, associations, and implications the author himself never fully develops. According to Levinas's skeptical assessment of our Western philosophical and political systems of knowledge, the function of identity—as both a separation from its participation in elemental otherness and a perpetuation of the subjective possibility of freedom—must overlook, as if it did not also proceed from, the relation to the other. Every premise by which we lay claim to knowledge is already caught up within a cultural politics of power to which theorists such as Nietzsche and Foucault finally gave their assent with Hobbesian enthusiasm, but from which Levinas recoils as though all political and cultural systems fixing identity within a totalizing logic might degenerate at any moment into totalitarian applications of the system against the person. One might rehabilitate Nietzsche and Foucault to liberalism or to the post-liberal praxis of the late-twentieth-, early-twenty-first-century Western state by emphasizing the need to construct political citizenship as not only requisitely implicated in political structures of power but also dependent on certain minimal conditions for access to power. Yet in Levinasian ethics the other remains beyond the social construction of her rights, and so recalls, even as she demands our response to it, the practical reality whereby she is left outside the parameters of ethical concern or the benefits of sociality as thus far enacted.

It is in this respect that the stranger, not unlike the victim, seems a particularly resonant figure within Levinasian ethics, calling to mind the one who enters into relation as someone already estranged from the benefits of cultural heritage and from those rights pertaining to any individual through the society to which he belongs naturally. In the praxis of a state or some other communal affiliation, ethics would be contained through the persistent structures of belonging by which we generalize our responsibility—for strangers, foreigners, homeless people, for the politically oppressed and economically destitute of our country, every now and then (though not often enough) for the politically oppressed and economically destitute of Third World countries. Even when the stranger is another citizen within our society, she occurs to the subject firmly ensconced in culturally determined identity as an exception to ordinary logic and knowledge; she is not yet or perhaps no longer the neighbor whom one habitually recognizes. Thus, the dichotomy of *stranger/neighbor* is also significant within Levinas's work because it provokes contradictions, especially in later writings in which the neighbor replaces the stranger as the preferred trope for figuring relation to the other. Far less paradoxical, it would seem, than to speak of the memory of the stranger would be to contemplate our memory of neighbors or to speculate on the memories they share with us. I want to inquire whether there can be a memory of the stranger that does not lead back to presumptions of commonality and belonging that are largely responsible for the exclusion of strangers in the first place. Can the stranger possibly signify more than the precise moment of her impingement upon a self-contented consciousness? And, if she can be meaningful other than as a reminder of our own potential to be alienated (temporarily, we hope) from structures of belonging, what would such admission of her importance do to our enduring construct of the neighborly other?

THE STRANGER, METAPHORICALLY SPEAKING

In the essay "The Moral Life of Metaphor" (1986), which makes no direct mention of the Holocaust, Cynthia Ozick argues that what Greek culture could neither anticipate nor make allowance for—precisely because it was so confined by the alternatives of inspiration or intellectualism, always choosing between the radical spontaneity of extraordinary identification and a system prepared to answer (in advance) the contents supposedly apprehended in moments of inspiration—was the experience of the foreigner. While Ozick does not entirely disavow the legacies of Greek culture (to which, for example, we at least owe the university), she does accuse the Greeks of failing to develop a compassionate politics for including strangers, as a consequence of their commitment to a religion enraptured with spontaneity and to immediate, contemporary matters of the polis. Accounting for this persistent parochialism of the Greeks, who were proud of despising their enemies and perceiving the foreigner as barbaric, Ozick insists that they lacked a "heritage of a common historical experience" from which they might have universalized an ethic of pity or developed "the imagination of reciprocity."[5] By contrast, the Jews (perhaps, she admits, only because they were politically less fortunate) developed a version of historical consciousness remembering their own people's experience of bondage and, by means of that memory, became capable of discerning in strangers a potentially similar fate of subjection, disavowal, or political persecution. Arguing that Judaism contributed to the world a language that cleared the ground for a paradigm shift in Western culture's imagination of the stranger and pointed our way toward a truly universalistic ethos, Ozick indulges a dichotomous rhetoric of Jew versus Greek that implicitly recalls an array of unstated historical grievances: the ancient Israelites' quarrel with pagan culture, the historically vexed Hellenization of Judaism, Christianity's development of Hellenistic modes of rhetoric and proselytization in its long struggle to wrest the claims of covenant from the Jews, and a host of modern philo-Hellenic emphases in Western culture, not least of which were Nietzsche's and Heidegger's deep infatuation with the Greeks and rejection (at least culturally) of the Jews.[6] Although there is more than a hint of nostalgic sentimentality in

Ozick's own implicit historiographical opposition between Jews and Greeks (as though the Hebrew Bible, while putting forward a great many injunctions to love the stranger, did not also fiercely elaborate hatred of hostile foreigners and annihilative violence against the Israelites' historical enemies), what is perhaps most peculiar in her method is that while giving credence to a few idioms of collective memory, such as Leviticus 19:34, Ozick treats them as though they were in fact rigorous reflections on historically documented cultural practices.

Throughout her essay, in other words, Ozick confuses metaphor and history, even mistaking metaphor for history. As she sets the idioms of biblical language against the idioms of Greek culture and reads into them discernible, realized historical differences, she fails to admit a possibility evident in her own interpretive imperative—namely, that the language in which a community expresses itself, whether we speak of biblical Judaism or mythic Hellenism, may be compensatory or idealizing in a manner having little to do with historical reliability. It is rather oddly appropriate (if not altogether intended) that Ozick should commit herself to such wishfulness, since her central claim in the essay is that metaphor—which is the capacity for ambiguity, for imagining what it is to be someone else, for developing a politics of reciprocity—was the particular capacity bequeathed by the Jewish tradition to Western culture. Considering also that Ozick focuses on the specific metaphoric relationship of the stranger to the community, one might go so far as to say that, in Ozick's view, it is the Jewish community's metaphoric love for the stranger that centers the historical privilege of Judaism. Arriving at Leviticus 19:34 with confidence that she has "penetrated to history and memory," precisely as the Greeks had failed to do, Ozick discerns in the command to receive the stranger as though he were "homeborn among you" a threshold moment of culture in which memory became truly metaphoric (279). By emphasizing further that this command to love the stranger appears thirty-six times in the Pentateuch, Ozick merely repeats what is already remarked upon by much Rabbinic commentary. In Rabbinic lore, which characteristically substitutes metaphoric or fabulous morals for history, this command holds special significance through its frequent repetition, as though the number of times the ethic was pronounced gave evidence of the sentiment's sincerity and historical application.

Such a generous interpretation of biblical precedence is, however, an idealizing resolution of the wide-ranging, often troubling texts that make up the Bible. Take, for example, the Book of Numbers, which I choose simply because it refers to the stranger more frequently than any other book of the Torah except Deuteronomy and because these specific references must be reckoned as part of the Rabbis' tally. Whether the stranger is designated by a word deriving from the Hebrew root *goor* or *zoor*, each of which evolves from an original verbal connotation of turning aside, in the Book of Numbers strangers are labeled as such sixteen times, with two-thirds of such references proposing an ethic that surpasses mere tolerance (frequently the emphasis in Leviticus) to foresee a politics of genuine cooperation between the community and its alien residents, some even going so far as to specify ways in which the stranger might be integrated into the religious life of the community. Nevertheless, on the first two occasions in which Numbers mentions the stranger (1:51 and 3:10), as well as in three additional references interspersed throughout the text (16:40, 18:4, and 18:7), the stranger is put to a particular ban, his cooperation on the question of worship determining whether he will live or die. Each of these references arises in some relation to a description of priestly codes and the privilege given to the Levites before the "tent" in which Yahweh abides. In 1:51, for example, a simple warning follows the statement that the Levites will take down and put up the tent: "And the stranger (*zoor*) who comes near shall be put to death." Even if the stranger here bears a metaphoric emphasis, serving to reinforce boundaries between God and the people quite as though they have been drawn to protect the ark from falling into unconsecrated, foreign hands, the ban necessarily recalls interreligious rivalries and the harm that foreigners would do, at least potentially, to Israel's God. As the one who etymologically turns aside from the road and seeks lodging in a land not his own, the stranger (*zoor*) is by extended connotation one who is profane (in the sense that he is not part of the sacred aura of his host community) and may therefore profane that which is not his own (thus, the word *zoor* can also mean "to commit adultery," because the adulterer profanes what has not been consecrated to him). No matter how generously the Book of Numbers anticipates the stranger's sojourn, he is also the locus of a terrible anxiety about faithfulness to the requirements of Israel's God and, as such, may intimate the waywardness of the Israelites themselves. In the biblical tradition, as well as in the idealizing strains of Rabbinic commentary and Ozick's further elaboration of an ideally Jewish code, the command to love the stranger cannot entirely suppress this basic uneasiness a stranger provokes.

What Ozick's optimistic reading of that metaphoric love of strangers inherited through the Hebrew Bible correctly intuits, then, is the sense in which any stranger, as metaphor, must pertain even in the biblical text to an image of self or communal identity. In this respect her reading of the biblical stranger shares much with Kristeva's interpretive resolution to the historical scandal of strangers, based in the conjecture that the love one potentially shows the stranger can be generated most effectively as a symptom of self-remembrance. Since the stranger has been remembered as a figure for the exilic condition of the Jews, Ozick approves a narrative in which the memory of the stranger gets internalized as part of communal heritage. Whether articulated as a sign of an uneasiness with self endemic to communal identity (roughly, Kristeva's supposition) or developed from the concern for what the community has undergone at the hands of others (Ozick's view), the stranger is the very sign of the reign of culture—or, more precisely, of a cultural logic developed through a set of identifications structured to refine commonality and belonging. In biblical idiom the stranger may continue as one who is set apart, subject to hostility or to a temporary hospitality, or he may be incorporated, although perhaps not entirely, into the ritual, civil, and political life of the community. What is interesting is that the tension between these two options defines a threshold specifically associated with the function of metaphor: for the stranger who remains entirely other seems always to challenge the community as already constituted, implicitly provoking anxiety and hostility, but the fate of the stranger who becomes like the neighbor can be religiously pronounced upon because she has remained nearby long enough for the rules of the community to have been imposed upon her. In Numbers this is the ultimate sign of democratic generosity extended to the stranger—the supposition, in 15:26, that the alien will be considered no differently from the native when it comes to a violation of the community's religious laws, even to the point of incurring the possible penalty of being cut off from its privilege. It is quite as though the stranger were to reach a point where she could be mistaken, in both her own knowledge of communal identity and the community's expectations of her, for a native.

At least part of my reason for recalling Ozick's essay is that Levinas is often supposed to have conducted a similar de-Hellenizing critique of Western thought, and he frequently cites the biblical mandate to love the stranger as an ethical prooftext.[7] In an interview with François Poirié published in 1986 (the same year Ozick's piece first appeared in *Harper's*), Levinas cites this verse in its codified form, fully aware of its Rabbinic legacy and fully capable of differentiating his own technique of invoking biblical texts from the Jewish tradition's interpretive imperatives. After insisting that his willingness to employ a biblical verse in philosophical writing depends typically on one of two conditions, either that the verse serves the purpose of illustration or that even in its "religious context" it already bears a "philosophical accent," Levinas next cites Pascal as seriously as any biblical verse and then returns to yet another biblical example, this time from Psalms:

> All the same, "Thou shalt love the stranger," which is found in the Bible thirty-six times, exclusively in the Pentateuch—thirty-six times, according to a talmudic text which adds, "and maybe even forty-six." When it says "thirty-six and maybe forty-six," this is to say, maybe fifty-six, maybe sixty-six. This is a manner of saying that it is important to feel it, outside of any statistical interest in the tradition. And one ends up understanding this formula, "Thou shalt love the stranger," not as an anti–Le Pen politics,

but as the audacious and true affirmation that love itself, affectivity itself, and feeling itself have their initial place in the relation with the other, with the stranger which every man is for every other man. After all, everyone is a stranger. "I am a stranger on earth," says a verse of the Psalms, "Give me your law" (Ps. 119:19). There too is a verse that is philosophical from the start. Not only the avowal of a people without soil, but the signification of that presence on earth, of an exile behind the autochthonous, which is the definition of the pure transcendental subject and the primordial necessity of a moral law in that exile.[8]

Whereas Ozick (seemingly as a matter of course) invokes a meaning her tradition attributes to the Leviticus text, Levinas brings the verse and its corollaries to mind by explicitly distinguishing himself from the authority of heritage per se (he does this if for no other reason than that he is trying to demonstrate to his non-Jewish interlocutor, François Poirié, that his own philosophical texts are not primarily confessional utterances). Intuiting the sense in which merely reiterating or multiplying the same idea can seem an act of interpretive elaboration, Levinas conjectures that the Rabbis' fondness for numbers is deliberately inexact, the rough idiomatic equivalent of any interlocutor's exasperated attempt to remind us of a premise so fundamental as to be taken for granted—as if the Rabbis meant to say, *As I have said to you now for the umpteenth time.* Expressing less interest in tradition's authority than in a kind of proto-humanistic truth, the Rabbis turn biblical verse into philosophy through their lack of concern for exegetical or historical exactitude (or, as Levinas sees it, they do what he is also doing).[9] Even if the discussion in Numbers is framed by a memory of suspended violence against the stranger, the ethical command remembers the foreigner's predicament as though it gave rise to the very question of ethics, promoting as far as Levinas is concerned the same emotional inquietude in identity that, for instance, the death of the other or the irreferential bad conscience also inspires.

When Ozick binds history to memory as though the influence of empiricism and the techniques of scientific inquiry had not largely transformed the praxis of historians in the post-Enlightenment era, she approves, as though it were irrevocable, an attachment of historical consciousness to a politics of identity. As I have previously suggested (especially in chap. 1), this is at least in part the source of Levinas's underlying quarrel with history writing in his philosophical project: because history is, by definition, a superimposition of victorious consciousness, it cancels not only the witness of the victims but also their ethical demand upon us. Even an oppositional political stance espoused by an oppressed people, insofar as it relies upon an identity that longs eventually to be victorious, will depend upon an occlusion of the interrogative force of alterity. Whether one wishes to retrieve Hellenism or Hebraism as a corrective, by the logic of antinomy one already supposes that choosing sides or embracing heritage (which is roughly akin to a fixation upon the purportedly knowable, though also wishful, past) inspires the act of history. For Ozick, even as the Jews suffered exile as an estrangement from their rightful land and before the eyes of others, they remembered and so preserved their communal identity as an inviolable heritage. It is by extending this two-layered memory, of what one already knows for certain about oneself and of the suspicion with which different peoples have regarded you, that exilic history gets converted into an imaginatively negotiable metaphor.

To remember oneself as estranged or one's community as strangers upon the land is already to perform an imaginative conversion of the phenomenology of estrangement and to see it, as it were, from the converse side, from the perspective of the exile who has found at least temporary refuge—which is to say, simply, from a perspective no longer strictly a stranger's. Moreover, since from the perspective of the host community, the stranger arrives upon any scene as someone about whose past the community knows nothing definite, as a phenomenon of pure alterity, there is always a hermeneutical response to the stranger, enacted as a kind of conversion, whereby he or she is rendered a symptom of what is already culturally knowable. Levinas acknowledges the cultural force of such a process. In the earlier passage, for example, does he not commit himself to a technique of metaphorizing that shares many of the same cultural imperatives by which Ozick abides? In assessing the biblical verse "I am a stranger on earth" as philosophical, he too interprets it as though the memory of exile foresaw or were fulfilled by the universalistic connotations of an experiential estrangement belonging to every person. Especially if we expect metaphor to perform a genealogical erasure of its original context, expanding a point of reference associatively until it has been de-literalized to the status of mere figure, Levinas's assumption that "everyone is a stranger" involves an obvious deracination of the verse from its historical *Sitz im Leben*. By conceding the historically denotative basis for the Psalm and yet moving beyond that to a philosophical and metaphoric meaning generated not from an avowal of the exilic past but in witness to the "exile behind the autochthonous," he interprets the verse as metaphor. There is, as it were, an exile more original than the historical crisis of being cast out from a homeland. Having already presumed a metaphoric connotation testifying to the claim of ethics, Levinas discerns in the Jewish historical experience of being dispossessed of land the always anterior vulnerability of the other person, who as stranger or exile or refugee has not as yet been sustained by the project of culture. To a submerged layer of reference within our basic conceptions of culture and exile, Levinas responds by overhearing a clarion call, generated from necessity, for "moral law."

There is, then, a universalistic horizon for Levinas's project, but one that is unduly criticized or inadequately explained by simply locating Levinas in the Jewish tradition, by accounting for his apparent uncanniness within the Western philosophical project as a species of Jewish plaintiveness.[10] Rather, Levinas's conjoining of universalized humanity with an ethics defined as the relentless demand imposed upon each person in her humanity discovers an aspect of strangeness in the ethical relation itself. It is only through the signifying act of going toward or facing the other that our humanity comes to be described in quasi-universalistic terms, primordially defined for us. Signified always as that which also eludes any basis in cultural knowledge, the universalized Levinasian subject does not inherit her identity, nor is she capable of a self-sustaining act of remembrance by which any subject might be derived as both a symptom and realization of her cultural heritage. The estrangement determining ethics does not suppose a prior commitment to a cultural project such as the Jewish tradition, which would suffer an exile added to the premises of original identity and might then (as Ozick supposes) remember its own experience of foreignness as a hypothesis to be bestowed upon every stranger's condition of violated identity. Neither does the situation of ethics repeat an alienation within ourselves objectified by our treatment of others, projecting (as Kristeva insists) an inherent abjection onto the real-life figure of the foreigner. In Levinas the stranger, though neither his first nor final metaphoric description of the ethical relation, is yet one more sign of the alterity that demands from the subject the posture of responsibility.

Whenever Levinas evokes the figure of the stranger, an ambiguity thus presides over his referentiality: does he refer to historical experiences of strangers to emphasize the urgency of ethics, or does he imagine the universalized connotation of strangeness in each ordinary ethical encounter? Perceiving in the allure of historicity a corollary reduction to simplified essences and identities (what might almost be described as a cultural naturalism that has come increasingly into vogue since Nietzsche, exercising its influence on almost all critical theories of ethnic identity), Levinas would imply that the connection Ozick derives between history and memory, between political hospitality and heritage, is the necessary consequence of every attempt to interpret the stranger through a cultural standard into which she might be yet again incorporated. In this sense historicity always proves liable to the particular biases of a cultural moment and context, which necessarily enact a reduction of the ethical relation to the located perception; and, against this reductive, contextualized view of a readily situated other, Levinas positions the stranger as that figure for the other who is significant even though, or precisely because, she is also at a distance.

If we inquire about the implicit politics of such an estrangement from history, we might say that Levinasian ethics necessarily poses a challenge to politics as the realm of already constituted relation or even to the principles of fairness we might develop through what John Rawls calls the "original position" of the just society.[11] For Rawls proposes a fundamental political description of politics that does not depend upon already realized history but instead refers to a plausible, if also ideal, condition to which the citizens of society, as reasonable persons, would give their consent. Even according to such a flexible hypothesis, within which the liberal society would not be simply reducible to the imperfect, irrational, or unjust practices upon which it is historically based, there is an assumption that the one who might conduct herself in line with the principles of justice already partakes of its fundamental principles, if not all of its contingent privileges. Levinas dehistoricizes politics not by way of a hypothesis according to which society might better align itself with a justice to which it already aspires, but by way of reference to the other for whose benefit a society is not obviously oriented. There may be no getting around the fact that Levinas's act of de-historicizing the stranger fails to track a stranger's suffering as a contingent, variable historical fate and thus also fails to bestow upon her the benefit of politically construed interpretations of her condition. Yet the political is never irrelevant to the stranger's condition, if only because she is the site of a liminality by which the politics of the nation-state establishes its own boundaries of rights. Nor can the political as such be irrelevant to Levinasian ethics, if only because ethics must eventually cede to the practical negotiations of justice insofar as a subject must answer competing responsibilities for multiply triangulated others, who simultaneously and continually make demands upon each of us.

THE MEMORY OF THE STRANGER

What Ozick has proposed as a collective memory of the stranger, predicated upon the supposition that the Jews having once been strangers upon the land might hold the memory of estrangement in themselves as a complementary function of identity, could be challenged on multiple grounds—with regard to what she assumes about strangers, what she assumes about identity, or what she assumes about memory. Such a critique might proceed by upholding one term at the expense of the other or might revise one of these terms along very different lines. Yet what I want to assert here, so as to mount a challenge to any definition of the stranger formulated by way of identity, is the necessary interrelation of all three of these terms. According to the challenge the stranger imposes upon any plot of memorable or memorializing identity, I wish to emphasize that by Levinas's terms it should be impossible to speak of the memory of the stranger as productive of identity.

For Levinas memory is characterized as significantly by what it resists as by what it enfolds into the coherent system. Memory, as though it constituted the *I* in its literality, offers a first resistance to ontology or systemic knowledge.[12] I made the point in chapter 1 that, by attributing to the interiority of the *I* its own recusant materiality and its signal function of withstanding, say, "the totality of the historiographer," Levinas credits memory with a temporally connoted interruption of history's capacity to render each of its objects as "nothing but past" (*TI* 56). Signaling a psyche's discontinuity with an ideal order, memory performs an inversion according to which the nonreferentiality of the *I* in historical time designates, as it were, the material reality of interiority. The *I* must not be measured directly by its results in history for the simple reason that such an obvious structuralism, whether its justification be idealist or materialist, would necessarily submit humanity to a long view, either protentive or retentive in Husserlian terms, that emphatically overlooks the present. Insofar as it evades the present by always situating immediacy within an ongoing logic, history is unable to account for that which does not obviously exhibit itself in history.[13] In this respect Levinas would dissent from our contemporary vogue for assuming, as a matter of course rather than even as an accepted first principle, that one must at all costs reconcile culture and its diverse byproducts to an organizing, historicizing logic.

Lest we misconstrue Levinasian ethics as though it were charted simply on this side of memory and against history, it is important to recall that in Levinas's canon *memory* as a term does not typically fare, despite all its resistance to history, much better. What can be remembered—specifically, what we might recall as the specific content of memory—also falls into history, reconciled to the suppositions on which all cultural knowledge depends. Only insofar as memory signals the psyche's capacity to except itself from the recollective, dialectical plot of knowledge does it receive Levinas's temporary approval; yet, even while defining an exceptional interval within continuous historical time, memory must be complemented by that which is independent of and exterior to it, so as to proceed toward truth. In Levinasian hermeneutics truth does not recollect or get returned to an ideal order. It is, rather, the very principle of force exercised upon the psyche as though, even in its apparent self-sufficiency, the *I* still required what is other to it. Levinas makes a somewhat slippery, perhaps more analogizing than logical, move when he supposes that just as *desire* is an inordinateness searching beyond all happiness, *truth* is the search for that which is exterior to consciousness as though the search were inspired by, even issued from, the point of exteriority. In other words, desire corresponds to the movement of truth, suggesting a vocation of the *I* greater than what can be said of it through any systematic accounting.[14] Like Saussure or Derrida, Levinas comes close (*TI* 62, 64–70) to saying that everything is language, but he breaks with Saussure's stable, synchronic scheme as with Derrida's emphasis on the exorbitant influences of textuality in order to suppose that language is itself tantamount to relationship—the situation of being commanded by the other, of being called into communication as though speech discovered its vocation in ethics, as yet undetermined by an act of volition. Only via this symptomatic resistance of the other to the *I*, which by definition resists systematic elaboration, does Levinas finally arrive at his first principle: namely, an other who is absolutely anterior to every supposition of knowledge or representation, to every conclusion reached through the pragmatics of language usage.

Among the governing conceits of section 1B of *Totality and Infinity* is the metaphorically resistant, yet nevertheless influential, stranger. Indeed, this figure of the stranger effectively bridges the categorical divide between the otherness aimed at in desire and the other as the particular locus of language's communicative mission. In section 1B2 Levinas revises Plato's dictate that all desire tends ultimately toward immortality in order to suggest that the "objective of the first movement of Desire" is, rather than immortality, "the other, the Stranger [*L'immortalité n'est pas l'objectif du premier mouvement du Désir, mais L'Autre, l'Etranger*]" (*TI* 63; *TEI* 35).[15] This odd imbrication of impersonal otherness (Levinas had not yet foregrounded the particular relation to the *Autrui*) with the singular, quasi-mythic stranger already suggests the degree to which otherness will be characterized by the other, and not vice versa (as it is, for example, in Martin Buber). Perhaps even more important, what desire anticipates is precisely that which cannot be accounted for in relative ways. With specific allusion to Plato's own rejection of the myth of formerly whole beings who, having once been severed, forever seek reunion, Levinas insists that desire does not proceed toward originative sameness: "It does not rejoin beings preliminarily married to one another [*Il ne rattache pas des êtres au préalable apparentés*]" (*TEI* 35, my trans.; see *TI* 63). It is not clear to me whether the stranger seems more significant here as the aim or as the supposition of desire, but either way foreignness tropes that which is absolutely other, intimating in its incontrovertible alienation the very forcefulness of ethics.

Yet a short while later this aspect of foreignness is invoked to characterize the interlocutor "whose *way* consists in starting from himself, foreign and yet presenting himself to me [*dont la* manière *consiste à partir de soi, à être étranger et, cependant, à se présenter à moi*]" (*TI* 67; *TEI* 39). As a praxis undoing the reign of sameness, speaking must engage the *I* as though it were mastered by presence or determined straightforwardly by an interlocutor who, even were he to lie, still "abides in the relation of absolute frankness" (*TI* 66). Perhaps the cultural distrust of foreigners as

deceptive, as exuding politeness only insofar as they are dependent and must therefore fashion themselves to the expectations of the host, informs the slide from lying
to foreignness within Levinas's argument, especially if we recall Nietzsche's point
that truth is founded upon lies that have been collectively instituted so as to maintain society and that our persecution thereafter of so-called liars pertains to the challenge they always pose to our instituted truths.[16] At least part of the figurative valence
of lying, as of foreignness, suggests the waning of subjectivity's self-confidence in
its most basic mode of apprehension. By allotting to individuated thinkers the full
credit of reason even while simultaneously disavowing an account of reason as based
in its correlations to a rationally orchestrated system, Levinas worries that any
description of the thinker as an emanation of her moment and context necessarily
argues for a coherence that would make subjective expression tantamount to a suppression of the other, and he then insists upon the expressiveness of language as
simultaneously maintaining the other through the function of address. Thereafter
offering (in sec. 1B5) an almost transparently speculative account of language,
Levinas perceives in it an implied transcendence generated by the "the strangeness
of the interlocutors," which leads to a further quasi-genealogical speculation: "In
other words, language is spoken where community between the terms of the relationship is wanting, where the common plane is wanting or is yet to be constituted.
It takes place in this transcendence. Discourse is thus the experience of something
absolutely foreign. . . ." (TI 73). It is as though Levinas were here to say—revising the
Greek tradition of caricaturing the foreigner's language as barbarism or a nonsensical flow of sound likened to grunts of *bar! bar!*—that language comes most basically
from the foreigner. What is already known, what is familiar or common, entirely
lacks the urgency of communication.[17]

Also remarkable in *Totality and Infinity* is Levinas's imbrication of freedom with
the other qua stranger (although this emphasis on the freedom of the other will be
qualified so as not to give permission to the subject's own arbitrarily exercised will,
and to emphasize that the other must be understood as constituting ethics simultaneously by a relation of mastery or teaching that challenges freedom). In supposing
that only free beings can have this relation to one another, of a dependence that is
not already mutual, Levinas seems influenced by the currents of existentialist
thought in that he presumes that freedom is predicated upon some degree of estrangement from custom. Linked to existentialism by his reactions to the phenomenology
of Husserl and the ontology of Heidegger, by his indebtedness to his revered teacher
and friend Jean Wahl, by the existentialists' incorporation of a philosopher such
as Kierkegaard into their fold, or by the quasi-existentialist overtones of Buber's
thought, Levinas cannot in 1961 bring to mind strangers and the question of freedom

without implicit reference to Albert Camus's novel *The Stranger* (1942).[18] It is even possible that his capitalization of *L'Étranger* in section 1B2 is a direct allusion to Camus. Levinas would discern in Camus's social allegory a philosophical emphasis in which strangers are associated with conceptual or categorical otherness, never quite realized for us as persons who stand, at least potentially, also in our presence. In this sense one might say *stranger* much as one might learn through contemporary race or gender theory to say *the other*, speaking always of those persons deemed to be other than normal or normative.

The ostensible lesson of Camus's *The Stranger*—though certainly, much like Oscar Wilde's *Picture of Dorian Gray* (1891), it proceeds by way of its formal, moral framework to question the validity of all moralistic storytelling—is to instruct us about the influence of behaviors, whether socially or psychically constructed, that arise as though produced from outside of intention. The stranger, an Arab on the beach, inspires a response unmotivated by personal malice, thus prompting the paradox of unpremeditated murder, a hypothesis that all Western legalism maintains even as our rational dictates (by which we prosecute such obviously criminal behaviors) would severely limit the conceptual space of the undeliberated action, if only because such actions seem so fundamentally anarchic or uncontrollable. The murder of someone who is completely unknown tests the very definition of freedom, exhausting freedom by revealing its own absurdist, even violent exigencies, so that the purely unmotivated action seems the supremely contingent event. If society ultimately cannot permit freedom to be exercised in this way, there is little question but that, in not permitting a subject's freedom at the expense of others, the liberal society both restricts and contradicts an irrefutably existentialist whimsicality that inheres in the very possibility of individual freedom.

Thus in Camus it seems, the arbitrariness of intentionality is part of the very social texture of freedom. In existentialist terms freedom is absolutely dependent upon individual will and the capacity to act against norms. Meursault's murder bears the memory of Kierkegaard's violent Abraham, who is heroic in his capacity to follow antisocial, transcendent dictates, even if they prove or seem murderous. By the terms of Camus's novel, which similarly wishes to read the unmotivated murder as inspiring a question or doubt about transcendent meaning, we might say that a stranger is someone upon whom a subject can act not only murderously but as though his own actions were arbitrarily determined. It is for this reason, I think, that Camus absolutely refuses to draw his hero back toward a notion of responsibility based in the recollection of motive, as though a plot of personally triggered causation might too readily support theories of socially determined hatred. Although Camus probably does not expect us to banish altogether the consideration that Meursault's seemingly arbitrary act might be motivated by currents of social prejudice (no doubt the novel should be read, at least in part, as expressive of Camus's ambivalence about France's continuing colonialist enterprise in Algeria), nevertheless the philosophical conundrum of the novel arises insofar as Meursault cannot trace his own motivations.[19] Or, to put it another way, it is because the Arab remains unknown and hostile in his unknowability that Meursault does what he does. (Is the Arab's decision to draw his knife an act of aggression or self-defense?) To murder a neighbor would be to act out a grudge, to be subject to feelings of slightedness, to be the product of a prejudice with a particular prehistory by which it might also be rationalized. But the animosity directed at the stranger can remain, in proportion to his purported anonymity, pure—which is to say, resistant to the agent's capacity for self-reflection.[20] A stranger permits of an unmotivated violence that does not immediately contradict a community's own self-regarding premises, so that, according to the plotted illogic of Camus's novel, the Arab on the beach functions sacrificially as one whose death generates the hero's existentialist crisis.

Among the most ethically questionable moves made by Camus is to have interpreted the modern condition of alienation through the stranger's situation of vulnerability. As one who has murdered a stranger and been imprisoned for his motiveless crime, Meursault is alienated from his own society, unable to examine his own motives to much the same extent that he cannot search the premises of justice in his society. Thus, the novel's plot depends upon a mechanism of usurpation, a tactic of metaphoric remembrance whereby the situation of alienation is hypothetically experienced by the person who has done another violence. The scenario of murder is not directly invoked in section 1B of *Totality and Infinity* (although elsewhere in this work and others, as I have previously observed, Levinas casts the scene of murderous violence as archetypal for the institution of ethics). Still, many of the section's other metaphoric terms recall Camus's imbrication of freedom and estrangement, of existentialist conundrum and a stranger's seeming asociality. Having invoked the stranger as the signifying force of otherness, Levinas proceeds to a description of how alterity arrives at ethical signification through language, privileging "the strangeness of the Other, his very freedom!" as the locus for a transcendent, uncancellable dignity (*TI* 73), and he continues thereafter with a meditation (perhaps obliquely inspired by the fact that the Arab of Camus's novel is murdered under a severe sun on a desolate beach) on the nudity of things versus the nudity of the face. With some debt to Buber, Levinas deplores what can be said of things when they are unadorned—which is to say, unabsorbed in form: "For a thing nudity is the surplus of its being over its finality. It is its absurdity, its uselessness, which itself appears only relative to the form against which it contrasts and of which it is deficient. The thing is always an opacity, a resistance, an ugliness" (*TI* 74). For Levinas the literality of the material is its uselessness, and, insofar as persons might be defined within a system of knowledge making no final distinction between persons and things, every person might degenerate into just such a crudely objective uselessness. What the nudity of the face presents is an alternative posed through language, according to which we "[enter] into relationship with a nudity disengaged from every form" (*TI* 74).

Levinas briefly considers an additional meaning of nudity, which would be derived through a social anxiety about the body's modesty, in other words as a question of shame, but he quickly decides, not so much by argument as by assertion, that such a meaning is entirely consequent upon the "nakedness of the face." At the very least, what this brief digression supposes is that there is a sociality to nakedness, since immediately upon emphasizing the body's spectacular vulnerability he proceeds to assert an ethical meaning in the situation of apparent shamefulness, such that true nudity, which pertains purely to the face, can never be reduced to a shame equated with modesty.[21] Into this hypothesis he also introduces the figure of the stranger: "The transcendence of the face is at the same time its absence from this world into which it enters, the exiling [*depaysement*] of a being, his condition of being stranger, destitute, or proletarian. The strangeness that is freedom is also strangeness-destitution [*étrangeté-misère*]. Freedom presents itself as the other to the same, who is always the autochthon of being, always privileged in his own residence. The other, the free one, is also the stranger. The nakedness of his face extends into the nakedness of the body that is cold and that is ashamed of its nakedness" (*TI* 75). Much as Camus's narrative of senseless crime and punishment gestures vaguely toward the vast scale of motiveless malignity that the Nazis stood for in occupied Europe, Levinas's figurative language slips here from within the privilege of residence to the destitution of nakedness, as though, to borrow Giorgio Agamben's terms, the universe of the concentration camps had revealed the condition of bare humanity as the fundamental object of aversion upon which all politics is constructed.[22] But for Levinas the situation of extremity is less an atavistic sign of political origins from which the Western state can never quite separate itself and according to which it might always lapse from law into the state of exception than the paradoxical site for ethics, even perhaps its raison d'être. Shame, as I suggested in chapter 2, does not presume ordinary moralizing valences so much as the extraordinary situation of ethics, which is also universal and systemic. According to this revalued connotation, then, shame is the corollary of nudity, either term meaningful only insofar as it designates the condition of others for which we must all, as ethical and therefore social beings, be responsible.

In this way, strangeness is at some level exemplary, demonstrating the separation of beings from each other and from the systemic logic upon which any theory of freedom depends. But in their strangeness persons are not existentially universalized such that we might altogether overlook the political conditions producing alienation. Exile is a not uncommon term in Levinas's figurative arsenal, and both Abraham and Odysseus are favorite personages exemplifying different aspects of the Western project of consciousness as an exilic adventure. In the immediately prior example, the association of the face's nudity with the exilic connotation of the other's strangeness suggests the stark reality of the French term *depaysement*, in which we hear historical echoes of a denuding, or particularized disfranchisement, that coincides necessarily with every political act of de-patriatization. By appositionally equating the exile's condition to destitution and to proletarian exploitation, Levinas relies upon the political parameters of all exilic experience, refusing to allow the metaphoric import of estrangement, which he is simultaneously reclaiming for ethics, to lose its hard edges. But Levinas's metaphoric usage is also inconsistent. How it is that the stranger retains his privilege and freedom even as he arrives in destitution, already bereft of those very same privileges, is never explained. At least part of the point, I take it, is that the exilic stranger must occur politically, as ethically, as a sign of his own destitution, someone who cannot return in reality or even in memory to other welcoming, distant shores where we are not responsible for him. According to its familiar French connotation, *depayser* (which is at the heart of *depaysement* as exilic experience) means to take the other out of his element or, by metaphoric generalization, to mislead. Suggested here is an etymological origin for that aspect of lying sometimes projected by hosts onto foreigners, in order to rationalize the political agency that begets exile. Any theory trying to reclaim the exile's subjective experience as beneficial or productive, such as Edward Said's contemporary revaluation of exile as a site of critical consciousness, already diminishes the exilic stranger's most basic meaning—which is that some community (the one he has left or the one into which he is potentially received) must remain, if only in an unrealized way, responsible for his existence.[23]

There is, however, a sense in which the experience of exile cannot be generated from identity as the product of memory. For Levinas neither the stranger's own subjective self-possessing memory nor the outgoing memory of indigenous or naturalized citizens regarding foreigners presently or formerly in their midst can secure again those traces of familiarity we always hope to find, even in the midst of radical estrangement. There is, of course, a long tradition of valuing the Jewish exilic perspective as a hypothesis of impartiality, encouraging detachment because it confers other imaginative and cultural possibilities. When Said infers the intellectual or critical benefits of exile, he draws implicitly upon a metaphoric prestige of the term bequeathed by Judaism, and so too when Daniel and Jonathan Boyarin overtly advocate a politics consequent upon exilic Jewish identity, finding it especially necessary in an era in which the Zionist project has recuperated the Jews to nationalist belonging, they intuit the ethical limitations of all too readily located attachments.[24] Whereas the Boyarins propose an exilic emphasis such that the memory of the stranger would sustain a critique from within identity, Levinas attributes ethical meaning to the figure of the exile insofar as it designates the relation to someone purely other, to the foreigner as someone about or for whom a subject can never presume partiality.

In response to the position I have here associated with Ozick, Levinas would suggest that exile cannot serve in history as a lesson for others, even if the one who has undergone exile would like to offer a lesson based upon her remembrances. Exile opposes not just normative identity (as it does for Said when he presumes that the oppositional stance of exilic consciousness will serve as its own anchoring counter-identity) but any social theory that would proceed from the stability of identity. Clearly, Levinas operates within a tradition of exilic Jewish consciousness that Berel Lang suspects of being inseparable from theories such as Freud's hypothesis of projective fantasy or Sartre's elaboration of the irreality that produces all antisemitic antagonisms—in other words, from theories (Kristeva's is yet another of the same type) in which the one who is maltreated, hated, or persecuted cannot in the moment of her persecution also be a person whose subjective experience is firmly moored in identity. The danger, say, for exiled Jews is that consciousness of self-as-alien must follow from the cultural logic of other-as-alien, never to be generated in the first place by the Jewish people themselves.[25] What Lang asks of all who value exile's opposition to identity, such as the Boyarins or Levinas, is whether it is possible that one could ever deny oneself in order to affirm oneself.

One might answer Lang's query with a question absolutely contrary to its premise: *who said anything about affirming oneself?* For, regardless of when and how often affirmation is necessary, or how we account for the difference between a pragmatic psychology of self and a social theory in which such an affirmation could only proceed from strong group ideology, or whether we doubt that what sometimes makes for good psychology has continuous value once translated into the realm of politics, for Levinas one thing is clear: ethics is not affirmation. This is nowhere more clear than in the essay "No Identity" (1970), written at least partly as a response to the revolutionary fervor of France in 1968, as a reflection upon an intellectual climate Levinas feared had become governed by apocalyptic platitudes. Even as he attempts to reclaim for humanism some of the prestige it had formerly bestowed upon phi-

losophy and ethics, Levinas rejects any nostalgic clinging to a humanism still reverently enamored of self-possessed identity. Gladly conceding the basic argument of
Nietzsche, Marx, and Heidegger that a certain philosophical conception of the self
as capable of coinciding with itself and initiating its responsibility in the world has
come to an end, Levinas nevertheless objects to the conclusion reached by all structuralist critiques of the human sphere insofar as they suppose that the pronounced
end of our capacity for self-coinciding must altogether destroy the vitality of *the
human* as a measure of ethical and political existence. By associating humanistic
vitality with youthfulness (his revisionary figure for the student movements of 1968),
Levinas suggests that the energy within the category of the human is instead generated by a lack of self-coinciding, that subjectivity might "signify precisely by its incapacity to shut itself up from the outside" (NI 145).

Significantly for my argument, much of the essay "No Identity" is shaped by
Levinas's metaphoric elaboration of the conceit of the stranger or foreigner. When
Levinas interprets the end of metaphysics as the end of *being* insofar as it is grounded
upon "native land" and refers instead to the "foreignness of man in the world, his
stateless condition" (NI 144), he is carrying on an argument with a Heideggerian,
existentialist characterization of the modern condition of alienation, refusing by way
of an allusion to the stateless Jews of the middle twentieth century to allow history
to become metaphorically interchangeable with a crisis of the individual soul.[26]
There is a basic question as to whether "subjection to this foreigner" is to be experienced only as self-alienation and not, instead, as a self-accusation having the very
structure or substitutive crux of ethics, described here through Rimbaud's phrase "I
is an other" (NI 145). It as though the foreigner could make consciousness foreign to
itself. Interpreting "the deportation or drifting of identity" testified to by pronouncements of humanism's end (NI 145), and wondering whether humanity's youthful
vitality is exhausted by such apparent evidence, Levinas recalls the historical severity of political exile, his usage of *deportations* remembering the nationalist imperatives of Nazism by which Jews were forcibly extracted from their homes. What
Levinas intuits is a construct of history to be gleaned through our politically determined structural relation to those estranged others who might otherwise become
mere metaphoric fodder for the soul. Still, there can be little doubt that Levinas also
reads this defeat of identity opportunistically, even perhaps sacrificially (in the terms
of my previous chapter) as a reminder of subjectivity's strange election, which is to
be for the other.

A similar dialectical tension is maintained when Levinas cites in this same essay
a biblical verse that exemplifies the ethical crisis the stranger poses to identity. Invoking Hebrew scriptures, suggesting that "the Greek scripture of the philosophers" is

not in simple opposition to biblical imperatives but rather perhaps in the position of deciphering "a writing hidden in a palimpsest" (NI 148), Levinas's allusion is doubly revisionary (he revises philosophy from the perspective of a tradition implicitly revised and contained by philosophic writings). Notably, he does not arrive at a direct affirmation of the privileges of Jewish identity. Instead he cites biblical verses in which Israel's experience is desperately exilic and yet paradigmatic of human possibility. Levinas quotes, for example, the verse from Psalm 119, "I am a stranger on the earth, do not hide from me your commandments," suggesting that, even if such a dictum dates from the Hellenistic period, already influenced by Plato's conception of the soul as exiled in the human body, it also recalls Leviticus 15:23: "No land will be alienated irrevocably, for the earth is mine, for you are but strangers, domiciled in my land" (NI 148). Since the land cannot possibly belong to the people, the situation of exile is perpetuated, indicative even in Levinas's revisionary reading of biblical myth of the "difference between the ego and the world," by obligations incurred to others via the condition of exile. Only human beings who cannot finally be sure they belong anywhere will find themselves involuntarily thrown again and again into encounter. Persons who coincide with their own self-conception, who seem capable of possessing themselves much as they possess the land, would be capable also of turning from their obligations and defining themselves by closing off what is outside or foreign. By contrast, Levinas decides that "the condition (or the uncondition) of being strangers and slaves in the land of Egypt brings man close to his neighbor. In their uncondition of being strangers men seek one another. No one is at home. The memory of this servitude assembles humanity" (NI 149).

Just how different, we may ask, is this from Ozick's proposal? The memory of being a stranger upon the land plays a constructive role in Levinas and does seemingly bequeath, as in Ozick, a legacy of generosity to others. But there is a fundamental difference between Ozick's and Levinas's respective formulations. For Levinas never presumes an identity formerly possessed of itself, which was once capable of recuperating its own elective capacity. Rather, he suggests a point at which memory simply will not line up with identity, at which it will not lend itself out even in remnant form, in this way refusing to exercise a reifying influence on what an individual or group might possess according to its self-constituting premises. Thus, the phrase I have been employing here, "the memory of the stranger," is (according to the Levinasian hermeneutic) firmly paradoxical, blurring the properties of the subjective and objective genitive. For the stranger is the one who bears evidence of memory's unreliability, someone who, in his objective "uncondition"—according to what Levinas a little later calls the "unreal reality of men persecuted in the daily history of the world"—does not belong to memory or to what normative memory reclaims for the province of identity (NI 150). Even in their individual memory of servitude, persons are cast toward what is outside of inherited knowledge and familiar experience—the *I* defined not through identity but rather as a "stranger to itself" (NI 149), disquieted by history and the real presence of others. Only in its estrangement from self as in its dedication to imperfectly remembered strangers is the *I* thrown into necessary relation with those who are also neighbors.

SOMEBODY'S KNOCKING AT THE DOOR . . .

En route, as it were, to *Otherwise than Being* (1974), with its more severely unpleasurable figures for alterity, Levinas wrote a subtle yet powerful essay called "Enigma and Phenomenon" (1965) which evokes the dichotomy of *stranger/neighbor* in a not altogether consistent manner.[27] Although it might well seem a transitional essay, in which Levinas begins to experiment overtly with conceiving the other of ethics newly as *neighbor* (or perhaps no longer as quite such a stranger, since she is also nearby), it is not clear in this essay that the other as stranger ever quite gives way to neighborly familiarity. In the first half of Levinas's career, during which his primary idiom for alterity was infinity, he consistently invoked the figure of the stranger to speak of the other.[28] "Enigma and Phenomenon" is an in-between work in every sense, for not only does it show Levinas reformulating his earlier philosophical conception of the other as extreme exteriority in order to articulate a responsibility that arises especially in proximity, but it describes an other who exists precariously or enigmatically between arrival and departure, as if at every turn at which responsibility for the other might become apparent the other were to withdraw and, in so doing, estrange the very conceptual rubric by which we might recognize him.

The prevailing conceit of Levinas's essay is determined by its epigraph from Eugène Ionesco's play *The Bald Soprano* (1950): "In short, we still do not know if, when someone rings the doorbell, there is someone there or not. . . ."[29] Directly invoked several times over the course of the essay, this central moment in Ionesco's play figures the larger philosophical problem of the enigma, or trace, as a resistance within being, knowledge, or experience (read also: ontology, epistemology, or phenomenology). As an echo of what Levinas already calls the Saying and predicting his further development of this concept in the essay "Substitution" (1968) and in *Otherwise than Being* (1974), the enigma is a mode of signifying that withdraws from its own apparent significances. In its argumentative reach "Enigma and Phenomenon" develops Levinas's friendly quarrel with the philosophical school of phenomenology (from Husserl to Jean-Luc Nancy and Paul Ricoeur), as he sets the ethical dimension of language apart from — and in tension with — both the resolutions of cognition and the manifest meanings of experience. Referring language to that which cannot be manifested in experience precisely because it resists its own intelligibility, Levinas conjures a "signification that would signify in an irreducible disturbance" (EP 67), even as he simultaneously admits that the notion of disturbance already supposes a phenomenon to be reabsorbed into knowledge, into the realm of perpetual sameness.

In *The Bald Soprano* a couple named the Martins, who can barely remember each other, visit their friends the Smiths, who claim to be surprised by these unexpected guests and yet also to have been waiting for them for four hours. In the midst of their polite, nonsensical small talk a doorbell rings three times in a row, but when the door is answered no one is there. Only when it rings a fourth time is there somebody on the step, a fire chief who claims to have been waiting for entry for forty-five minutes but also denies having rung the bell the first two times (although he admits to having rung it the third time and to having thereafter hid himself from view). A debate quickly ensues about whether one can conclude that when a doorbell rings someone will be at the door, and Mrs. Smith, who answered the door the first three times but not the fourth, even proposes, based on her own experience, that when a doorbell rings no one will ever be there. Levinas's first invocation of Ionesco focuses specifically on the problem of whether the other person can ever be introduced into the social order of knowledge except as a temporary disturbance, an interruptive, presumptuous claim that troubles all of a subject's presuppositions: "Someone unknown to me rang my doorbell and interrupted my work. I dissipated a few of his illusions. But he brought me into his affairs and his difficulties, troubling my good conscience. The disturbance, the clash of two orders, ends in a conciliation, in the constitution of a new order which, more vast, closer to the total, and in this sense ultimate or original, order, shines through this conflict" (EP 68). In Levinas's revisionary formulation, a doorbell rings and a door gets answered, leading to a seemingly ordinary conversation during which the guest and the host temporarily have an impact upon one another (dissipating illusions or dispelling good conscience) before having, eventually, to enact a conciliation that is less about their relation to one another than about functioning within a cultural system. The element of difference that inspires conversation cannot hold; any sense of the absoluteness of alterity subsides.

In the very next paragraph Levinas once more revisits the implicit scene from Ionesco, this time imagining the encounter with the other at the door as if it already eluded the realization of thoughts or words, as though meeting were itself an evasion: "The strident ringing of the bell is reabsorbed into significations; the break in my universe was a new signification that came to it. Everything is understood, justified, pardoned. And what of the surprise of that face behind the door? That surprise will be denied" (EP 68). Again in quasi-Hegelian terms, the facticity of surprise gets suppressed, or at the very least accounted for, within the general progress of our knowledge. Yet by Ionesco's absurdistly insistent hypothesis, as here by Levinas's implicit adoption of it, an incident in which a doorbell rings without giving way to a person on the doorstep is every bit as significant as the historically verifiable fact of the fire chief's conventionally announced arrival. His act of remaining long enough to be received would chart the relation between ringing the bell and entering a house as though it were a realized intentionality, whereas the specter of withdrawal from even such minimal intentionality suggests (if it is anything more than a child's game of ding-dong-ditch raised to the level of absurdist parable) an other who might ring doorbells without knowing ahead of time whether they'll be answered or even whether he'll stick around long enough to find out whether he'll be invited in or turned away. Such a withdrawal denotes the other's behavior as enigmatic, and the quality of the *enigma* obtains the character of a mock-transcendence, as Levinas sympathetically elaborates Kierkegaard's conception of a religious truth valid only insofar as it is persecuted by the "universally evident truth" (EP 71), so as to approximate the absurdist paradoxicality of existentialism. Responsibility, according to such an absurdist connotation, is a responsiveness never entirely parallel to the prospect of answerability in its predictable connotations. One must still go to the door, even if one does not believe someone is there.

In refusing *The Bald Soprano*'s refusal to consider the possibility that the fire chief might have been lying about the first two incidents (recall that he denies having rung the bell the first two times), we may wonder whether the ringing of a doorbell announces the arrival, and perhaps immediate withdrawal, of a stranger or of the neighbor. With Ionesco's scene as resonant subtext, Levinas considers the metaphorical person at the door under both aspects of alterity. Still worrying about a trajectory according to which disturbance will always tend to subside, Levinas asks whether the event of "abrupt coming," functioning here again as an implicit allusion to Ionesco, might signify under the aspect of approach rather than result. "Did not a neighbor approach?" he queries, with an obvious yet deeply resonant pun on the *neigh-bor* as one who is nigh, *le prochain* as the "one who is near" or "the next one" (EP 69). Apologetically, Levinas also glosses his adoption of this more familiar term for the other in a footnote: "Formerly we refused this term [*prochain*], which seemed to us to suggest community by neighboring. Now we retain in it the abruptness of the disturbance, which characterizes a neighbor inasmuch as he is the first one to come along" (EP 178–79). Referring to one who is immediately nearby, the term *le prochain* supports a double function, designating someone who both approaches, even in a situation wherein he is already near, and also alienates us from what we know about him. Since the pure stranger is someone never truly encountered, Levinas refers ethics to the situation of nearness as though the approach of the other intimated a responsibility that could not, at least not in good conscience, be refused. Every time the other comes along he usurps the place of priority as though there were no difference between his being the first ever to come along and the first within a certain perceptible block of time—say, a week, a day, or fifteen minutes—to make a demand upon the subject merely by having approached her. In coming near again as if for the first time, a neighbor disturbs the presumptions of cultural knowledge by which he was previously defined and by which the subject's responsibility for him was mediated and delimited.

Much of this connotation too seems borrowed from *The Bald Soprano*, specifically with regard to Ionesco's technique of defamiliarizing characterization. During a protracted scene in the first half of the play, after the Martins have paid their expected yet surprising visit to the Smiths, they sit in the living room talking to each other while their hosts dress for dinner offstage. Over the course of their conversation they seem puzzlingly familiar to one another, even as they repeatedly pronounce themselves unable to recall how it is each knows the other. Reviewing their individual recent histories, they soon establish that they have often been in the same place at the same time—sitting across from one another on the train this afternoon, living at the same house and sleeping in the same bed, and each having raised a daughter whom through the logic of coincidence each admits to having parented. Only after charting their elaborately parodic course through a recognition scene modeled on the reunion of Penelope and Odysseus (in which the description of a shared bed also plays a central role) are the Martins able to declare themselves husband and wife, whereupon Mr. Martin proposes that they "try not to lose each other anymore" (20).

What Ionesco offers us in this scene is a parable of history without memory, a mutual past veering toward uselessness as heritage precisely because the outstanding social characteristics uniting the couple are so extraordinarily banal, their intimacy having been charted only by superficial markings, by their having again, after brief confusion, aligned themselves on the side of social convention. It is as if Penelope's fantastic testing of Odysseus, which precipitates the emotional plot of reunion in *The Odyssey*, were to happen every day in the lives of this couple—a version of which plot has been exploited for its comedic, yet sentimentally affirming potential by recent Hollywood films such as *Groundhog Day* (1993) and *Fifty First Dates* (2004). Made to seem strangers to themselves, able to reenact mutuality only by a protracted remembrance of the social factors that identify them as a couple, the

Martins seem to diminish reunion to the point where their declarations of affection caricature all the anxious urgency involved in losing track of a loved one, even temporarily. Perhaps just as significantly, their inadequate knowledge of one another prefigures the announcement of the *neighbor/stranger*, who a short while later rings the doorbell, approaching without necessarily arriving. For Ionesco every movement toward familiarity, dependent upon the basic presumption of knowing another person, is disrupted by the difficulty any of us has in sustaining the social form of familiarity—or, should we say, achieving it even once more.

Just such an ironic reservation is implicit in Levinas's own early wariness about the term *neighbor*, and it is largely what we cannot know even about our neighbors that shakes Levinas free of his reservations. If I read him correctly, Levinas's wariness stems from the economically predefined nature of neighborliness, which as a construct of familiarity sets specific boundaries for perceiving others. Levinas would employ the term *neighbor* more freely in his later writings—and sometimes (as in a 1985 discussion about the politics of Israel) in ways surprisingly reliant on just such a cultural economy of limitations. For the most part, however, in this 1965 essay and in his developing articulation of *proximity*, the Levinasian neighbor approaches a subject through the metaphorical possibility of being someone who is alien even in his proximity and seeming familiarity. Initially interpreting Ionesco's doorbell ringer as a neighbor, Levinas openly wonders how it has been possible for the neighbor "to tear himself up from the context" (EP 69). The problem posed here is whether it is possible for the other to connote a responsibility not resolved in advance by the cultural constructs of identity or a social system attributing value to people by order and rank. In response, as he speculates further about whether relationship can signify apart from the indications of the present order, Levinas introduces the idea of *the trace* in the same essay. As that mode of signification marking a relational depth that does not fully arrive in the present tense, the trace is for Levinas an empty, desolate, and forgetful sign emphasizing an ethical paradoxicality according to which the "dereliction" of reference suggests a relationship interrupted even before contact. Responsibility does not measure merely that which has been asked directly of us. Rather, Levinas modifies Ionesco's conceit of the stranger/neighbor who rings but perhaps cannot wait to be received in order to describe the trace as a "solicitation that does not have the effrontery to solicit." It is even a "beggar's solicitation" (EP 69–70), signifying one who would by the very fact of her existence beg the question of our responsibility and whose departure might be predicted from the condition of inequality between us, by the fact that he is someone who requires neither tactics of familiar welcoming nor mutual comfort but rather a response inspired by the radical disparity between two parties.

From the outset I have maintained that the particular species of immemorial remembrance Levinas links to ethics has to do with the memory of injustice, and yet an injustice that is not constituted according to the grievance of a single party speaking from the knowledge of its woundedness and recuperating its identity by measuring what it has lost. Any grievance readily negotiated within and as part of cultural currency has already become a conceptual property, a resource for identity. In this sense the capacity to refer to a past that will not amount to the present is the peculiarly unfulfillable calling of the trace, which marks a disturbance not chartable as a conflict within the order of knowledge leading eventually to conciliation. According to the pattern of Hegelian conceptualization, thought must arrive at the present, even if only by pointing toward the future of the present.[30] By this very logic thought and identity correspond through a dialectical trajectory, which, while being subjected to farcical caricature in Ionesco's couple, seems nevertheless to predict their reconciliation. Rededicating themselves to the appearance of reinforcing mutuality, as though they realized with Nietzsche that truth is simply the revaluation of a lie collectively agreed upon for the good of society, Ionesco's couple, the Martins, enact a social identity (even if it is, as the Maid hints, a false one) they plan to extend into the future. By contrast, the trace can neither propose nor suppose any stable order. It deposes the very idea it would seem to bring forth, much in the manner of a "movement that already carries away the signification it brought" (EP 70).

In building so adamantly upon a vignette from *The Bald Soprano*, Levinas might almost be accused of taking Ionesco's absurdism too seriously, of earnestly flattening out the play's irreverent ironies and rendering them as sincere philosophy (after all, it is entirely possible that the fire chief, who does finally appear on the door claiming to have been there for forty-five minutes and to have hid only the third time, is a mere liar or trickster, someone playing a game of withdrawal that is, since deceitful, also transparently unethical). But Levinas declares language itself to be given over to such an absurdist scenario—"someone rang, and there is no one at the door: did anyone ring?" According to an "enigmatic equivocation," which intuits responsibility even from within the social scenario of seeming irresponsibility, language is always a beckoning both oracular and extravagant, which presumes the other through whom and for whom it speaks (EP 70). For Levinas, much as the face-to-face relation must designate a sincerity overruling even a murderer's self-rationalizing intentions, the other who withdraws before any encounter has taken place necessarily stands, in his implicit earnestness, for a demand that will be reduced neither to the simultaneity between what he says and what he stands for nor to a similarity between what he signifies and what the subject understands him to signify. To withdraw before encounter is to signify in advance the meaning of ethics as that which eludes our interpretations of responsibility.[31]

At the same time Levinas cannot, however, forgo the connotation of the stranger as the one who more than merely unsettles rationality, and so he switches from calling Ionesco's constantly withdrawing bell ringer a "neighbor" to referring to him as a "stranger": "And yet disturbance is possible only through an intervention. A stranger is then needed, one who has come, to be sure, but left *before* having come, ab-solute in his manifestation." Perhaps because neighbors never appear to us as having newly arrived—they have always been there, haunting our doorsteps as familiar places, if only intermittently noticed by us—Levinas instead invokes the stranger who intrusively arrives as one who cannot reasonably have been expected. The particular appeal of the stranger is that he is one who, since "the past of the Other must never have been present," absolutely cannot be accounted for as the object of common memory (EP 72). Then too strangers withdraw more absolutely than neighbors do. If one does not respond to the call of the stranger, if one does not answer the ringing bell, she recedes into an unknowability entirely consummate with her alterity.

Just such an outcome is intimated when Levinas refers a little later in the essay to the saying that remains unheard, wondering what it is that one can hear by "listening at the doorway of language" even as "it closes on its own apertures" (EP 74). The suggestion is that what does not enter into language as speech, what does not arrive finally at the moment of mutual understanding, is every bit as important as that which language directly pronounces upon. To confine ourselves only to what we have heard or expected to hear, to answer the door only when we feel like it, is to be guilty of an inhospitality to the very meaning of language; though such an action may seem reasonable, it is hardly ethical. "It is perhaps reasonable to respect the decency of this closed door," Levinas says ironically, already supposing that our social codes of privacy shut out the realm of larger responsibility by ignoring the beggar, refugee, or perhaps desperate neighbor who is on the doorstep. Language, he asserts, must always be positioned on a threshold of meaning, at a "door thus both open and closed," which Levinas also calls "the extra-ordinary duplicity of the Enigma." In the essay's most emphatic statement of the enigmatic, estranging aspect of responsibility, Levinas characterizes the stranger precisely as the one who has arrived to contradict a subject's expectations but also his desire: "The enigma, the intervention of a meaning which disturbs phenomena but is quite ready to withdraw like an undesirable stranger, unless one harkens to those footsteps that depart, is transcendence itself, the proximity of the Other as Other" (EP 74). Seemingly reticent in her trespass, unwilling to provoke the subject in his complacency, the stranger has perhaps intuited the extent to which she must, by definition, be that which is not already desired. Only the subject's necessary pursuit of a disturbance already in remission ensures the vocation of ethics.

"Enigma and Phenomenon" is of interest to me, then, not only because Levinas reluctantly adopts the term *neighbor*, even while falling back upon the figure of the stranger, but also because the very fact of such an ambiguous shift in terminology constitutes the admission of a problem. There is perhaps something inherently abstract in the notion of the stranger, who either remains truly unknown to us or in arriving sets himself apart from the neighbor by his non-belonging, by his aberrance from the norms of our culture. In the 1960s, as he began more frequently to deploy the idiom of proximity and substitution, supposing partly in response to Derrida that ethics must devise an insistence not connotatively metaphysical (which is to say, not purely exterior to the cultural system of knowledge), Levinas conjured ever more frequently the surprising possibility of a neighbor who might approach almost as if she were a stranger. "Enigma and Phenomenon" charts almost too neatly this transitional stage. Levinas first describes the hypothetical other at the door as neighbor, modulates into speaking (as in an already practiced ethical key) of him as stranger, and then at the end of the essay again refers to him as the neighbor. In retrospect one already hears "the strident ringing of the bell" in the first half of the essay as the insistent tones of a stranger or at the very least a desperate neighbor, the beckoning of someone alienated by circumstance from the rhythm of ordinary expectation. Within the figurative logic of the essay, the stranger and neighbor eventually become imbricated, almost as though each were to take turns ringing the bell and withdrawing, overlapping to the point where we cannot be sure which is which.

There is, we might say, following the essay's figurative logic, a discernment of a spectral stranger within every neighbor; and even if Levinas's figurative progression were to be deemed relatively unintentional, it nevertheless predicts a conflicted connotation unavoidable in his future work. On this note it is worth again recalling that in Ionesco's play the person appearing on the doorstep the final time is the fire chief, who may be nothing more than an alarmist. Announcing that he has been commissioned to put out all fires in the city and deducing therefore that it his duty to put out the fire in the Martins' kitchen stove, the fire chief is utterly unable to distinguish the situation of emergency from a condition of normalcy. Yet, as Levinas incorporates Ionesco's threshold scene, employing it as figurative conceit or submerged moral philosophical anecdote, he implicitly revises the fire chief's alarmism into a kind of ethical vigilance. Every time a doorbell rings it might as readily portend a predictable encounter, a false alarm, a waste of my time, or perhaps an emergency affirming the very reason I must answer all stridently rung doorbells, searching out my responsibility for a stranger or neighbor who has perhaps already withdrawn from her request. The doorbell rings at any hour; it might be the mail-man, a fire chief, a beggar or homeless person, a refugee fleeing Nazism, perhaps only a vacuum cleaner salesman, or perhaps a stranger such as Kitty Genovese, the woman who in 1964, in a series of attacks near and in her own apartment building in Queens, New York, was raped and knifed to death while calling for help, without a single neighbor's door being opened to her. While creatively adopting a scenario from Ionesco's *Bald Soprano* and flattening out the play's absurdist ironies into a parable of responsibility, Levinas never quite concretizes the scene of ethics he would implicitly construct. There is, however, just enough metaphoric residue in other pieces of his figurative language to suggest that the distinctive circumstance imagined by Levinas in this essay pertains to the plight of the refugee. Levinas refers on one occasion to the "exorbitant proposition" one diplomat makes to another and then later appraises the ethical signifyingness of the enigma as that which "does not take refuge" in an already constituted sphere to be grasped by prepared conceptual solutions (EP 70, 75). According to such subtly allusive figures, there is always some-one who arrives as a stranger and demands to be encountered as though from within the idiom of the neighbor. Whoever might be at the door having already withdrawn from it—whether a refugee, a persecuted citizen with but minimal time in which to make her request, or a familiarly oppressed citizen who has not yet plumbed the abyss of her destitution—the occasion of beckoning arises as an excessive responsi-bility within sociality. It is the demand according to which sociality is construed as a structure of relationship never to be stabilized, or put to rest, by the social order.

LEST WE FORGET — THE NEIGHBOR

Although throughout this book I have attempted to draw out Levinas's conceits in order to elucidate their implication for his ethical thought, I would nevertheless be reluctant to ascribe to such figurative language a simply determinative influence on the philosophical speculations in which it participates. And yet Levinas's subtle interrogation of the stranger/neighbor antinomy does amount to a philosophical argument conducted at the level of figurative language. With regard to his use of fig-urative language, Levinas typically avoids the question of imaginative mediation by employing what I want to call, paradoxically, a *metaphoric literalism*. What makes figurative language suspect, coinciding with the fault of the aesthetic imagination per se, is that it always recedes from immediacy as from the direct signification of the face-to-face encounter.[32] In contrast, Levinas's ethicofigural language imposes a reality of ethics prior to the cognitive and imaginative acts through which the ethi-cal situation is conceived and acted upon. Thus, for example, the Levinasian conceit of tearing the bread from one's mouth to offer it to the other never gives the slightest hint that we should understand it as merely analogical. The bread torn from one's mouth is supposed to be a literal inscription of a demand impressed upon us before any act of sharing could even be conceived. In this example, which at the same time annihilates its anecdotal function, Levinas executes a transposition of those situational examples ordinarily employed by moral philosophy, situations that more typically turn toward general or universal applications. As the conventional trajectory of metaphor's trespass is abrogated by Levinas, the particularity of taking bread from one's mouth comes to stand not as symbolic of an ethical situation but as though it were a sign of the literal moment of ethics itself. This aspect of literalism in Levinas's language draws the critique of Derrida, who argues that Levinas puts himself in a double bind by so frequently employing the copula *to be* in his description of ethics, even while the aim of his entire project is to define ethics as otherwise than being and thus, presumably, as free from a language of essence characteristically dependent on declarative statements and copula constructions.[33] I would emphasize, rather, that a technique of rhetorical compression characterizes the Levinasian style, functioning, as it were, as the very idiom of the ethical in his work and thus demonstrating a remarkable consistency between the style and content of Levinasian ethics. For Levinas the term *proximity* articulates the way in which the other presses upon me as "a suppression of distance [that] suppresses the distance of consciousness of . . . ," so that Levinas's highly compressed syntax and metaphoric literalism amount to a stylistics of proximate constructions, within which grammatical copulas and appositions compound the multiplicity of terms that name the ethical (*OTB* 89).

Ethics itself is a structure of infinitely compounded relation. The conceit of proximity, which sometimes takes on a persecuting intensity, seems especially fitted to the syntax of Levinasian ethics, indicative of his almost infuriating habit of stringing clauses together appositionally, of piling phrase upon phrase in relations of seemingly endless modulation and elliptical parataxis (a technique probably indebted to biblical parataxis, which similarly abbreviates the logical arrangement of its rapidly conjoined clauses). If we were to define it by its own emphatic redundancy, we might say that proximity is especially a relation to the neighbor's nearness. In this respect proximity is not quite the same thing as the idiom of neighborliness. Supposing a nearness more strangely immediate than any conceptualization, a position inside of all familiarity, Levinas's proximate neighbor might well be imagined along the lines of the infamous "close-talker" from the sitcom *Seinfeld*, the guy who (for a single episode) dates Elaine and habitually stands too near to her and to everyone else with whom he is conversing.[34] The close-talker is incapable of discerning social boundaries. Over the course of the episode he befriends Jerry's visiting parents and treats them, the parents of a friend of a woman he is only casually dating, as though they were longtime intimate acquaintances, even taking time off from work just to ferry them around New York. What makes the close-talker so comical is that he stands on the hither side of a social awkwardness we all potentially inhabit. To the extent that the social codes presiding over our linguistic conduct are variable, open to subtle interpretive shifts, and always subject to violation, any of us might fail to uphold the cultural rules and boundaries by which they are preserved. If the close-talker were a foreigner—perhaps from the Mediterranean, the Middle East, Africa, or Latin America, any culture known for its extremely other-than-Anglo social codes, for communicative mores that impinge upon Anglo-American sensibilities—his ignorance of social custom would perhaps account for his slightly aberrant relation to language and his New York neighbors. But on *Seinfeld* the fact that the close-talker carries with him a hint of the foreigner's ignorance, while lacking any such excuse for his ignorance, makes him absurdly comical. Alienated from social routine even while standing, at least by all appearances, entirely within it, the close-talker is nevertheless utterly sincere; he is almost too sincere, as though sincerity could admit of degrees. To stand inside of language's comfort zones, impinging upon a speaker before she has spoken, one's every breath as impressive as, say, one's facial expression or bodily appearance, all of one's manners already contextualizing what one will say before it has been spoken—this is to realize proximity as the absolute condition of all communicativeness.

As with foreigners and awkward users of language, so also for proximate speakers: they remind us of the extent to which language is based already, even perhaps uncomfortably, in ethical relation. All of us are proximate speakers, Levinas supposes, no matter how close or how far away we stand. Perhaps the primary metaphoric function of the neighbor for Levinas is to signify this necessarily importuning function of ethics as set against language's neutral, philosophical objectivity. In a passage, for instance, in which Levinas interprets the suppression of distance as tantamount to the occurrence of the highly proximate other, he contends that the neighbor already excludes himself from "the thought that seeks him" and that ethics is the positive denotation of this exclusion: "my exposure to him, antecedent to his appearing, my delay behind him, my undergoing, undo the core of what is identity in me" (*OTB* 89). We observe here the use of a tripled appositional structure (though Levinas is certainly capable of stringing together many more clauses than this), as if grammatical compactedness could connote language's implication in relationship, mimetically enacting the point that the ethical relation is, par excellence, a severe closeness to the other. If ethics is an inrushing of alterity, it must be signified in part through a variety of precognitive moments failing to assemble into the ordinary temporal or clausal relations that help position the others around us into preconceived social narratives or cognitive schemes.

Already in "Enigma and Phenomenon" Levinas borrows the stranger's signifying alterity for the neighbor, attributing the stranger's unknowability even to the one with whom a subject is already in relation, and as he speaks of an "approach beyond thought" (EP 67) likens the signifying force of the trace to that absolutely unrealized approach of the stranger-like neighbor at the door. More and more frequently after 1965, the *neighbor* signifies for Levinas the other with whom one has contact characterized not so much by familiarity as by an aspect of proximity that beckons, renewedly. In essays such as "Language and Proximity" (1967) and "Substitution" Levinas develops the ethical connotations of proximity as central to his project. In the latter of these two essays he associates the trace with the construct of proximity in order to describe the ethical relation as that which will not resolve itself in words, an "invisibility that becomes contact" (S 80). Further emphasizing the anarchical force of proximity as a relationship "without the mediation of any principle or ideality," he immediately thereafter speaks of proximity as describing "my relationship with the neighbor" insofar as that relationship is prior to any sense brought to bear upon it by consciousness (S 81).

As someone who is already there, even before a subject formulates an idea of her, the neighbor preoccupies every thought one could have about her, and also intimates, strangely enough, a relation to those one does not know: "It is the summoning of myself by the other (*autrui*), it is a responsibility toward those whom we do not even know. The relation of proximity does not amount to any modality of distance or geometrical contiguity, nor to the simple 'representation' of the neighbor. It is *already* a summons of extreme exigency, an obligation which is *anachronistically* prior to every engagement" (S 81) Taking care to argue against the modality of distance through which one might expect to conceptualize proximity (if only as the fact of limited distance), Levinas efficiently leverages the terminological echoes of the stranger, who has seemed perhaps too easily classified by degrees of separation — as though she were always just enough at a distance to remain outside of immediate responsibility, either not obviously insistent in her demand or having seemingly withdrawn before she could become insistent. The neighbor, however, summons the subject before an other who is already in place, in the very same place in which the subject finds herself, and it is precisely this connotation of hypothetical replacement that becomes so central in the essay, since the other is someone for whom, in whose place or in whose stead, a subject must stand to the extent that she is also responsible.

In the extremity of her summons, a neighbor surprises us by summoning our responsibility regardless of any social knowledge we have of her identity, even independent of any voluntary intention we might adopt toward her: "The intentionality of consciousness certainly does not refer solely to a voluntary intention. And yet it does retain the initiating and inchoate motif of a voluntary intention. Thought recognizes and invests its very project in the given which enters it. The given manifests itself a priori—from the first, it re-presents itself—but it does not knock at the door unannounced, allowing, across the interval of space and time, the leisure necessary for welcome" (S 82). Here in "Substitution" Levinas treats the other who knocks at the door or rings a bell as though such a scenario were the archetypal situation for ethics, within which the ethical meaning of the other must be maintained as distinct from any resultant welcome that might follow. Against the hypothesis of a predictable visit that always suits the welcoming disposition of the subject, Levinas supposes that one might answer the door only to find oneself persecuted by the other, pursued by a responsibility far in excess of what one has been prepared to do for the other. By thus inflecting the emergency scenario with the additional force of persecution, Levinas intuits a responsibility persisting in every situation into which a neighbor is introduced as if for the first time. Along these lines, having already established the ethical necessity of passivity and having associated it with an incarnational suffering perceived under the sign of persecution, Levinas declares in the fourth chapter of *Otherwise than Being* (revising his 1968 essay) that passivity deserves "the epithet of complete or absolute only if the persecuted one is liable to answer for the persecutor." In the previous chapter I elaborated the sacrificial connotations embedded in this attitude, but it is worth remarking additionally that, according to Levinas's figurative typology, it is the neighbor and not the stranger who most often assumes the role of a persecuting other: "The face of the neighbor in its persecuting hatred can by this very malice obsess as something pitiful" (*OTB* 111). What Levinas appears to intuit is that only the neighbor can enact hostility with genuine malice.

Since the relation to the stranger is largely imaginary and always in some sense impersonal, the hypothesis of hostility, which is sometimes projected onto strangers as though it originated in their will, is always challenged once they enter into familiar terms—which is to say, once they have been converted from their alien status. Such a hypothesis is frequently revisited in the Hebrew Bible, as the potential hostility of the one who is received gets converted, through hospitality, into a hypothesis of intimacy: look, the menacing stranger is really a messenger from God; look, it is really only Joseph who is here before us! More disturbing, in biblical terms, is an opposite potential for the perception through familiarity to be deceptive. In the account of Jacob's usurpation of Isaac's birthright or the story of Leah's being substituted for Rachel so that Jacob does not know which woman he has slept with until morning, there is a touch of comical nihilism. What has been taken for granted, what was produced within the conventions of lineage and descent, can be at any moment alienated from expectation. Even the family is not immune to the influence of estrangement, to the deceptive play of willfulness, even of animosity, that preoccupies all human relationship. In Levinas, since the most consistent figurative value attributed to the stranger is a remoteness suggesting transcendence, the practical interruptive force within human relationship occurs via an unpredictable, proximate neighbor. Even more so than the stranger, perhaps only because the opportunity or occasion is always so near, the neighbor becomes the one who signifies interruption rather than order. Such neighborly disturbance (already alluded to in the footnote from "Enigma and Phenomenon" I mentioned earlier) is conveyed eloquently by Levinas's phrasing in a later essay, "Peace and Proximity" (1984), in which he insists upon discerning responsibility as consequent upon the neighbor's *approach*, which is, simply put, the coming near "of the first comer in his or her proximity as neighbor and unique."[35]

A neighbor more so than the stranger is likely to be this first comer, and she cannot await the subject's responsibility as if it were a vocation dedicated only to what is unusual. Responsibility must always be founded in the immediate moment, brought to bear by whoever occurs to us first, whoever now draws near, time and again demanding our response as if for the first time. This is what Levinas means when he speaks of the impossibility of evading the neighbor's call. Again, *Seinfeld* exemplifies a surprising degree of ethical meaning for a television show ostensibly about nothing. Kramer is not just the quirky neighbor who borrows and breaks things, who violates etiquette by drinking and eating without compunction all Jerry's groceries; he embodies the very force of the neighbor as someone persistently disturbing in his nearness, always entering without knocking, with an urgency conveyed in his kinetic intensity—indeed, Kramer frequently seems as surprised by himself as Jerry ought to be (but no longer is) by all these interruptions. Only occasionally does Jerry mutter Kramer's name under his breath when something has gone wrong or lament "Kramer!" with an exasperation already attuned to its own futility, as Kramer yet again bursts in without knocking. Jerry concedes each interruption as if it were necessary, since Kramer (unlike Ionesco's reticent bell ringer) is incapable of a stranger's withdrawing. "Don't you knock?" is sometimes the response, and many a time Jerry walks out of the bathroom or bedroom of his small apartment to find Kramer already there, enjoying Jerry's food.[36] What the materiality of self finally means is that one is already enmeshed in relationship, with the sharing of resources or of one's own livelihood seemingly prior to any competitive cultural formulation about how one ought to obtain and preserve for oneself what others might also enjoy. Here is the structure of sensibility as defined by the "proximity of the other," our every enjoyment referred, in Levinas's view, to its capacity to be "altered by the immediacy of contact" (*OTB* 74).

In Levinas's formulation the movement to conceptualize a self's ordained satisfactions and rights is contested seemingly in its original space. Thus, Levinas speaks of a "committed freedom" (*liberté engagée*) proceeding from the "proximity of contact" (*OTB* 76; AQE 95).[37] The redundancy of the determining phrase (*la proximité du contact*) suggests an emphatic literality, as if touch could only refer to itself via a synonymous, not-yet-conceptual term such as *proximity*.[38] A footnote offered at this point in his argument traces the metaphoric anxiety behind Levinas's formulation. Contending implicitly with materialist philosophy, in which the quality of the material world becomes meaningful only when taken up as possession, Levinas finds even in things a meaning that does not reduce, as in Marx or Heidegger, to their implementation: "It is as possessed by a neighbor, as relics, and not as clothed with cultural attributes, that things first obsess. Beyond the 'mineral' surface of things, contact is an obsession by the trace of a skin, the trace of an invisible face, which the things bear and which only reproduction fixes as an idol" (*OTB* 191). Here, again, the neighbor is the bearer of a conceptual ambiguity. Even as he functions within community, as the owner of objects that soon obtain the cultural status of property, already there is an unintended act of generosity signified in his use of those same things an *I* might also have used.

Levinas continues the same footnote by imagining a breaking up of consumption that would be consequent upon a sense of things tied to a neighbor's proximity: "the thematized disappears in the caress, in which the thematization becomes a proximity. There is indeed a part of metaphor in that, and the things are taken to be true and illusory before being near. But is not the poetry of the world prior to the truth of things, and inseparable from what is proximity par excellence, that of a neighbor, or of the proximity of the neighbor [*la proximité du prochain*] par excellence" (*OTB* 191). As thematization gives way to the proximity from which it arises, Levinas's metaphoric literalism suggests a reversion to the thing itself arrived at through redundancy. When Levinas speaks of the "poetry of the world," this phrase has to be understood as the capacity to understand the world not as virtual poetry but rather as a poetry synonymous with the world itself. What he means, in other words, or in less poetic words, is that there can be an immediacy even in things, even within the concepts by which we express and thereby conceptually reduce the urgency of relation. The metaphoric literality of this phrase gets us that much closer to proximity itself.

Finally, proximity as closeness haunts the order of things, intimating that someone nearby uses them with material urgency. The very priority Levinas attributes to *proximity* relies upon yet another redundancy, neatly expressed in the French phrase "la proximité du prochain," which is perhaps best rendered in translation as "the nearness of the one who is near." As someone who stands already inside the conceptual frames and conventions by which we order nearness—even as we may be deciding that a close-talker stands too close or that Kramer is too often already there eating Jerry's food for either to be considered entirely respectable, conventional citizens—the neighbor exemplifies the meaning of ethics as that which cannot be avoided. The neighbor is one from whom we cannot turn easily away by finding words to express our right to privacy or to formulate social boundaries and etiquette that postpone our sense of obligation for him or her.

THE COMMUNITY OF NEIGHBORS—IS IT A GOOD THING?

Much of Levinas's shift in vocabulary from *stranger* to *neighbor* has to do, then, with the importance he newly attached to proximity as an absolute situation in which the other can neither be put off by way of reference to prior knowledge nor gathered into a conversation that would ultimately extend the formal priority of cultural knowledge. By the 1980s the shift in terminology I have here described was more firmly in place, so that the neighbor most often announced the privileged place ethics must be given in any description of sociality. In a work such as *Of God Who Comes to Mind* (1986) it is not surprising to find, therefore, that the neighbor foregrounds what Levinas calls the twentieth-century shift from a "philosophical tradition of the unity of the I or the system" to a "philosophy of dialogue" (137).[39] Levinas does not perceive the concentration of philosophical knowledge in the knowing *I* to be simply a historically flawed emphasis derived through a Western hermeneutic culminating in the ideology of bourgeois individualism. Rather, collectivity is by all philosophical accounts inscribed upon an *I*, which expresses its own experiences and its group identity. Collectivity, in other words, is the converse of every *I*, the seeming opposition of these two terms in the particular moment eventually reconciled in the long view under the cultural system of knowledge. In effect, Levinas casts every attempt to ascertain identity as privileged experience, whether of the group or of the individual, as a suspect endeavor. Experience (most credibly theorized under Husserlian and Heideggerian phenomenology) must necessarily be rendered as a property of thought, describing a state of sociality in which "the relations with the neighbor, the social group, and God would again be collective and religious *experiences*" (138).

At least one of the questions we must ask, therefore, is whether the neighbor, even as Levinas defines her in radical proximity, can ever elude the communal patternings by which we prefer her as someone who is near (*prochain*) to those who are not. The question of the near and far—or, of the neighbor versus the stranger—is as old as the question of responsibility. In almost any society we could remember or imagine, nearness has held the advantage. Our fellow citizens are, at least by an easy metaphoric association, also hypothetically our neighbors. Historical factors such as racism, xenophobia, and nativism have contributed, for example, to a long history of political discourse in the United States, according to which some citizens have been deemed less worthy of neighborliness than others. Segregation, as a matter of law or as a persistent cultural practice, supposes that many citizens have refused to admit entire categories of people among us to the familiarity of neighborliness. With a kind of primitive tribalism hard to distinguish from superstitious ideas about contagion, white Southerners in the United States held to Jim Crow laws, refusing well into the 1950s and 1960s to drink from the same water fountains or to share the same toilet seats with black citizens who should have been, even by the standards of a reluctantly progressive liberal society, at least by the time of the late twentieth century worthy of being treated as neighbors. According to the sentiments of liberal society, such refusals of civility or neighborliness must seem atavistic, signaling a failure to keep pace with the trajectory of the nation-state's purportedly democratic culture, in which human rights must be consistently complemented by civil rights that practically guarantee some aspects of neighborliness (say, the right to move in next door and become a bigot's neighbor) whether the prevailing public sentiment of the community is there to support it or not. Each time society lapses from its progressive orientation or fails for too long to move into the future, there is a suspicion that we will never become civil enough in our social praxis to merit the rights promised by democratic culture.

Of course, with each historical event demonstrating a resistance to the politics of greater inclusiveness we also glimpse the rites of neighborly exclusion. Although it may well be accurate to speak of the neighbor as a basic social unit of liberal citizenship that competes with familial obligation for primacy, what the privilege given to nearness and kinship also suggests is that there are, in effect, only so many people we will admit to being not just national citizens but also real or even imaginative neighbors. So emphatic is this narrowing construction of neighborliness that it hardly seems a solution to declare, as Levinas does, that ethics means recognizing "a desire of the stranger in the neighbor," as if the coexistence of far and near qualities in people we encounter could all by itself revise our too-limiting constructs of sociality (*OTB* 123). The neighbor's rejection of strangers, motivated (according in part to the long misuse of Darwinian theory in American democratic culture) by seemingly elemental, quasi-naturalistic impulses, is a fiercely abiding stance. What neighborliness always encourages is a communal posture of self-sufficiency, such that anyone who threatens to violate the wellbeing of those who are at the center of the community's benefits might be cast imaginatively outside its purview. The ease with which fellow citizens can assume the aspect of foreignness is remarkable. As soon as others demand too much or too greatly alter the quotient of normalcy, native-born citizens revoke the fragile premises of neighborliness, reminding us that there are too many strangers in our midst, even for a liberal society. Unlike the stranger, a neighbor is someone who in her basic self-sufficiency does not frequently disturb (if I'm lucky, perhaps never bothers) the premise of my own autonomy. In the 1980s, as the social epidemic of homelessness became ever more visible, advocates for the homeless population invented the acronym NIMBYism (Not in My Backyard) to name an attitude exposing the economic supposition by which most neighborhoods were constructed. People who were not necessarily against social services for the downtrodden nevertheless did not want homeless people living next door in temporary housing, driving down property values in the neighborhood, and many of these same people were willing to lobby their politicians, counteracting the efforts of homeless advocates, in order to make sure shelters and the people served by them stayed where they belong—at a distance.

In a plain sense the idea of *neighbor* always tends toward a reduction in identity. It suggests the concentrating, delimiting function of identity, according to which each person is identifiable through a pattern of social affiliations, readily positionable according to cultural functions such as race, class, religion, gender, or ethnicity. According to these diverse factors delimiting identity and producing it as a function of social ideology, according also to the quasi-involuntary criteria through which other citizens can be identified, we are able quickly to choose which citizens make good neighbors. Identity as such coincides with the basic social construct of limited access to others, which is in turn reified as a social contract limiting the access of others to us. In such a view of sociality, ethics must arise as though its priority were concentrated on what is near. According to the definitional antinomy of ethics and politics made famous by Hegel, ethics stands on the side of intimacy, attached to a realm of familial, private commitments that cannot be dishonored except at great cost to our being. In Hegel's terms Antigone would be almost unnatural if she did not worry so extensively about getting proper burial for her dead brother, if she gave him up to the indifferent laws of the state. Hegel's Hellenism also presumes that the realm of politics orders human relations through a set of ideas not determined by intimacy per se but nevertheless given over to an impersonalism that promotes social order. Still, as Benedict Anderson has suggested, politics is always also an extension of what we have already valued largely through the conceits of community and thereafter recognized because it was produced in nearness.[40] The idea of nation is constructed via metaphors of community that are themselves troped by familial, narrowing logics of obligation. In the movement, say, from family to neighbors to community to nations, there may well be a broadening of our construct of nearness but always also a fundamental stinginess, as though at some point a threshold might be crossed and a realm entered from which we could not return to have ourselves again closed off and entire.

Typically, nativism gets a bad name in retrospect as we become better capable, in our historical responses to past eras, of lamenting anti-immigrant postures that proved so costly during, say, World War II. Still, there is no getting past the fact that nativistic currents are inherent to the ideology of nationalism, as the no-longer-so-far-right in the United States continues to prove. In the primary campaign for a U.S. Senate seat in Illinois in 2004, a prominent Republican candidate aired a commercial in which he spoke from a helicopter hovering over Soldier Field in Chicago, informing his constituents that the number of illegal immigrants entering their country each week could readily fill the football stadium below him. Not lost on the candidate was the stadium's symbolic status as a nationalist monument honoring those who died to keep their country safe—ostensibly, to keep it safe from people who might invade it by war or overrun it by other means. Thus, the political commercial closes with the politician's suggesting that he can think of ten thousand reasons today, with his reasons having become straightforward metonyms for illegal immigrants, why Illinois residents should vote for him—and he'll have ten thousand more the next day and ten thousand more the day after that. One might be thankful voters rejected such obviously nativist sentiment, if it were not for the fact that his victorious Republican opponent's most prominent television spot also contained a fiercely xenophobic, nationalistically stingy message.

In that commercial for the eventual winner of the primary, the candidate sits comfortably on a suburban sofa, with his remote control in hand, watching television like any hardworking American who needs to wind down. But his relaxing day keeps getting interrupted by a ringing doorbell. Each time he opens the door, a newly arrived caricature of liberal causes makes a plea for money. There's even a seal-loving, hippy-styled woman anachronistically typecast to suggest that it's never too late to dump on the sixties, and a conspiratorial foreigner with a vaguely Soviet accent who proves that the Cold War is never over and that all American money spent on foreigners involves us in their nefarious, antidemocratic ways. After the candidate promises not to waste our money on government programs that support

such dubious causes, the doorbell rings a final time as he says, with apparent self-sat-
isfaction, "That better be the pizza guy." It is almost as if the commercial were savvy
enough to allude to *The Bald Soprano* and suggest that, rather than being abused by
unarriving visitors or unpredictable neighbors or too predictably intrusive solicitors,
doorbells should be rung by people who facilitate commercial culture, bringing services to our door only when we want them.

   That representing oneself as a stereotypical American who just wants to be left
alone should have such broad appeal—presumably, those who voted for the win-
ning candidate, Jack Ryan, in the Republican primary Senate race more or less identified with his couch-potato aspirations—would almost seem surprising were it not
so culturally persistent. In an era when the socialistic vestiges of welfare government have come entirely under attack, Americans prove capable of rejecting all
reminders that democratic culture must concern itself with the economically unfortunate within its ranks. Ryan's political ad can caricature overseas spending as waste-
ful in much the same way that his defeated opponent can appeal to primitive nationalistic fears about keeping the alien hoards at bay, because there is no compelling
mainstream political discourse to suggest that conventions of refuge, whether they
refer to our own citizens or to extra-nationals, are fundamental to our notion of rights.
So, when in late March 2004 television talk show host Bill O'Reilly reported on a
case brought to the World Affairs Court by the Mexican government contending
that fifty-one Mexican citizens had been sentenced to death by U.S. courts without
being allowed (per the 1963 Vienna Convention) contact with Mexican officials, he
voiced contempt for any argument granting extra-national citizens roughly the same
protection under the law as American citizens. Caricaturing the internationalist perspective as though it were a matter of feeling sympathy for murderers, he declared,
referring to the Mexican extra-nationals in his stylized, provocatively flat voice, "I
don't care about them." When his liberal interlocutor, a woman lawyer obviously (in
O'Reilly's estimation) with a misguided heart, insisted, "You have to," and tried to
persuade him that, if the rights of these apparent criminals were not respected, at
some point O'Reilly's rights might not be either, the talk show host paused briefly as
if to consider the point and repeated that he did not care about the Mexicans. They
came here and murdered American citizens. What would be really interesting to
know was how many of them were here illegally, he ventured, but we'd probably
never get that information. Apparently, the liberal lawyer's suggestion that O'Reilly
might feel differently about honoring internationalist conventions if he were accused
of a crime while abroad and thrown in a Mexican jail was also not persuasive. No
doubt O'Reilly was secretly comforted by America's imperialist might and by his
own so far nonmurderous history, but my basic point here is that his proclamation

of indifference is inarguable. The host pronounces a limit to his care and consideration, seemingly bringing to an end not only all rational arguments about fairness but any construct of obligation not to be conceived as rooted in nationalistic, neighborly loyalty.

What the ethical vocabulary of nearness already supposes, then, and this is the very reason Levinas confesses in "Enigma and Phenomenon" that he had prior to 1965 sought to avoid the term, is a narrowly, even perhaps chauvinistically construed notion of community. Although the neighbor in her singularity may represent only a concrete instance of responsibility, what she also intimates is the very social structure by which individual consciousness is positioned on the threshold of its communal investments. In this sense the apparent narrowness of ethics, as conceived by Hegel or by Fredric Jameson, must already be located within a socially organized system of memory, as part of what Maurice Halbwachs called collective memory. Among the most difficult and controversial tasks of recent cultural theory has been the attempt to formulate an adequate conception of what we mean by collective memory—precisely where it has its start, how far it ought to reach, and how many have to remember an event before it has become collectively significant. What I want to highlight within this debate is the implicit significance of the neighbor, who introduces herself as someone shaped by the influence of a collective memory that pertains to me and for whom I am therefore responsible precisely because of what we already hold in common. Obviously, and only more obviously during wartime, Americans are on the whole those who are most important to Americans. They are certainly more important than, say, suspected Muslim terrorists detained at Guantánamo Bay or Mexicans convicted without recourse to international conventions. We don't care about them—or at least, we don't have to care about them.

In *The Ethics of Memory* (2002) Avishai Margalit argues that just such a delimiting hypothesis of care may be at the center of our vocabulary for ethics. Positioning the intersection of ethics and memory along the axis of the near and far, or what he calls "thick" versus "thin" relations, Margalit wonders how the language of obligatory remembrance arises and in what sense remembering and forgetting might be terms subject to evaluations of praise and blame. Everything, he decides, depends upon how one understands the "we" of remembrance, whether memory is truly collective or distributive. Revising the Hegelian opposition between ethics and politics into a division between ethics and morality, Margalit associates ethics with "our relations to the near and dear" (parent, friend, lover, countrymen), whereas morality delineates principles of obligation that are generalizable and also less personally compelling, "our relations to the stranger and the remote."[41] Memory holds thick relations together, and, by a necessarily circular logic, communities of memory are

places for thick relations and thus for ethics. But the realm of thin relations is supported only by the general commonality of being human—say, of being a woman or
of being sick. Margalit finds that there is indeed an ethics of memory but little
morality of memory. There are cases, he decides, when morality should also be concerned with memory—with regard, for instance, to Nazi crimes that were inspired
by an ideology denying our shared humanity. Yet even here, since humanity itself is
not a community of memory, a question will arise as to who should carry out this
moral memory on behalf of humanity. Since any public discourse of memory will
be more effective if it has a genuine community of memory supporting it, Margalit
implies that all remembrance is generated from experiential authority, with the
result that the events meriting our moral remembrance—and for Margalit these are
especially sufferings as the consequence of extreme systemic evil—will implicitly
carry over the techniques of communally concentrated, thick memory.[42]

With regard to Margalit's argument for ethics' correlation with memory, what I
want to call attention to is the neighborly logic of it all. In one sense the neighbor
is someone fully within the territory of memory, but he is also, as a function of the
group, a vehicle for remembrance. At least some of the difficulty I have with Margalit's model arises from the link it supposes between memory and identity—in other
words, from the assumption that memory depends upon and also inspires identity.
Yet we must admit that no matter how effectively the sociologist or cultural critic
points out the arbitrary, selective bindings of identity or the obvious sources of their
cultural determination, each individual does adhere, much as Margalit supposes, to
her own experiential memory as though it marked an existential threshold of self.
Although constructs of identity privileging, say, family and a limited sphere of thick
relations severely limit our attempt to move ethics beyond the Hegelian antinomy
of ethics versus politics and to find for ethics a meaning other than its service to the
already extant privileged relation, nevertheless each of us inherits an identity proscribed by relations that have seemed to us, in the first light of experience, to be the
way things really are and perhaps also the way they ought to be. And this culturally
defined sense of reality is initially, perhaps even characteristically, perceived as though
it were an entirely natural response to an inalterable reality. All of us who would be
critics of a culturally espoused set of often oppressive relations seem to be voicing
our criticisms after the fact, always put in the position of being naysayers to an accu-
mulated history that has worked well enough to get us to where we are. To offer mere
qualifications or amendments to an original social, if not altogether natural, fact is
to prove oneself capable, at least in the popular view, of seeing only in hindsight
and of observing only that which is flawed, never what is commendable about one's
own culture. Already we appear to be susceptible to the preemptive strategy of the

George W. Bush White House, which relentlessly accused its critics of pessimism when they objected to a unilaterally, imperialistically enacted war in the Middle East or the torture taking place in U.S. military prisons.

Or one need only recall the paroxysms and the genuine loss of political stature that followed from Hillary Rodham Clinton's use of the aphorism "It takes a village to raise a child" to be convinced that the ideological commitment to certain cultural premises becomes so entrenched as to mistake itself for moralistic naturalism (which should be an oxymoronic phrase from almost any perspective other than certain pervasive currents of American conservatism). As long as reactionary political sentiment remains ascendant in a culture, even while seeming outmoded, it will paradigmatically determine much of the political reality for individuals within that same culture. It hardly seems worth mentioning that Hillary Clinton's aphorism only minimally expanded the central principle of belonging upon which familially constructed identity is based. The village is still a tribal unit, extended but slightly beyond endogamy. It reaches only as far as the neighbor in its quest to define who will count as meaningful. What quickly becomes apparent is that the familial conceit privileging nationalistic nearness is as inescapable on the mainstream left as on the right. So, in offering his regalingly satiric jeremiad against the conservative right, *Lies and the Lying Liars Who Tell Them—A Fair and Balanced Look at the Right* (2003), Al Franken responded to the preposterous charge that liberals do not "love America enough" by accusing conservatives of a regressive, infantile mode of loyalty about which liberals are simply more sophisticated, thus ratifying a predominant cultural logic by disobeying it only so far: "They don't get it. We love America just as much as they do. But in a different way. You see, they love America the way a four-year-old loves her mommy. Liberals love America like grown-ups. To a four-year-old, everything Mommy does is wonderful and anyone who criticizes Mommy is bad. Grown-up love means actually understanding what you love, taking the good with the bad, and helping your loved one grow. Love takes attention and work and is the best thing in the world."[43] To criticize without first giving assurance that the attention paid to what you criticize cannot impair your esteem for that which you already love must violate, Franken supposes, a basic grammar of our political culture. Such a stance seems not only altogether unfamilial but also, as Sacvan Bercovitch has suggested with critical precision, un-American.[44] To paraphrase Bercovitch, we might say that, insofar as critique of a predominant cultural paradigm must follow closely upon a statement of professed loyalty to virtually the same paradigm, any transformative, revisionary capacity of critique is greatly diminished.

My point, then, is a straightforward one: insofar as critique depends upon the attempt to extend normative terms as if they were sometimes limited but infinitely correctable, or perhaps upon a hindsight exposing an injustice concealed within conditions we took to be relatively fair, it is not only caught playing a game of catch up without the capacity to alter the rules; it is also always susceptible to the indifference of those who see it differently, perhaps only because it is more convenient for them to do so. If TV show host Bill O'Reilly doesn't care about those others, whoever they may be, what exactly are we to do about it? In a free country his opinion, so he adamantly believes, is as good as anyone else's. As I emphasized in my introduction, there is no genuine force in ethics. Indifference to the plight of others is the very stuff of freedom, and freedom as such is formulated as a natural instinct, a loyalty to the modes of belonging to which one already adheres. The one who speaks critically of those who are near and dear, the one who dares to criticize family, can expect hostility—almost as if she spoke barbarically, as if she spoke for, about, and like foreigners. Thus, Franken's decision to include himself within familial love for America is far more than incidental. It depends upon a basic cultural supposition that, even while we draw distinctions between the private and the public realm or differentiate, as Hegel does, between familial duties and political responsibilities, there must be metaphoric continuity between the superficially opposed terms of family and nation. What O'Reilly's indifference and Franken's corrective witticism alike point to is how unlikely it is that any of us could begin to imagine or theorize a community of strangers. It is one thing to conceive of a predominant, liberalized paradigm, such as the one Ozick imagines Judaism has bequeathed to the Western world, according to which we might make room for the stranger almost as if she were one of our own. It is another thing altogether to harbor a fundamental alienation at the center of our construct of community.

Could we ever conceive of a social logic—or, in ethical terms, should we be willing to do so—that is not predicated upon constructs of belonging necessarily reverting, even if only metaphorically, to familial notions of privilege? In *Smothered Words* (1987) Sarah Kofman interprets Maurice Blanchot as having said yes to my question, of having speculatively intuited, with historical perspicacity, the sense in which community can only be meaningful if the possibility of closeness already honors radical heterogeneity. More so than any of the major poststructuralists, Blanchot explores a language of alterity seeming to surpass even the relatively predictable cultural play of difference, as he inherits from Heidegger that sense in which language dedicates Being to a phenomenology of difference and reads this toward a sociality serving the hypothesis of the potentially unincorporable alterity.[45] In Kofman's reading of Blanchot's anti-story "The Idyll" (1936) as an allegory for the totalitarian state that nevertheless cannot account for Auschwitz, she intuits the sense in which Blanchot deploys the camp as a conceit not only for governance under a fascistic state but, perhaps more generally, for the assimilationist imperatives of the nation-state.[46] In this pre-Holocaust story and in his later work *The Unavowable Community* (1983), which seems to Kofman a fuller elaboration of the story's metonymic possibility, the stranger becomes the very type of the alienated being, who was ideologically reified by Nazi ideology and then further attacked as if to prove that the merely remnant humanity perceptible in all strangers could be abolished.

In "The Idyll" a stranger arrives from a country he will not name, and in a caricature of hospitable reception he is asked to scour the dirt from his body in prolonged showers and is then detained until he can be assimilated (SW 23). Already the hypothesis of reformation, of remaking others into beings as homogeneous as our neighbors, allows for a possibility never in fact permitted under Nazi ideology. The stranger lives in a barracks with other men, occasionally does forced labor, and over the course of the story attempts to interpret the marital happiness of the camp's director and his wife, eventually trying to naturalize himself through marriage and partake of the domestic idyll that has been modeled for him, only to endeavor a last minute escape that results in his death. Kofman's strongest exegetical insight into Blanchot's story is that the model couple's ambiguous affection for one another serves as evidence that their misfortune is "to have mistaken—and to have wanted others to mistake—hatred for love, death for life, and to have believed that proximity, fusion, and the absence of difference and distance are constitutive of love, whereas, as Empedocles taught, the affinity of the same for the same is governed by hatred, while love consists in the union of the heterogeneous, the lack of relation, the infinite separation" (SW 28). It is not hard to hear in such a passage the possible influence of Levinas himself, whose own reaction to the insistent phenomenology of sameness presiding over Western thought is as dramatically contentious as Blanchot's or, in her interpretive paraphrasing of Blanchot, Kofman's.

Kofman's dissent from a beloved precursor is mostly honorific, but she nevertheless seeks to qualify and contain the value Blanchot bestows on estrangement, as though the figure of the stranger inherently demanded the movement we also see in Levinas back to a contemplation of what we owe to neighbors. Kofman's response to Blanchot charts at least in part the rationale for Levinas's own heightened embrace of the conceit of neighborliness. As Kofman paraphrases Blanchot's claim that only what remains at a distance is capable of authentic relation, we hear traces of Levinas's own deployment of the stranger as a figure for the other with whom one enters into relationship, and, as she suggests that Blanchot's esteem for the necessary distance inscribed upon relationship depends upon a paradigmatic scenario—"the relation must be broken; for only the foreignness of that which can never be held in common can found the community" (SW 30)—her misgivings run parallel to Levinas's own qualification of a former emphasis in his project. In the first half of his career Levinas challenged the Heideggerian project by reversing the order of Being so that beings were to be philosophically anterior to their subjection to ontological meaning, a reversal that depended in large part upon the extraordinary influence of exteriority. Notably, Levinas's affinity with Blanchot is perhaps most remarkable during the first half of his career, during which strangeness prevailed as the figure for the other. Eventually, Levinas tried to take up the challenge of the subject's bifurcated signification within responsibility, and much of the importance of what I described in the last chapter as the sacrificial connotation of substitution attaches to the project of locating the subject as the irremissible site of its responsibilities, as individuated by what places a demand on it immediately, not only as from the outside but as though from inside the identity it takes for granted.

Kofman's challenge to Blanchot charts a similar tension between the signifying force of estrangement and the value of what is already near. As Blanchot envisions a community that relies upon a commonality with absolutely no metaphysical, nationalist, or biological ground, he travels to such an imaginative terrain as though the dystopic universe of national idylls could only be countered by a utopian vision of community (for has such a community ever truly existed?) that proceeds from what is uncommon to us all, from our respect for one another as foreign. In modifying this formulation, Kofman mournfully invokes the memory of her father, who died in the camps, and then turns to Robert Antelme's memoir *The Human Race* (1947), relying on Blanchot's own deferential respect for Antelme to legitimate her revisionary strategy. Her focus is especially on Antelme's hard-nosed humanism. Amidst descriptions of the overly determined world of the concentration camp, Antelme emphasizes the determination of prisoners to find a cultural or simply a materialist basis for their humanity, and Kofman decides that this also counts for what we must imagine community to have become for us. In her vision of community after Auschwitz, she supposes that language, even between those who did not speak the same language, functioned to thread together the inmates of the camps. Interpreting Antelme, Kofman declares that even "in this situation of abject distress"—and here she interrupts herself to cite Blanchot's description of a situation in which the human being reduced to the "extreme destitution of need" became "an interchangeable sign, a stranger to himself and to first-person existence"—it was possible to give voice to lived experience, to designate a realm over which Nazi power could not have final say (SW 51).

Kofman's parenthetically framed paraphrasing of Blanchot is central to her often submerged argument. For Kofman the specter of estrangement looms overabundantly in Blanchot, and so she is forced to locate what binds us (perhaps not unlike Todorov's solution in *Facing the Extreme*) in the efforts made by prisoners to be bound to one another, even to the SS, by whatever evidence they could bring to mind. Sometimes, she observes, this amounted to nothing more than being commonly degraded and calling attention ironically to this shared degradation as human beings forced to piss and shit in the camps' beyond-filthy latrines. Kofman qualifies Blanchot's avowal of estrangement because she perceives an implicit danger in any attempt to make the permanently estranged a social site for the difference by which we might all be held together, and this danger is simply that a construct of alienated identity implicitly coincides, perhaps by its own deliberately revisionary analogy, with the efforts of the SS to dig an abyss "between man and man" (SW 59).

In response to such a possibility, Kofman opts for what she calls a "new humanism," a solution not unlike that of Jean Améry or Primo Levi. I would argue further that her softening of Blanchot's prescription of binding alienation provides a clue to Levinas's own increasing preference throughout the 1980s for the other who is, at least metaphorically, a neighbor. There are many ways in which Levinas is, like Kofman, invested in the recuperation of humanism, as he comes to use the term more freely in the latter half of his career, most obviously in the collection of essays entitled *The Humanism of the Other Man* (1972).[47] For Kofman such a recuperation of humanism depends at least in part on the overcoming of strangeness, whereas for Levinas any recovery of humanism would depend upon a paradigmatic shifting from the philosophical language of subjectivity and the political discourse of rights to a focus on that privilege a subject always yields to the other. As he says in an interview with Roger Pol-Droit, mounting an argument against the inherent ethics of contestation in the Heideggerian system: "Now, humanism is altogether different. It is a response to the other that cedes him first place, that gives way before him rather than combating him."[48] The question we have also to ask—partly as a result of the shift in Levinas's own vocabulary—is whether this means ceding first place to another who is a neighbor and so already cooperative with the social place an *I* now holds or whether it means ceding first place to a stranger who might be usurping social places already allotted by the political order. To the extent that Levinas's humanism is largely a reinvention of the term in its historical parameters, naming a possibility that might have been and might still be, we have also to worry that it is bound up with the Kantian question Levinas takes up haltingly in the latter half of his career, of whether it is possible to imagine a harmony between ethics and the nation-state, in which case the renewable prestige of humanism might still depend on a preference for the other who is not quite so different from us after all.

HOW WELL DO I KNOW MY NEIGHBOR?
THE EXIGENCY OF ISRAEL AND THE HOLOCAUST

By exposing a conservative tendency embedded in our appreciation of neighbors, evident at the very least in *neighbor* as a communally, nationalistically bound terminology, I have not wished to foist upon Levinas the charge of an obviously reactionary turn in his own politics. The question of whether the biographically defined (or undefined) political positions of an author should be the final measure of his thought is a real one. With regard to Levinas I do not believe, however, that the concrete ideological shortcomings of several aspects of his philosophical language, nor the statements he failed to make as an international citizen, can be read as though they gave the lie to his extensive revaluation of ethics. The politics of Levinas the man, even if they can be intuited reliably through his philosophical writings, do not exhaust the political implications of his ethics, especially given how consistently a Levinasian definition of ethics offers itself as a critique of the most persistently oppressive dimensions of Western culture. As we offer correctives to real limits in Levinas's work, which are matters not just of his personal belief but also of his philosophical language, we need to consider how the implicit trajectory of Levinasian ethics, in its revaluation of Western cultural, ideological, and philosophical patterns of thought, might be greater than the mere sum of its apparent flaws.

Nevertheless, the political shortcomings of Levinasian ethics are not few. Perhaps most famous by now—brought to light at an early point in his career by contemporaries such as Simone de Beauvoir, Jacques Derrida, and Luce Irigaray—is the extent to which Levinas's language is bound up with patriarchal categories of gender derived in part from the traditions of Judaism.[49] Then, too, not only are there critics, such as Badiou or Žižek, who suppose that Levinasian ethics is not significantly enough set apart from the political norms of liberal ethno-nationalism, but there are others such as Gillian Rose who lament the political impracticality of his poststructuralist vocabulary and still others, such as Derrida, Haar, and Paul Ricoeur, who perceive a paradoxical valuing of violence or cruelty inscribed at the center of Levinas's description of the ethical relation. Certainly, Levinas's dependence on and contribution to the politics of the left are not always easy to discern. His use of quasi-socialist idioms are perhaps more common in the early half of his career, and, as I have previously conceded, it is never entirely obvious how his philosophical method would help us explicate inequalities in present social structures. In favor of the progressive view of Levinas, however, it has to be said that his statements about ethics as a responsibility for those who are disfranchised by political systems, especially the oppressed peoples of the Third World, endure in the writings of the late 1970s and 1980s. Additionally, Levinas makes several overt statements against the kind of parochial ethnic attachment of which Badiou would accuse ethics, and he rejects any nostalgic, quasi-tribal abhorrence of modernity and its technological capability (a position frequently associated with Heidegger), as when Levinas declares, for example, in one of many interviews given throughout the 1980s, that technology provides us with the possibility of becoming politically responsive to the misery of the Third World.[50]

To draw attention to the troubling intersection of neighbors and nations in Levinas's work, with the concern that such a logic might predict a political horizon preempting only most obviously an abiding ethical concern for the stranger, is not therefore to work entirely against the grain of Levinas's own work. Nor is it to favor the early Levinas over the late Levinas (if anything, this book has given more emphasis to the late Levinas). For, as the idiom of the neighbor becomes more prevalent and uncritical statements about the nationalistic politics of Israel also come to light, Levinas simultaneously deepens the vocabulary for a responsibility that is, by so many of his figurative terms, responsible for other people's sufferings. Although there are indeed contradictory political valences in Levinas's work, by the method I have employed throughout this book, which perceives a complex imbrication of the ethical relation and the responsibility for political structures in his figures for ethics, it would seem irresponsible to Levinas not to consider the hazards that might befall his ethics were the neighbor to be granted an inordinate, concrete priority over more distant others. Indeed, such a declared privilege might expose the political shortcomings of Levinas's own revaluative ethics and more generally much of Western ethical thought.

The implicit nexus between the Holocaust and Israel in Levinas's thought is perhaps the most obvious focus for those distrustful of the political implications of Levinasian ethics, since it locates Levinas within range of the suspicion I discussed in the introduction, that the prevalence of Holocaust memory is owing to a variety of nationalist and ethnic priorities and that Levinasian ethics might be read as a philosophical legitimization of basic cultural preferences for *us* as opposed to *them*. When Margalit supposes that it is basic to the structure of ethics to prefer memories of the hurt done to ourselves to memories of the hurt we do to our enemies, he suggests how readily the construct of obligation might be reconciled to a notion of communal identity and to an ethics that is universalist only by preferring, as Badiou explicitly laments, those who are already like us to those who clearly are not. Within the context of the Palestinian-Israeli conflict, the temptation for the Holocaust to be invoked as a metaphor exempting a Jewish nation-state from international judgments or from the memory of injustices it has also perpetrated is a persistent one. Not a few of Levinas's interviewers tried over the years to draw him out with regard to his political views about Israel, and he for the most part chose a course of considered reticence. Nevertheless, by his own testimony we know that Levinas wrote a letter in 1964 to Jean-Paul Sartre encouraging France's most famous philosopher, if he visited with Egyptian president Gamal Abdal Nasser, to propose peace with Israel, and in 1979 Levinas wrote an essay at Sartre's request for *Les Temps Modernes* called "Politics, After!" specifically addressing the situation in Palestine. In a 1990 interview for *L'Express* Levinas would say that he had "never leaned toward an active Zionism" but that the already constituted Jewish state seemed to him a political necessity, "the subsistence of the Jews as such" depending as he saw it "on the continuation of this task, and under a particular form."[51] In the same passage Levinas refers to the prophetic dimensions of Zionism, which must be oriented, as he puts it, "to create upon Israeli soil the concrete conditions for political invention, and to make or remake a state in which prophetic morality shall be incarnate, along with its message of peace." Such a turn to biblical rhetoric overlooks the pragmatic secular reality of Israel as a modern nation-state, and it leads Levinas to the verge of an exceptionalist logic: "but Israel represents a security in a world where politics count, and where the cultural depends on the political. On this point, they have enough problems without our adding to them" (*IIRB* 198). On the one hand, Levinas implies that the state of Israel is a concession to political reality: we might all like to be visionary, but doesn't the very category of the cultural depend upon the order of nation-states? On the other hand, having offered at least this much in a pragmatic vein while having previously advocated a prophetic vision of Israel, Levinas decides that it is best that *we* (here he means France, having previously in the interview invoked his adopted homeland as a model for a democratic state) should not add to Israel's problems—presumably, by rendering internationalist judgments upon *their* political affairs.

Any argument for exemption (according to the terms of my argument in chap. 3) necessarily bears a sacrificial logic, such that some would be spared judgment but not others, such that even those exempted from judgment, such as Christ or Israel, must be paradoxically enfolded into the trajectory of sacrificial necessity. Such a logic is strangely manifested in Levinas's references to Auschwitz as the "Passion of Israel" in which the turn to Christian metaphor marks Israel as a sign to the Christian nations. "I am thinking notably," Levinas says in a 1985 interview, "that the Passion of Israel at Auschwitz has profoundly marked Christianity itself." Shortly thereafter, Levinas proceeds to a brief discussion of the Temple as having marked the moment in which sacrifice yielded to prayer in Jewish theology, with the conceptual carryover being simply that prayer is always an offering, specifically, to God. Yet Levinas also says: "There is an exception when one prays for persecuted Israel. In that case one is praying for the community, but this is a prayer for the people who are called to reveal the glory of God" (*IIRB* 226).[52] The messianic destiny of a singular people can have, of course, no preeminent authority in a truly internationalist, secularist articulation of justice. But Levinas's phrasing raises a more specific doubt—namely, whether the exceptional regard for a particular persecution has not always preoccupied the vocation of prayer or what we might call, to put this wholly in secular terms, a mythical adherence to identity sanctioned by metaphysical, suprarational principles such as blood and God. By such cultic logic—which in the eighteenth and nineteenth centuries Christian historicist biblical criticism too self-servingly attributed to the Jews in order to distinguish a progressive, universalist Christian teleology from Jewish parochialism—prayer reifies the logic of sacrifice: one appeases God as a foundational principle for community itself. By offering to the gods, a community proves its claim to the land and its right to extend itself in time. Even when the form of prayer suffers a long history of disconsolation, there may be implicit in it an exorbitant sign of affirmation, a reification of belonging perceived perhaps only in an intracommunal or intercommunal mutuality based on what has not been achieved.

Levinas also says in the 1990 interview for *L'Express*: "I have said that the *shoah* was felt by Jews with a depth that is understood by Christians staggered by the Passion of Jesus. One wonders afterward if it is still possible to uphold something" (*IIRB* 197).[53] Already, this speculation about what might still be upheld reconstitutes a sense of belonging to be based, if upon nothing else, in a common desire for that which is already extant among us and might yet be upheld. In the same interview Levinas says that Judaism nevertheless always supersedes its own cultic ratification. The Torah addresses itself to all men, advocating a universalism that makes tribalist, nationalist preferences recede. At this very point the interviewers from *L'Express* pose their question about Israel, to which Levinas responds by suggesting that he has not been an active Zionist but nevertheless believes in the pragmatic necessity of Israel. The obvious question (never entirely answered here) is how far, and when exactly, cultic preference and the politics of nationalist identity should recede.

For Levinas, I want to suggest, the Holocaust provokes and delays the answer to such a question. Although he cannot bring himself to offer any practical political criticism of Israel (and it has to be said in fairness that Levinas does not typically interpret it as his task to offer practical criticisms of any political structure), there is more informing such reticence than mere cultic loyalty. No doubt part of Levinas's willingness to exempt Israel from internationalist judgment is his suspicion that the court of international opinion is no further beyond nationalist prejudices than the nascent Jewish state, and Levinas's confidence in a prophetically humanist vision of Israel allows him to believe that there is a self-corrective mechanism within the discourse of Zionism, which, according to biblical logic, must eventually give priority to the other man. In short, the exceptional vocation of Israel devolves from its envisioning itself as a state that foresees its own universalistic supersession. As John Llewelyn points out, much of Levinas's discourse about Israel resembles a mode of cabbalistic exegesis according to which *Israel* comes to stand as the one who is chosen for responsibility and thus as an emblem of universalist fraternity; but, as with all allegorical interpretation of scripture, we have every reason to worry that an immediate, literal level gets overlooked for the sake of a symbolic—in this case, messianic—connotation.[54] At some level the Holocaust might seem only to give a new valence to this eschatological vocation of Israel's uniqueness among the nations, as the only state that by virtue of its own founding discourse, or at least within the prophetic strains of such discourse upon which Levinas focuses, is not primarily about its own sovereignty. For, in Levinas's view, Israel is the nation-state that must by definition, whether it has yet done so or not, deconstruct its most fundamental principles of belonging.

At the same time the imperatives of Holocaust remembrance persist in Levinas's revisionary ethical figures as signs of general, albeit perhaps not conceptually generalizable, human obligation. In political terms there is a tension here that informs every de-particularized, slightly decontextualized account of injustice, for the revisionary response to the fact of injustice, which would still preserve it in memory against the status quo structures of power, may involve an aspect of overlooking some injustices for the others one considers most important. In Levinas's Jewish writings, such as *Difficult Freedom*, Israel remains the sign of a universalistic progressive meaning, which is perhaps more attuned to the tones of biblical prophecy than to the contemporary realpolitik of modern nation-states. Although Levinas speaks of the "notion of Israel" as designating an elite among peoples, the elite is significant only insofar as it is an "open elite," allowing us "once and for all to get rid of the strictly nationalist character that one would like to give to the particularism of Israel" (*DF* 83). By this logic Israel should supersede its own ethnic codes and proceed toward what we would call a kind of hyper-universalism, a mode of universalist discourse constantly referred to the other—whether as victim, stranger, or neighbor—as the only site upon which, in Levinas's terms, the renewal of humanism could be based.

In this sense, too, the Holocaust ought to disconcert our conventional affection for nearness. So, for example, when Levinas dedicates *Otherwise than Being* in memory first to those "who were closest among the six million assassinated by the

National Socialists" and then immediately proceeds to recall millions of other victims "of the same hatred of the other man, the same anti-semitism," he defines the figurative trajectory of proximity in his work.[55] As I have stressed, the other who impresses herself upon the subject as an anterior obligation and as the very source of signification is proximate in a manner having little to do with kinship, cultic, or nationalist norms:

> Proximity is not a state, a repose, but, a restlessness, null site, outside of the place of rest. It overwhelms the calm of the non-ubiquity of a being which becomes a rest in a site. No site then, is ever sufficiently a proximity, like an embrace. Never close enough, proximity does not congeal into a structure, save when represented in the demand for justice as reversible, and reverts into a simple relation. Proximity, as the "closer and closer," becomes the subject. It attains its *superlative* as *my* incessant restlessness, becomes unique, then one, forgets reciprocity, as in a love that does not expect to be shared. (*OTB* 82)

The emphasis on utopian dis-location is intended to prevent the prospect of coming again to rest or returning home, as though ethics were indeed a description of what Margalit calls "thick relations." Levinasian proximity should not amount to the embrace of familiarity but must bear within it a thinness or strangeness, peculiarly manifested in the subject's own restlessness, as if even here, close to the one for whom he ought to be responsible, the subject cannot subside into normalized obligations. Unlike the love of family or kin or even of neighbors, proximity does not produce reciprocal love but the urgent demand of a version of love, much as Kierkegaard also imagined it, that can never be adequately answered.

The subject's restlessness in proximity is similar to the inquietude provoked by the death of the other, and not only does such language recall for us the abiding influence of the mournful connotation of Levinasian ethics, but it puts us in mind of Holocaust scenes such as those described by Primo Levi in *Survival in Auschwitz* (1958), in which the violent contact among the victims of a deportation train and then later between Levi and an anonymous yet familiar bedmate revise the very possibility of ethical meaning:

> Our restless sleep was often interrupted by noisy and futile disputes, by curses, by kicks and blows blindly delivered to ward off some encroaching and inevitable contact. (*SA* 14)

> I do not know who my neighbour is; I am not even sure that it is always the same person because I have never seen his face except for a few seconds amidst the uproar of the reveille, so that I know his back and his feet much better than his face. He does not

work in my *Kommando* and only comes into the bunk at curfew time; he wraps himself in the blanket, pushes me aside with a blow from his bony hips, turns his back on
me and at once begins to snore. Back against back, I struggle to regain a reasonable area
of the straw mattress: with the base of my back I exercise a progressive pressure against
his back; then I turn around and try to push with my knees; I take hold of his ankles
and try to place them a little further over so as not to have his feet next to my face.
(SA 52–53)[56]

The promiscuity of contact—which is beyond choice, which is encroaching and
inevitable—predicts the lost repose of the Levinasian subject. In Levinas the other
drawing always "closer and closer" as though from "outside of the place of rest" is
not necessarily the victim of the deportation trains, but in light of Levinas's other
Holocaust-inspired figures it is hard to put such a possibility altogether out of mind.
When Levi describes a woman who has been bodily "crushed against [him] for the
whole journey" (SA 14), how far is he from the traumatic contact Levinas considers
as that which precisely cannot be refused in ethics, "as though the sensibility were
precisely what all protection and all absence of protection already presuppose: vulnerability itself" (OTB 75).[57]

Then, too, Levi's declaration in the second passage just cited, "I do not know who
my neighbor is," could almost be read as an epigraph to Levinas's revisionary formulation for relation to a neighbor. Eliding the difference between encroachment
and ordinary nearness, Levinas associates responsibility with a vigilant regard for the
death of the person who is immediate, with being arbitrarily thrown into the situation of immediacy, already liable by a mournful inflection for the final end of
another. If this is "not an attitude which regards the death of a being already chosen
and dear, but instead the death of the first one to come along," Levinas supposes that
the privilege of the neighbor, as conceived in familiar terms, has already lapsed. "To
recognize that I let the other—whoever he might be—pass before I do," Levinas says
in a 1982 interview, "that is the ethical" (IIRB 129).[58] There is an allusion here to
Genesis 32:24–29 that is also relevant in Levi's text. For Levi's futile wrestling with a
bigger, anonymous bedmate (as he tells us, "it is all in vain"; he cannot move the
heavier man) quite plausibly recalls Jacob's wrestling with the unnamed man at
Peniel: "Jacob was left alone; and a man wrestled with him until daybreak. When
the man saw that he did not prevail against Jacob, he struck him on the hip socket;
and Jacob's hip was put out of joint as he wrestled with him. Then he said, 'Let me
go, for the day is breaking.' But Jacob said, 'I will not let you go, unless you bless
me'" (NRSV, Gen. 32:24–26). In the biblical story the fact that Jacob does not get a
direct answer when he asks the man's name leads him to the conclusion that he has

wrestled "face to face" with God (Gen. 32:30), but we have no reason to believe his interpretation. Many biblical interpreters have tried to turn the episode into an anticipatory dream, according to which the man would be the spirit of his brother Esau and the entire scene would depict Jacob's wresting the birthright a second time from him but now by more honorable means. There is no necessary reason that this should be true either.

The genuine uncanniness of the passage is best accounted for by the man's surprisingly proximate and also anonymous physicality, and it is precisely this sense of the passage that Levi picks up on. The bedmate he cannot budge is an anonymous neighbor, and the intimacy between the two men is contentious according only to their limited physical space and their desire for an autonomy that each spatially reminds the other he cannot have. If in Genesis and Levi we register the desire for autonomy through the central protagonist (Jacob or Levi himself), each passage also depends upon the severe limitation of such predetermined preference. The mysterious man at Peniel will not yield, nor will Levi's bedmate budge, and each of these nocturnally veiled others forces upon Jacob and Levi, respectively, a grudgingly ceded acknowledgment of the place of alterity.

Notably, the reluctantly bestowed blessing is absent from Levi's text. According to his desperately materialist humanism, the ethical implications of proximity are never quite fortunate. In many ways such an emphasis sounds a Levinasian note, as unpleasure marks the moment of another's importance. Yet Levinas's rendering of the same text, as a demystification and deconstruction of the privileges of nearness, does result in a revised version of the Genesis text's recuperative blessing, by which Jacob would reclaim his dignified autonomy at the last minute (Gen. 32:29).

For Levinas, however, the arrival of the other who is the first one to come along and the implication in his death are what produce a version of strictly humanist blessing—an act of recognizing the other and letting him pass, regardless of his identity, before the *I* does. *Recognition* is not Levinas's favorite term, since it implies the privileging of cognitive systems of ordering, but here it especially furthers the allusion to the Genesis text. Letting another "pass before I do," whether or not one has first wrestled with him and implicitly begrudged him his place, which is also mine, results in an involuntary acknowledgment. The other earns my respect, with the full implication being that I am reluctant to give it. To derive ethical meanings either implicitly from Holocaust texts (Levinas) or from within the apparent non-sense of the Holocaust (Levi) is to grant a meaningfulness to humanity in the face of suffering and to be unwilling to look beyond suffering for the moment when meaning might be achieved. Accordingly, the proximity of another person provokes a vigilance in every subject, as if one were waiting for a return—an anterior time in which significance were complete or full—only to find that it is always and necessarily suspended. As Levinas says several times, subjectivity attains its ethical meaning and its true signification in its "incapacity to shut itself up from the outside," in its basic defenselessness before the other, in the persecuting intensity of a moment in which one who is already near comes nearer still: "In the approach (*l'approche*) I am instantly a servant of the one who is near (*du prochain*), already late and guilty of being late. I exist as though I were put in order (*ordonné*) from the outside (*dehors*)" (AQ 110, my trans.; see also OTB 87). The particularity that comes from the outside is not to be overcome. Again, we discern here the note of the stranger, what Levinas persistently refers to as the alterity or strangeness of the Other. In the moment of ethical impingement the neighbor is also unknown as in Levi's text, a stranger whose desires cannot be predicted. By such a logic the subject who is defined by the ethical relation (and not the other way around) partakes of the meaning of his own passivity, yielding to "an unendurable and harsh consent that animates the passivity and does so strangely despite itself" (NI 146). This estrangement within the ethical project, based in the alienating influence of the other, suggests that identity is already altered by that which is exterior to it.

What we know of ourselves in culture is inadequate before the other's need or superiority, before her generosity or violence. Much as mourning seems for Levinas an inescapable yet humanizing influence, there is perhaps a note of fatalism in his metaphoric recasting of the stranger even in the situation of nearness, quite as though Levinas were to take for granted sharply perceived cultural differences (which often result, for example, in the hostile treatment of foreigners) and nevertheless reimagine the shock of a foreigner's strangeness as generated by an otherness basic to all interpersonal relationship. When Levinas speaks of the stranger which every man is for every other man, he is no longer speaking just about those forcibly exiled from habitation upon the land, violently estranged from their host communities. As always with such metaphoric usage (much as I had worried in chap. 3 that the historical experience of victimization can be universalized to the point of irrelevance if employed as paradigmatic for subjectivity), when every person, even the neighbor, seems potentially, inherently a stranger within ethical relation, the particular scandal of the stranger may get torn from its historical context.

Generally speaking, we can say, Levinas is willing to violate historical context, although not to the point of final ahistoricism. By embedding historically concrete scenarios in his figurative language for ethics, he attempts to make ethics the very structure by which responsibility for hateful, harmful histories might be assumed. The Holocaust proves no exception to this rhetorical habit. Even as it preoccupies Levinas's tremendous revisioning of proximity, the Holocaust serves to emphasize the urgency of ethics. In several interviews there creeps into Levinas's language, despite his own assertions in "Useless Suffering" that the *shoah* proves only the final uselessness of another's suffering, a hint of sacrificial opportunism. Envisioning in a 1987 interview a new threshold in Judeo-Christian relations, Levinas credits the Holocaust with having, unfortunately, brought about this opportunity: "Then something new came along, and one called it the Holocaust. The great 'experience' of Judaism" (*IIRB* 137).[59] Immediately thereafter he refers once more to the Passion of the Jews under Adolf Hitler as analogous to the Passion of Christ. And, to recall the 1985 interview with Myriam Anissimov mentioned above, he says: "The injustice committed against Israel during the war, that one calls the *shoah*—the passion of Israel in the sense in which one speaks of the passion of Christ—is the moment when humanity began to bleed through the wounds of Israel. Someone asked me the other day if, as a Jew, I didn't feel like an outsider in France. I replied to him that wherever I am, I feel like I'm in the way, and I quoted a Psalm: 'I am a stranger upon the earth' (Ps. 119:19). Strangeness is situated in relation to the earth."[60] The compactness of Levinas's conjoinings in this passage—of the *shoah* and Israel, of the sufferings of Israel and Christ's passion, of exile and a universalistic vision of human estrangement—speaks to many of the issues with which I have been concerned. By alluding to Israel as a nation that precedes its historical moment of inception and by metonymically naming all the Jews who perished under Hitler, whether Zionists or not, as citizens of such an imaginary country, Levinas evades practical criticism of contemporary Israel. The preexistent biblical mandate to reconstitute Israel determines the extent to which the Jews suffer as a nationalistically constructed people (an idea not altogether inconsistent with the persecuting logic of Nazism) almost as though, by a teleological trajectory, it were a productive passion.

There is a hint here of what Tom Segev has observed with regard to much early Zionist rhetoric concerning the Holocaust—that, insofar as it supposed a continuity between the Holocaust and Israel, it often cast the *shoah* as a nationalistic opportunity.[61] Most likely, Levinas would refute this line of interpretation, but his figurative language is nevertheless implicated in such nationalist mythology, in what I have described as a preference for familiar neighbors (according to Margalit's notion of thick relations) over someone, even such a circumstantially estranged neighbor as the man whom Levi lies beside in Auschwitz, whose claim upon the subject is not prescribed by communal belonging. What may be most significant nevertheless about Levinas's invocations of the Holocaust as a quasi-paschal sacrifice in association with his infrequent statements about Zionism is that they reveal his commitment to modes of a belonging that compete with the originary claim he attributes to ethics. In this vein, returning to the question of Israel as a sign of contested nationalist belonging, we might also account for Levinas's disturbing remarks from a 1982 radio discussion, "Ethics and Politics," aired on Radio Communauté in the wake of the war crime perpetrated by Phalangist militias introduced by the Israeli military into the Palestinian refugee camps of Sabra and Shatila in Lebanon, where they proceeded to massacre several hundred people over two days while the Israeli army did nothing to intervene.[62] The incident provoked international outrage, and the radio program—which also featured Alain Finkielkraut, himself a Levinasian-minded social critic—addressed itself to Israel's responsibility for these specific actions and implicitly to its antiterrorist/anti-Palestinian military policy in Lebanon. Throughout this interview Levinas comes off as highly evasive. He several times emphasizes the outrage within Israel and among the international Jewish community over these events as a sign of the ethical, but he also consistently deflects responsibility for the specific political crimes by speaking of a general notion of responsibility, such that the supervening spirit of internationalist responsibility might appear to cast a veil over obviously nationalistic crimes of state. Along the way Levinas's hyper-rigorous formulation of ethics as responsibility even for that which one has not done gets bizarrely flipped such that Levinas can insist upon speaking, even in the context of a heinously enacted political crime, "of the responsibility of those 'who have done nothing'"—as if this formulation applied to the state of Israel in the immediate case (LR 290). Even as Finkielkraut tries to steer the conversation toward an indictment of Israel for these specific actions and worries about what he calls the "temptation of innocence," according to which the Jewish people's long history of victimization might incline them to an attitude of innocence from within which they might refuse to be held responsible for others, Levinas defends Israel's relative innocence as a nation and explicitly exempts the Jewish state from practical criticism, invoking the potential contradiction between ethics and politics in such a way that his politics seem to lag grossly behind the rigor of his ethics. As was the case with Elie Wiesel, who spoke in the era from the late 1960s until the 1980s so passionately as a witness to the plight of Russian Jews, refugee Cambodians, starving Ethiopians, and the victims of apartheid in South Africa but for the most part refused to address the Israeli-Palestinian conflict, with Levinas also (whose philosophy, while not as directly addressed to such internationalist issues of grave political injustice, is often eloquently interfused by concern for them) the trauma of the Holocaust appears to have made him fearful of making any statement that might render the Jewish people especially vulnerable to the priorities of other people's nationalisms.[63]

Even if we allow for such inconsistency between the central tenets of Levinas's ethical thoughts and his occasional political applications, what remains disturbing at a deeper level is the degree to which Levinas's own apparent evasion of responsibility—his failure to criticize specific political actions taken by the state of Israel on ethical grounds—forces him throughout the 1982 interview into dramatic convolutions with regard to his own thought. Implicitly apologizing for Israel's military policies in Lebanon under the rhetoric of besiegement, he goes so far as to associate the recent actions with a necessary attitude of militaristic defense, justified not through self-interest per se but, rather, by self-defense in the name of the neighbor—as he says, "of those close to me, who are also my neighbours" (*LR* 292). Further on in the conversation he makes explicit what I have described as the always potentially nationalistic emphasis in the discourse of the neighbor, arguing that to defend the Jewish people is to defend your neighbor and admitting that there is a limit to the relevance of ethics when it comes to affairs of the state. When reminded by Shlomo Malka that he is supposed to be the "philosopher of the other" and asked whether politics was not to be the very site for the encounter of the other and whether in a basic sense the Palestinian was not the most obvious other for the Israeli citizen, Levinas gives what Howard Caygill describes as a "chilling" reply that "opens a wound in his whole oeuvre" (192): "My definition of the other is completely different. The other is the neighbour, who is not necessarily kin, but who can be. And in that sense, if you're for the other, you're for the neighbour. But if your neighbour attacks another neighbour or treats him unjustly, what can you do? Then alterity takes on another character, in alterity we can find an enemy, or at least then we are faced with the problem of knowing who is right and who is wrong, who is just and who is unjust. There are people who are wrong" (*LR* 294).[64]

In fairness to Levinas, this response is not entirely incompatible with his attempt in the later sections of *Otherwise than Being* to recover the ground of politics as a response to ethics via the role played by the third person in mediating the irreconcilable demands exercised by every other within the immediacy of the face-to-face relationship. Moreover, if we recall the story of Jedwabne with which I opened this chapter, it is not hard to imagine how the memory of such a historical incident might force us to establish boundaries for the unlimitedness of ethical responsibility. It will not get us anywhere, at least not anywhere we want to be ethically, to speak of Nazis or of Poles incited to undertake a pogrom as misunderstood strangers; and at one point in the interview Levinas turns to the Holocaust to make the point that, though it cannot be an excuse for any action, it nevertheless suggests "that all those who attack us with such venom have no right to do so," clearly referring here not to terrorist acts but to international criticisms of Israeli reprisals against real and perceived threats offered by its neighboring nations (*LR* 292).

And yet throughout much of Levinas's ethical project, he does speak of a responsibility that extends from the hypothetical perspective of the victim to include responsibility for the persecutor, using language that I have suggested it is impossible to disentangle from the implicit status of Holocaust memory in his work. The extensive responsibility of the victim, I suggested in chapter 3, traces a deep complicity with sacrificial narratives, but so also is any argument for the victim's absolute innocence—and seeming exemption from responsibility—deeply implicated in this problematic sacrificial construction of language and culture. On the whole Levinas's philosophy prefers to emphasize the responsibility even of the innocent, even beyond pragmatic standards of reason, and he makes this point several times in the radio discussion. So why does Levinas also deploy the language of political opposition as an exemption from the inherently unreasonable calling of ethics on this occasion? Why refer with obliquity and yet also unmistakable directness to the Palestinians as an "enemy" precisely at a historical point when Israel has just played host or sponsor to a war crime? I do not think the answer is to concede that here we see Levinas's sense of realpolitik kicking in and to charge, as Caygill does at least initially, that such a description of the other as enemy is "thus entirely consistent" with a "reading of Levinas's ethics" (193).

By my own reading of this 1982 radio discussion, which seems symptomatic of Levinas's more general reticence on the Israeli-Palestinian conflict, Levinas's language on this occasion must be judged inadequate to the terms of his own ethics. To the extent that Levinas's willingness to interpret the other as enemy recalls an archaic meaning of the stranger as one who is hostile (in Latin *hostis*), this must strike us as ethically problematic. To allow the meaning of strangers to serve as an excuse for preemptively defensive hostilities or to allow the priority of the neighbor to supersede and in effect to displace the claim of the stranger—neither of these options remains true to the radical meaning of responsibility Levinas helped to introduce into post–World War II ethics. Such an episode poses a challenge to the understanding of the interrelationship between politics and ethics I have been arguing for in this book, but we cannot characterize, as I have also emphasized, an entire philosophy by selective examples of the philosopher's applied—or in this case mostly unapplied—politics. In my view Levinas's failure to address the Israeli-Palestinian crisis constitutes a relatively singular example of self-interpretation and quite possibly also a bad application of his own ethics. In this sense—although it may be risky to put it this way—what seems most troubling to me about the 1982 radio discussion is not the nationalistic inflection to Levinas's politics per se but, rather, the philosophical contradiction brought about by Levinas's language. The twentieth century's greatest defender of generosity proves here to be, quite simply, philosophically ungenerous.

By my account, however, this highly symbolic failure of ethical discourse is also not entirely inexplicable, for Levinas uses language in the radio discussion that coincides with what I have also described as a contradictory valence brought to bear on Levinasian ethics by his use of the term *neighbor* (*le prochain*). Asked to give a practical interpretation of his ethics in a situation that would seem to call for at least some criticism of Israel, Levinas instead interprets his own ethical project through a terminology he reluctantly introduced in the mid-1960s and then over time elaborated with dialectical sophistication, effectively metaphorizing the status of nearness, wresting it from its apparently primary connotations as proximate kinship and parochialism. Responding to Shlomo Malka, Levinas restrictively and somewhat surprisingly defines the other as neighbor even as he also defined neighbors largely in the terms Western culture at least since the era of nationalism has traditionally used to define them—not necessarily as kin, although they can be, but in any case suggesting the extent to which responsibility is economically and only gradually extended from inside the boundaries of what is already dear to us. To be for the neighbor is to be for the other—this sounds more like jingoism than ethics. What I hope to have demonstrated in this chapter, however, is that even as Levinas's adoption of the term *neighbor* represents a compromise within his project by which he struggles to reconcile the alienating force of alterity to the possibility of a practical responsibility executed from within range of the subject's reach, he has simultaneously preserved the play of estrangement necessary to the signifying force of responsibility in revisioning the terminology. The neighbor is one who approaches through an unsettling proximity; and in this sense the conservative, nationalistically inflected privilege we persistently grant to the ones who are nearest—even when we find Levinas himself falling back upon these hard-to-excise cultural habits—is simply not the best reading of what Levinas himself meant by *le prochain*, who is always other and also at least residually, possibly more radically, a stranger within Levinasian ethics.

Levinas seems better able to provide a ground for the critique of our commitments to cultural identity and the exclusionary modes of systemic knowledge when he is not speaking about Israel. To sanctify the wounds of Israel through Christological language—at one point in the 1982 radio discussion he speaks of Israel as a "political ordeal" and refers cryptically to "the Passion of this war" (*LR* 293)—will not bring us closer to radical ethical critique. In the 1982 discussion Levinas also offers what is perhaps only an oblique response to his own complicity in nationalist mythology, but that commitment is as conspicuous when he speaks in his 1985 interview with Myriam Anissimov of an exemplarily democratic France as when he speaks of a preexistent Israel. But in that interview he also offers an illustrative corrective to the premise of nationalist belonging, evoking memory of the Holocaust as a mode of exilic consciousness that disenchants all nationalisms. Having been asked whether he feels like an outsider in France, Levinas says with a vaguely confessional pathos, resonant with post-Holocaust consciousness, that he always feels like he's in the way and then quotes Psalm 119—"I am a stranger upon the earth." Perhaps Anissimov hoped to win from Levinas a critique of France's own nationalist bigotries or a political confession of exilic consciousness along the lines Edward Said or the Boyarins have espoused in the United States or perhaps a confession that as a Jew Levinas's true loyalty is to Israel. But Levinas admits to estrangement only insofar as it is a representative human experience, as if the limited notion of nationalist neighborliness were already preempted by the Hebrew Bible's prescient humanism. The estrangement from the land undoes nationalist attachment: this is a very old, even perhaps proto-internationalist sentiment, embedded within Jewish tradition, and Levinas for the most part remains faithful to it. To remember the stranger, then, is necessarily to rely upon—as in mourning, in bad conscience, and in our response to victims—a vigilant memory never to be reconciled to fixed cultural premises. Our memory of injustice must proceed, in Levinas's view, as though it came from what happens to a stranger, even upon anyone's land.

Ethics versus History

Is There Still an Ought *in Our Remembrance?*

In *The Shape of the Signifier* (2004) Walter Benn Michaels reminds theorists of post-Holocaust memory as well as all advocates of ethnic or racial heritage that, strictly speaking, what they can remember of the historical past is nothing.[1] As he addresses himself to a contemporary vogue for blurring the motives of memory with the causes behind history, and even traces an ostensibly antitheoretical movement such as New Historicism to the performative dimensions of deconstruction or testimony theory in supposing that the value attributed to the past is implicit in the possibility of its being once again experienced, Michaels offers a clarifying caveat: our contemporary desire to make history function as memory, to instill that version of the past a collective population might claim as properly its own, depends upon the supposition that memory only obtains value for the sake of identity. Moreover, our concern for history characteristically retains history's causal ramifications as though they were part of our own experience: "It is only when the events of the past can be imagined not only to have consequences for the present but to *live on* in the present that they can become part of our experience and can testify to who we are" (SS 139). In challenging the orthodoxy of a wide variety of posthistoricist (which is to say also, poststructuralist or postmodern) hermeneutics, and by further suggesting how deeply inscribed such theoretical imperatives are within what now passes for historicism, Michaels ultimately questions why our capacity to address political injustice should depend at all upon the memory of how a present state of inequality came to be. Once we prove capable of naming a contemporary injustice, he finds "that no one's history need be taken into account, that the recognition of inequality makes the history of that inequality irrelevant, and that the question of past injustice has no bearing on the question of present justice" (SS 166).

According to this explicitly contentious argument, history does not—despite all our proclamations about the usefulness, value, or necessity of remembering the past—as easily convert into memory as we might like to assume, nor should it. Most of our attempts to chart why history must be remembered depend upon obscuring, mystifying interstices, frequently figured as ghostly presences or some imprecisely metaphoric collective soul, through which we are encouraged in a largely delusive belief that any one of us, as a sign of the many, might have experienced that which none of us actually did experience in historical time. There are indeed people who remember the Holocaust, although they become far fewer as the twenty-first century advances, as there were also African Americans who could remember slavery (up until the time, say, when a person such as the fictional Jane Pittman would have died, in the late 1960s), but all those who claim to remember slavery or to revere the memory of the Holocaust now depend upon recollections that have been passed to them by others.[2] In lieu of memory's properly experiential relation to an event, the possibility of laying claim to history—not simply as knowledge of the past but, rather, through a special feeling for it—serves to provide a cultural foundation for identity. By such a logic history is elevated to a value. And, precisely because history is nowadays so often theorized as though it were valuable, it is delimited from the start by the necessarily relativistic influence of cultural contexts and traditions by which any past event might be deemed worthy of remembrance. In Michaels's account, as our historicism abides by the doctrines of posthistoricism—the one represented by recently resuscitated arguments for nationalistic liberalism offered by, say, Arthur Schlesinger Jr. or Richard Rorty, and the other by conservatives pronouncing the end of ideology or intellectuals who claim to have discovered the impossibility of universalistic modes of truth—the result is that most historicist praxis, insofar as it fails to consider the past under the aspect of impersonalist knowledge, becomes one with a culture ordered by memory. Thus, abiding by imperatives coded either explicitly as corporate-capitalistic nationalism or only slightly more covertly as a politics of cultural heritage that is nonetheless foundationally a kind of ethnonationalism, culture is that which substitutes for nationalistic belonging and yet remains, theoretically, a version of it.

In the post–Cold War, post-ideological era, Michaels conjectures, we no longer demand that our beliefs should aspire to universalistic truth, since, if we did, our beliefs would remain not only worthy of disagreement but subject to refutation. In a former ideological era ideas were contestable, and it was precisely because a belief should also be true that one held passionately to it. In the post-historical era, however, when we defend the values of the United States, we no longer have to defend them as more truthful than, say, socialism. Instead, we defend them automatically—

because they are our values and because we reflexively defend what is our own. The presiding supposition in this argument, according to what philosophers often refer to as the noncognitive approach to morals, is that a value is not subject to skeptical or empiricist inquiry. One either accepts a value and lives by it, ordering one's identity in accordance with it, or one fails to accept it, perhaps most basically because one is already altogether outside the given province of the value. If one is not an American citizen, perhaps one cannot see why President George W. Bush or U.S. troops should be supported, right or wrong. (In a *Saturday Night Live* skit from fall 2004, a year and half into the war in Iraq, the actor Jude Law impersonated British prime minister Tony Blair backing up his friend and ally President Bush at a White House press conference, playing the part of the Bush administration's eloquent, Anglican lackey, the only formidable representative of the "coalition of the willing," who must therefore be paraded before American audiences to keep up national morale about the war. Of course, as the skit cleverly acknowledged, American nationalistic morale was never really in question, so that, when the prime minister fields a question about how the discovery that there were no weapons of mass destruction in Iraq—Bush and Blair's original rationale for invading the country—hurt his standing with the British people, he sputteringly admits that his approval ratings have plummeted but then says that he thinks it's great that "you Americans" continue to support "your president" no matter what.) Any value that coincides with the function of the group precedes and so also preempts the evidence by which it might be challenged. In this sense all theorizations of history as a mode of cultural heritage abide by the very same logic of nationalistic belonging, according to which identification with the group defines both what one holds dear and how (or why) one remembers history. To the extent that history, under the presiding influence of memory, is marked as significant largely because of its value for the community (even, perhaps especially, when that history is one of great suffering or oppression), Michaels's underlying premise seems irresistible: "We learn about other people's histories; we remember our own" (SS 133). And if this is true, it seems only natural to conclude that the only history that matters to us is our own.

Given what I have suggested in the preceding pages about the ethically construed memory of injustice, there are at least two questions we might pose to Michaels's critique: whether memory must have a mystificatory function in relation to the historical content to which it refers; and whether memory necessarily revisits and reenacts concerns that are properly our own. According to a basic conceit behind even our contemporized constructs for remembrance, *memory* reverts to a premise operative in the Latin verb *memoro*, meaning "to call to mind." Although already in classical Greco-Roman culture *memoria* also refers to records and historical accounts, the experiential core at the basis of *memory* makes such terms as *collective memory* and *cultural memory* seem only metaphoric expansions of a capacity traceable to a specifically identifiable mind. Neither Michaels nor any of memory's various contemporary critics would be likely to deny that late-twentieth-century theorists of memory made efforts to overcome the connotations of memory as a construct owing its prestige to the mythic foundations of Western liberal, bourgeois culture, and thus to an individualistic framework. Nevertheless, as Michaels emphasizes, sounding not unlike Alain Badiou when he enfolds the "ethics of difference" into the reign of identity politics, what we commonly mean by memory abides by a primary cultural value associating the past with its relevance to identity.[3] Even as the skeptical evaluators of memory suspect memory's arbitrariness and contingency, they continue to perceive memory as a concept dependent for its origins upon the conceit of mindfulness. Memory as such relies for its authority on what an individual—or particular group—retains of experience, usually supposing that such selectively remembered contents tell the truth, or at least part of the truth, about what has happened in history.

Insofar as our relation to the past would be constructed as a question of heritage, much of my interpretation of those aspects of ethics that resist memory, identity, and normative knowledge proves compatible with many of Michaels's contentions. For, to the extent that any language of cultural heritage depends upon normative notions of inheritance, as if memory itself were a property, what we have always to suppose is a technique whereby transmission of the past can be achieved via established lines for identity, say, through norms privileging familial relations or giving legal sanction to preferences determined by bloodlines or DNA coding. One might consider, anecdotally, the rage on daytime television, on the talk show *Maury*, for example, and on soap operas such as *Passions*, for technologies such as DNA testing or for the dramatic sorting out of bloodlines so that the cultural plot of responsibility can be read correctly. In the typically sensationalist scenario of the daytime talk show, the woman who has slept with more than one man is onstage with both of them (or, better yet, one or two more), each perhaps denying paternity, the woman with only an intuition of who the real father is, while the centrally suspect father denies his paternity even more fiercely than the other lovers. Before revealing the results of the DNA testing, the show's host, Maury Povitch, typically asks the man a question along these lines, "If it's positive, are you prepared to do the right thing and be a father to this child?" By such a cultural logic (already considered in the last chapter) responsibility pertains only to that which is properly our own. These are the same cultural norms that preclude, perhaps as a necessary corollary, obligations to foreigners, to others in the Third World, to those destitute in our own country who are not obviously our next-door neighbors. Anyone who would prefer foreigners to neighbors, who might esteem a village as much as a family or a foreigner's homeland as much as the dwellings of American families, who could possibly care for dead Iraqis or imprisoned extranational Mexicans as much as the military dead of the United States, would seem to be unnatural. Even our purported reverence for multiculturalism subsides, whenever it must, to nationalistic priorities (in a national survey from December 2004, 44 percent of Americans favored at least some restriction of the civil liberties of Arab Americans).[4]

Although theories of ethnicity have become increasingly complex and sophisticated in the last few decades, they can never altogether suppress the original function of ethnicity as a cultural substitute for nationalist loyalties, that historical sense in which ethnicity becomes important to a group according to its displaced, even diasporic relation to a homeland or nation-state. If the ethnic group's relation to its homeland is especially recent or exceptionally active—as with, for instance, German immigrants in the United States during World War I or contemporary Latin American immigrants who send portions of their wages to extended families south of the U.S. border—there may be concern that ethnic or linguistic adherences are, at least potentially, signs of disloyalty in relation to the new homeland of the naturalized immigrant. Certainly, much of what informs contemporary ethnic loyalties falls under the category of nationalist nostalgia, and recent diasporic and transnationalist theory has tried to suggest that this structure of divided loyalty can introduce a significant dissonance into the imperialistic, homogenizing discourses of Western nation-states. Yet such modes of seemingly productive resistance may prove limited as political critique because, as Michaels has also suggested, they typically depend on mystificatory notions of belonging.

What becomes an even more difficult question, I have supposed, is whether the unwanted, undesirable historical memory—pertaining to events such as slavery and the Holocaust—functions properly as the inspiration of identity. To assume that the primary signifying function of such memories is to promote the cultural politics of heritage, as Peter Novick emphatically declares about Holocaust memory in the United States and Michaels suggests more generally about all rhetorical appeals to past injustice, is to come to a conclusion highly selective in its emphasis.[5] The very fact that such memories have now become politically acceptable, and are even slightly in vogue if one accepts Novick's terms, overlooks a recent past in which they were once thoroughly rejected by the American mainstream and, in many cases, by the particular groups directly affected by these past injustices. The immediate impulse to suppress knowledge of political injustice and to turn from the recent evidence of suffering determines the eventual reception of slavery or of the Holocaust in the

United States, and therefore must also be accounted as a crucial part of the meaning of such belated remembrances. Not wanting to dwell on the past is almost as American as it is Nietzschean, and Novick's appeal to a universalistic ethos, when ethnic or religious groups did not vie for political authority by appealing to the historical wrongs done to them, seems nostalgic for an era of pragmatic political forgetfulness. Of course, it also means invoking the 1950s, an era of anxiously pitched Cold War politics in which enthusiastic American nationalism was positioned against an international, totalitarian threat, as though it were implicitly normative. Ought we to reject a rhetoric of heritage fully implicated in nationalist nostalgias only to arrive at an open espousal of the public discourse encouraged by the nation-state, with its long history of perceiving others as enemies, categorizing foreigners or extra-nationals as external threats always potentially violating the nation's internally self-sustaining premises?

It may well be that a kind of moral capital has accrued to groups in our contemporary political context by way of the memory of past injustices. In this vein the grafting together of heritage and past injustice depends upon a rhetoric of compensation, what we might construe as an almost gratuitous balancing of justice's scales in the light of historical grievances. By arguing for group rights based in what has been previously withheld or violently taken from any particular group, contemporary advocates of ethnicity have assumed that compensation ought to be a term of political justice, that, if democracy is going to mean what it says, it cannot simply declare its premises to be actual but must admit its failures and do something about them. To those who see in all of this merely an opportunity for minority groups to advocate permanent grudge holding and to nurse their wounds as a vehicle for political power, the esteem for victims would appear to have led us down a path possibly foreboding the end of democratic culture, suspending the possibility that we might honestly address the contemporary causes of inequality and oppression.[6]

In one sense what all such recent criticisms hold in common is a distrust not only of the reign of memory but also of the very realm in which it has become significant—which is to say, culture itself. At least since Theodor Adorno, the techniques of cultural criticism have been governed by a peculiar ambivalence, according to which a critic must first establish the importance of observed phenomena and attribute them to the determining influence of what gets called "culture," but must also thereafter pose a critique of the workings of culture. In consequence, one might be led to doubt whether any genuine value attaches to the imprecise perceptions or ideological workings of what counts as culture. Culture gets defined by the workings of a culture industry (there is at least this much of Adorno in Novick's argument), or, as Geoffrey Hartman has conjectured, it serves as a displacement of lived political reality.[7] If, then, the memory of injustice gets treated as though we might answer for the past by esteeming a once despised or persecuted culture, the political imperatives we derive from the perception of injustice will have been displaced into a merely perceptual realm. Indeed, we might almost imagine that merely thinking better of a past we once disavowed might itself stand as a genuine political intervention. Recent attacks on Affirmative Action programs in the United States have proceeded precisely along such lines, as superficial cultural perceptions about race came to be substituted over time for a critique of the socioeconomic conditions proving the endurance of racism even in our contemporary moment. Although the cultural critique of racism began as an attempt to discover the deeply embedded cultural, ideological underpinnings of an injustice so much taken for granted that it might almost have seemed tantamount to the legacy of Western liberalism, quickly added to such a critique were what we might call the sentimental vestiges of Victorian philanthropy, according to which benevolent attitudes and cultural gestures seemed to compensate for the history of injustice, even perhaps to cancel our perception of abiding contemporary imbalances. Clearly, the history of Affirmative Action's dismantling is more complex than this, but we find ourselves nevertheless in a political culture within which conservatives continue to assert that racism is no longer systematically operative in the United States and to argue that we have achieved a conceptual equity in our ideas about race, if not genuine socioeconomic equality. Similarly, as part of a general attack on the welfare state begun by the Reagan administration but legitimated by so-called new Democrats under President Bill Clinton, contemporary America has decided that enough cultural attention has been paid to the poor and to minority communities.[8] The logic in both cases is simple: even if things are not yet fair, they ought to be by now.

THE MEMORY OF INJUSTICE

Throughout this book I have tried to wrest Levinasian ethics free of the charge that it depoliticizes the causes of injustice and our perception of the reasons for injustice. Not least among the qualifications we might offer the skepticism directed at multiculturalism and identity politics by Rorty or Michaels is simply this: there need be no necessary relation between the memory of injustice and a politically narrow definition of the group identity upon which harm has been inflicted. If we ought to be on the watch against any impulse to remember injustice by mystifying irrationality and thereby sentimentalizing oppression itself, we require such vigilance because all languages dependent upon the premise of an identity violated by oppression, much like all remembrances that would confer rights retrospectively upon those who lacked them in history, are compensatory untruths told against the fate of the victim. The memory of the victim or of the foreigner is not a place of identity; it is the terrible absence at the center of all cultural histories, the place to which the benefit of group belonging, in its self-protective function, cannot extend. Memory accounted as such cannot confer rights in retrospect—and this is simply because it cannot amend what has been done to the other in the space of violence, in the historical moment in which rights were exposed as mere cultural fictions guaranteeing nothing. What we need also to consider is precisely the extent to which the memory of injustice, by not aligning with the ordinary usage of memory in culture (as part of, say, the orthodoxy of identitarian self-concern), preoccupies the meaning of memory with a responsibility that is supremely political in its implications. To suppose that the memory of injustice serves to promote solidarity and to foster continuity in the group (whether through the nationalist valences of American memory or the cultural roots of African-Americanism or the ethnic subtleties of, say, Latin-Americanism or Italian-Americanism or the religious and cultural necessities of post-Holocaust Judaism) is to override the radical discontinuity that every event of violence imposes upon history.

Just such a shift in the very meaning of memory is designated by Levinas's persistent use of the term *immemorial*, which disquiets memory where it lives and veers the conventional trajectory of memory off its course. In order to argue for the political value of this shift, I began by tracing the mournful cast of Levinasian ethics. The figure of mourning in Levinas is that which turns the subject away, time and again, from the concern that is properly one's own. As such, the memory of injustice is related to mourning and requires mourning's unresolved vigilance. When mournful rhetoric becomes nostalgic, when it seeks to go back in time and imagine a condition of identity already intact, as if our capacity to appreciate the fullness of the victim's culturally located identity would enhance our sympathy for his fate, it adheres to a logic that would value injustice as a function of cultural perceptions rather than according to its socioeconomic or politically oppressive literality (thus we arrive at the cultural manifestations and uses of mournful memory to which Badiou, Novick, and Michaels object). Yet, with every such attempt to make the suffering of others useful, it is as though we would distinguish implicitly between our understanding of victims who had full lives with much to lose and those whose lack might almost seem to have precipitated the harm that befell them, as though we simply cannot trust ourselves to care enough about victims who are not fully identified in some other way as persons of significant cultural value.[9] Although it is possible for the self or group (as nation or as a culture within the rubric of nationalism) to construe meaning from its own suffering, nevertheless if the suffering of the other is to be understood ethically, Levinas insists in "Useless Suffering" (1982), it must remain absolute in its uselessness, calling us to a responsibility for the other's suffering without finding ways to make it meaningful.

Thus, we begin to glimpse much of Levinas's relevance to contemporary debates about the moral valences attached to the Holocaust or the benefit individuals and groups might garner through the memory of injustice. Another way of putting this is to suggest that as soon as injustice is recollected in such a way that it might be made to appear beneficial, it is no longer a memory of injustice. It is altogether plausible to assert that the memory of injustice is sometimes put to beneficial uses; and, indeed, we might well conclude that any liberal or (better yet) socialistic society demands a conception of justice as also compensatory, amending at least symbolically not only what it has failed to address in the past but also those histories of oppression, persecution, or atrocity with which the Western nations, their respective constructs of cultural self-esteem, and perhaps all our evolved rights and privileges have been historically complicit. Within every movement toward recompense or reciprocity, however, the memory of injustice also persists as the negative of our construct of justice, demanding our vigilance in and through time, demanding that we examine the present moment as a sign of the violences that have preceded it and continue to influence it. This negative meaning of injustice seems in a basic sense more original than justice itself. Injustice is not a deformation of social contracts enacted between powerful parties capable of justice (as Nietzsche would imagine), but rather the very means by which we begin to elaborate what rights can possibly mean. To remember violence is to insist upon the "thou shalt not" dimension of rights. Not being murdered, not being raped or tortured or taken hostage, not being subjected to famine and severe economic deprivation, not being made the object of an ideological hatred that becomes so extreme that its advocates seek to eradicate an entire people—these are the historical imperatives of ethics. If we would like to believe they are also rights, any historically minded political view should suggest that we are far from proving such rights to have obtained in history, either in our own contemporary Western societies or at the broader international level, including all those Third World countries shaped by the West's imperialistic appropriation of subaltern resources and markets. However else one thinks about the violent circumstances wherein rights have not begun to obtain, we should be hard-pressed to describe the situation of genuine social injustice as though it opportunistically capitalized on exploitation and automatically conveyed rights through the facticity of suffering. There is too much unanswered misery in our recent history and in our contemporary international culture for injustice to seem only one more marketable reality within capitalistic commodity culture. What most characterizes injustice is perhaps its tendency not to be remembered or not to be recognized in the first place; and yet injustice, as the very structure of a contrariness within memory, as a facticity to which memory insofar as it is ethical always objects and upon which it therefore relies in order to become meaningful, poses a challenge to any social order perpetuating forgetfulness about what it already neglects. The same challenge also interrogates the suppositions of a memory—immersed in that same social order and its varied, competing premises of identity—that might reclaim injustice as a validation of heritage.

One way of characterizing my argument in this book would depend, then, upon a rather Levinasian question—namely, whether responsibility begins from the same place as rights. In presuming an answer of no, my goal is not to overthrow the discourse of rights but rather to discern the extent to which ethical and political responsibility must be constructed *not* as an original hypothetical balancing of all parties in question, but as a response to historical imbalances and to perpetrated injustices perpetually marginalized by our discourse of rights. In Badiou the alignment of responsibility with rights is taken as a matter of course, as though the stuff of responsibility were always an emanation of extant rights and thus a reification of the rightness of the Western culture that sponsors them. The obvious insight here is that if responsibility is to have any political will behind it, it must be developed from an already legitimated discourse. What sense can we make of responsibilities that fall outside the sphere of extant politics within which established or contested rights are already part of a system? Along these lines it is worthwhile to investigate the space devoted to the spectacle of natural disaster in the American media. For it seems easy enough to argue that the willingness to turn our attention to victims of an earthquake in India or of famine in Africa or of a tsunami in Southeast Asia depends upon the lack of political controversy at stake in such exceptional, wide-scale suffering (although hardly a trained scholar, rock star Bob Geldof, who in 1986 was awarded an honorary knighthood by the queen of England for his work on behalf of famine relief, nevertheless came to a conclusion entirely against the currents of popular understanding in the West—that famine in Africa *is* political). By our ordinary accounting, the natural disaster sets aside political differences and makes us discover what is common in our humanity.

Considered politically, our responses to such spectacularly unperpetrated suffering may feed a perception that the everyday socially determined causes of suffering are to be accepted as though they were part of the normative natural order or, according to an even more self-justifying Western rationale, as though they gave proof of the complicity of those who suffer from them. Even the Third World poor, perhaps with the exception of the children, seem responsible for what befalls them in a way the rest of us are not, if only because their fate is happening to them and, as far as we can tell, we're not directly responsible for it. Every supposition along these lines altogether suppresses the function of responsibility as a sign of the internationally systemic relations between nation-states, developed as a consequence of the West's historical, imperialistic accrual of wealth, of its ravaging of Third World resources, and of its oppression of subaltern, less-powerful peoples. Yet even the natural disaster, which encourages depoliticized compassion, does not adhere only to its apolitical meaning. The very fact that we believe we should care for the suffering we have not caused—that we continue to turn, as it were, automatically to the spectacle of suffering as though it mattered to us—suggests an alternate etiology of responsibility, one not to be derived through the language of rights. Just as it would be absurd to declare that one believes one's government should offer money, resources, and people to earthquake victims in India because it is every person's right not to be oppressed by earthquakes, it ought to be as absurd to say that one can only be responsible for the victim of political oppression to whom rights, through the Western construct of national sovereignty, have already been extended.

The challenge, then, is to politicize our impulse for responsibility, to argue that it cannot be selectively chosen, applied only when we feel like it or when some extraordinarily disastrous event has commanded our sympathy, or only because it falls into line with our duty perceived as a function of identity and of rights established by the conventions of group belonging. To answer for those persons who are already within the structure of the group is only to extend to them rights they already possess, which may have been violated but which were also already extant. The one who suffers political persecution does not necessarily or even typically undergo her suffering as a being who is conscious of the rights being refused her (although it certainly remains possible for a victim to experience an added degree of outrage from the consciousness that someone who by rights should have helped is now hurting her). In extreme suffering the extant categories are never good enough. If a victim becomes a survivor—though our responsibility must be answerable for him whether he survives or not—his experience of suffering may eventually seek resolution in the discourse of rights. What motivates such an entry into the justice decided by political convention, however, is the premise of a responsibility, which begins with an event of suffering that lies behind all conceptual response.

Responsibility in this view is that which is generated from the victim's suffering and falls to those who stood by, who might have done or might still do something on his behalf. It already obligates. It is, in Levinas's terms, the preoriginal fact of relationship. Everyday life readily allows for the refusal of such inordinate responsibility.

Star athlete Michael Jordan and former television personality Kathie Lee Gifford can respond to the knowledge that they have endorsed products manufactured in sweatshops in differing ways. Jordan can say that this is a matter that does not concern him; he is only an athlete celebrating basketball shoes. Or Gifford can say, these facts cannot be true because she loves children and wants to help them. (Of the two Gifford's response, although patently more ridiculous, at least apprehends the matter as pertaining to her moral character.)[10] Politicizing our responsibility involves a willingness to see ourselves as functioning within extensive political systems, to understand the free market as a highly regulated system that always benefits those who set it up and regulate it through power. From a historical standpoint we have to see the connections between and continuity of systems, especially insofar as they are also oppressive, in order to be able to address them politically. In this respect Michaels's supposition that the fact of inequality in the present ought to be good enough for our discourse of political justice is also not quite good enough. Even a basic understanding of the interrelation and interdependency of nations in history would make it entirely impossible to imagine Third World nations as constituted in the present as distinct from the oppressive conditions that presided over their emergence and would make it necessary for us to consider the current deprivation of peoples in other countries to be also our responsibility according to, if nothing else, the function of history.

NOBODY HAS TO REMEMBER

We are used by now to declarations in the imperative mood equating the Holocaust with a duty to speak, to remember, to testify. Oftentimes, as in Sarah Kofman's *Smothered Words*, such declarations are pronounced in close proximity to an author's observations that moral categories and ordinary language have been contested, even invalidated, by the Holocaust's reality. After espousing the post-Holocaust devolution of storytelling and yet positing her father's own faithful, dignified exemplariness in the death camps ("My father, a rabbi, was killed because he tried to observe the Sabbath in the death camps" [SW 34]), Kofman arrives at the paradox of post-Holocaust language: "If no story is possible after Auschwitz, there remains, nonetheless, a duty to speak, to speak endlessly for those who could not speak because to the very end they wanted to safeguard true speech against betrayal. To speak in order to bear witness. But how?" (SW 36). According to the ambiguity of Kofman's text, the fragment "To speak in order to bear witness" hovers ambiguously between the efforts made by those within the camps and a received imperative—or is it merely a desire?— of those who live after the knowledge of 1945. A trope of transmission is already

embedded in her conceit of obligation, as Kofman's perception of daughterly duti-
fulness gets generalized as the "duty to speak" even of what is unspeakable. All of
this is closely tied to the cultural plot of identity, as though the family were the foundational construct for loyalty, as if we were always taking our cues from an Antigone
who cannot be quieted while her brother's body lies unburied, while his memory is
violated by the actions of the polis.

On an episode from the cable television comedy show *Sex and the City* from the
2003 season, the Protestant character Charlotte confronts an obligation conceived
precisely along the lines of such familial necessity. After her Jewish lover informs her
that he has promised to raise his children in the Jewish tradition because his mother
"lost family in the Holocaust," the spectral cliché of post-1945 memory compels her
to concede to his desires, as she says, "Well now I can't say anything because you
brought up [she pauses] *the Holocaust.*"[11] Her reverence is forced in every sense,
and there is supposed to be as much humor in the fact that his filial vow preempts
all other rational considerations as in the fact that she can say nothing to refute a
duty framed in this way. Playing upon sacralizing sentiments that suggest silence is
the only appropriate response to the Holocaust, *Sex and the City* figures the perception of obligation—and perhaps the Holocaust itself—as silencing. It is yet
another cultural version of the "race card," of a statement pertaining to identity that
absolutely trumps any argument not already positioned within the rubric and corollary assumptions of the identity in question.

According to Kofman's filial formulation and *Sex and the City*'s caricatured ren-
dition of such traditionalism, obligation and identity constitute a hermeneutic cir-
cle, each term presuming and reifying the hold of the other. Just as filial duty guarantees the transmission of a memory (on *Sex and the City* all we have left is a form
of memory, a transmitted vow to adhere to what should have been remembered), the
occasion of obligatory transmission enacts the filial bond, even perhaps assuring the
continuity of family. By such a logic duty gets naturalized: it seems practically
impossible to separate filial loyalty from the rhetoric of obligation. Second-genera-
tion Holocaust narratives often depend on the same terms, assuming in advance that
the cultural category of identity (whether concentrated in familial transmissions or
upon ethnic or cultural group identifications) already enacts an inheritance and so
reconstitutes a realm, as Amy Hungerford has argued, in which our most significant
memories seemingly must continue to happen.[12] Yet, as soon as one admits a potential in the second generation for indifference or even hostility toward the inherited
memory—which is certainly part of the point Spiegelman makes by exaggerating his
own callousness in relation to the father's story in *Maus I* and *II*—the technique of
transmission is characterized by its fragility, having become entirely dependent

upon conceptions of duty that may seem antiquated to a postmodern, post-Holo-caust, post-memory generation.[13]

It is important to recall again that a language of moral obligation can compel us to do nothing. No matter how much we might agree with David Hume that implicit prescriptive categories always preoccupy our descriptive evaluations, the language of *ought*, when pronounced as separate from reality and not disguised within codes of scientific realism or political pragmatism, must refer us to that which is hypo-thetical and therefore particularly susceptible to forgetfulness. For Nietzsche the realm of justice was originally and should always be free of the restrictive contrac-tual schematization of morality, and, as I have argued, he worries that the language of *ought* coincides too neatly with memory, interpreting the condition of relative incapability in a weaker party and encoding a debt as a promise to be honored under penalty. In Nietzsche's genealogical narrative a threat of punishment became over time tantamount to a language of obligation, but it is not as though Kant failed to intuit just such a potential vulnerability in obliged parties and in our language of obligation. Kant simply turned morality's apparent disadvantage—versus, say, the law or politics—into a conceptual advantageousness. The law proscribes actions and compels them in anticipation or retrospection, yet it lacks the truest sense of duti-fulness, which must proceed as toward an imperative not transparent from the out-set. For Kant moral law supersedes legalism precisely to the extent that it imposes obligation as a dialectic between involuntarism and voluntarism, defining a space in which what we wish to do immediately does not necessarily square with what we ought to do. The impasse between Kant and Nietzsche has largely to do with the value we attach to that which is exterior to us in a manner never fully reconciled to our will, and of course it is by way of this impasse that Levinas becomes most rele-vant to our conversations about obligation.

When we say we must remember—inspired by Kofman or perhaps by Elie Wiesel or Maurice Blanchot or by countless others who have reminded us of what we need to be mindful of after 1945—we already presume a value in memory itself. From a Kantian perspective it might even be the case that, lacking such a capacity for remembered obligation, we altogether lack a vocabulary for value. The statement "Never forget" is tantamount to the expression "You have to care," and it already admits the everyday reality of its own negation—the possibility of saying, "I don't care about them" or perhaps "I won't care about them." The one who says, "I don't care about them," not only seemingly brings to an end all rational arguments about fairness but pronounces himself immune to any construct of obligation not to be conceived as rooted in nationalistic, neighborly loyalty. For in a basic sense the order of caring presumes preferences, which are, by definition, also exclusions. Any attempt to generalize the ethics of caring may be rendered suspect by the impossibility of sustaining genuine memories of all those whom we care about. Thus, when Avishai Margalit recounts in *The Ethics of Memory* (2002) the example of a military officer who fails to remember the names of men who have died in battle under his command and might therefore be accused of not caring about them, the point of the anecdote is that remembrance as such—even the mere remembering of names so as to prove basic esteem—is a standard that becomes impossible in inverse proportion to its original constrictiveness. If we take Margalit's example and give it a slightly different emphasis, we might suggest that the aphasia of names is symptomatic of a greater crisis in our contemporary structures of obligation. Feeling besieged by (too much) knowledge that we would hypothetically convert into memory, we are overcome by forgetfulness, which preoccupies the center even of our most personal remembrances. In this respect contemporary trauma theory, despite a hermeneutical overreaching that projects the therapeutic scenario onto the purported pathologies of the public realm, might be understood most sympathetically as an attempt to answer the inherent forgetfulness of contemporary culture. What trauma theory proposes as a new mode of historiography is a forgetfulness implicitly full of memory, finding in our most basic structures of avoiding knowledge residues of history as trauma and in that sense also the implicit imperatives for subsequent acts of remembrance—to be elicited from a past we are always in the process of forgetting. By Cathy Caruth's account, the traumatized themselves become witnesses to history, not by means of their own intentions but, rather, by virtue of the history they've suffered and thereby been marked by. The burden conceived in advance by trauma theorists is that memory's unreliability is yet another mode of representation that has failed us, and what the terrain of the trauma permits is a hermeneutical bypassing of memory's narrowness and selectivity. In such a view history might be imposed upon consciousness even in ways any singular consciousness has not yet or never quite imagined.

It is worth noting that Margalit's solution is not all that different from Caruth's. Framing an opposition between ethics and morality such that ethics pertains to familiar (or thick) relations and morality to all those generalized, public (or thin) relations, Margalit supposes that care is inherently limiting, even we might say conservative. We need morality, he says, in order to overcome our "natural indifference to others."[14] In the public realm, Margalit suggests, we have to understand what makes us reliable citizens, but there still is not much we have to remember particularly about the past. Nevertheless, there are exceptions to this basic premise. There are events such as the Holocaust, he supposes, that should concern us more generally and not just as individuals directly affected by memories or as groups of people living with the legacy of past experiences pertaining to those whom we hold dear through broader (yet narrow enough to be significant) collective structures for identity. To meet the challenge of the history that exceeds even group memory, Margalit proposes the category of the moral witness, that person who suffers history initially within a narrower, ethical rubric of concern, and whose experience as such enables her to stand for concerns relevant to a great many people. As Caruth and Margalit entrust themselves in divergent yet parallel ways to the figure of the witness, they recover a martyrological principle embedded in memory, implicitly remembering that the Latin verb *memoro* is indebted etymologically to the Greek verb *martureō*, "to be a witness" or "to bear witness," a hypothesis of experience seeming already imbricated in the responsibility of transmission. According to the martyrological premise inherent in memory, a witness possesses an event—or, in the traumatic formulation, is possessed by it—so as to share it with others.[15]

Margalit argues that the witness provides our most authoritative access to knowledge about an evil that attacks our general moral system, and the credibility of her act of moral witness will be increased when she speaks for others who are bound by a set of thick relations. With this move he returns the act of witness to a premise of identity. So, too, despite trauma theory's effort to bypass the limited terrain of memory and identity to elicit modes of knowledge not testified to in an ordinarily voluntary sense, it characteristically maintains the privilege of the singular witness who is the substitute vehicle for a knowledge not so readily conveyed. In each case, whether the commitment to a certain version of identity precedes the conclusion or whether the conclusion makes evident a latent assumption, the theoretical problem pertains to the act of transmission. Only the particular location within experience—whether one understands it via the realm of thick relations or fails to understand it because it is a violence one suffers—can guarantee the authenticity of testimonial speech. Each theory supposes that an experiential dimension presides over witnessing as an act of transmitted knowledge. Moreover, a mystificatory hermeneutic oversees the transmission—as the moral witness's thick-relational authority gets extended into the public realm; as the one who is traumatized and inherently implicated in violent history involuntarily passes on that history by implicating other listeners through an experience of virtual traumatization.[16]

In either case an element of hermeneutical mystification arises when the philosopher or theorist attempts to transfer the *ought* of individual or group experience. In consequence, the significance of memory becomes entirely dependent upon its own redundant imperatives: because the witness must bear witness, we must listen; or, because the witness is obligated by memory, her memories must also be significant to our general understanding of obligation. According to our prevailing constructs of memory and to the implicit ethical constructs in which memory's workings are signified as imperatives of one sort or another, what happens in memory is that an outside or radically exterior point of reference occurs as if it were within the mind's reach, fitted into a community of discourse or a specifically defined system in order to become meaningful.

The tendency of morally or politically systemic knowledge to reduce exteriority to a set of discernible functions internal to a psychic or social system seems one of the founding instigations for the Levinasian project of critique. The reach of concern in Heidegger was measured as an apprehension of subjectivity's limit and possibility, and, behind Heidegger, Nietzsche had declared with demystificatory insistence that every perceived obligation is merely a rationalization of the will's own disguised motives as well as its immersion in a set of power relations. Even in Kant obligation's imperative must correspond to an interior motive that acts for the sake of duty, presuming a categorical imperative that generalizes ahead of time each particular, historical exigency. Insofar as Levinas seeks a definition of ethics that proceeds as though the functional exteriority of obligation instituted reason itself, he characterizes a structure of obligation preceding all moral philosophical motivation, exceeding all cultural codification along the lines of pragmatic self-interest, and even superseding every translation of obligation into action. Responsibility preoccupies the subject, as though every glimpse we gain of our duty were only a partial realization of a preeminent vocation, which is why we must turn to the ubiquitous, systemically perpetrated facticity of injustice insofar as we wish to live as just or fair human beings. If, even while immersed in a culture of self-concern and of infinite distraction, we can yet recognize inequality or suffering, then so much greater must our responsibility be to have answered for it.

WHY SHOULD I CARE?

What seems finally most persuasive, even perhaps irrefutable, about Michaels's critique of the contemporary politics of cultural remembrance is his contention that, insofar as a concern for identity oversees our calculations about how justice should be calculated in the public realm, memory will attempt to retrieve the past as though it expressed that concern that is properly one's own—in effect, a concern that is tantamount to identity. Through an ingenious reading of Randall Robinson's book *The Debt* (2000), which calls for the United States government to make financial reparations to African Americans, Michaels suggests that, as Robinson argues for righting the historical imbalance set in motion by slavery, he wants in effect the 20 percent of African-American households earning under $15,000 to dip to 13 percent while the 7 percent of African-American households earning above $75,000 rises from 7 percent to 13 percent.[17] Never doubting that slavery and the history of racism have influenced such disproportionate numbers, Michaels simply wonders "how leaving the economic inequalities of American society intact while rearranging the skin color of those who suffer from and those who benefit from those inequalities counts as progress" (SS 164). Indeed, Robinson accepts the permanence of economic inequality as a precondition of his argument when he observes that "lamentably there will always be poverty" (8). By converting the phenomenon of injustice through an allusion to the gospels into a fact surrendered to platitudinous piety, Robinson declares economic inequality to be regrettable but not finally alterable. Carrying Robinson's argument to its logical conclusion, Michaels exposes a selective view of causality that has been filtered through the lens of a momentous historical suffering. Once reparations have corrected the injustice produced by slavery, the economic inequality with which we are left will be "lamentable," but, as Michaels says paraphrasing Robinson, "it won't be unjust" (SS 165).

Drawing attention to the oddity of Robinson's conclusion, Michaels emphasizes an irony whereby the remembrance of historical oppression would distort the very possibility of naming injustice in the present moment. Yet Michaels's ironic distinction also depends upon two presumptions—(a) that inequality is truly unjust; and (b) that we ought to care about injustice, not just its memory. The first of these he would frankly profess, and the second he would no doubt qualify, if not altogether reject. Nevertheless, what I have tried to suggest is how deeply interrelated the two claims must be and, furthermore, how dependent each—whether the progression is charted from b to a or from a to b—must be upon our ethical explication of the memory of injustice. Robinson deploys historical memory as a corrective to a deeply ingrained cultural imbalance, which ought to be in contradiction to liberal culture; but he also stops where liberal culture stops, refusing to address inequities based in the systemic distribution of wealth and the problem of rights as devolved through the construct of property. In response, Michaels highlights the inconsistency involved in stopping our conversation about injustice where Robinson stops it, but he thereby fails to admit what is also revealed by Robinson's selective critique of injustice. For it is precisely because our lives are so very much steeped in ideology—and, after all, it is Michaels's persistently ironical point that the so-called post-ideological age is anything but—that Robinson can reach his conclusion that economic inequality need not be unjust. As long as we remain citizens whose political reality is immersed in ideology and characterized in large part through culture, which is to say as long as we remain anything less than perfectly rational political citizens, our definitions of injustice will tend to reinforce those principles to which we are already committed. Justice will be characterized, as Nietzsche's preference for the truly strong who were capable of promising or Robinson's acceptance of poverty as a natural part of human existence would demonstrate, by the limits by which we draw our concerns. If injustice is only the failure of extant justice, then we will only be willing to trace the extent of that failure so far. To trace it all the way, to a point where we are responsible for those who have never been enfranchised by our state or experienced the privilege of a mode of justice working on their behalf, would mean admitting justice's historical irresponsibilities.

Another way of phrasing this point is to declare quite simply, *why should I care?* Why ought anyone to care about the injustice or inequality she cannot understand herself to have caused? *Because it's factual*, Michaels wants to say. *Because it's true*, Badiou wants to say, as he hypothesizes a truth that arises in contingency but gets sustained as fidelity to systemic transformation. Yet even that which is factual and that which is true need not be calculated, even when either or both also discovers a condition of inequality, insofar as it participates in that which is unjust. The recognition of injustice depends deeply upon a construct of ethics in which responsibility for the other, if only as a rhetorical possibility, matters also to our truthfulness. Indeed, to the extent that the question of why should we care gets imbricated with the question of why should we remember, the memory of injustice becomes interchangeable with a question about why we care for the suffering of the other in the present.

Put otherwise, we might say that the memory of injustice provides a dissenting force within the extant political structure as well as within the ideology by which it is rationalized, and that, moreover, the memory of injustice serves as a motivating force to enact responsibility for those who suffer under current political systems. How we think about history, the attention we pay to the injustice that is historical, I have proposed, actuates a space of critique within the present order. Among other things the memory of injustice, charted in its historical, systemic causations, provides an answer to the citizen who does not care because he cannot perceive himself to be causally responsible. It expands the principle of causation to a point where the subject accepts his positionality in a chain of causality. Levinas himself never emphasizes this important point, but his failure to do so is based perhaps in an intuition that responsibility must proceed from outside the logic of causality, as if from a place that is not already conceptually extant within the realm of obligation. By this logic it is precisely because ideology is so influential upon justice that Levinas must locate the radical of obligation even beyond what the subject may be capable of perceiving in her historical moment.

In Levinas the hermeneutic centered on the dutiful transmission of obligation is finally suspended. There remains a very strong sense that prescriptive suppositions (even biblically inspired prescriptive formulas) inhere in his descriptions of ethics, but the qualifications posed by utilitarianism, by cynical reason, or by pragmatic relativism are answered in advance by Levinas's assertion that obligation pertains to the facticity of the other. Consequently, a figurative system of obliging tropes, most of which are radically unpleasurable and several of which have been explicated in this book, comes to order all responsible subjectivity: mourning, obsession, bad conscience, standing as sacrificial victim, being taken hostage, persecution, even trauma. To quote again a passage cited in chapter 4 "In the approach (*dans l'approche*) I am instantly a servant of the one who is near (*du prochain*), already late and guilty of being late. I exist as though I were put in order (*ordonné*) from the outside (*dehors*)— traumatically commanded—without interiorizing by means of representation and concepts the authority that commands me" (*AQE* 139, my trans.; refer to *OTB* 87). To be defined so radically by obligations proceeding from the outside attributes to the ethical subject the apparently ineluctable position of a victim, or perhaps the foreigner who is unattached to or ignorant of social rules, someone who stands for responsibility even in the moment of her persecution or alienation.[18]

A responsible subject does not have recourse to the consolations of identity in order to say, *I choose to accept this responsibility, to refuse these others*. Levinas does not doubt that such choices must be made in the realm of politics, in the realm of justice, but ethics already precedes such regulatory social systems. For Levinas the ethical calling of reason would hark back to an openness never to be reasoned away.[19] When Levinas speaks paradoxically of the vulnerability of sensibility as an "aptitude," which every being in its "natural pride" would be ashamed to admit, ethics means suffering for another person with an openness that risks death, and not only does Levinas sometimes figure the ethical relation in implicit metaphorical terms whereby the other is persecutor and the subject the victim, but he even contends that "to suffer from another is to have charge of him," as though ethics remained revisionarily attached to, even as it also demystifies, the sacrificial logic of so much of Western culture (NI 146).[20]

What I have herein emphasized with regard to Levinasian ethics, then, is the implicitly obligating status of injustice. In mapping the previously uncharted significances of ethics, Levinas explicitly preempts the categories of moral philosophy (taking up Kantian questions about acting for the sake of duty by ironically suspending the question of the *ought*) because such a discourse must realistically entertain the hypothesis of a subject who freely refuses perceived obligations and as freely fails to perceive her responsibility. Moral philosophy must take talk show host Bill O'Reilly's refusal to care "about them" and his stance of indifference to heart. It must consider, as Bernard Williams has done so extensively, the extent to which our basic discourse of morality (for example, the entire language of values) can and probably should be demystified by offering a rigorous explication of the minimal conditions, which are synonymous with those personal or public matters we really do care about, that allow for an obligation to be enacted. By this logic much, if not all, of what we care for is predictable by our location in cultural systems. If identity is a symptom of the will to power or at the very least our implication in power relations, our values will typically affirm the premises of identity, which are themselves reifications of a preexistent social logic. Yet, even in the face of such normative cultural tendencies, Levinas insists that responsibility upholds itself as a competing system of valuation.

Then, too, there is still the question of *ought* that informs any decision to read Levinas: much as the Kantian categorical imperative depends on the sincere question "What ought I do and how ought I think about what I propose doing in order to act ethically?" the question of whether one ought to read Levinas already presumes some commitment to a worldview in which our relative capacity as responsible beings would be indicative of the very fact of our significant humanity. Levinas assumes we are already beings who find our responsibilities significant and then presumes to define the ultimate sense in which all responsibility must overrun our conventional perceptions, in which it must arrive from the outside and yet have already preoccupied the subject beyond her predictable intentions. And it is in the very same place of a responsibility that cannot be refused—in the very place another person occupies in relation to every subject as specifically that ethical meaning to which she is already dedicated—that Levinas has inscribed the memory of injustice.

At stake here is a fundamental question as to whether injustice is to be understood only as a negation of justice, as a condition of disadvantage, or whether the historical facticity of injustice requires us to frame a relation to suffering as other than the mere deficit of opportunity or advantage, apart even from our intuition of what life ought to have been for the other. All our cultural notions of the victim who gains an advantage depend upon a reading of the victim as though her experience could be normatively recuperated to the realm of self-interest, but Levinas's reading of the victim, his preference (at least early in his career) for the stranger over the neighbor, altogether inverts this way of thinking. It is not my victimization but the victimization of the other that is the matter for ethical responsibility. As Levinas's figures for ethics inscribe situations of conspicuous suffering upon the other's obligating intensity, he enfolds the memory of injustice into the very place from which ethics begins—the other's exteriority coinciding, as it were, with the exteriority of injustice. All ethical critique, which is also necessarily aimed at political structures, originates in the surplus of the other, who is dramatically, even magnificently, a sign of my requirement especially insofar as she is a stranger, insofar as he is also a victim. Lest politics should only concern itself with injustice as though it were a measurable imbalance in the present context, Levinas supposes that injustice is necessarily historical and, in a corollary sense, that the historical occasion of injustice occurs outside expectation, desire, or intention, and yet as such has already obligated us.

Ethics, even as its arises from the historical facticity of injustice, is always also supposing a location outside of conventional history, an event not adequately summarized by the already realized intentions or consequences of actions, be they benevolent or malevolent, measured in history. If we ask whether we must really be responsible for what we do not acknowledge or perceive to be our responsibility, Levinas has more than any other modern philosopher answered yes. And if we don't ask this question, Levinas implies, we cannot really be said to be moral beings. Bill O'Reilly doesn't have to care for anybody he doesn't want to care for, but he is still more responsible for such people than he thinks. This is not a matter of directed remembrance or even a matter of the declarative *ought*. In Levinas's own implicitly humanistic terms there is doubtless a slightly mystifying tendency to speak of obligation as a necessity. I cannot leave the other alone to his death, he tells us. But of course I can—it is because I can do this that Levinas has to enjoin a universalized subject *not* to do such a thing. There is no necessity or even natural momentum to morality. There is no ontological essence, or even a reliable structure of identity, that precedes or contains our responsibility. Responsibility is always a slightly desperate language, but for Levinas these desperate tones are weighted by the subtle structure of obliging memory, what I have herein called "vigilant memory," which functions as a persistent demand for our response to the historical exigency of injustice. Which is not nothing.

Notes

1. Geoffrey Galt Harpham, "Ethics and Literary Study," *Shadows of Ethics: Criticism and the Just Society* (Durham: Duke University Press, 1999), 18–37, 18.

2. See, for example, Jonathan Kandell's dismissive obituary for Derrida, "Jacques Derrida, Abstruse Theorist, Dies at 74," *New York Times*, Oct. 10, 2004; Stephen Moss, "Deconstructing Jacques," *Guardian*, Oct. 12 2004; Amelia Hodsdon, "What to Say about . . . the Death of Derrida," *Guardian*, Oct. 12, 2004. Cf. Terry Eagleton's outraged reply to the "set of bemused, bone-headed responses to the death of Jacques Derrida" collected in the Oct. 12 story for the *Guardian*. Eagleton, "Don't Deride Derrida: Academics Are Wrong to Rubbish the Philosopher," *Guardian*, Oct. 15, 2004.

3. See Jeffrey Shandler, *While America Watches: Televising the Holocaust* (New York: Oxford University Press, 1999), xi–xviii, 211–56.

4. Lawrence Langer, *Preempting the Holocaust* (New Haven: Yale University Press, 1998), 4–13. See also Tzvetan Todorov, *Facing the Extreme: Moral Life in the Concentration Camps*, trans. Arthur Denner and Abigail Pollak (New York: Henry Holt, [1991] 1996). For a discussion of the ideological system that made victims cooperate with their fate, see Zygmunt Bauman, *Modernity and the Holocaust* (Ithaca: Cornell University Press, 1989), 117–50.

5. Also a forerunner for Todorov, Levi spoke honestly, even sociologically, about the behaviors of the victims, who were made to seek their survival often by imitating or aspiring to the condition of the truly privileged, the Nazi perpetrators who oversaw the camps or the *capos* who were their intermediaries. But he also insistently preserved the distinction between the moral categories of "victims" and "perpetrators." See Primo Levi, "The Gray Zone," *The Drowned and the Saved*, trans. Raymond Rosenthal (New York: Simon and Schuster, [1986] 1988), 36–69.

6. Giorgio Agamben, *Remnants of Auschwitz: The Witness and the Archive*, trans. Daniel Heller-Roazen (New York: Zone Books, [1998] 2002), 63.

7. It is generally assumed, of course, and with good reason, that there is a difference between the experience of moral choice for those who were outside the camps and those who were victims of the camps. Although the terror of the Nazi totalitarian state certainly altered the ordinary structure of the citizen's agency as premised upon democratic political institutions, the pressures exerted on morality from within the ranks of Nazism or upon those who

to one degree or another collaborated with the Nazi regime were simply not the same as the devastation of morality from within the camps. My point, however, is that with regard to arguments insisting that the camps prove not to be so much an exceptional place as a historical moment that forever altered the categories of morality—and in fact the Holocaust persistently functions as such in both intellectual analyses and popular understanding—the terms of retrospective moral judgment might seem less plausible. Thus, David H. Jones attempts to demonstrate that the choices proper to morality were still largely possible within the ordinary functionings of the Nazi state, and, more controversially, Todorov tries to make a case for what yet remained of morality even from within the camps. Jones, *Moral Responsibility in the Holocaust: A Study in the Ethics of Character* (New York: Rowman and Littlefield, 1999); Todorov, *Facing the Extreme*. It should be noted that, if we are speaking strictly from the standpoint of historicism about de Man's deplorably antisemitic writings, the author most likely did not yet have knowledge of the full eliminationist project of antisemitism the Nazis were undertaking—which is only to say that, even if in popular cultural understanding we often fail to make such distinctions, his wartime writings, although apologetic for Nazism and conventionally antisemitic, were not yet inflected by the historical inevitability of the Holocaust.

8. For an exemplary discussion of the tension between ordinary techniques of representation and the extraordinary demands exerted by the Holocaust on representation, and for a theorization of the way in which this tension enacts itself as a tension between different regimes of representation that sometimes constitute a new hybrid genre, see Michael Rothberg, *Traumatic Realism: The Demands of Holocaust Representation* (Minneapolis: University of Minnesota Press, 2000).

9. A first version of the essay was printed as "Violence et métaphysique, essai sur la pensée d'Emmanuel Levinas," *Revue de Métaphysique et de Morale* 69:3 (1964): 322–54; and 69:4 (1964): 425–73. Derrida revised the essay and included it three years later in his major monograph, *Writing and Difference*. See Derrida, "Violence and Metaphysics: An Essay on the Thought of Emmanuel Levinas," *Writing and Difference*, trans. Alan Bass (New York: Routledge, [1967] 2001), 97–192. See also Robert Bernasconi, "Skepticism in the Face of Philosophy," *Re-Reading Levinas*, ed. Bernasconi and Simon Critchley (Bloomington: Indiana University Press, 1991), 149–61.

10. Harpham describes Derrida's belated efforts to clarify the deconstructive enterprise as a mode of reading in which the critic began, first, with a faithful reproduction or mimesis of fact and then proceeded through those elements that were undecidable or indeterminate in a specific text (in large part because of the free play of language in its cultural context) to arrive at the minimal conditions for responsible reading. See Harpham, *Shadows of Ethics*, 22; see also Critchley, *The Ethics of Deconstruction: Derrida and Levinas* (Cambridge, MA: Blackwell, 1992).

11. Alain Badiou, *Ethics: An Essay on the Understanding of Evil*, trans. Peter Hallward (New York: Verso, [1993], 2001); hereafter referred to as *E*.

12. See Walter Benn Michaels, *The Shape of the Signifier: 1967 to the End of History* (Princeton, NJ: Princeton University Press, 2004), esp. 19–81; Francis Fukuyama, with responses by Harvey Mansfield et al., "Second Thoughts," *National Interest* 56 (Summer 1999): 16–33.

The argument for ethics as a turning from politics is, of course, that of Badiou. See Badiou, *E*, esp. 8–10.

13. For Levinas's most concise statement about such a relation between ethics and politics, see Emmanuel Levinas, *Ethics and Infinity: Conversations with Philippe Nemo*, trans. Richard A. Cohen (Pittsburgh: Duquesne University Press, [1982] 1985), esp. 80–81. For studies of the interrelation of ethics and politics, see Don Awerkamp, *Emmanuel Levinas: Ethics and Politics* (New York: Revisionist Press, 1977); Critchley, *Ethics of Deconstruction*, 188–247; Bettina Bergo, *Levinas between Ethics and Politics: For the Beauty that Adorns the Earth* (Boston: Kluwer Academic Publishers, 1999), esp. 241–57; and, most thoroughly of all, Howard Caygill, *Levinas and the Political* (New York: Routledge, 2002).

14. For instance, Gayatri Spivak gave a 2004 seminar titled "Is Levinas Use-less?" at the School of Criticism and Theory at Cornell University.

15. Within moral philosophy *critical ethics* is sometimes used as a synonym for *meta-ethics*. I have in mind a connotation framed by the theoretical context for ethics and infused with the spirit of political critique along the lines of the approach framed by Rainsford and Woods in *Critical Ethics: Text, Theory, and Responsibility*, ed. Dominic Rainsford and Tim Woods (New York: St. Martin's Press, 1999).

16. Dennis King Keenan, *Death and Responsibility: The "Work" of Levinas* (Albany: State University of New York Press, 1999), 24.

17. In other words, skepticism is refuted insofar as it would stand for the truth of its negation while at the same time denying the positivity of truths and, moreover, insofar as it would stand for its negating truth within the same system of rationality that upholds those (now contested) truths. At the same time, when skepticism proves the impossibility of a stated truth, it must, as Levinas precisely puts it in *Otherwise than Being: or, Beyond Essence*, "*realize* this impossibility by the very statement of this impossibility," since the skeptic is bound to language, to representation, to confession or expression, and so always speaks within the medium of, indeed according to the very idioms he would lament. See Levinas, *Otherwise than Being or Beyond Essence*, trans. Alphonso Lingis (The Hague: Martinus Nijhoff, [1974] 1981), 7; hereafter referred to as *OTB*.

18. This atemporal temporality gets figured frequently, as Dennis Keenan points out, as a strangely posterior anteriority. As Keenan observes, an "atemporal temporality" structures every instant, an aspect of "dead time" within the event of truth or obligation giving us the theoretical idea of the *trace* (24). When we search for the cause of being in knowledge, we know it, Levinas says, "by its effect *as though* it were posterior to its effect." See Levinas, *Totality and Infinity: An Essay on Exteriority*, trans. Alphonso Lingis (Pittsburgh: Duquesne University Press, [1961] 1969), 54; hereafter referred to as *TI*.

19. In order to proceed beyond the all-too-familiar impasse of skepticism, Levinas has to retain and reformulate the principle by which the value of skepticism, as also the things that skepticism devalues, must constantly return. Although skepticism is pure critique, as Dennis Keenan argues, "at the very moment of critique, what is critiqued (comprehension, production, and possibility) retains all of its value and therefore returns" (24). For Levinas what skepticism also signifies is a plot of diachrony according to which *being* is structured despite itself—despite its claims to realized presence, despite its having codetermined an already con-

stituted order of knowledge and meaning, despite its adherence to the inherently conservative politics of the Western nation-state.

20. John D. Caputo, "The End of Ethics," in *The Blackwell Guide to Ethical Theory*, ed. Hugh LaFollette (Malden, MA: Blackwell Publishers, 2000), 111–28; *Against Ethics: Contributions to a Poetics of Obligation with Constant Reference to Deconstruction* (Bloomington: Indiana University Press, 1993).

21. Caputo, *Against Ethics*, 1–19. Caputo says that "things only start to get interesting when you get past duty," punning upon the etymology of *inter-esse*, of the relational in-between-ness that is not dutiful and yet defines ethics ("End of Ethics" 123).

22. Bernard Williams, "*Ought* and Moral Obligation," *Moral Luck: Philosophical Papers 1973–1980* (New York: Cambridge University Press, 1981), 114–23.

23. All that is left, finally, to distinguish the moral *ought* are two notions pertaining to the unrealized act: blame (attributed retrospectively to an agent who ought to have done something that was not done) and deliberation (which occupies a space between the customary set of psychological motivations and any hypothetical, still-to-be-realized event). When Williams proposes that "the class of moral obligations in the wider sense" pertains significantly to the arena of blame (121), he links blame to the basic possibility of finding an external reason, altogether distinct from practical considerations, for our moral actions. Whatever else blame may be, it cannot describe a motivating force within the moment of decision since it does not compel a subject to act so much as remind her of actions she failed to commit or realize.

24. Walter Benn Michaels and Steven Knapp, "Against Theory," *Critical Inquiry* 8:3 (Spring 1982): 723–42.

25. Slavoj Žižek, *Did Somebody Say Totalitarianism? Five Interventions in the Mis(use) of a Notion* (New York: Verso, 2001).

26. See, for example, Critchley, *Ethics of Deconstruction*, esp. 217–25.

27. See, for example, Caputo's interlinking of Levinas and Kierkegaard precisely along these lines. Caputo, *Against Ethics*, 8–16.

28. Allan Bloom, *The Closing of the American Mind* (New York: Simon and Schuster, 1987).

29. Kevin Hart, "Forgotten Sociality," *Discerning the Australian Social Conscience*, ed. Frank Brennan (Sidney: Jesuit Publications, 1999), 53–71.

30. Levinas's relative absence from the American theoretical conversation about difference is illustrated, for example, by the fact that Barbara Johnson fails to mention him even once in her award-winning, definitive study of the then emergent critical discourse of difference, *A World of Difference* (Baltimore: Johns Hopkins University Press, 1987).

31. According to Jill Robbins, we need to avoid reading Levinasian ethics as if it were declined from the Holocaust. Such a determinist approach might too readily construe an ethical horizon from the Holocaust, as if there were moral lessons to be learned from atrocity. Robert Eaglestone acknowledges the relative absence of a represented Holocaust in Levinas's work but nevertheless emphasizes the allusive relation of Levinasian ethics to that history it cannot quite revisit. See Robbins, *Altered Reading: Levinas and Literature* (Chicago: University of Chicago Press, 1999), xv; Eaglestone, "From behind the Bars of Quotation Marks: Emmanuel Levinas's (Non)-Representation of the Holocaust," *The Holocaust and the Text: Speaking the*

Unspeakable, ed. Andrew Leak and George Paizis (New York: Saint Martin's Press, 2000), 97–108. For Eaglestone's fuller elaboration of Levinasian ethics as defined by post-Holocaust sensibility and shaping the discourse of postmodernism, see *The Holocaust and the Postmodern* (New York: Oxford University Press, 2004). For another expert view of the influence of the Holocaust on Levinas's views on suffering and evil, see Richard A. Cohen, *Ethics, Exegesis, and Philosophy: Interpretation after Levinas* (New York: Columbia University Press, 2001).

32. For an insightful discussion of the motif of the "hostage" in Levinas, see Thomas Keenan, *Fables of Responsibility: Aberrations and Predicaments in Ethics and Politics* (Stanford: Stanford University Press, 1997), esp. 19–23, 27–28. For a looser discussion of the vocabulary of unpleasure in Levinas, see Susan A. Handelman, *Fragments of Redemption: Jewish Thought and Literary Theory in Benjamin, Scholem, and Levinas* (Bloomington: Indiana University Press, 1991), esp. 271–75. See also Helmut Peukert, "Unconditional Responsibility for the Other: The Holocaust and the Thinking of Emmanuel Levinas," in *Postmodernism and the Holocaust,* ed. Alan Milchman and Alan Rosenberg (Atlanta: Rodopi, 1998), 155–66.

33. Levinas's famous resistance to rhetoric seems largely coextensive with his resistance to poetry and literature, split between a Nietzschean suspicion of all moral persuasiveness and a Platonic suspicion of the seductive lure of the poetic imagination to set up a competing, false reality. See Robbins, *Altered Reading,* 75–90.

34. With Robbins, then, I assume that Levinas's own overtly rhetorical rejection of rhetoric naïvely underestimates the ethical efficacy of rhetoric, most especially his own. Although I am not proposing, say, a deconstructive reading of Levinas along the lines of Derrida's charge that Levinas remains continuous with Heidegger and complicitous with metaphysics, I wish to perceive Levinas's misnaming of his own complicity with rhetoric as symptomatic of what he himself describes as a perpetual unease within language. As leaders of the deconstructive movement, Derrida and de Man might be taken to represent different aspects of the critique of language. Derrida emphasized the extent to which all language depended on a play of oppositions that construed reference only through *différance,* without the possibility of making a direct designation of presence except by evoking an authoritative convention or a supplemental rhetoric, whereas de Man gave special emphasis to the rhetorical properties of language, examining the literary manner by which every figure obtains only through what we might call a double deferment, by functioning as a figure of the figure. De Man's deconstructive hermeneutic seems so literary, as it treats the rhetorical appeal of the text as a self-consciousness about figurative referentiality in which the text returns to its ownmost perception of conventions to elicit its effect, that from a Levinasian standpoint it would seem overly mired in the realm of self-sufficient representation, as though theory and literature were only different ways of characterizing language's potential for absolute autonomy, marking the threshold at which language is no longer returnable to ethics. Although Jill Robbins has effectively brought much of Paul de Man's deconstructive hermeneutic to bear on Emmanuel Levinas's work in a manner that elucidates rather than distorts Levinas's project, there is little evidence in Levinas of a direct encounter with de Man. On the other hand, Derrida's critique of *Totality and Infinity* profoundly shaped the course of Levinas's later work, demanding that Levinas account more thoroughly, or maybe just more accurately, for his dialectical break with Heideggerian metaphysics (among Derrida's major concerns was how readily Levinas's ethical

language seemed to be drawn back within range of the metaphysical categories he purported to overthrow). See Derrida, "Violence and Metaphysics," esp. 147–92. For Levinas's direct response to Derrida's critique of his work, see Levinas, "Wholly Otherwise," in *Re-Reading Levinas*, 3–10. For the framework of Robbins's own somewhat deconstructive approach to Levinas's use of figurative language, see Robbins, *Altered Reading*, esp. 39–55.

35. Although sometimes retrieved in our post-high-theoretical moment as though he might cooperate with contemporary efforts to recall the context of ethnic particularisms or collective identities ignored by theory's generalizations, Levinas (as I have already intimated) is a rather troubling interlocutor in debates about the politics of identity and can be used only imperfectly as an advocate of, say, an ethnic construct of Jewish identity. However we interpret the Judaic quality of Levinasian ethics, the force of his argument about ethics will not resolve itself in a privileged positioning of the author's own Jewish identity, hypothetically inserted, in our larger cultural debate about the context and heritage that inform identity, as one among other possible sites for authoritative speaking. To argue thus is not to underestimate Levinas's deep interaction with Jewish tradition or even to deny what Susan A. Handelman has referred to as the prophetic resonance of the Levinasian voice; it is, rather, to respect Levinas's own insistent separation of his so-called Greek and Jewish writings and to refuse to interpret the Greek writings (the metaphoric label often given to his major philosophical texts) as though the key to them were to be found in his somewhat more transparent essayistic engagements with Judaism such as his expositions of the Talmud. It is too simple and simply too misleading to interpret Levinas the philosopher as a Jew writing in Greek, someone occupying the realm of foreigners as though he were the exile who is forever clear-sighted, if not altogether clairvoyant, about the failures of Greek culture because he is able to see by the light of Jewish conscience (which, as a privileged site for knowledge, would necessarily borrow its authority from the tradition's rootedness in revelation). Although she emphasizes Levinas's own terminology and his attempt to distinguish between his Greek and Jewish writing and then traces some of the larger context of Jewish thought informing Levinas's work, Handelman perhaps overemphasizes the extent to which Levinas's philosophical texts can be understood to be implicitly explained by his Jewish writings, thus making Levinas's Jewish identity a hermeneutical key to his philosophical difficulty. See Handelman, *Fragments of Redemption*, esp. 263–305. See also Tamra Wright, *The Twilight of Jewish Philosophy: Emmanuel Levinas's Ethical Hermeneutics* (Amsterdam: Harwood Academic Publishers, 1999), esp. 141–72.

36. A number of too pat critical terms—such as the phrase "myth of the Holocaust" employed by those who question the ideological incentives for the cultural canonization of the Holocaust in North America or Europe, or the punning expression "Shoah business" invoked often by those who study the Holocaust to express skepticism about some of its particular representations in popular, capitalist culture—are barometers for the emerging prevalence of such discourse. The term *Shoah business* operates more from within the community of scholars who worry about what responsible representation of the Holocaust might entail, so that, for example, Michael E. Staub discusses with sympathetic wryness the obvious implication of *Maus I* and *II* in capitalistic commodity culture and explicates Art Spiegelman's aesthetic strategies for coping with his own love/hate affair with the commercial marketplace. See Staub, "The *Shoah* Goes On and On: Remembrance and Representation in Art Spiegelman's *Maus*," *Melus* 20:3 (1995): 33–46. For a highly polemical thesis casting doubt on the signifier

"Holocaust" (without doubting the veracity of the historical event) and interpreting it as commensurate with its *mythic* cultural function, see Norman G. Finkelstein, *The Holocaust Industry: Reflections on the Exploitation of Jewish Suffering* (New York: Verso, 2000). For a more moderate critique of the commercialization of Holocaust memory which nevertheless brings together some of the language about the "myth of the Holocaust" with the suspicion of "Shoah business," see Tim Cole, *Selling the Holocaust: From Auschwitz to Schindler; How History Is Bought, Packaged, and Sold* (New York: Routledge, 1999).

37. I am thinking here especially of Richard Rorty's critique of multiculturalism, in which he supposes that multiculturalism has damaged the legacy of liberalism as concentrated on practical questions about the distribution and redistribution of wealth, a topic upon which Rorty lectured widely throughout the late 1990s. See *Achieving Our Country: Leftist Thought in Twentieth-Century America* (Cambridge, MA: Harvard University Press, 1998).

38. The work of Peter Novick best represents this conflation. See Novick, *The Holocaust in American Life* (Boston: Houghton Mifflin, 1999).

39. Consult also Tina Chanter, "Traumatic Response: Levinas's Legacy," *Philosophy Today* 41, supp. (1997): 19–27.

40. For an emphasis on the socio-structural dimensions of evil, see Raul Hilberg, *The Destruction of the European Jews*, rev. ed. (New York: Holmes and Meier, 1985), esp. 1187–94; Bauman, *Modernity and the Holocaust*, esp. 151–200.

CHAPTER 1: ETHICS AS UNQUIETED MEMORY

1. For a particular application of this very principle in relation to the political economy by which political refugees are accounted, see my article "The Ethical Uselessness of Grief: A Reading of Randall Jarrell's 'The Refugees,'" *PMLA* 120:1 (Jan. 2005): 49–65.

2. Levinas, "Dying For . . . ," in *Entre Nous: On Thinking-of-the-Other*, trans. Michael B. Smith and Barbara Harshav (New York: Columbia University Press, [1991] 1998), 207–18; hereafter referred to as D.

3. Levinas, "As If Consenting to Horror," *Critical Inquiry* 15:2 (Winter 1989): 485–88; hereafter referred to as AICH. For the intersection between Levinas's philosophical revisioning of Heidegger and the questions raised about Heidegger after the publication of Victor Farías's book *Heidegger and Nazism*, trans. Paul Burrell and Gabriel R. Ricci (Philadelphia: Temple University Press, [1987] 1989), see Tina Chanter, *Time, Death, and the Feminine: Levinas with Heidegger* (Stanford: Stanford University Press, 2001), 4–8.

4. For an exploration of Levinas's dissent from Heidegger as figured especially through questions of time, see Chanter, *Time, Death, and the Feminine*, esp. 23–36, 140–88.

5. Levinas's objection to Heidegger's silence culminates with a quotation from an unpublished lecture given by Heidegger in which he declares the Nazis' "manufacture of corpses in the gas chambers and the death camps" to be consistent with practices of the agriculture industry and modern technocratic governance. Seeming rather like his too casual retrospection of the Holocaust, Heidegger's equation of genocide with technological efficiency seems to Levinas "beyond commentary," and yet the obvious implication is that he has normalized Nazism as a representative species of cultural ideology without ever lamenting his own ideological complicity in such ideology. See Levinas, AICH 487.

6. Without (I hope) greatly distorting Heidegger, I have nevertheless maintained here a Levinasisan slant in my reading of Heidegger. For a critique of Levinas's slant on Heidegger, see Jacques Derrida, "Violence and Metaphysics: An Essay on the Thought of Emmanuel Levinas" (1964), in *Writing and Difference*, trans. Alan Bass (New York: Routledge, 2001), 79–195; Chanter, *Time, Death, and the Feminine*, esp. 140–69, 224–40.

7. David Krell, *Intimations of Mortality: Time, Truth, and Finitude in Heidegger's Thinking of Being* (University Park: Pennsylvania State University Press, 1986), 157.

8. For eloquent readings of the way in which Holocaust history speaks from trauma, even as it demands the therapeutic response of historiography, see Dominick LaCapra, *Representing the Holocaust: History, Theory, Trauma* (Ithaca: Cornell University Press, 1994); Saul Friedlander, *Memory, History, and the Extermination of the Jews of Europe* (Bloomington: Indiana University Press, 1993).

9. In order for expressiveness to be again objectified in the world, the ego yields to new attachments and, through an act of healthy mourning, passes beyond the limiting effect of grief to exorcise the compelling past. See "Mourning and Melancholia," *The Standard Edition of the Complete Psychological Works of Sigmund Freud*, ed. and trans. James Strachey (London: Hogarth Press, 1953–74), 14:239–58. Elsewhere I have argued for Freud's basic inability to keep mourning and melancholia separate as a sign of the necessarily ethical meaning, partly glimpsed by Freud, of mourning itself. See *The Ethics of Mourning* (Baltimore: Johns Hopkins University Press, 2004), esp. 47–52. Also compare Judith Butler's reading of the imbrication of mourning and melancholia along the lines of the cultural plot of subjection by which any psychic subject emerges in *The Psychic Life of Power: Theories in Subjection* (Stanford: Stanford University Press, 1997; and consult Eric L. Santner's discussion of the melancholically severed objects of history in *Stranded Objects: Mourning, Memory, and Film in Postwar Germany* (Ithaca: Cornell University Press, 1990).

10. See Levinas, *TI*, esp. 111–13.

11. Des Pres, *The Survivor: An Anatomy of Life in the Death Camps* (New York: Oxford University Press, 1976); Todorov, *Facing the Extreme: Moral Life in the Concentration Camps*, trans. Arthur Denner and Abigail Pollak (New York: Henry Holt, [1991] 1996).

12. Consult Giorgio Agamben's astute reading of the way Bruno Bettelheim's and Terrence Des Pres's reciprocating critiques of the remnant heroism by which each abides exposes its mutual implication in the cultural requirement of mastering shame in sections 3.2–3.5 of *Remnants of Auschwitz: The Witness and the Archive*, trans. Daniel Heller-Roazen (New York: Zone Books, [1999], 2002), 89–95.

13. Although Todorov is somewhat skeptical about the epochal shift in ideological and philosophical climate that Des Pres argues for in claiming that all heroic codes have lapsed in the era of post-Holocaust consciousness, nevertheless in Todorov's account the testimonies that emerge from the camps prove the moral resourcefulness of human beings under the most extreme conditions and thus suggest the irrevocable sense in which humanity lives with renewed knowledge after totalitarianism of its moral possibilities. See Todorov, *Facing the Extreme*, esp. 31–70.

14. As Levinas asks what resistance is really possible to the will, having altogether abrogated the categories of a stoicism that withdraws from the affective struggle to be greater than fate, he focuses specifically on what the "acceptance of death" means in the extreme situation

of a "struggle unto death" in which the refusal to acquiesce to a foreign will provides no guarantee that the self will not have served the "murderous will of the Other." Since heroism coincides with the expression of a will that history necessarily loses sight of, it also suggests how a will resists the anonymity of knowledge and any use of the will's own work in or by history. See Levinas, *TI* 220–32, 230.

15. For many years after World War II this mythicized misperception was so fiercely held to by the French citizenry that one might have imagined here and there a few Frenchman collaborating with Nazism but certainly not the relatively autonomous government of Vichy presiding over the entire southern region of France in cooperation with the Nazis. For a discussion of the distorting effects of the myth of resistance upon memory of the Holocaust, see Alain Finkielkraut, *The Imaginary Jew*, trans. Kevin O'Neill and David Suchoff (Lincoln: University of Nebraska Press, [1980] 1994), 3–34, esp. 9.

16. I hear the influence of his former teacher Maurice Halbwachs in Levinas's emphasis here insofar as his conception of memory's opposition to history resembles an emergent sociological argument about collective memory, which interprets the past according to the terms and needs of the present, refusing the distance of historical time and putting the fact itself back into question. In *Totality and Infinity*, however, memory's reversal is most significantly the activity of an *I*, separating itself from the anonymous elements as also from any preexistent idea. Compare Halbwachs, *On Collective Memory*, ed., trans., and intro. Lewis A. Coser (Chicago: University of Chicago Press, 1992).

17. In other words, by rendering history incomplete, "memory realizes impossibility" (*TI* 55). There is here an overlap with Derrida (most likely the result of a Levinasian influence on Derrida) but yet also a difference, since Levinasian memory peculiarly refuses to remain purely in the aftermath of the event. See Derrida, *Memoires for Paul de Man* (New York: Columbia University Press, 1986).

18. See sections 3.12–3.24 in Giorgio Agamben, *Remnants of Auschwitz: The Witness and the Archive*, trans. Daniel Heller-Roazen ((New York: Zone Books, [1998] 2002), 109–35.

19. See Agamben, *Homo Sacer: Sovereign Power and Bare Life*, trans. Daniel Heller-Roazen (Stanford: Stanford University Press, [1995] 1998), esp. 119–80.

20. This is true even though, according to his discussion of the will in section 3C2 of *Totality and Infinity*, Levinas readily admits that the willful articulation of interiority in work brings a requirement of sacrifice upon the inner life. Levinas is not perfectly consistent with his terminology, so, although *memory* is sometimes used in a more conventional sense that links it with retrospective knowledge, it is just as often a resistant force within the order and time of representation and history/historiography. In "Violence and Metaphysics" Jacques Derrida was among the first to charge Levinas with inconsistencies with regard to his use of terminology, arguing specifically that certain concepts to which Levinas had objected returned with uncanny frequency in the pages of *Totality and Infinity*. Although Derrida does not emphasize Levinas's use of *memory*, he might well have. Levinas does not retrieve a previously abandoned concept so much as he works toward a greater critique of its necessary implication in the structures of knowledge that conform alterity (of the past itself or of the person) to the imperatives of present being. In *Totality and Infinity*, perhaps under the influence of Maurice Halbwachs, Levinas credits memory with a resistance to the time of historiography. As it aligns with the capability of interiority, memory reverses what has been accomplished, the very

"weight of fatality," and puts back into question the past to which it refers: "Memory realizes impossibility: memory, after the event, assumes the passivity of the past and masters it. Memory as an inversion of historical time is the essence of interiority" (*TI* 56). Over a decade later, in *Otherwise than Being*, Levinas is harder on the capabilities of subjectivity and memory, associating memory more often with the work of identification and the recuperative assembling of the past as a differing within identity (e.g., *OTB* 32; and also D 215).

21. Levinas, "Death and Time," a 1975–76 lecture series given at the Sorbonne, *God, Death, and Time*, trans. Bettina Bergo (Stanford: Stanford University Press, [1993] 2000); hereafter referred to as DT.

22. Plato, *Loeb Classical Library: Euthyphro; Apology; Crito; Phaedo; Phaedrus*, trans. Harold North Fowler (Cambridge, MA: Harvard University Press, 1999). This reading might be strengthened by the fact that Phaedo also refers to Apollodorus as having been "quite unrestrained" (*Phaedo* 204; hereafter referred to as P).

23. Although Levinas repeats the gendered stereotyping of the Greek world and strongly associates Apollodorus with Xanthippe (an association made by analogy rather than declaration in the *Phaedo* itself), it is nevertheless significant that he lets the discounted and unauthoritative feminine voice speak as an irony against the philosophical resolve advocated by Socrates himself. Which is to say, grief engenders a conflict in rationality that puts the so-called masculine sensibility at odds with itself, and, however culturally typed it may seem here, the feminine serves to trace a responsiveness that is at the very heart of ethics. See Derrida's famous challenge to Levinas's gendered language in the essay "At This Very Moment in This Work Here I Am," trans. Ruben Berezdivin, in *Re-reading Levinas*, ed. Robert Bernasconi and Simon Critchley (Bloomington: Indiana University Press, 1991), 11–48. See also Tina Chanter, "The Alterity and Immodesty of Time: Death as Future and Eros as Feminine in Levinas," in *Writing the Future*, ed. David Wood (New York: Routledge, 1990), 137–54.

24. This is one of those uncommon moments in which Levinas alludes directly to a contemporary, invoking here Derrida's notion of the supplement as the moment in which the rhetorical argument draws its force from its statement of excess. See Jacques Derrida, *Of Grammatology*, trans. Gayatri Chakravorty Spivak (Baltimore: Johns Hopkins University Press, [1967] 1976).

25. Precisely this sense of excess in mourning, which corresponds to the mourner's dissatisfaction with the world and the metaphysical or political principles by which it is ordered, is what I designate as the constitutive ethical force of mourning in my previous work. See Spargo, *Ethics of Mourning*, esp. 81–86, 120–27.

26. In the Heideggerian view, although anxiety denotes a being's fear of annihilation, it also signifies the existential truth of being's *pouvoir*. In the Sorbonne lecture course Levinas offers accounts of Aristotle, Bergson, Hegel, and Heidegger, concentrating by and large on those aspects of their thought most central for himself. The encounter with Heidegger runs more consistently throughout the lecture course, but I have drawn here especially from the series of six consecutive lectures on Heidegger on November 28, December 5, 12, and 19, 1975; and on January 9 and 16, 1976. See Levinas, DT, 22–49.

27. Levinas, "Time and the Other" (1947), *Time and the Other, and Additional Essays*, trans. Richard A. Cohen (Pittsburgh: Duquesne University Press, [1979] 1987); hereafter referred to as TO.

28. Whereas a subject depends, through the set of familiar relations and through the possessive reach of representation, upon its capacity to render objects knowable, death is the very instance of radical alterity insofar as it refuses to enter into "what is already known." In the 1987 lecture "Dying For . . . ," with all of his vocabulary on the subject finally in place, Levinas argues that death is the necessary question asked in order that the relation with infinity, or time, may present itself. Functioning as that before which all provisional arrangements with alterity must collapse, death resists every language of capability—the virility of the Heideggerian subject as well as the recuperative complexity of the Freudian ego. Yet, as early as the 1957 essay "Philosophy and the Idea of Infinity," Levinas had cast the resistance of the other to systems of thought in the terms of infinity. "Ethical resistance," he says, "is the presence of infinity" (55). Revising the Cartesian idealism that constitutes the transcendent possibility of consciousness in its cognitive relation to infinity, Levinas speaks of an infinity that breaks up cognition precisely because it is "not proportionate to the thought that thinks it" and comes as a thought that "thinks more than it thinks" (56). See "Philosophy and the Idea of Infinity," first published in *Revue de Métaphysique et de Morale* 62 (1957): 241–53; reprinted in Levinas, *En découvrant l'existence avec Husserl et Heidegger*, 2d ed. (Paris: Vrin, 1967); published in English in *Collected Philosophical Papers*, trans. Alphonso Lingis (Dordrecht, Neth.: Martinus Nijhoff, 1987), 47–59.

29. Levinas says, "This is the equivocal language in which dying, in its mineness, becomes a neutral public event, a news item. The They effaces the character of death as ever possible by giving it the effective reality of an object. We console ourselves as if we could escape death. Public life does not want to let itself be troubled by death, which it considers a lack of tact" (DT 48). If death must remain in service of being, what this means in the everyday life of the individual being is that the question of death is abstracted. Immersion in the everydayness of life, as Heidegger describes it, permits any individual being to live inauthentically in flight from death, yet authentic being can only be lived in the anguish of one's own death, bringing one a fuller sense of human possibility and locating one inside structures of care for the other, by which a being answers its inevitable inscription in being-toward-death. Here Levinas identifies in Heidegger an analysis of what Ernest Becker would call the "denial of death." If in Heidegger the cultural evasion of death arises from the empirical certainty of death which marks the limit of all possibility, Levinas rejects this strategy because it is a symptom of empirical facticity, which relies on secondhand observation of the dying other with death marked strictly as the end of the other's experience and expressiveness.

30. Levinas, "The Philosopher and Death," a 1982 interview by Christian Chabanis, originally published in Chabanis, *La mort, un terme ou un commencement?* (Paris: Librairie Arthème Fayard, 1982), 341–52; trans. Michael B. Smith, in Levinas, *Alterity and Transcendence* (New York: Columbia University Press, 1999), 153–69; hereafter referred to as PD.

31. Levinas, DT 13. Specifically, Heidegger locates anxiety as the fount of being, to be precise, as a relation to the anti-conceptual realm of nothingness, a realm with regard to which being and the work of intentionality can have nothing to say.

32. Rosalyn Diprose, *Corporeal Generosity: On Giving with Nietzsche, Merleau-Ponty, and Levinas* (Albany: State University Press of New York, 2002), esp. 125–44.

33. Levinas, "Dialogue on Thinking-of-the-Other" (1987), *Entre Nous: On Thinking-of-the-Other*, trans. Michael B. Smith and Barbara Harshav (New York: Columbia University Press, [1991], 1998), 201–6, 202.

34. See Michel de Certeau, *The Practice of Everyday Life* (Berkeley: University of California Press, 1984), 86–87.

35. Derrida, "At This Very Moment in This Work Here I Am," trans. Ruben Berezdin, in *Re-Reading Levinas*, ed. Robert Bernassoni and Simon Critchley (Bloomington: Indiana University Press, 1991), 11–48, 46.

36. Søren Kierkegaard, *The Concept of Irony, with Continual Reference to Socrates: Together with Notes of Schelling's Berlin Lectures*, ed. and trans. Howard V. Hong and Edna H. Hong (Princeton, NJ: Princeton University Press, 1989).

37. Jill Robbins has explored the paradoxical status granted to the words "Thou shalt not kill" as a kind of "primordial lexicon" for Levinasian ethics. For an extended reading of murder as a conceit for Levinasian ethics, see Robbins, *Altered Reading: Levinas and Literature* (Chicago: University of Chicago Press, 1999), 63–72.

38. For example, in section 3C3 of *Totality and Infinity*, again wrestling with the legacy of Heidegger's assertion of being-toward-death as an agon with nothingness, Levinas cites the Cain and Abel story to declare, "the identifying of death with nothingness befits the death of the other in murder" (*TI* 232). Employing a fabulous and allegorical etiology of murder as a proof-text, Levinas reasons that, if death and nothingness were synonymous, Cain should have possessed the knowledge of death once he slew Abel. There is an odd inference here that Cain's intention, like the intention of every murderer for whom he stands, has been to achieve annihilation, almost as if a murderer's intention were philosophical.

39. Recalling his own association of death with alterity in early work such as "Time and the Other" (1947), Levinas casts this association as even more ominous when he notes that the other is "inseparable from the very event of transcendence" and "situated in a region from which death, possibly murder, comes" (*TI* 233).

40. See Levinas, PD 163.

41. Levinas is directly invoked by Finkielkraut in the chapter "From Novelesque to Memory" in *Imaginary Jew*, 52. Finkielkraut's influence is in turn discernible in Levinas's "Useless Suffering" (1982). Finkielkraut's simultaneous critique of the old assimiliationist model of universalism and what he perceives as the newly fashionable and superficial appreciation of cultural difference among French Jews bears an intriguing relation to Levinas's work. Until perhaps the early 1980s Levinas had offered a universalistic Holocaust in the philosophical writings, which came to be only slightly qualified in keeping with Finkielkraut's expressed misgivings about the way the French left seemed all to happy, for example, to forsake the memory of the destroyed Yiddishkeit so fundamental to European Jewish culture and to disparage unforgetful Jews as promoting nostalgia to the detriment of present injustices.

42. See, for example, Pierre Nora, *Realms of Memory*, trans. Arthur Goldhammer (New York: Columbia University Press, 1996); Michel de Certeau, *The Writing of History*, trans. Tom Conley (New York: Columbia University Press, 1988); Hayden White, *The Content of the Form: Narrative Discourse and Historical Representation* (Baltimore: Johns Hopkins University Press, 1987); Dominick LaCapra, *History and Criticism* (Ithaca: Cornell University Press, 1985), *Representing the Holocaust*, and *History and Memory after Auschwitz* (Ithaca: Cornell University Press, 1998).

43. For a concise discussion of the way such a position quickly turns into or turns upon a cultural narrowness, see Robert Bernasconi, "Philosophy's Paradoxical Parochialism: The Reinvention of Philosophy as Greek," in *Cultural Readings of Imperialism: Edward Said and the Gravity of History*, ed. Keith Ansell Pearson, Benita Parry, and Judith Squires (New York: St. Martin's Press, 1997), 212–26.

44. See Derrida, *Of Grammatology*, trans. Gayatri Chakravorty Spivak (Baltimore: Johns Hopkins University Press, [1967] 1976), esp. 30–44.

45. Jean-François Lyotard, *The Postmodern Condition: A Report on Knowledge*, trans. Geoff Bennington and Brian Massumi (Minneapolis: University of Minnesota Press, 1984).

46. Lawrence L. Langer, *The Holocaust and the Literary Imagination* (New Haven: Yale University Press, 1975).

47. Maurice Blanchot, *The Writing of the Disaster*, trans. Ann Smock (Lincoln: University of Nebraska Press, [1980] 1986), 47.

48. Hartman's engagement with Blanchot's philosophical thought was expressed early in his career in an essay "Maurice Blanchot: Philosopher-Novelist," *Beyond Formalism: Literary Essays, 1958–1970* (New Haven: Yale University Press, 1970). His more direct engagement with Blanchot as an interpreter of the Holocaust occurs in "Maurice Blanchot: Fighting Spirit," in *Witnessing the Disaster: Essays on Representation and the Holocaust*, ed. Michael Bernard-Donals and Richard Glejzer (Madison: University of Wisconsin Press, 2003), 221–30; "Maurice Blanchot: The Spirit of Language after the Holocaust," in *The Power of Contestation: Perspectives on Maurice Blanchot*, ed. Kevin Hart and Geoffrey H. Hartman (Baltimore: Johns Hopkins University Press, 2004), 46–65.

49. For links between Blanchot and Levinas, see Robbins, *Altered Reading*, esp. 150–54; and also, concerning the interrelation of their thought on alterity and death, see Alain P. Toumayan, *Encountering the Other: The Artwork and the Problem of Difference in Blanchot and Levinas* (Pittsburgh: Duquesne University Press, 2004), esp. 44–84.

50. Compare Bernard-Donals's discussion of the sublimity of much Holocaust discourse in "Between Sublimity and Redemption: Toward a Theory of Holocaust Representation," *Mosaic* 34:1 (Mar. 2001): 61–74. To the extent that Blanchot and poststructuralists seem to have special bearing on Levinas's thought, this is because for Levinas also the Holocaust inspires an interrogation of basic conventions of historical and representation referentiality, always referring us beyond reference as to that which could not be contained by knowledge nor apprehended either by imagination or memory.

CHAPTER 2: THE UNPLEASURE OF CONSCIENCE

1. Gillian Rose, *The Broken Middle: Out of Our Ancient Society* (Oxford: Blackwell Publishers, 1992).

2. Robert Bernasconi and Bettina Bergo after him have discussed the intersection of Hegelian dialectic with the Levinasian project in a manner that does not suppose that Levinas's postmodernism (as Gillian Rose might argue) simply cancels the validity of Hegelian dialectic. See Bernasconi, "Hegel and Levinas: The Possibility of Reconciliation and Forgiveness," *Archivio di Filosofia* 54 (1986): 325–46; Bergo, *Levinas between Ethics and*

Politics: For the Beauty That Adorns the Earth (Boston: Kluwer Academic Publishers, 1999), esp. 277–94.

3. Here I am following Bergo's concise and exemplary account of Hegel's response to Kant with regard to those details especially anticipatory of the Levinasian project. See Bergo, *Levinas between Ethics and Politics*, esp. 280–83.

4. Judith Butler, *The Psychic Life of Power: Theories in Subjection* (Stanford: Stanford University Press, 1987); hereafter referred to as *PLP*.

5. Although subjection is always complicit with the structure of power by which it is produced, Butler reminds us, a constitutive ambivalence toward power always also preoccupies subjectivity. See Butler, *PLP*, esp. 82–95.

6. Jean Wahl, *Le Malheur de la conscience dans la philosophie de Hegel* (New York: Garland Publishing, [1951] 1984).

7. Levinas, "Israel and Universalism" (1958), *Difficult Freedom: Essays on Judaism*, trans. Seán Hand (London: Athlone Press [1963, 1976] 1990), 175–77, 175.

8. Ricoeur, *Oneself as Another*, trans. Kathleen Blamey (Chicago: University of Chicago Press, [1990] 1992), 188–94.

9. Cohen charts the parallels in the careers of Levinas and Ricoeur, foregrounding the esteem each held for his peer before elaborating their philosophical rift over the very status of selfhood—a rift Ricoeur clearly described throughout the 1990s, first in *Oneself as Another* (1990) but also in *Autrement: Lecture d'Autrement qu'être ou au-delà de l'essence d'Emmanuel Levinas* (Paris: Presses Universitaires de France, 1997). See Cohen, "Ricoeur and the Lure of Self-Esteem," *Ethics, Exegesis, and Philosophy: Interpretation after Levinas* (New York: Cambridge University Press, 2001), 283–325.

10. Among those pockets of postmodern thought especially dependent on Nietzsche's demystification of morality (and Foucault would seem only the most obvious descendant of Nietzschean thought in this regard), Levinas's insistence on a language of severe difference may bring to mind archaic institutions of morality in which pain had been imagined as a vehicle for memory and responsibility derived only by internalizing contractual codes, which were themselves reflective of positions of power. For a discussion of the importance of Nietzsche to French poststructuralism and for the suggestion that Lyotard's turn to Kant and Levinas quite possibly marked the waning of Nietzsche's influence, see Alan Schrift, *Nietzsche's French Legacy: A Genealogy of Poststructuralism* (New York: Routledge, 1995), esp. 104–11.

11. See Friedrich Nietzsche, *On the Genealogy of Morals and Ecce Homo*, trans. and ed., with commentary by, Walter Kaufmann (New York: Random House, 1967), (sec. 4–7) 62–69; hereafter referred to in the text as *GM*.

12. Nietzsche clearly describes the "bad conscience" as evolving from the weaker party's guilty feeling of indebtedness. See Nietzsche, *GM* (sec. 2:14–2:20), 81–91. Levinas, "Nonintentional Consciousness" (1983; hereafter referred to as *NC*); and "From the One to the Other: Transcendence and Time" (1983, 1989), *Entre Nous: On Thinking-of-the-Other*, trans. Michael B. Smith and Barbara Harshav (New York: Columbia University Press, [1991] 1998), 123–32, 133–54, esp. 127–32 and 140–44.

13. See also Berel Lang, *Heidegger's Silence* (Ithaca: Cornell University Press, 1996); Dominick LaCapra, "Heidegger's Nazi Turn," *Representing the Holocaust: History, Theory, Trauma* (Ithaca: Cornell University Press, 1994), 137–68.

14. *Salvador,* dir. Oliver Stone, 1986; *Schindler's List,* dir. Steven Spielberg, 1993.

15. None of this is to say that Oliver Stone did not set out to make a political film indicting American foreign policy in Central America under the Reagan administration. What I mean to suggest, rather, is that insofar as the film avoids portraying a thoroughgoing American bad conscience, it also deflects or refracts its critique in such a way that it seems not so much soft on communism (as Stone is afraid he might be deemed) as soft-going on American Cold War politics. In a crucial scene in the film the photojournalist Rick Boyle (played by James Woods) turns over photographs he has taken while in the FMLN-occupied countryside to two American military intelligence advisors, who are dressed in nonmilitary garb and who instantly accuse him of holding out on them, which he is in fact doing. Even as he characteristically spins a cover story for himself, stuttering and fast-talking with the manipulative ease of a con artist, Boyle lapses into passionate, even ponderous sincerity, defending himself against the charge of being a liberal/pinko, insisting on the difference between liberals and communists. "You people never can tell the difference," he tells one of the advisors. Boyle then charges that the death squads are a "brainchild of the CIA," that the American involvement is "some kind of post-Vietnam experience," and that the American military is creating a "major Frankenstein" down here. His labyrinthine quest to get himself beyond complicity with American aid to and covert involvement with an oppressive regime and to breathe the clean air of the righteous conscience corresponds to his avowed love of America. "I don't want to see America get another bad rap," he says, a phenomenon he witnessed firsthand when he was covering Vietnam. Declaring his patriotism—"I believe in America, I believe we stand for something"—and associating the spirit of America with the constitution and human rights, Boyle performs for the film's audience their own hypothetical innocence, divorcing himself (as we might also) from the secret shenanigans of the Reagan administration. The more sympathetic of the two advisors feels put upon by Boyle's accusation and, even as he self-professedly looks to his conscience, he achieves for himself a vision of innocence remarkably parallel to Boyle's: "You know I am often asked by people like yourself to examine my conscience, and every now and then I do examine it." When Boyle asks him what he sees there, the advisor declares that in his view whatever "mistakes we make down here, the alternative would be ten times worse." Clearly, this highly artificial scene of self-examination is presented in a satirical light by Stone, and in this sense what Stone portrays is precisely the absence of a bad conscience in someone who should feel guilt over the policy he is unofficially overseeing in El Salvador. Yet the fact that the film insists upon the contrived separation between Boyle's innocently motivated outrage and the advisor's hypocritical declaration of innocence—the former being more or less accurate, the latter rendering bad conscience in caricature as a bad faith expression of ideology—suggests that the rigorous structural critique of the bad conscience, while having been gestured at, has not truly been taken up.

16. It is worth noting that this scene was specially contrived by Spielberg for the film and does not appear in the source text, Thomas Keneally's documentary novel *Schindler's Ark* (London: Hodder and Stoughton, 1982).

17. In order to overcome our natural forgetfulness, we developed quite remarkably what Nietzsche calls a "mnemotechnics"—or cultural techniques for making memory—in order to keep us mindful of our promises. What brings the promise to mind and will not let it recede

is a parallel threat of violence, manifested in the example set by cruelty. Nietzsche, *GM* (sec. 2:3), esp. 61.

18. The bad conscience, which is the negative complement to promising a somber transaction, comes into being based in an economics of compensation—that a pain could be suffered in proportion to injury, a carryover from the contractual relationships of credit and debtors. Punishment is based on a pre-intentional economy, or an equivalence between pain and injury, and injury might be held in check but also paid back through punishment. Nietzsche, *GM* (sec. 2:3–2:6 and 2:12–2:15), 60–67, 76–83.

19. Nietzsche, *GM* (sec.2:11), 73–76.

20. Punishment, even as it presides over the false history of morality, instituting a feeling of guilt as a substitution for the real historical memory of an economic transaction or cultural relation of power, also traces a direct expression of power and the power to hurt. Nietzsche argues against genealogists (such as Duhring) who explicated justice as a reactive expression and an elaboration of the aggrieved impulse to take revenge. For Nietzsche the perception of injustice begins only within the legal antinomy of the just and the unjust. No injury or assault can be unjust unto itself since life operates through injury, assault, and exploitation and could not be imagined without these qualities. Greek culture, especially before Socrates and Plato, had articulated a concept of justice, with its emergent legal codes and conventions, expressing the perspective of those who viewed injuries from a position of power. If we recall the origin of justice in relations of equivalence (although admittedly an equivalence between superior and powerful parties), there is a horizon for human relationship, according to Nietzsche, in which reciprocity rather than disadvantage might serve as the central economic principle. Over the course of time this good start came to many bad ends. The most persistent confusion involved an intermingling of punishment with justice, two spheres with distinct genealogies that ought to have remained separate but did not. Most often the utilitarian misunderstanding of punishment, which supposes that punishment is an institution whose purpose is to awaken feelings of guilt in the guilty party, is mistakenly added to the concept of justice. See Nietzsche, *GM* (sec. 2:5), 24–31.

21. Nietzsche, *GM* (sec. 2:16–2:17), 84–87.

22. See Butler, *PLP* 63–82.

23. As Gregory Zilboorg emphasizes, however, in his introduction to the Norton edition of *Beyond the Pleasure Principle, unpleasure* is an imperfect, slightly neologistic rendering of Freud's German term *Unlust,* the force of which is already diminished in translation. Sigmund Freud, *Beyond the Pleasure Principle,* trans. James Strachey, intro. Gregory Zilboorg (New York: W. W. Norton, 1965, 1971).

24. Freud, *Beyond the Pleasure Principle, The Standard Edition of the Complete Psychological Works of Sigmund Freud,* trans. James Strachey, 24 vols. (London: Hogarth Press, 1955), 18:7–64.

25. This hypothesis might be phrased more accurately if one conceded the suspicions of those who contend that an unremembered, unrepresented, and finally private experience of a historical event lacks all the properties we associate with rational history and that a trauma can never return history in all its literality, if only because the distorting filter of the psyche has already represented the event unconsciously. What we can say, giving a slightly Levinasian connotation to the trauma's signification, is that the trauma indeed signifies as a responsibil-

ity for history, and as such it makes a claim that—for all the clarity and apparent causality offered by those representations of events we call history—history itself cannot require. As soon as one states, for instance, that those who ignore history risk repeating it or that we must study a particular history, such as the Holocaust, so that it might never be repeated, one strays—from the empiricist's perspective—into a philosophy of history or a moral rationale for historiography. When trauma theory makes the private traumatic apprehension stand for a larger history, it infuses historical consciousness with the pseudo-moralistic imperatives of the private self. At least part of the impulse to let the trauma stand for history may arrive through a conflation of the separate signifying strains of unpleasure—that sense in which the requirements of the collective are encountered as unpleasure having been mixed with the more esoteric signification of an individual's traumatic unpleasure. See Caruth, *Unclaimed Experience: Trauma, Narrative, and History* (Baltimore: Johns Hopkins University Press, 1996).

26. In Caruth's terms the function of the trauma is not to mystify irrationality but to acknowledge a certain rupture in the procedures of knowledge and the transmission of responsibility—perhaps brought about in part by the Holocaust but absolutely as relevant to a wide range of extremely oppressive, violent realities that have a hard time making their way into the public discourse. See Caruth, *Unclaimed Experience*, esp. 7–9, 65–72, 100–107. See also Michael Rothberg, *Traumatic Realism: The Demands of Holocaust Representation* (Minneapolis: University of Minnesota Press, 2000), 1–24.

27. In *Otherwise than Being* especially, Levinas insists that it is only through responsibility that we arrive at the facticity of a subject, since subjectivity is grammatically and existentially defined in the accusative case, that is, as *subjectum*. Although Levinas undertakes a critique of subjectivity running oddly parallel to the Nietzschean suspicion of historical consciousness, it would be a mistake to read the Levinasian critique of subjectivity as representative of the general post-Nietzschean and poststructuralist assault on the subject of moral, individualistic, and bourgeois history. For a succinctly normative account of the commonly perceived contrast between the two, see Schrift, *Nietzsche's French Legacy*, esp. 104–11.

28. There is a break here with both the Kantian and Nietzschean formulation of responsibility as obligation, since the Levinasian subject does not become ethically meaningful through its dutifulness in either the good or bad faith connotation of that word. Levinas shifts the imperative and categorical grounds of responsibility in Kant to a consideration of ethics as an accusative and signifying structure that comes before its conceptualization. See Levinas, *OTB*, esp. 121–29.

29. Emmanuel Levinas, "Diachrony and Representation" (1985), in *Entre Nous: On Thinking-of-the-Other*, trans. Michael B. Smith and Barbara Harshav (New York: Columbia University Press, [1991] 1998), 159–77, 172; hereafter referred to as DR.

30. Here and elsewhere Levinas suggests that our conceptual or intentional constructs of ethics are belated. Levinas's re-direction of meaning helps us arrive at what he has a few lines earlier called "an inveterate obligation, older than any commitment" (DR 172). With each mention of a phrase functioning in effect as a negative substitution that alienates its normative and familiar conceptual meanings, Levinas's repetitions and turns of language guide us toward the paradoxical sense of a commandment wherein the content is seemingly immaterial, since it is always tracing an anterior ethical signification.

31. Besides appearing in "Diachrony and Representation," the *mauvaise conscience* is also a central trope in "Nonintentional Consciousness" and "Uniqueness." See Levinas, "Uniqueness" (1986), *Entre Nous*, 189–96. For a view of how this critique of benevolence might apply more broadly to a field such as cultural studies, see Rey Chow, *Ethics after Idealism: Theory, Culture, Ethnicity, Reading* (Bloomington: Indiana University Press, 1998), in which Chow employs the term *non-benevolence* to disassociate her method from idealistic renderings of cultural identity. Chow's suspicion of the idealizing narratives of multiculturalism because they recapitulate the positivist, universalist, and essentialist claims of the traditional constructs of liberal discourse not only traces a debt to poststructuralist critique but suggests the recalcitrance of our cultural idealisms.

32. At least in this respect, Levinas departs from Kant without traveling all that far. Levinas is engaged in a similar critique of the concept's divergence from the humanity it would serve. For, as Paul Ricoeur has observed, the premise of autonomy so fundamental to the Kantian agent's capacity to posit itself and act reasonably under the dictates of the law is already compromised by its necessary relation to an outside, by the need a self has to position itself via an extrinsic principle in order to find the truth in its course of action. The danger in Kantian responsibility, as both Levinas and Bernard Williams perceive it, is that the agent must insist on an obedience to what is only seemingly outside of the self, for in its utter reasonability the Kantian agent recognizes the imperative as an intrinsic function of its own rational desire. What is outside is both prescribed, written as a function of law, and inscribed, written within the function of reason. As Williams contends, the morality system's concentration on what is purely moral—which is to say, equivalent to a moral category or principle—is most often registered subjectively through the concepts of guilt and self-reproach, and this process of internalization tends to conceal the real sense "in which ethical life lies outside the individual," which for Williams is the sense in which ethics refers to the shared values or network of relations in which considerations are influenced and troubled by other moral agents. Whereas Williams poses questions about practical necessity to the Kantian model, asking how it is, realistically, that an agent interprets her particular situation through the demands of moral law, Levinas revisits the metaphysical suppositions or idealistic structures in Kantian thought. As such, Levinas might almost be said to offer, at times, a clotûral reading of Kant, in which the very categories of Kantian thought Williams seems most content to abandon (such as the radical exteriority of moral obligation) are repeated in order to be reclaimed under newer, revised connotations. Indeed, Derrida accused Levinas of such an unpaid debt to Kant and Heidegger in the essay "Violence and Metaphysics," in *Writing and Difference*, trans. Alan Bass (Chicago: University of Chicago Press, 1978). In speaking of Levinas's clotûral reading of Kant, I follow Simon Critchley in perceiving a great deal of overlap between certain techniques of reading in Derrida and the writing of ethics in Levinas. See Critchley, *The Ethics of Deconstruction: Derrida and Levinas* (Cambridge, MA: Blackwell, 1992), esp. 1–58.

33. See my discussion in the introduction on the problem of the extrinsic force of morality in the Kantian scheme and for the terms of Bernard Williams's critique of Kant.

34. Levinas, *Autrement qu'être ou au-delà de l'essence* (The Hague: Martinus Nijhoff, 1974); hereafter referred to as AQE.

35. See Levinas, "No Identity" (1970), *Collected Philosophical Papers*, trans. Alphonso Lingis (Dordrecht, Neth.: Martinus Nijhoff, 1987), 141–52; hereafter referred to as NI.

36. See Levinas, NC, 123–32. As he sets out to describe how the relation to the other imposes itself as meaning in a manner distinct from the structures of knowledge and rule of intentionality Husserl had elucidated, Levinas argues that the Husserlian phenomenological project is characterized by "a privilege of the theoretical, a privilege of representation, of knowing," notwithstanding the emphasis of Merleau-Ponty, who, drawing on Husserl, had given emphasis to nontheoretical intentionality, the life world, or the role of the lived body (NC 124). Although the phenomenological method espouses an interrelation between the object of thought and the thought that thinks it and thus would aim at concreteness (specifi-cally, of the object it proposes to the mind), it nevertheless depends upon the realm of the the-oretical or an order of thought to which the object must always be returned. So, whereas Husserl brought to our attention how the horizons of meaning arise out of and are at the same time obscured by the object's absorption in that order of thought through which it is con-ceived, Levinas contests the Husserlian system because it cannot attest to a meaning of thought other than that which is strictly dependent on what is already known.

37. My reinterpretation of this story in the context of Levinas's thought is strongly indebted to Jill Robbins's insightful exegesis of the story as a conceit for Levinasian thought, although my departure from Robbins on several key points should also be apparent. See Robbins, *Altered Reading: Levinas and Literature* (Chicago: University of Chicago Press, 1999), 63–72.

38. Jean Halpérin, André Neher, et al., *La conscience juive: face à l'histoire: le pardon* (Paris: Presses Universitaires de France, 1963).

39. So disturbing is God's initial rejection of Cain's sacrifice that many readers see it as determinative of his actions. For example, Regina Schwartz reads the original rejection of Cain as a sign of the stingy economics of monotheistic thought. See Schwartz, *The Curse of Cain: The Violent Legacy of Monotheism* (Chicago: University of Chicago Press, 1997).

40. According to the mournful posture I have associated with Levinasian ethics, the non-coincidence presiding over one's responsibility for the other often resembles the pecu-liar temporality of elegiac belatedness. See my discussion of the trope of belatedness in *The Ethics of Mourning* (Baltimore: Johns Hopkins University Press, 2004), esp. 31–32, 135–42, 176–77.

41. As though the Genesis text predicted the horizon of sociality as based always in part upon Cain's desire, as though the world upon which Levinas tries to impose an immemorial ethical meaning were always already Hobbesian or Nietzschean or even Hitlerian, Levinas interprets even the ordinary proximity of the neighbor as necessarily entailing an oddly mur-derous connotation according to which one becomes responsible for the other's death as though one were also its cause. See Levinas, DT 117.

42. See Tzvetan Todorov, *Facing the Extreme: Moral Life in the Concentration Camps*, trans. Arthur Denner and Abigail Pollak (New York: Henry Holt, [1991] 1996), esp. 47–58, 71–90, 285–96; David H. Jones, *Moral Responsibility in the Holocaust: A Study in the Ethics of Character* (Lanham, MD: Rowman and Littlefield, 1999), 15–96; Lawrence Langer, *Preempt-ing the Holocaust* (New Haven: Yale University Press, 1998), 4–10. Jones's rehabilitating assess-ment of character as a valid category for examining questions of responsibility within Holo-caust history readily lends itself to a critique along the lines of the one Lawrence Langer has leveled at Tzvetan Todorov.

43. See Jones, *Moral Responsibility in the Holocaust*, 28–29.

44. In Nietzsche's view all expressions of moral obligation tend to be in bad faith because they imaginatively adopt the perspective of the one who is in debt, exorcising the specters of weakness or vulnerability by reclaiming a compromised social position as though it were dutifully chosen and thereby dedicated to a teleologically oriented good. Thus, when Jones locates the center of his moral philosophical argument in the deliberations of perpetrators, he cooperates with a basic liberal premise that Nietzsche would find entirely suspect. According to Nietzsche's demystifying genealogy, there is no necessary reason why the moral conscience should cooperate with expressions of the political will, and the relative sincerity attributed by Jones to the perpetrators—as a capacity to have recognized the error of their ways—would be merely a function of cultural convention.

45. Jean-François Lyotard, *The Differend: Phrases in Dispute*, trans. Georges Van Den Abbeele (Minneapolis: University of Minnesota Press, [1983] 1988).

46. See Eli Cohen, *Human Behavior in the Concentration Camp*, trans. M. H. Braaksma, (New York: W. W. Norton, 1953); and Bruno Bettelheim, *The Informed Heart: Autonomy in a Mass Age* (Glencoe, IL: Free Press, 1960).

47. See Giorgio Agamben, *RA* (sec. 3.3–3.5), 92–95.

48. See the extended discussion of the inhuman in Agamben, *RA*, sec. 2.6–2.7, 51–54.

49. Auschwitz subsumes Nietzscheanism under the new imperative of testimony because, with regard to the experience of the camps, it is impossible to imagine how a subject could possibly answer the question Nietzsche poses in *The Gay Science*—"Do you want this to happen again, again and again for eternity?"—in the affirmative. See section 3.7 of Agamben, *RA*, esp. 99. This tendency to interpret Auschwitz at least partly in line with the historical trajectory of the Nazis' experiment, as though the meaning of the camps must be accounted by way of their horrible yet irrevocable contribution to the biopolitical meaning of state power, as well as his willingness to read the writings of the proto-fascistic philosopher Carl Schmitt as elucidating the historically shaped ontological meaning of human existence, has made Agamben a not uncontroversial figure.

50. Cynthia Ozick, "Rosa" (1983), *The Shawl* (New York: Random House, 1990), 38.

51. Primo Levi, "Shame," *The Drowned and the Saved*, trans. Raymond Rosenthal (New York: Random House, [1986], 1989), 86; hereafter referred to as Sh.

52. See Levinas, *OTB* 114.

53. Levinas, "Useless Suffering" (1982), *Entre Nous: On Thinking-of-the-Other*, trans. Michael B. Smith and Barbara Harshav (New York: Columbia University Press, 1998), 91–102; hereafter referred to as US.

CHAPTER 3: WHERE THERE ARE NO VICTORIOUS VICTIMS

1. Joseph A. Amato, *Victims and Values: A History and Theory of Suffering* (New York: Greenwood, 1990); Shelby Steele, *The Content of Our Character* (New York: St. Martin's Press, 1990); Charles J. Sykes, *A Nation of Victims: The Decay of the American Character* (New York: St. Martin's Press, 1992). During the same period Naomi Wolf coined the phrase "victim feminism" to refer somewhat dismissively to the politics of previous generations of feminists, and the so-called third wave of feminism, featuring besides Wolf figures such as Katie Roiphe and Rene Denfeld, eschewed any politics that might cast women into the role of victims. Rene

Denfeld, *The New Victorians: A Young Woman's Challenge to the Old Feminist Order* (New York: Warner Books, 1995); Katie Roiphe, *The Morning After: Sex, Fear, and Feminism on Campus* (Boston: Little, Brown, 1993); Naomi Wolf, *Fire with Fire: The New Female Power and How It Will Change the 21st Century* (New York: Random House, 1993). For an assessment of the third-wave feminists and their relation to Nietzsche's critique of *ressentiment*, see Rebecca Stringer, "'A Nietzschean Breed': Feminism, Victimology, Ressentiment," in *Why Nietzsche Still? Reflections on Drama, Culture, and Politics*, ed. Alan D. Schrift (Los Angeles: University of California Press, 2000), 247–73.

2. See Sykes, *Nation of Victims*, 19–20.

3. O'Reilly led in to the segment by lamenting, with apparently stunned sincerity, that a natural disaster could be politicized, code in his vocabulary for any so-called liberal criticism of official American policy under the George W. Bush administration. By dumbing down the debate to the question of whether Americans were generous or not—without considering questions about the proportion of American giving to its consumption of the world's resources or worrying about points raised, for example, by the secretary-general of the United Nations, Kofi Annan, about how this surge of generosity compared to ordinary patterns of American charitable giving for other international injustices—O'Reilly presumed in advance that responsibility for others must always coincide with the United States's image of itself as the benevolent nation. See *The O'Reilly Factor*, January 6, 2005.

4. Peter Novick, *The Holocaust in American Life* (Boston: Houghton Mifflin, 1999).

5. For a sense of the range of political meanings of the Holocaust within Jewish-American culture and especially with regard to the legacy of Jewish liberalism, see Michael E. Staub, *Torn at the Roots: The Crisis of Jewish Liberalism in Postwar America* (New York: Columbia University Press, 2002).

6. Jean-François Lyotard, *The Differend: Phrases in Dispute*, trans. Georges Van Den Abbeele (Minneapolis: University of Minnesota Press, [1983] 1988).

7. Maurice Blanchot, *The Writing of the Disaster*, trans. Ann Smock (Lincoln: University of Nebraska Press, [1980] 1986), 47.

8. Such emphasis on rationality's failing protection resonates with Levinas's own mournfully inflected assessment of a vulnerability that defines all responsibility, as though the impossibility of fulfilling guardian thoughts were to guarantee the primordial significance of ethics as a demand surpassing its implementation. See my discussion of the function of vulnerability in constituting mourning's orientation to the other as ethical in *The Ethics of Mourning: Grief and Responsibility in Elegiac Literature* (Baltimore: Johns Hopkins University Press, 2004), esp. 1–4, 29–30.

9. My debt here to Stanley Cavell's fundamental conceit for responsibility as a play of recognition between counting and accounting should be obvious. See Cavell, *The Claim of Reason: Wittgenstein, Skepticism, Morality and Tragedy* (New York: Oxford University Press, 1979), esp. 329–496.

10. As perhaps the most popular advocate of silence in response to the Holocaust, Elie Wiesel supposes that such final failure of speech approximates the canceled perspective of the Holocaust's most central victims—those whose lives were extinguished in the gas chambers. For an account of how Wiesel's position, most famously stated in *A Jew Today* (1977), results in a paradoxical hermeneutic of secrecy, see Colin Davis, *Elie Wiesel's Secretive Texts*

(Gainesville: University Press of Florida, 1994), 1–30, 141–84. Nevertheless, any response sanctifying reverence also treats history as if its potential extraordinariness were supernatural, an exception in the flow of experience not to be readmitted to the terms of rationality, hardly seeming a reality produced by responsible human agents. For a helpful discussion of this "exceptionalist" dimension of Holocaust discourse, see Alan Mintz, *Popular Culture and the Shaping of Holocaust Memory in America* (Seattle: University of Washington Press, 2001), esp. 36–84. What Lawrence Langer and Geoffrey Hartman have tried to do, the one working in the vein of pragmatic skepticism and the other in the phenomenological tradition, is to allow survivor testimony to fill the gap between rationality and disaster, as though only the one who suffered history in its extremity could offer us a mode of speech—perhaps only through the fissures in speech, through the ruptures of silence, the brokenness of voice or remnants of language—upon which we could reconstruct a language from within which we could begin to imagine these events. Between silence and testimonial speech there is a great distance, and the part either plays in the construction of history seems to depend largely on an ethical privilege granted to the victim's perspective, even perhaps a late-twentieth-century crediting of authenticity for which the credentials are primarily negative. Langer, *Holocaust Testimonies: The Ruins of Memory* (New Haven: Yale University Press, 1991); Hartman, *Scars of the Spirit: The Struggle against Inauthenticity* (New York: Palgrave/Macmillan, 2002).

11. By way of qualifying my own position, I should mention the work of John Rawls, who as perhaps the most influential political philosophers of American liberalism formulates the idea of the "original position" of justice that is necessarily of a hypothetical nature. In this way Rawls admits into political theory the inequities that codetermine the establishment of justice, even as he allows the hypothesis about conditions of equity and fairness to endure as usable ideational content in the face of the less than ideal political reality to which justice must address itself. See Rawls, *Justice as Fairness: A Restatement*, ed. Erin Kelly (Cambridge, MA: Belknap Press of Harvard University Press, 2001), 14–17, 80–134.

12. Alain Badiou, *Ethics: An Essay on the Understanding of Evil*, trans. Peter Hallward (New York: Verso, [1993], 2001), esp. 10–13.

13. Lang, *Act and Idea in the Nazi Genocide* (Chicago: University of Chicago Press, 1990), xiv; hereafter referred to as *AING*. Lang's moral philosophy would have us discern a broader cultural or moral hermeneutic permitting perpetrators to mistake their historical interrelation to victims for a politically obfuscating mutual implication in the event, as though perpetrators and victims might become indistinguishable.

14. By alleging morality's inextricability from pragmatic consequences within history, and by further insisting upon a proportion between act and idea to be measured by results, Lang thwarts the perpetrator's retrospective hypothesis that his own intention might have been contrary to his actions and might thus escape their consequences. Yet even the formal limitation of deliberative decision making does not alter a perpetrator's basic fullness of knowledge, which functions for Lang as a central figure for responsibility. This argument contrasts with the approach of David H. Jones, who has offered a moral philosophical account of responsibility from within the context of the Holocaust by insisting upon the perceptions and deliberative discernments of individual agents. Jones, *Moral Responsibility in the Holocaust: A Study in the Ethics of Character* (Lanham, MD: Rowman and Littlefield, 1999), 15–96.

15. Identifying three stages of deliberation in the agent of genocide, Lang suggests that each stage of deliberation corresponds to a process of reflection. These are the three stages of

deliberation upon which the reflections are based: (1) identifying individuals according to generic or collective categories that permit of no exception; (2) the claim that this generic essence represents an imminent danger; and (3) the conclusion that extermination of the danger is the only appropriate response to it. They result in the following stages of rationalizing reflection: (1) the agent of genocide denies in the potential victim a capacity for individual agency; (2) then denies any alternative response from within the group to the threatened action, and; (3) by converting genocide into a principle finally rejects the argument that he as agent proceeds from self-interest. See *AING* 13–22.

16. Much of Lang's argument is waged against explanations of the Holocaust that would derive the Nazis' ideas about their actions from a utilitarian rationale, such that the metaphors of disease employed by the Nazis in reference to the Jews might become indicative of a utilitarian conviction—however deluded and irrational—that they were acting consistently for the good of society as they understood it. Yet one of the reasons the disease metaphor (the Nazi belief that Jews as an inferior race had to be exterminated much as one might treat by extreme measures a disease-ridden organism) fails to be a persuasive indication of utilitarian conviction is that in their genocidal project the Nazis were so often willing to act against the utilitarian good of Germany. See also Martin P. Golding, "On the Idea of Moral Pathology," in *Echoes from the Holocaust: Philosophical Reflections on a Dark Time*, ed. Alan Rosenberg and Gerald E. Myers (Philadelphia: Temple University Press, 1988), 128–48. Taking seriously the intersection of moral reasoning and pathological states of cooperation, Golding argues for the German citizen's cooperation with Nazi authority as a "moral pathology" perhaps necessarily embedded in most social morality and operative, to some degree or another, in every society. In German society the conditions heightening such a pathological tendency were extraordinary. For Lang malevolence seems the more reliable category for proving intention, since the malevolent act cannot refuse its consequences by way of a merely hypothetical intention.

17. According to Hilberg, for example, the bureaucratic dimensions of the Nazi genocide created a system in which individual agents could function efficiently in service of an awful political end, often without understanding themselves to be significant agents in the crimes of the Nazi state. Responding to Hilberg's historiographical account of the bureaucracy without which the massively successful and systemic genocide of the Nazis could not have taken place, Zygmunt Bauman has further theorized the sociological conditions of this history. See Raul Hilberg, *The Destruction of the European Jews* (New York: Holmes and Meier, 1985); Bauman, *Modernity and the Holocaust* (Ithaca: Cornell University Press, 1989), esp. 83–116.

18. Raising the question about whether the events of the Nazi genocide follow from a corporate intention or a set of fragmentary and possibly accidental intentions, Lang takes up the Functionalist/Intentionalist debate within Holocaust studies, especially skeptical about the potential correspondence between social-deterministic views and the exonerating aegis of ideological principle by which Nazism was purported to replace individual intention. One of the sticking points in the debate between Functionalists and Intentionalists has been the lack of a documentary record of a "Hitler order" setting in motion the extermination of the Jews. In the chapter entitled "The Knowledge of Good and Evil" Lang argues that the pattern of concealment in Nazi language reveals an aspect of shame, a wish to hide the act from the outside world, from the German people, and even from many of the perpetrators themselves that neg-

atively proves a consciousness of right and wrong. Accordingly, the lack of the Hitler order might be explained itself by the shameful possibility that Hitler went to great lengths to distance himself from association with the practical implementation and execution of the genocide (*AING* 42). Lang elaborates his relation to this debate more clearly and especially expands his critique of the chronological premise of intention in *The Future of the Holocaust: Between History and Memory* (Ithaca: Cornell University Press, 1999), esp. 65–76. Arguing that "Functionalists turn out to be Intentionalists" who dispute the evidence of intention, Lang concludes that what both models of intention share is an "External Model of intention" requiring two principal conditions that define intention: (1) that the intention be explicitly related to an object; and (2) that the intention chronologically precede its enactment. Against this, Lang proposes a view of intention, based in Wittgenstein, G.E.M. Anscombe, and philosophical psychology, that he calls the "Contextual Model of intention," pointing out that, in the first place, intentions are most often read back onto acts and considered reliable even when no prior, "external" evidence exists (as, say, in the case in which one concludes that a fire that started in various parts of a building derived from intention, even if one is without further documentation of intention), and as an extension of this point, he says, intentions evolve as functions of actions, actions that are as often as not previously unenvisioned by the agents themselves. Even when we have professions of intention available to us as evidence, Lang reminds us, we admit the possibility that groups could lie about their intentions and so investigate such professions to find corroboration for them in what has actually been done. Ultimately, Lang argues against the Functionalist view because it endangers a historiography that would locate cause too simply in the agents, and he says even in the absence of a prior decree to implement the Final Solution, "there *was* an intention in the relation joining the individual parts of the policy" (*Future of the Holocaust* 75). For a critique of the debate between Intentionalists and Functionalists that claims that the antimony is too schematic and that the Nazi genocide is better portrayed by a more dialectical account of the relation between intention and function, see Christopher Browning, "Beyond 'Intentionalism' and 'Functionalism': The Decision for the Final Solution Reconsidered," *The Path to Genocide: Essays on Launching the Final Solution* (New York: Cambridge University Press, 1992), 86–121.

19. Each line of thought is implicit in interpretations that treat Nazi thought as a flawed application of utilitarianism or as a pathological, aberrant, or deluded ideology. Lang argues that the horizon of such arguments is to say that, although the Nazis were "punishable on the grounds of culpable ignorance or negligence," as long as one insists that they did what they thought was right, they cannot be "guilty in the more radical sense of having done something that they were aware of us as wrong" (*AING* 35). Ideology cannot be allowed, in Lang's view, to relax responsibility under the proviso first established by Plato that no one does evil knowingly. As Lang says, "There obviously are occasions when moral agents act in or out of ignorance, and there are rarer instances when such agents act out of general moral blindness. In the tradition of philosophical rationalism, these explanations account for all acts of wrongdoing: there is no instance in which the wrongdoer has full or genuine knowledge that he ought not to do what he chooses to" (*AING* 28).

20. Jean Améry, "Resentments," *At the Mind's Limit: Contemplations by a Survivor on Auschwitz and Its Realities,* trans. Sidney Rosenfeld and Stella P. Rosenfeld (Bloomington: Indiana University Press, [1966] 1980), 62–81.

21. This distinction with regard to Améry's work is either lost on Giorgio Agamben or seems to him entirely unpersuasive. See Agamben, *RA*, sec. 3.7, 99–103.

22. Girard, *Things Hidden since the Foundation of the World*, research undertaken in collaboration with Jean-Michel Oughourlian and Guy Lefort, trans. Stephen Bann and Michael Metteer (Stanford: Stanford University Press, [1978] 1987), 27.

23. Of course, Ryan supposes that victims should no longer be blamed and that already some victims (the undeserving poor, for example) are not so severely blamed, but the seemingly inexplicable loathing for victims he observes must be accounted for, at least in part, as a residual effect of the very cultural category of *victim*. See William Ryan, *Blaming the Victim* (New York: Pantheon Books, 1971).

24. Girard, *Violence and the Sacred*, trans Patrick Gregory (Baltimore: Johns Hopkins University Press, [1972] 1977).

25. Lang defines *genocide* as a distinct act of destruction intended against a group of people who cannot be exempted from the objectively enclosing group-category because of the allegedly natural criteria by which they have come to be included in it—in short, as a crime against reified identity. Lang's definition of *genocide* seems especially shaped to the historical particularity of the Holocaust, with the effect that some of the other aspects of the definition formulated by the Geneva Convention (such as the intentional devastation of a culture) seem less emphasized. For his discussion of the degrees that differentiate genocide, see Lang, "Degrees of Genocide—and Evil," *The Future of the Holocaust*, 15–25.

26. Much as a robber may want what the victim has, even when he is a thief stealing for pleasure, so too—and here Lang seems indebted to an emergent discourse of victimology, which details scenarios involving bad choices made by victims—a murderer "*may be* responding (however disproportionately) to something his victim possesses or has done as an individual" (*AING* 19; emph. added). Even with regard to the victim of sexual violence, Lang supposes, the logic of precipitating conditions (popularized by criminology) may apply. Lang's own conditional language ("may be responding") suggests a sensitivity he does not maintain with enough rigor, for the victims of criminal violence as often as not fail to participate in any precipitating condition or may get classified by the bogus sociology of a criminal whom criminologists are obliged to take seriously. So, for example, a woman may be identified as a victim by a rapist based on the mere fact that she is a woman and appears to be vulnerable. And just such a perceptive structure is at work in the categories the agent of genocide applies to his victim.

27. Even what Lang says about genocide, that "all sense of individual agency in the victim—choice, deliberation, the potentiality for change—is denied" (*AING* 19), is of course not perfectly true for Holocaust victims, as Primo Levi famously explicated degrees of complicity with the negative of concentration camp victims and survivors, even if such "gray" moral behaviors were not to be reckoned by any conventional tribunal. Levi, "The Gray Zone," *The Drowned and the Saved*, trans. Raymond Rosenthal (New York: Simon and Schuster, [1986] 1988).

28. Levinas's project diverges from Lang's moral philosophical approach in any number of ways, not least of which is Levinas's critique of the long-standing idealist and ontological premises informing the moral philosopher's conception of agency. With regard to Lang's attempt to make the genocidal act adequate to the claims of moral knowledge and thus to

refute any effort to exempt genocide from the order of rationally discernible moral intentions, Levinas would insist that violence is inherent in our every attempt to claim the other through knowledge, in the metaphysical premises upon which our knowledge is premised, and perhaps especially apparent in such a rationalized reconciliation of the other qua victim to the plot of a perpetrator's intentions. See, for example, Derrida, "Violence and Metaphysics: An Essay on the Thought of Emmanuel Levinas," *Writing and Difference*, trans. Alan Bass (New York: Routledge, [1967] 2001), 97–192.

29. As Hent de Vries has noted, responding to Jacques Derrida's famous critique of the violence that persists in Levinas's more than vestigial metaphysics: "Critiques of violence are not without violence. They are successful only if they turn violence inside out, if they are somehow violent in turn, turning good violence against bad or worse violence" ("Violence and Testimony: On Sacrificing Sacrifice," in *Violence, Identity, and Self-Determination*, ed. Hent de Vries and Samuel Weber [Stanford: Stanford University Press, 1997], 27). In short, a language resistant to violence will be characterized by violence, if only by the violent rejection of a dominant pattern of cultural violence. On a slightly different note, Derrida argues in "Violence and Metaphysics" that the danger in Levinas's revisionary recapitulation of a metaphysics of signification is that by employing a figurative hypothesis of sacred nonviolence Levinas masks history and, more specifically, the cultural narrative of sacred history, with its mystification and promotion of violence. Metaphysics is a categorical violence grounding our immersion in violent cultural narratives, and, just as Heidegger before him returned to metaphysics by way of ontology, Levinas also fails to escape the very thing he set out to investigate. In his relentlessly immanent critique of signification Derrida denies that there can be an exception to this cultural rule of violence.

What Derrida fails to account for is the pervasiveness of violence in so many of Levinas's figures for ethics, and I would point to the violence of his figures as an effort to acknowledge the cultural rules of violence. Already in *Totality and Infinity*, we observe this pervasiveness of the figure of violence, but it emerges even more remarkably in *Otherwise than Being*. It may well be, as Colin Davis (*Levinas: An Introduction* [Cambridge: Polity Press, 1996]) has suggested, that *Otherwise than Being* should be read in part as a response to Derrida's critique, in which case one aspect of Levinas's response was to revisit what Derrida had seen as the metaphysical veiling of the relation to violence through metaphysics and to bring the signs of cultural violence more directly into play in his figurative presentation of the other. My larger point, however, is that although we should worry about the way metaphysical logic arrives at or determines patterns of cultural violence, Levinas begins from the literality of a violence already incurred, so that his turns against violence are not simply refutations that fail to escape a necessary immanence in violence but are, rather, acknowledgments of the ways in which the ethical relation is signified from within or despite violence, and even more surprisingly, by the very exigency of the condition of violence, a move that brings with it a whole new set of concerns—perhaps most specifically, that victims are hardly ever imagined as far from the perpetrators who harm them. In charting a figurative play between the perpetrator and victim and by considering, if only hypothetically, that their roles might be interchangeable, Levinas acknowledges the seemingly irrefutable cultural logic that inscribes the rule and order of violence.

30. Levinas, *Difficult Freedom*, trans. Seán Hand (London: Athlone Press, [1963, 1976] 1990), 8; hereafter referred to as *DF*.

31. See Lang, *AING*, esp. 19–20.

32. Levinas, "Freedom and Command" (1953), *Collected Philosophical Papers*, trans. Alphonso Lingis (Dordrecht, Neth.: Martinus Nijhoff, 1987), 15–23; hereafter referred to as FC.

33. The face becomes a figure for what Robbins calls the "originary donation of the law, in all the literality of its imposition," and, when the murderer takes violent aim at the face by not truly facing it, he interprets the face as a mask (a reduction of its ethical meaning), but he also "loses face." Reading the connotations of Genesis 4:5 in which Cain's "face fell" (*waniphlo panav*) as a prolepsis for his act of murder, Robbins draws out a connotation of the "face" which would necessarily return its significance to the subjective pole of the figuratively imagined perpetrator. Robbins's emphasis on the figural takes a different direction from my own, since she is especially concerned with the "intercontamination of the governing oppositions of Levinas's discourse" on the face. See Robbins, *Altered Reading: Levinas and Literature* (Chicago: University of Chicago Press, 1999), 67–68. Tracing Levinas's resistance to rhetorical figuration precisely because it would suppose that the face-to-face relation can be compromised by the dissimulations of the social world—the play between what Paul de Man in "Criticism and Crisis" (1967) identifies as "the distinctive privilege of language to be able to hide meaning behind a misleading sign" and "the distinctive curse of all language, as soon as any kind of interpersonal relation is involved, that it is forced to act this way"—Robbins unpacks the "semantic destination" of the face as figure in Levinas's analysis (60, 67). It is especially in the paradox of the speaking face, whose only word is the "no" to murder, which Robbins identifies the slippage of the un-rhetorical *droiture* (or "straightforwardness") of the face Levinas insists upon. De Man, "Criticism and Crisis," *Blindness and Insight: Essays in the Rhetoric of Contemporary Criticism*, 2d ed. rev. (Minneapolis: University of Minnesota Press, 1983), 11.

34. See Levinas, *TI* 84; hereafter referred to as *TI*. In this sense Lang's attempt to preserve the intentionality of the perpetrator for the sake of moral responsibility may seem susceptible to Levinas's critique of the metaphysical and ontological claims made by knowledge, the difference between these two philosophers working in different traditions perhaps nowhere more evident than with regard to their slightly divergent connotations of intentionality. Yet even here they share something in common, for although Levinas's critique of intentionality depends upon an expansion of "the word intention" in Husserl's phenomenological discourse, he argues that, as an intuitive fulfillment of meaning greater than the willed aim of a subject, intention "bears the trace of the voluntary and the teleological" (*OTB* 96). In both the morally philosophic and the phenomenological trajectory, there is the premise of a subjective orientation to be satisfied by the seizing of its object, and with this comes a corollary supposition—that the object of moral attention or phenomenological interest can be made adequate to the significance attached to it through the projective play of intention. The difference between Levinas and Lang begins precisely at the point that Levinas finds intention—whether defined through phenomenology or moral philosophy—inadequate to responsibility.

35. Or, as Maurice Blanchot says, violence changes the other "into an absence but does not touch him." *The Infinite Conversation*, trans. and foreword by Susan Hanson (Minneapolis: University of Minnesota Press, [1969] 1993), 61. See also Robbins, *Altered Reading*, esp. 65–66.

36. Philippe Nemo, *Job and the Excess of Evil*, with a postface by Emmanuel Levinas, trans. with a postscript by Michael Kigel (Pittsburgh: Duquesne University Press, 1998), 196.

37. For Levinas's relation to Jewish biblical sources, see Oona Ajzenstat, *Driven Back to the Text: The Premodern Sources of Levinas's Postmodernism* (Pittsburgh: Duquesne University Press, 2001), esp. 64–84, 201–75. See also Susan A. Handelman, *Fragments of Redemption: Jewish Thought and Literary Theory in Benjamin, Scholem, and Levinas* (Bloomington: Indiana University Press, 1991); Tamra Wright, *The Twilight of Jewish Philosophy: Emmanuel Lévinas' Ethical Hermeneutics* (Amsterdam: Harwood Academic Publishers, 1999).

38. Such norms in their neutrality cannot bring us close to the intention and responsibility inherent in evil, Nemo supposes, and in this regard his concern anticipates Lang's similar objection to the ideological explanation of evil. Within the collectivist view there is a final incapability of "coming to the aid of victims who are useless for the survival of the group" (Nemo, *Job and the Excess of Evil*, 2) — which is to say, in Nemo's view, that genocide is not the worst that can happen to a person simply because genocide is what happens to the group and not to the person.

39. Levinas, "Transcendence and Evil," in Nemo, *Job and the Excess of Evil*, 165–82; hereafter referred to as TE. Levinas's essay first appeared in *Le Nouveau Commerce* 11 (1978): 55–75, was reprinted in *Of God Who Comes to Mind* (1982), and was first translated into English as a freestanding essay in Levinas, *Collected Philosophical Papers*, trans. Alphonso Lingis (Boston: Kluwer, 1987), 175–86.

40. See, for example, Galatians 5.

41. For a discussion of the imbricated origins of Jewish and Christian martyrdom and their symbolic modes of nonparticipation in the Roman cultural milieu, see Daniel Boyarin, *Dying for God: Martyrdom and the Making of Christianity and Judaism* (Stanford: Stanford University Press, 1999), esp. 67–92.

42. For a reading of Levinas's application of Christian "passion" language to the historical fate of Israel, with a critical eye focused on the sacrificial politics of the Western nation-state, see Howard Caygill, *Levinas and the Political* (New York: Routledge, 2002), 162–66.

43. Levinas, "Substitution" (1968), trans. Peter Atterton, Simon Critchley, and Graham Noctor, in *Basic Philosophical Writings*, ed. Adriaan T. Peperzak, Simon Critchley, and Robert Bernasconi (Bloomington: Indiana University Press, 1996), 79–96; hereafter referred to as S.

44. See René Girard, "A propos du film de Mel Gibson, *La Passion du Christ*," *Le Figaro Magazine* (Mar. 2004); "On Mel Gibson's *The Passion of the Christ*," *Anthropoetics* 10:1 (Spring–Summer 2004).

45. For a contemporary Christian reading that would resemble aspects of Levinas's own hermeneutic (by accusing Job of being guilty precisely for trying to preserve his good conscience while others suffer) see Gustavo Gutiérrez, *On Job: God-talk and the Suffering of the Innocent*, trans. Matthew J. O'Connell (Maryknoll, NY: Orbis Books, [1986] 1987).

46. For the Christian theological elaboration of this theme, based in part in the Gospel of Matthew's reference to humanity's debt and in Romans 3:24 to the naming of Christ as a ransom, see Calvin, *Institutes of the Christian Religion*, ed. John T. McNeill and trans. Ford Lewis Battles (Philadelphia: Westminster Press, 1960), bk. 3, chap. 20:45, 910–15.

47. Levinas, "Interview with Myriam Anissiomov," first published in *Les Nouveaux Cahiers* 82 (1985): 30–35; trans. Jill Robbins and Thomas Loebel, in *Is It Righteous to Be? Inter-*

views with Emmanuel Levinas, ed. Jill Robbins (Stanford: Stanford University Press, [1984] 2001), 92. This book of interviews will hereafter be referred to as *IIRB*.

48. For a reading of the nationalistic narratological dimensions of covenant in relation to the Samuel narrative and this scene in particular, see David Damrosch, *The Narrative Covenant: Transformations of Genre in the Growth of Biblical Literature* (San Francisco: Harper and Row, 1987).

49. Karl Barth, *Church Dogmatics*, ed. G. W. Bromiley and T. F. Torrance, vol. 4, pt. 1: *Doctrine of Reconciliation*, trans. G. W. Bromiley (Edinburgh: T. and T. Clark, 1956), 550; hereafter referred to as *DR*.

50. In Barth's view Christ represents the future of man as redeemed and the past of man in his sinfulness, our wrong and death having been relocated to the past through Christ's intervention, so that in a "positive sense Jesus Christ lives in our place, for us, in our name." See Barth, *DR* 555.

51. For a historicist-minded, contemporary Catholic account of modern Christological debates, see John P. Meier, *The Mission of Christ and His Church: Studies on Christology and Ecclesiology* (Wilmington, DE: M. Glazier, 1990).

52. See Rudolf Karl Bultmann, *The History of the Synoptic Tradition*, trans. John Marsh (Oxford: Blackwell, 1963); *Jesus Christ and Mythology* (New York: Scribner, 1958).

53. Cf. John Llewelyn's discussion of Levinas's intersection with Nietzschean "atheology." Llewelyn, *Emmanuel Levinas: The Genealogy of Ethics* (New York: Routledge, 1995), 149–61.

54. For an attempt to bridge the conceit of embodiedness in Merleau-Ponty and Levinas, see Rosalyn Diprose, *Corporeal Generosity: On Giving with Nietzsche, Merleau-Ponty, and Levinas* (Albany: State University of New York Press, 2002), esp. 173–85.

55. A skeptical reading might suggest these verses from Matthew are the evangelist's composition, meant to enhance a voluntary drama that is crucially embedded in a plot of involuntariness, since Jesus has no choice but to offer himself up. From a theological perspective already inscribed in the gospel, there cannot be any contingency in the event of crucifixion.

56. See J.N.D. Kelly, *Early Christian Doctrines* (New York: Harper and Row, 1959), 138–62.

57. A short while later Levinas refers to the "kerygmatic logos" with an almost entirely metaphorical implication, rendering transparent the doctrinal, programmatic trajectory of the logos as rationalist, secularist discourse, since it must always bear the memory of Plato's insistence on the eternal properties of matter conditioning all discourse. See *OTB* 110.

58. In hindsight the quasi-Christological dimensions of Job's sufferings seem almost too obvious. Referring to a long tradition of Christian biblical commentary, according to which Job's suffering is placed within the context of previous and subsequent biblical stories, Philippe Nemo states clearly, "Job's dereliction recalls, and therefore in retrospect seems to announce, Christ's solitude on the cross" (*Job and the Excess of Evil*, 4).

59. See E. P. Sanders, *Jesus and Judaism* (Philadelphia: Fortress Press, 1985).

60. Such revisionary representation of "Jews on the cross," as David G. Roskies has effectively charted, was an artistic convention predating the Holocaust but also proved useful for many Jewish writers after the war in their imaginative responses to the Holocaust. See Roskies, *Against the Apocalypse: Responses to Catastrophe in Modern Jewish Culture* (Cambridge, MA: Harvard University Press, 1984), 258–310.

61. Yaffa Eliach, "Jew, Go Back to the Grave!" based on author's interviews with Zvi Michalowski and other people from Eisysky, *Hasidic Tales of the Holocaust* (New York: Oxford University Press, 1982), 53–55.

62. Consult Alain Finkielkraut, *The Imaginary Jew*, trans. Kevin O'Neill and David Suchoff (Lincoln: University of Nebraska Press, [1980] 1994), esp. 3–34.

63. Emil Fackenheim, *God's Presence in History: Jewish Affirmations and Philosophical Reflections* (New York: New York University Press, 1970), 69–70.

64. Arthur Allen Cohen, *The Tremendum: A Theological Interpretation of the Holocaust* (New York: Crossroad, 1981).

65. Anthony Hecht, "More Light! More Light!" *The Hard Hours* (New York: Atheneum, 1967).

66. For fuller explications of Levinas's critique of theodicy, see Richard A. Cohen, *Ethics, Exegesis, and Philosophy: Interpretation after Levinas* (New York: Cambridge University Press, 2001), esp. 266–82; Richard J. Bernstein, *Radical Evil: A Philosophical Interrogation* (Malden, MA: Polity, 2002), esp. 168–74.

67. Dan Pagis, "Written in Pencil in the Sealed Railway-Car," *The Selected Poetry of Dan Pagis*, trans. Stephen Mitchell, intro. Robert Alter (Berkeley: University of California Press, 1996).

68. Drawing our attention to writing without a communicative medium, an implausible final wish to speak from within violence, Eve bears the very onus of responsibility of which Levinas so often speaks. She is the subject figured as what Levinas would call an "irreplaceable hostage" (*OTB* 124), her responsibility described in persecution.

CHAPTER 4: OF THE OTHERS WHO ARE STRANGER THAN NEIGHBORS

1. See Jean-Paul Sartre, *Anti-Semite and Jew*, trans. George J. Becker (New York: Schocken Books, [1946] 1948); Julia Kristeva, *Strangers to Ourselves*, trans. Leon S. Roudiez (New York: Columbia University Press, [1989] 1991).

2. See Freud, "The Uncanny," *The Standard Edition of the Complete Psychological Works of Sigmund Freud*, ed. James Strachey, vol. 17 (London: Hogarth Press, 1955).

3. For an influential overview of this position (although I agree with much of his reporting of the cultural symptoms of this phenomenon but only inconsistently with his interpretation of the ideological reasons for it), see Peter Novick, *The Holocaust in American Life* (Boston: Houghton Mifflin, 1999), esp. 39–59.

4. That said, Robert Eaglestone has argued for just such a hermeneutic, characterizing much of what we call postmodernism by a post-Holocaust and also a post-Levinas sensibility in *The Holocaust and the Postmodern* (New York: Oxford University Press, 2004), esp. 249–78.

5. Cynthia Ozick, "Metaphor and Memory," originally published as "The Moral Life of Metaphor," *Harper's*, January 1986; reprinted in *Metaphor and Memory* (New York: Alfred A. Knopf, 1989), 276, 277.

6. For an even-handed evaluation of Nietzsche's stance in relation to Jews and Judaism as one of genuine ambivalence, taking account of his polemics against Judeo-Christian religious heritage and his tendency to caricature Jewish tribalism but also his staunch criticisms of the new *völkisch* brand of German antisemitism represented especially by a figure such as Wag-

ner, see Siegfried Mandel, *Nietzsche and the Jews: Exaltation and Denigration* (New York: Prometheus Books, 1998).

7. In a late essay such as "Philosophy and Transcendence" (1989), with all the major components of his thought in place, Levinas accuses Greek thought of a failure to conceive of the possibility of a "transcendence in sociality itself," the signification of an absolute that has its meaning "in proximity rather than in ecstasy." When he also adds that such an idea has remained "foreign to Greek thought," there is in this an implicitly Judaic suspicion of polytheistic culture, of religion conceived as the ecstatic loss of identity only to reinforce culture as the place where identity reigns. See Levinas, "Philosophy and Transcendence" (1989), *Alterity and Transcendence*, trans. Michael B. Smith (New York: Columbia University Press, [1995] 1999), 3–38, 8–9. Levinas nevertheless credits Greek thought with having traced, albeit reluctantly, a dissatisfaction in metaphysical aspiration. In a real sense, then, it is the failure *within* Western knowledge that designates the meaning of ethics in the Levinasian project.

8. Levinas, interview with François Poirié, first published in *Art Press* (Mar. 1986) and thereafter in Poirié, *Emmanuel Levinas: qui êtes-vous?* (Lyon: La Manufacture, 1987), 63–136; trans. Jill Robbins, Marcus Coelen, and Thomas Loebel, in *IIRB* 23–83, 63.

9. In one sense, then, Levinas proves the better exegete than Ozick simply because he is better able to discern the tradition's unhistorical usage of its most fundamental texts. And yet, as he follows the precedent of the Talmud, he sides with metaphor against both historical and traditionally delineated meanings. For a discussion of Levinas's dependence on Talmudic strategies of interpretation, see Oona Ajzenstat, *Driven Back to the Text: The Premodern Sources of Levinas's Postmodernism* (Pittsburgh: Duquesne University Press, 2001), 201–75.

10. As I emphasized in the introduction, there has been a tendency among Levinas's most sympathetic and unsympathetic readers to apply his Jewish heritage as a hermeneutical key to understanding his complaint with Western philosophy. Such a view is implicit in criticisms of his prophetic, metaphysical voice. For a reading especially emphasizing the continuity between his Jewish identity and Levinas's philosophy, see Susan A. Handelman, *Fragments of Redemption: Jewish Thought and Literary Theory in Benjamin, Scholem, and Levinas* (Bloomington: Indiana University Press, 1991).

11. John Rawls, *Justice as Fairness: A Restatement*, ed. Erin Kelly (Cambridge, MA: Belknap Press of Harvard University Press, 2001), 14–17, 80–134.

12. In the logical progression of section 1B of *Totality and Infinity* Levinas challenges the primacy of ontology by emphasizing the separation of the ego, which posits itself under a hypothesis of autonomy, separate from what it lives from, maintained in discourse as though it is apparently self-standing. There is a corollary function with regard to truth, which must pertain to objects in their objective distinctiveness rather than as situated in an idealizing flow or preconditioned categories. Such a seemingly materialist break with ontology has ample precedent in the currents of twentieth-century antiphilosophical thought inspired by Marx and Nietzsche, except that, for Levinas, following Buber and fearing the trajectory of Heideggerianism, we cannot put our trust in the finality of things.

13. For Levinas's understanding of the relation between history and phenomenological praxis, see Levinas, *TI* 65.

14. Breaking with the structuralism of our knowledge, motivated by the face of the other, Desire reaches toward and speaks with another, already supposing our situatedness in lan-

guage. This resistance to structuralist phenomenology might be called vaguely metaphysical, since it refers language to that which can never fully enter into language or social knowledge, thus refusing structuralism's basic premise that all meaning is culturally constructed. On this point there is a possible link between Levinas and Lacan, insofar as Levinasian desire is by definition inordinate and Lacan also emphasizes the signifying absence of the other as consequent upon desire's basic structure of dissatisfaction. For a discussion of affinities between the two infrequently compared French contemporaries, see Drucilla Cornell, "Rethinking the Beyond of the Real," in *Levinas and Lacan: The Missed Encounter*, ed. Sarah Harasym (Albany: State University of New York Press, 1998), 139–81; Davis Ross Fryer, *The Intervention of the Other: Ethical Subjectivity in Levinas and Lacan* (New York: Other Press, 2004).

15. For the original French, see Levinas, *Totalité et infini* (The Hague: Martinus Nijhoff, 1961); hereafter referred to as *TEI*.

16. See Nietzsche, "On Truth and Lies in a Nonmoral Sense," in *Philosophy and Truth: Selections from Nietzsche's Notebooks of the Early 1870s*, trans. and ed. D. Breazeale (Atlantic Highlands, NJ: Humanities Press, 1979).

17. Thus emerges Levinas's most radical challenge to contemporary theories of identity. In its capacity to impart what is not already obvious or latent, the subject presumes a relation of instruction, and only that which is absolutely other, only the facticity of another human being who is by definition unknown, foreign to any subject's project of identity or self-understanding, can truly *in-struct* us (*L'absolument étranger seul peut nous instruire* [*TEI* 46]) in the sense that we would be defined according to the very structure of relationship into which we are—just now but also already—entered. What the stranger emphasizes, since he is someone encountered as though he were "wholly by relation to himself" (*TI* 74), is that there is always a quality of what Paul Ricoeur has called "irrelation" inscribed upon the relationships by which we are bound ethically. See Paul Ricoeur, *Oneself as Another*, trans. Kathleen Blamey (Chicago: University of Chicago Press, [1990] 1992), 188–94, 189.

18. Albert Camus, *The Stranger*, trans. Matthew Ward (New York: Vintage International, [1942] 1989).

19. Camus was of course a French national who lived more than half of his life in Algeria, never having learned Arabic but nevertheless writing sympathetically about the poverty and underdevelopment of the indigenous Algerians in his journalism throughout the 1930s. In launching a modern nationalist literary tradition, Algerian writers often perceived Camus as one of their own and also as a colonialist, even if a relatively sympathetic one. See Christiane Achour, "Camus and Algerian Writers," in *Camus's L'Étranger: Fifty Years On*, ed. Adele King (New York: St. Martin's Press, 1992), 89–100. When the Algerian crisis escalated in the 1950s and France attempted violent suppression of the natives, Camus expressed willingness to fight for France if necessary, a statement which may seem retrospectively to color the nature of Meursault's ambivalence in the novel. During the first twenty years of its reception, at least in part because of the influential interpretation put forward by Jean Paul Sartre, *The Stranger* was read as though it were the quintessential expression of the metaphysical crisis in identity provoked (or merely expressed?) by the literary-philosophical movement of existentialism, as the highly symbolic, colonialist connotation of the violence on the beach was largely overlooked. All of that started to change shortly after Camus's death. The earliest challenges to the orthodox existentialist reading were presented by Pierre Nora, Henri Kréa, and

Ahmed Taleb Ibrahimi. See Nora, "Pour une Autre Explication de *L'Étranger*"; and Kréa, "Le Malentendu Algérien" in *France-Observateur*, Jan. 5, 1961, 16–17; Ibrahimi, *De la décolonisation à la révolution culturelle (1962–1972)*, 3d ed. (Algiers: Société Nationale d'Edition et de Diffusion, 1981); original remarks made in 1967 lecture. For the first book-length study concentrated on reading the implicit colonialist allegory embedded in the novel, see Conor Cruise O'Brien, *Camus* (London: Fortuna/Collins, 1970). For an overview of this shift in reception, see Alec G. Hargreaves, "History and Ethnicity in the Reception of L'Etranger," *Camus's L'Étranger: Fifty Years On*, 101–12. I am suggesting that insofar as Levinas's implicit 1961 interpretation of the figure of the stranger is influenced by Camus, it is not just the existentialist themes of Camus's text but its more or less obvious exilic resonances that are registered by Levinas's allusion.

20. According to René Girard's hermeneutic, a stranger would slide easily into the role of scapegoat since he permits the mythic or communal commitment to remain unrecognized. If a stranger serves a binding function and does in fact reinforce identity, the hostility directed at him does not present itself as motivated by any such self-justifying logic. See René Girard, *Violence and the Sacred*, trans. Patrick Gregory (Baltimore: Johns Hopkins University Press, [1972] 1977), esp. 39–67, 250–73.

21. This aside is posed as though Levinas intuited the kind of commonsensical, psychoanalytically pitched objection that would find Meursault's violent action too symbolically located on a beach, with the repulsively, immodest body of another person shockingly there before him and, lest we forget, his relation to his mother still not worked through.

22. See Giorgio Agamben, *Homo Sacer: Sovereign Power and Bare Life*, trans. Daniel Heller-Roazen (Stanford: Stanford University Press, [1995] 1998), esp. 160–80.

23. See Edward Said, *Culture and Imperialism* (New York: Knopf, 1993); Abdul R. JanMohamed, "Worldliness-without-World, Homelessness-as-Home: Toward a Definition of the Specular Border Intellectual," in *Edward Said: A Critical Reader*, ed. Michael Sprinker (Cambridge: Basil Blackwell, 1992), 96–120.

24. Daniel Boyarin and Jonathan Boyarin, "Diaspora: Generation and the Ground of Jewish Identity," *Critical Inquiry* 19:4 (Summer 1993), 693–725.

25. If we ask from whose point of view exilic status is first designated, Lang suggests, we must reply: from the point of view of someone who is not alien, who is already safely at home in the world, who merely reacts to whatever disturbs the familiar network of relations. If the representation of Jew as alien comes from outside, it is enjoined upon his self-understanding, even superseding whatever identity he has chosen for himself. Yet, according to Lang, the very endurance of the hypothesis of Jewish identity must have depended upon other resources than the purely negative experience of persecution and should not be originally characterized by estrangement, as in accounts, such as Sartre's, in which Jewish identity seems engendered by the antagonism of antisemitism. No doubt, Lang says, external views can be adopted by a person, but could such assimilation account for the persistence of the Jews as a community? See Lang, *AING*, esp. 110–11.

26. Through Heidegger and others, philosophy had rendered political exile and the human condition seemingly interchangeable metaphoric terms. By tracing existentialist alienation back to a metaphoric basis in foreignness and by further reminding us of the political statelessness that generates exilic consciousness, Levinas discerns a different emphasis in alienation.

Identity is indeed still alienated in the Levinasian view but precisely to the extent that an unknown term has exercised a force "alienating my identity."

27. Levinas, "Enigma and Phenomenon" (1965), first published as Levinas, "Enigma et Phénomène," *Esprit* 33:6 (June 1965): 1128–42; trans. Alphonso Lingis, rev. Robert Bernasconi and Simon Critchley, *Basic Philosophical Writings*, ed. Adriaan T. Peperzak, Simon Critchley, and Robert Bernasconi (Bloomington: Indiana University Press, 1996), 65–78; hereafter referred to as EP.

28. It is remarkable how often the other is troped as stranger in the era of *Totality and Infinity* (say, 1958–64), while Levinas typically conceived the challenge of the other's alterity along the lines of transcendence and supra-Cartesian infinity, as that absolutely untranslatable divide presiding over every communicative situation.

29. Eugène Ionesco, *The Bald Soprano, and Other Plays*, trans. Donald M. Allen (New York: Grove Press, [1950, 1958] 1982).

30. For a discussion of the Hegelian background in Levinas's work, see Tina Chanter, "Reading Hegel as a Mediating Master: Lacan and Levinas," *Levinas and Lacan*, 1–21; Bettina Bergo, *Levinas between Ethics and Politics: For the Beauty That Adorns the Earth* (Boston: Kluwer Publishers, 1999), 277–94.

31. Remembering the theatrics of the absurdist movement in order to trace his debt to and simultaneously move beyond the existentialist phenomenality of Sartre or Wahl, and behind them the theosophic irrationality of Kierkegaard, Levinas supposes that all absurdist resistance fails precisely because, as a symptom of irrationality, it cannot pose an abiding interruption to the system of rationality. Irrationality as such must be defined as an aberrant normality, a deviation already accommodated to that from which it deviates. Although there is much that is owing to Kierkegaard in Levinas's philosophical formulation of an obligating transcendence, he distinguishes himself from Kierkegaard by worrying that there is an element of mystificatory participation of irrational exuberance in Kierkegaard's "leap of faith." See Levinas, "Kierkegaard: Existence and Ethics," *Proper Names*, trans. Michael B. Smith (Stanford: Stanford University Press, [1975] 1996), 66–74.

32. For an account of Levinas's complex and not altogether consistent estimation of aesthetics, see Eaglestone, *Ethical Criticism: Reading after Levinas* (Edinburgh: Edinburgh University Press, 1997), esp. 98–128.

33. As deconstructive linguistic critique, Derrida's point is certainly accurate, yet we have to bear in mind that Levinas fully allows for the apparent ubiquity of ontology, even as he subjects it to a rhetorical strategy. See Derrida, "Violence and Metaphysics" (1964), *Writing and Difference*, trans. Alan Bass (New York: Routledge, 2001).

34. *Seinfeld*, "The Raincoats, Part 1," season 5 (Apr. 28, 1994).

35. Levinas, "Peace and Proximity," trans. Peter Atterton and Simon Critchley, *Basic Philosophical Writings*, ed. Adriaan T. Peperzak, Simon Critchley, and Robert Bernasconi (Bloomington: Indiana University Press, 1996), 161–69, 166–67. The essay was first published in *Les Cahiers de la Nuit Surveillée*, no. 3: *Emmanuel Levinas*, ed. J. Rolland (Lagrasse: Verdier, 1984), 339–46.

36. In *Otherwise than Being* Levinas introduces the term *proximity* while discussing the primordial condition of sensibility, as that which occurs in relation to enjoyment or and under the aspect of suffering but is in either case concentrated on the body's materiality. See Levinas,

OTB, esp. 72–97. The key to sensibility is its fundamental passivity, which Levinas interprets as already signifying through a practical dedication of one-for-the other. Here, in the third chapter, Levinas describes the way enjoyment's self-satisfying complacency already turns or gets turned, through sensibility, toward another's need, even to the metaphorically literal point of "snatching the bread from one's mouth" (*OTB* 74). In several episodes of the TV sitcom *Seinfeld* Kramer finds a sandwich Jerry has already taken a bite from and asks, "Are you going to eat that?" Already sensibility has inscribed upon it a potential for displacement, whereby the other moves inside the apparent self-containment of every enjoyment to spoil or transform it, so that it is "not a gift of the heart, but of the bread from one's mouth, of one's own mouthful of bread." Such a meaning is not a choice to welcome or reject the stranger but, rather, an opening of "one's pocketbook" and "of the doors of one's home," as though the redistribution of wealth proposed by socialism were only a belated conceptualization of a fundamental principle implicit in us as sensible beings (*OTB* 74). Citing two verses from Isaiah 58, which command that bread be shared with the famished and that the wretched be welcomed into one's home, Levinas characteristically converts biblical moral codifications into quasi-natural, philosophical imperatives.

37. The emphasis in the French brings a political connotation to the fore, since Levinas refers at the end of this same sentence to the tendency to reduce engagement (*engagement*) to a construct of freedom: he may well have in mind existentialism or Marxism, or perhaps Sartre's conflation of the two; or he may be imagining primarily the conventional dictates of liberal individualism. See Levinas, *AQE*, 95.

38. The tendency toward what I have called "metaphoric literalism" is most obvious in Levinas's attempts to account for the force of proximity, as he speculates upon conceptualizing strategies for framing touch as "openness upon . . . , consciousness of . . . ," according to which touch might get formulated as an objective knowing of things. See Levinas, *OTB* 76.

39. What the new philosophy of dialogue permits is a discernment of the worth (*valoir*) of the other person glimpsed through an encounter that does not already depend upon our former experience of him. What we think we know of the other person is never sufficient to the meaning of encounter, which structures our language as for the other person even prior to the moment when he is, seemingly, brought within conceptual range of what the language of reason might say about him. Even dialogic philosophy does not propose a completely straightforward challenge, since, even in the twentieth century "philosophy of dialogue," best represented by Martin Buber or Franz Rosenzweig, dialogue brings us to the oneness of reason. In other words, the form of conversation already belongs to and reinscribes a sociality in which reciprocal alterity is suppressed. It is quite as though the construct of unanimity or of absolute consensus were the most dangerous of all social fictions, always in our time reminiscent of totalitarian structures of political thought. Perhaps the very hypothesis of unanimity, of a oneness to be obtained or again reclaimed, depends upon collective anonymity, always requiring a suppression of proximity according to which the other who, by ethical definition at least, puts herself forward finds herself in the political situation in which she cannot be brought forward to impinge upon social or individualized conscience. To the extent that the trajectory of reason depends upon the mythic premise of a former unity, of a sovereignty or divinity conditioning all knowledge, Levinas suggests that politics is always a reduction and suppression of responsibility. Can it be, he asks, that the hope of reason's peacefulness owes nothing perma-

nent to the other man, "to the social life with him which would be a relation to the neighbor?" See Levinas, *Of God Who Comes to Mind*, trans. Bettina Bergo (Stanford: Stanford University Press, [1986] 1998), 141. If not, Levinas fears, society must always constitute itself as straying from this basic ethical structure upon which it is based.

40. See Benedict R. Anderson, *Imagined Communities: Reflections on the Origins and Spread of Nationalism*, rev. ed. (New York: Verso, 1991); see also Alasdair MacIntyre, *After Virtue: A Study in Moral Theory* (South Bend, IN: University of Notre Dame Press, 1981).

41. Avishai Margalit, *The Ethics of Memory* (Cambridge, MA: Harvard University Press, 2002), 7.

42. Thus, the "moral witness" is Margalit's special hybrid term for one who testifies from direct experience about something all humanity is obliged to remember. See Margalit, *Ethics of Memory*, esp. 147–82.

43. Al Franken, *Lies and the Lying Liars Who Tell Them—A Fair and Balanced Look at the Right* (New York: Dutton, 2003), 24.

44. Critique is already compromised by what it can propose, insofar as the critic is committed to taking the good with the bad and to seeing the policies of the state as though they are akin to the character flaws of the individual, amendable only through the absolute presupposition of attachment. In the American context, for example, Sacvan Bercovitch has drawn our attention to the ways in which statements of political dissent must also be couched in a rhetoric assenting to America's mythic promise, perhaps to its revolutionary genealogy as a sign of abiding democratic process or to its system of constitutional law as a commitment to the future of justice, so that critique is always also a jeremiad, a renewal of the presumption of the nation's progressive narrative. Thus, Franken here ventures a language of critique safeguarded by his professions of vehement devotion to the United States, by his always faithful adherence to the nation's fullest potential. See Bercovitch, *The Rites of Assent: Transformations in the Symbolic Construction of America* (New York: Routledge, 1993).

45. For the interrelation of Blanchot and Levinas on the question of difference, see Alain P. Toumayan, *Encountering the Other: The Artwork and the Problem of Difference in Blanchot and Levinas* (Pittsburgh: Duquesne University Press, 2004), esp. 8–43.

46. Sarah Kofman, *Smothered Words*, trans. Madeleine Dobie (Evanston, IL: Northwestern University Press, [1987] 1998); hereafter referred to as SW. Kofman initially invokes Blanchot's story by remembering his 1983 afterword to a collection comprising this story and another pre-Holocaust story in which he warned of such stories' necessary insufficiency to the world of Auschwitz and further claimed that all stories must seem hereafter to come from a time before Auschwitz. Kofman disavows the possibility that any story such as "The Idyll" might speak of or in analogy to Auschwitz and yet proceeds to execute what might be called an analogical anti-allegory by way of this story, contrasting its pre-Holocaust descriptions of the scandal of the stranger and the designs upon strangeness executed by the so-called idyllic society to the impossible-to-anticipate, also impossible-to-represent horrors of Auschwitz. In her reading—no doubt informed by Blanchot's own right-wing sympathies at the time he wrote this story (though it must be said that the right-wing politics of Blanchot's early career were not perceptibly antisemitic and were in fact dedicated to a version of French nationalism specifically aimed at combatting the external threat of fascism)—Kofman appears unable either to interpret the story's persistent insistence upon the idyllic possibilities of community

as a mode of effective irony or to decide whether the hypothetical resistance of the stranger might intimate a real reordering of society. The figure of the Jew would become over the course of Blanchot's career the representative other, the sign of an exile fundamental to Blanchot's poststructuralist imaginings of the social. Kofman—offering what seems a deconstructive double reading—first speaks of her rabbi father's death in Auschwitz as a sign also of an attempt to honor "the absolutely Foreign," which is in this case God (SW 34–35), and then, elaborating on what she sees as the relative failure of the hermeneutics of honoring the stranger with regard to the world of Auschwitz, argues that even in Auschwitz there was the possibility of community based in the commonality of experience and the shared anti-language of the camps. See also Blanchot, "After the Fact" (1983), afterword to *Vicious Circles*, trans. Paul Auster (Barrytown, NY: Station Hill Press, 1985).

47. For an excellent account of Levinas's persistent commitment to humanism, especially to a mode of "biblical humanism," see Richard A. Cohen, *Ethics, Exegesis, and Philosophy: Interpretation after Levinas* (New York: Cambridge University Press, 2001), 216–65.

48. "The Awakening of the I," an interview by Roger Pol-Droit originally published in *Les imprévus de l'histoire* (Montpellier: Fata Morgana, 1994), 203–10; trans. Bettina Bergo and reprinted in *IIRB*, 182–87, 186.

49. See Luce Irigaray, "The Fecundity of the Caress," *An Ethics of Sexual Difference*, trans. Carolyn Burke and Gillian C. Gill (Ithaca: Cornell University Press, 1993), 185–217. For a discussion of the signifying status of the feminine in Levinas and a rigorous examination of Levinas's failure to take gendered difference as philosophically seriously as Heidegger had, see Tina Chanter, *Time, Death, and the Feminine: Levinas with Heidegger* (Stanford: Stanford University Press, 2001), 37–122.

50. "In the Name of the Other," a 1990 interview conducted by Luc Ferry, Raphaël Hadas-Lebel, and Sylvaine Pasquier for *L'Express*, July 6, 1990; reprinted in *Is It Righteous to Be? Interviews with Emmanuel Levinas*, ed. Jill Robbins (Stanford: Stanford University Press, 2001), 190; interviews hereafter referred to as *IIRB*.

51. "In the Name of the Other," a 1990 interview conducted by Luc Ferry, Raphaël Hadas-Lebel, and Sylvaine Pasquier for *L'Express*, July 6, 1990; trans. Maureen V. Gedney, reprinted in *IIRB*, 188–99, 197–98.

52. "Who Shall Not Prophesy?" a 1985 interview conducted by Angelo Bianchi, originally published as "Violence du visage," in *Hermeneutica* 5 (1985): 9–18; and reprinted in *Alterity and Transcendence*, trans. Michael B. Smith (New York: Columbia University Press, [1995] 1999); here trans. Bettina Bergo, reprinted in *IIRB* 219–27, 226.

53. For further commentary on Levinas's imbrication of Israel and Christ through the conceit of the Passion, see Howard Caygill, *Levinas and the Political* (New York: Routledge, 2002), 162–66.

54. John Llewelyn, *Emmanuel Levinas: The Genealogy of Ethics* (New York: Routledge, 1995), esp. 210–11.

55. There may be a degree of biographical confession operative here, as the language of closeness alludes presumably also to personal losses Levinas suffered at the hands of the Nazis (except for his wife and daughter, most of Levinas's family died in the Holocaust), in which case the confessional utterance tropes the very way in which the tribal priority gives way to concern for every other.

56. Primo Levi, *Survival in Auschwitz: The Nazi Assault on Humanity*, trans. Stuart Woolf (New York: Collier Books, [1958] 1961); hereafter referred to as *SA*.

57. If Levinas veils the allusiveness of his figures by arguing that such proximity is radically anterior and anarchic, so that "no site" is sufficiently a proximity but perhaps only a trace of proximity's more radical form, Levi's deportation train is nonetheless a referent that conjures the condition of existing outside of any sense of occasion or place. Levi says, "During the halts, no one tried anymore to communicate with the outside world (*di comunicare col mondo esterno*): we felt ourselves by now 'on the other side (*dall'altra parte*)'" (*SA* 14), defining a sensibility that has lost its familiar orientation in the world. For the Italian, see Levi, *Se questo è un uomo* (Torino: Giulio Einaudi, 1976), 18.

58. Here I cite for its emphasis an alternate translation of Levinas's interview with Christian Chabanis. See "The Philosopher and Death," trans. Bettina Bergo, IIRB 121–29.

59. "Being-Toward-Death and 'Thou Shalt Not Kill,'" a 1987 interview conducted in German by Florian Rötzer, originally appeared in Rötzer, *Französische Philosophen im Gespräch* (Munich: Klaus Boer Verlag, 1987), 89–100; trans. Andrew Schmitz, reprinted in *IIRB* 130–39, 137.

60. "Interview with Myriam Anissimov," IIRB 84–92.

61. Tom Segev, *The Seventh Million: The Israelis and the Holocaust*, trans. Haim Watzman (New York: Hill and Wang, [1991] 1993), 67–96.

62. Levinas, "Ethics and Politics," the transcript of this interview was originally published in *Les Nouveaux Cahiers* 18 (1982–83): 71, 1–8; reprinted in *The Levinas Reader*, ed. Seán Hand (Cambridge, MA: Basil Blackwell, 1989), 289–97; hereafter referred to as *LR*.

63. See Colin Davis, *Elie Wiesel's Secretive Texts* (Gainesville: University Press of Florida, 1994), esp. 113–24.

64. Caygill, *Levinas and the Political*, 159–98, 192.

AFTERWORD: ETHICS VERSUS HISTORY

1. Walter Benn Michaels, *The Shape of the Signifier: 1967 to the End of History* (Princeton, NJ: Princeton University Press, 2004); hereafter referred to as SS.

2. Michaels's contention relies upon a quasi-phenomenological understanding of memory and reacts to the crude contemporary uses to which memory, undergirded by tenets of popularized psychoanalytic psychology displaced into the realms of sociology, literary, and cultural studies, and even history itself, has frequently been put. For his explicit treatment of intersection of memory and history, see Michaels, SS 134–36.

3. See Michaels, SS, esp. 129–39.

4. "Nearly half (44%) of all respondents agree that at least one form of restriction should be placed on Muslim American civil liberties." "MSRG Special Report: Restriction on Civil Liberties, Views of Islam, and Muslim Americans," Media and Society Research Group, Cornell University, Ithaca, NY, 2004.

5. Novick, *The Holocaust in American Life* (Boston: Houghton Mifflin, 1999) esp. 170–203.

6. When such critics are not merely reactionary conservatives, when they fit the label of what we might call neo-liberals (here I am thinking of intellectuals such as Richard Rorty or Novick himself) or perhaps neo-Marxists (Michaels is not exactly a Marxist, but he shares

some of Marxism's hermeneutics), they aim to correct the fragmenting tendency of multicultural politics through a commonsense effort to describe and thereby enact a common ground upon which we might base a system of politics aimed at redressing the measurable terms of disadvantage and oppression (most urgently, the severe disparities in economic well-being that haunt Western society, to say nothing of devastated post-imperialized economies of Third World countries). While the contemporary currents of ethnic particularism seemingly dismantle a cultural discourse and political ideology in which the criticism of imbalances might find its corollary in corrective or compensatory agency, these cultural critics, who seem wholly as skeptical of poststructuralist critiques of post-Enlightenment rationality as they are of the chaotic melee of multiculturalism, recommend a restoration of pragmatic rationality as the proper discourse of the political sphere.

7. Geoffrey Hartman, *The Fateful Question of Culture* (New York: Columbia University Press, 1997).

8. In an era when the socialistic vestiges of welfare government have come entirely under attack, Americans prove capable of rejecting all reminders that democratic culture must concern itself even with the economically unfortunate within its ranks. Perhaps the real problem, we are asked to consider by the "welfare reformers," is that welfare created an ideological system of dependence, in which those who were politically oppressed were permitted to see themselves as culturally disvalued and, becoming victims in their own minds, have continued to act like victims ever since.

9. Here I find Michaels's critique especially cogent because he interrogates the grafting together of group identity and the memory of woundedness, exposing what I would describe as the sacrificial logic that enables such a conjunction. See Michaels, SS 140–58.

10. In April 1996 the news broke that the Wal-Mart clothing line to which Kathie Lee Gifford had given her name was produced in sweatshops exploiting child labor. To her credit, although many of her critics viewed these subsequent actions as a public relations campaign, Gifford testified before a congressional subcommittee later that summer advocating for stiffer regulations on child labor. See Eyal Press, "No Sweat: The Fashion Industry Patches Its Image—U.S. Clothiers and International Sweatshop Labor," *Progressive*, Sept. 1996; "Lost Childhood: Millions of Children Work under Slavery Conditions," *Current Events*, Sept. 1, 1996.

11. *Sex and the City*, season 6, pt. 1, episode 1, "To Market, to Market" (Home Box Office, 2004).

12. See Amy Hungerford, *The Holocaust of Texts: Genocide, Literature, and Personification* (Chicago: University of Chicago Press, 2003), esp. 97–121.

13. It is precisely for this reason that the logic or remembrance in Spiegelman's fictional/nonfictional text seems so suspect to Michaels and Hungerford, respectively. See Michaels, SS 129–33; Hungerford, *Holocaust of Texts*, 73–96.

14. Margalit, *The Ethics of Memory* (Cambridge, MA: Harvard University Press, 2002), 33.

15. Relevant here, again, is Giorgio Agamben's discussion of the bifurcated status of the witness, caught between the survivor and the spectral but true witnesses to genocide, those *Muselmänner* of the camps. See RA 1.14–2.4, 36–50.

16. Certainly, with regard to trauma theory, this has raised the concern even among certain proponents of traumatic discourse that to privilege the trauma is to subject our knowledge

to the realm of irrationality, to permit a mystificatory relation to violence that might almost resemble—as Dominick LaCapra supposes—the Nazis' commitment to sacrificial violence. See Dominick LaCapra, *Representing the Holocaust: History, Theory, Trauma* (Ithaca: Cornell University Press, 1994), esp. 13–17.

17. Randall Robinson, *The Debt: What America Owes to Blacks* (New York: Dutton, 2000); Michaels, SS 164.

18. The tropological function of *trauma* in Levinasian discourse remains distinct from psychoanalytic hermeneutics, but something of Levinas's sense of trauma as responsibility appears to have influenced Cathy Caruth's interpretation of trauma. In the absence of a hermeneutic that might rationalize the privilege of singular witness or foresee a return for identity, trauma for Caruth surprisingly singles out a subject for responsibility, declaring the elected dimension (in the sense of the biblical idiom) of every subject's relation to responsibility. See Caruth, *Unclaimed Experience: Trauma, Narrative, and History* (Baltimore: Johns Hopkins University Press, 1996), esp. 104–7.

19. In our "skin exposed to wounds and outrage" we take on responsibilities surpassing our immediate or ordinary capacities. In other words, the ethical subject has an aptitude for being wounded: it can be beaten; it can receive blows. In all of this, the subject who is defined by the ethical relation (and not the other way around) partakes of the meaning of his own passivity, yielding to "an unendurable and harsh consent that animates the passivity and does so strangely despite itself." Levinas, NI 146.

20. For the psychoanalyst similarly assumes that to suffer for another and to occupy the perspective of the victim is to have—or perhaps, more accurately, to take—charge of the other from whom one suffers. And this is so because the persecuting other functions as a strangely refracted image of the victim positioned as within the framework of the self's own aggressive desires. To dwell within a victimized perspective is unhealthy, according to the psychoanalyst, in part because one clings to an aggressive fantasy without claiming responsibility for it. Occupied by a memory one cannot quite remember, the self is given over to an unpleasure that postpones the very possibility of agency. For a subject to come into history, she must confront not only the private history that determines her intentions but also those places in which historical memory coincides with or interprets her own psychic predisposition. All knowledge as such is constituted through acts of remembrance, which are themselves greater and lesser examples of working through the losses that govern sociality and cultural significations. The responsible subject remembers herself at least potentially as an agent of the past, whether or not she has in fact been the agent of the events that haunt her. For an example of this psychoanalytic hermeneutical perspective on fantasy, see Jacqueline Rose, *The Haunting of Sylvia Plath* (Cambridge, MA: Harvard University Press, 1991), 205–38.

Index